European Cases in Strategic Management

Edited by

John Hendry
University of Cambridge, Cambridge, UK

Tony Eccles
London Business School, London, UK

with

Sumantra Ghoshal
INSEAD, Fontainebleau, France

Per Jenster
IMD, Lausanne, Switzerland

Peter Williamson
London Business School, London, UK

INTERNATIONAL THOMSON BUSINESS PRESS
I(T)P® An International Thomson Publishing Company

London • Bonn • Boston • Johannesburg • Madrid • Melbourne • Mexico City • New York • Paris
Singapore • Tokyo • Toronto • Albany, NY • Belmont, CA • Cincinnati, OH • Detroit, MI

European Cases in Strategic Management

Copyright ©1993 John Hendry, Tony Eccles, Sumantra Ghoshal, Per Jenster and Peter Williamson. (Individual chapters are under separate copyright).

 I(**T**)**P** A division of International Thomson Publishing Inc.
The ITP logo is a trademark under licence

British Library Cataloguing-in-Publication Data
A catalogue record for this book is available from the British Library

First published 1993 by Chapman & Hall
Reprinted 1993, 1994 and 1995
Reprinted 1997 and 1999 by International Thomson Business Press

Typeset by Best-set Typesetters Ltd, China
Printed in China.

ISBN 1-86152-577-X

International Thomson Business Press
Berkshire House
168–173 High Holborn
London WC1V 7AA
UK

http://www.itbp.com

Contents

vi   Contents

About the authors

Michelle Bergadaà is Professor of Sales and Marketing Strategy at the École Supérieure des Sciences Economiques et Commerciales (ESSEC) and Editor-in-Chief of *Marketing News* (the journal of the French Marketing Association).

Max Boisot is Professor of Strategic Management at ESADE, Barcelona, and Senior Associate at the Judge Institute of Management Studies, University of Cambridge. From 1984–88 he was founder Director and Dean of the China–European Commission Management Programme in Beijing, and prior to that was on the faculty of the Ecole Superieure de Commerce de Paris.

Gyula Bosnyak is Director of Strategic Management and Planning at the Taurus Hungarian Rubber Works.

Cliff Bowman is Senior Lecturer in Strategic Management at Cranfield School of Management and was formerly Head of the School of Business at Humberside College of Higher Education. He is the author of several books on strategic management, most recently *The Essence of Strategic Management* (Prentice Hall, 1990).

Pierre Dussauge is Associate Professor of Strategy and Business Policy at HEC, Paris. His most recent publications include *State-Owned Multinationals* (Wiley, 1987) and *Strategic Technology Management* (Wiley, 1992).

Tony Eccles is Professor of Strategic Management and Director of the Senior Executive Programme at London Business School. Originally a shop-floor engineer, he spent 10 years in factory management with Unilever before joining the faculty of Manchester Business School, and he later became the first holder of the Chair of Business Policy at Glasgow University. He has directed the Sloan programme and the Centre for Management Development at London Business School, and is a Director of two private media companies. Author of *Under New Management* (Pan, 1981), he is currently writing books on strategy implementation, and (with Douglas Wood) on wealth and competitiveness.

Sumantra Ghoshal is Associate Professor of Management and Digital Equipment Corporation Research Fellow at INSEAD. Following 13 years in mangement he gained doctorates from both Harvard and MIT and has since published a large number of articles and two books, most recently *Managing Across Borders: The Transnational Solution* (with Christopher Bartlett, Harvard Business School and Hutchinson, 1989).

Philippe Haspeslagh is Associate Professor of Business Policy at INSEAD and the author (with David Jemison) of *Managing Acquisitions: Creating Value through Corporate Renewal* (Free Press, 1991).

John Hendry is Director of the MBA Course at the Judge Institute of Management Studies and a Professorial Fellow of Girton College at the University of Cambridge. Before moving to Cambridge in 1990 he was Director of the Centre for Strategic Management and Organisational Change at Cranfield School of Management. His recent publications include *Innovating for Failure: Government Policy and the Early British Computer Industry* (MIT Press, 1989) and he is currently completing books on strategic change and management ethics.

José-Carlos Jarillo is Professor of Business Policy and International Strategy at IMD and was previously on the faculties of IESE and the Harvard Business School. He holds doctorates in both business administration and economics and has published widely in the areas of strategy formulation and international strategy.

Per Jenster is Professor of Strategic Management and Marketing at IMD, Lausanne. Born and educated in Denmark he holds a doctorate in strategic management and information systems from the University of Pittsburgh and was a faculty member of the University of Virginia before moving to IMD in 1989. Besides his academic work, Professor Jenster also has an extensive senior management consulting practice.

Jon Martínez is Professor of Marketing and International Business, and Director of the Business School, Valparaiso, University of Adolfo Ibanez in Chile.

Jozsef Poor is Chief Executive Officer of Hay International Consulting Group in Budapest. He was formerly Director of Consulting Services and Professor of Strategy and Policy at the International Management Centre, Budapest.

Raymond-Alain Thiétart is Professor of Management at the University of Paris IX–Dauphine and at ESSEC. His recent publications include *Strategie d'Entreprise* (McGraw–Hill, 1990) and (with J. Thépot) *Microeconomic Contributions to Strategic Management* (North–Holland, 1991).

Janos Vecsenyi is Professor of Strategy and Policy and Director of the MBA Programme at the international Management Centre, Budapest.

Peter Williamson is Dean of MBA Programmes and Associate Professor of Strategic and International Business at London Business School (LBS). He also directs 'Competing Globally: The view from Japan', an LBS course for senior executives held in Japan. Before joining LBS Peter worked with Boston Consulting Group and Merrill Lynch International, and he continues to act as consultant to a range of multinational companies. His research and publications include work on strategic planning, export strategy, international business, and strategies for an integrated Europe.

Joseph Wolfe is Professor of Management at the University of Tulsa. At the time of writing the cases in this book he was a Fulbright Fellow at the International Management Centre, Budapest.

Preface

The case teaching method has long been dominant in the teaching of strategic management, but the published resources to support this have been remarkably limited, typically to a single national, British or American context. At times it has seemed as if the rest of the world were confined to something called 'international business', which did not impinge upon 'strategic management' at all.

This volume stems out of a conviction that the world of business is essentially international, and that course material should reflect this, whatever the subject. At this stage in the development of the strategic management case body, the production of a truly global casebook still presents insuperable difficulties. There are still precious few usable cases from outside Europe and North America. The best cases from America are already available and cannot be economically reprinted. We have, however, reached the point where it is possible to put together a European casebook which, while still having a high proportion of British-based cases, is not dominated by them.

The 23 cases in this volume cover businesses based in eight different European countries. Nine of the companies are British-based, reflecting the fact that British business schools are still the main users and generators of cases in Europe, but most of these British-based cases are about companies, and issues, with a strong European dimension. Many of the cases are concerned with aspects of European integration, and four of them concern companies based in Eastern Europe.

The selection was made following a search and critical review of cases written within the last four years, and all are less than five years old. Some of them are, nevertheless, already established 'standards'. Others have not yet been disseminated significantly outside their originating institutions, but have been revised, polished and developed as a result of experience in those institutions. A few were completed only months before the volume went to press, but appeared to the reviewers and editors to have all the hallmarks of a first-rate case.

In making the selection, we had in mind three dimensions across which a good spread of cases was desirable: national culture; industry sector; and thematic focus. The fourth and overriding consideration was, however, the perceived quality of the cases as learning vehicles. Good teaching cases can always be supplemented by articles from newspapers and business periodicals, but a poor case, however desirable its focus and setting, is of little use to anyone.

In trying to balance these four criteria, within the space limits of the project, some difficult decisions were called for, and we have inevitably ended up with gaps on both the national and industry dimensions. We would have liked, for example, to include some cases on German-based companies, and some on financial services and the public sector. We hope that case writers will respond to these needs in the years ahead, and that any subsequent editions of the book will benefit as a result.

The book has its origins in two separate projects: one led by Tony Eccles at London Business School; the other by John Hendry, then at Cranfield School of Management. In bringing these projects together we have retained a number of our own cases, but what has really made this book possible is the support and co-operation of our fellow case authors. Throughout the project we have been impressed by the willingness of people to make their cases available, to supply the necessary support materials, and to meet the demanding deadlines that we have imposed.

John Hendry
Tony Eccles

Introduction

THE CASES

This book contains 21 cases in strategic management plus two separate industry notes. The companies described are based in nine different European countries and range from relatively small firms to large multinational corporations. Almost all are competing in international markets and the great majority incorporate international operations. All of the cases are under five years old. Most have been developed, over periods of between one and three years, on the basis of teaching experience in Europe's premier business schools. All have been carefully reviewed and, where appropriate, edited, before inclusion in the book. Apart from the most recent cases, all have accompanying current updates, either in the form of follow-up (B) cases or in the form of 'Notes', provided as part of the support package for teachers.

Between them these cases cover the full range of issues commonly addressed in courses on strategic management, business strategy or business policy, as well as a wide range of issues more normally addressed in courses on international business or international strategy. They will not, on their own, meet the needs of every teacher on every course in these areas, but they should provide a core resource to which appropriate supplementary material can be added so as to meet the particular demands of individual courses.

Guidance on how to use the cases is given in the support package for teachers, available from the publishers, but in the following table we have tried to give a rough categorization of the cases in terms of the themes and topics addressed. Since most of the cases are complex, they will lend themselves to a wide variety of uses. The table does, however, give a general indication of some of the main themes addressed by each case, and of the combinations of cases that might be used in putting together strategic management courses. All the cases are intended to serve as a **basis for class discussion**, and **not** to illustrate either effective or ineffective managerial practice.

	Implementation and the strategy process												Competitive strategy and strategic analysis										
Small business strategy	New business development	Mergers and acquisitions	Multinational operations	Strategic alliances	International joint ventures	Strategy implementation	Turnaround and strategic change	Corporate culture	Leadership	Strategies and styles	Strategy, structure and systems	Globalization	Core competencies	Diversification	Corporate strategy	Competitive advantage	Resource analysis	Generic strategies	Competitor analysis	Industry structure	Business environment	
									•		•					•	•					Amstrad
	•	•				•	•	•			•			•			•					Andersen Consulting
			•												•	•	•					Benetton
			•							•	•	•										Cadbury–Schweppes
						•										•	•	•		•	•	Csepel
					•																	DEC
																	•			•	•	DRG
		•				•	•									•				•		Electrolux
										•	•		•									GEC
										•	•		•		•							Grand Metropolitan
•	•										•					•						Infoservice
																				•	•	International Distillers
																•				•	•	Iskra
						•					•											J&M Airframes
																•				•	•	Nouvelles Frontières
							•							•				•		•	•	Rockware
									•							•	•	•	•	•	•	SAS
•					•																•	Sportis
		•						•	•					•								Storehouse
				•	•	•								•	•							Taurus

CASE SUMMARIES

Amstrad plc

Amstrad plc is a British-based multinational which designs, manufactures or assembles, and markets a range of personal computers and consumer electronics products. Founded in 1968 by the entrepreneur Alan Sugar, who remains the Chief Executive and driving force behind the company, it had grown by 1988 to have an annual turnover of £625 million and profit before tax of £160 million. However, the company had then stalled as a result of a number of concurrent problems. Some people attributed these problems to simple bad luck, others to changes in Amstrad's strategic focus, and still others to the inappropriateness of its management structure for the size of company it had become. Whatever the causes, urgent treatment was needed if the company was not to slide further downhill in a worsening economic recession.

Andersen Consulting (Europe): entering the business of business integration

By 1990 Andersen Consulting was the largest consulting company in the world, with over 20 000 professional staff in 50 countries engaged mainly in information systems consultancy. In the late 1980s it had commenced a new strategic thrust towards 'business integration', building up new practice areas of strategic services and change management alongside the well established and still dominant information systems practice, with a view to bringing together all these skills to address complex problems of business integration and strategy implementation. The case study focuses on the problems Andersen EMEA (Europe, the Middle East, and Africa) faces in seeking to implement its own strategy and to achieve the necessary internal integration across culturally distinct national and professional groupings.

Benetton SpA

With the Benetton family still owning 90% of the company, by 1987 Benetton was a major international player in the clothing industry, active in the design, manufacture, distribution, and retailing of fashion clothing. Though the company itself employed 1500 people and turned over in excess of 1000 billion lire, it was unusual in contracting out the bulk of its work. Most of the design work was produced by freelance designers, and the manufacturing by a network of 350 dedicated sub-contractors, mainly in Italy. Distribution was also carried out mainly by outsiders, and less than 10 of the 4500 Benetton shops worldwide were owned by the company, the rest being owned by independent franchisees. As the company had grown rapidly through the 1980s, the management and control of this complex network of activities had presented it with increasing problems, and by 1987 it was clear that significant restructuring would be needed if Benetton was to continue its rapid global expansion into the 1990s. It had recently diversified into financial services, and was now looking to build up this side of the business alongside a new global manufacturing system. The Benetton case is a classic study of multinational operations, core competencies, and diversification issues.

Cadbury Schweppes plc (A)

This case study addresses the problems facing Cadbury Schweppes in 1989. A British-based multinational food and drinks group with a turnover of £2.4 billion and a range of global chocolate and soft drinks brands, the company had emerged from a period of extensive restructuring. Since 1986 it had sold its non-confectionery foods businesses, acquired one major American soft drinks company, Canada Dry, taken a substantial stake in another, and set up a joint venture with Coca-Cola to handle all Coke and Schweppes brands in the UK. In the view of the Chairman, Sir Adrian Cadbury, these changes had laid the foundations for the long-term success of the company in the international confectionery and soft drinks markets. But the prospect for long-term profits had been secured at the expense of short-term profits, and this made the group vulnerable to takeover. General Cinema, an American holding company, had already built up an unwelcome stake of over 18% and a balance had to be struck between defending against further hostile moves and continuing to build for the longer term. **Cadbury Schweppes (B)**, supplied as part of the support package, focuses on the development of the strategy by Sir Graham Day, following Sir Adrian Cadbury's retirement, including key acquisitions in sugar confectionery and soft drinks markets, and associated management and organizational changes.

Csepel Machine Tool Company

The Csepel Machine Tool Company is an autonomous Hungarian company which, until 1986, was state-owned; it was then transformed into a publicly-held shareholders' corporation. In 1989 it employed about 1200 people and had a turnover of 2600 million forints, of which 20% represented domestic sales and the remainder was divided equally between CMEA (Soviet trading block) and non-CMEA exports. Entering 1990, it faced major and unpredictable changes in its business environment, and serious questions over its choice of strategy and operational performance. This case can be used either to explore the particular problems facing corporations in Eastern Europe or as a general case on competitive strategy and strategy implementation.

Digital Equipment Corporation International: competing through co-operation

In 1985 Digital Equipment Corporation (DEC) International Europe, an operating division of the large American computer manufacturer, entered into an experimental, multilevel, joint software development project with ITT Telecom in Europe. Eight months into the project, in early 1986, there was growing unease within DEC International. The costs of the project had yet to be matched by any visible benefits, and there was concern that DEC might be giving away its core technical expertise. The case study presents the complex issues facing senior DEC executives as they reviewed the future of the project and sought to develop a corporate policy on strategic alliances.

DRG Plastic Films: the European stretch film industry

In 1987 DRG Plastic Films was the second largest producer of poly-ethylene stretch film in the UK and the fourth largest in Europe – a position it had achieved within five years of entering the market. With the market continuing to change rapidly, however, there was no room for complacency. Though applications for stretch film were proliferating, DRG's home market was approaching saturation. It was still a small player in those countries in which stretch film had yet to achieve significant penetration, and while it could at present rely on its quality advantage to give it a competitive edge, this was likely to be eroded as the technology matured. The case study reviews the market structure and DRG's main competitors, as well as DRG's existing strategy, and raises the question of whether this strategy is appropriate for the next stage of industry development.

Electrolux: the acquisition and integration of Zanussi *and* note on the major appliance industry in 1988

By 1988 the Swedish-based Electrolux group was a Skr.70 billion turnover conglomerate with over 140000 employees. It was also one of the world's largest manufacturers of major domestic appliances, which accounted for over 40% of its sales. The group had been built up over a 20-year period through an aggressive acquisitions strategy including, in 1983, the acquisition of Zanussi. The second largest privately-owned company in Italy with its core business in domestic appliances, Zanussi had suffered from a costly programme of unrelated diversification and wound up in serious financial difficulties. By 1988 Zanussi was back in profit and the task of integrating its activities with those of Electrolux was well under way. But it was far from complete and a number of problems were surfacing which threatened to undermine the group's fight for leadership in the emerging global major appliances market. The case studies focus on the implementation of the Zanussi acquisition and Electrolux–Zanussi integration, and on the competitive environment of the major appliance industry.

GEC plc

GEC is a British-based multinational electrical, electronic, and defence manufacturer with a £6 billion turnover and 160 000 employees. Built up through a series of mergers and acquisitions in the 1960s, it was run by the Chief Executive, Lord Weinstock, as a federation of 160 operationally independent subsidiaries. But the headquarters acted as a banker to the units, controlling cash, capital investment plans, and acquisitions. The **GEC (A)** case study focuses on two budget meetings, at which unit managers presented their reports and proposals for the scrutiny of Lord Weinstock. These provide the basis for a detailed analysis of GEC's corporate strategy and strategic management style. **GEC (B)** focuses on the company's corporate strategy in the second half of the 1980s and early 1990s, and describes a series of acquisitions, partial mergers, and joint ventures established in that period, before coming back to the questions of organization structure and strategic management style. It can be used to build on the analysis of the (A) case, and to extend that analysis into the area of international joint ventures and strategic alliances.

Grand Metropolitan plc (A)

Grand Metropolitan is a large, British-based, multinational conglomerate with a turnover in excess of £8 billion. Originally a hotel group, it had been built up in the 1960s and 1970s through a series of major acquisitions in catering, foods, gambling, brewing, and spirits. In the early 1980s a series of American acquisitions had taken it into cigarettes, pet foods, soft drink bottling, fitness products and a range of branded services. This aggressive growth strategy had made Grand Metropolitan the 'darling' of the stock market, but by 1986, when Alan Sheppard took over as Chief Executive, things did not look so good. Profits were stagnating, and the group lacked direction. Sheppard's response was to refocus on a philosophy of global branding and on a narrowed portfolio of four core activities, continuing to make strategic acquisitions but selling peripheral businesses, even when they were thriving. The case study provides the basis for an analysis of both corporate and business level strategies, as well as of organizational philosophy and the role of corporate headquarters.

Infoservice: strategic decision-making simulation game

Infoservice is a small but fast-growing and successful French software development company. Founded in 1978, it had grown to 55 staff by

1990, and had by then embarked on its fourth generation of products. But like many growing firms in fast-moving industry environments, it was encountering a number of strategic and organizational problems. The character of the firm had changed with growth and many of the staff seemed dissatisfied. The structure no longer seemed adequate to ensure the co-ordination needed if Infoservice was to compete effectively. Industry restructuring in anticipation of the single European market posed strategic problems of market focus and technical standards. Having raised these issues, the case study gives the views of 15 different Infoservice staff. Besides giving substance and depth to the issues facing the company, these allow the case to be used, if desired, as a role-playing exercise.

International Distillers and Vintners (A)

International Distillers and Vintners (IDV), a subsidiary of Grand Metropolitan, is the largest wines and spirits company in the world with 10 of the world's top 100 spirit brands. In recent years the industry has become increasingly competitive and concentrated, with competition focused on the battle for global brand dominance. This case study describes the development of the world wine and spirits industry, and the positioning of the leading competitors. It raises the question as to whether IDV's strategic approach, highly successful in the mid-1980s, is appropriate to the changing environment of the 1990s. The case can be used for industry and competitor analysis, and for the analysis of competitive advantage. For the latter purpose it can be used either on its own or in conjunction with **Grand Metropolitan (A)**, also in this volume. **IDV (B)**, included in the support package for teachers, follows the most recent developments of IDV and its industry sector, and raises further issues of international brand strategies and strategic alliances.

Iskra Power Tools

Iskra Power Tools is a medium-sized Yugoslavian manufacturer of portable electric power tools, such as drills and angle grinders, and accessories. It has established joint venture relationships with a number of Western European power tool manufacturers, but has had to pull out of similar arrangements in Eastern Europe. As the economic geography of Europe underwent massive and rapid changes in 1990–91, Iskra found itself caught between two worlds. Following its bad experiences in Eastern Europe, the general manager saw the future of the company as lying in Western Europe, but he knew that Iskra could not match the quality and efficiency of its Western competitors. Having shown losses for the last two years, the company needed a firm strategic direction, but it was far from clear which of the possible routes open to it would be most likely to succeed.

J & M Airframes Ltd

J & M Airframes Ltd is a pseudonym for an aircraft manufacturer in the process of moving from being a single-product firm manufacturing a successful bomber aircraft to being a subcontractor manufacturing a wide range of assemblies. This change has put severe strains on the company's staff and on the organization structure and systems, and the case study raises the question of how the company and its operations might be restructured to suit the new conditions.

Nouvelles Frontières

Founded as a student travel organization in the mid-1960s, Nouvelles Frontières was, by 1990, the second largest tour operator in France, with its own network of exclusive travel agencies. The privately owned business had been built up on the strength of this exclusive network and of a sophisticated computerized reservation system, with air transport being purchased from third parties. In 1989, however, the company had bought a stake in a charter airline. It had also begun, in the late 1980s, to build up an overseas operation and to expand into tourist services such as hotels and language schools. The case study discusses the strategy and operations of Nouvelles Frontières in the context of the developing air traffic market, and can be used for the analysis of business environment, industry structure, and competitive advantage.

Rockware plc (A)

Rockware is one of the largest UK manufacturers of glass bottles. In 1983 the company faced extinction as a result of declining demand, massive industry overcapacity, and increasing foreign competition, and also as a result of its failure to capitalize on earlier diversifications into related packaging materials. Returning as Chairman after seven years running the state-owned British Rail, Sir Peter Parker was faced with the need to take drastic action to turn the business round and limit its losses, and then to establish a viable strategy for its future survival in a hostile industry environment. Rockware (A) discusses the turnaround package and leaves students with the problem of analysing the industry context and the competitive responses available to Rockware. **Rockware (B)**, included in the support package for teachers, reports on the strategy adopted and raises the further issues of diversification that arose as Rockware sought to establish a corporate growth strategy for the longer term.

Scandinavian Airlines System in 1988 *and* note on the European airline industry

Between 1981 and 1988, under the guidance of Jan Carlzon, Scandinavian Airlines System (SAS) had achieved a remarkable turnaround. From being a loss-making national carrier with declining market share it had emerged as one of the world's leading airlines, with the second highest operating revenues in Europe and the highest profit margins in the world. Looking to the future, however, it faced major problems if it was to face up to the challenges posed by a rapidly changing international business environment, an ageing fleet, and an inherently high cost structure. The case studies provide the basis for a detailed analysis of the business environment and industry structure in which SAS must operate, and of the strategic options open to SAS within its competitive environment.

Sportis: challenge and response in post-communist Poland

Sportis is a private Polish company with 160 employees, specializing in the manufacture of life-jackets and protective clothing. The political and economic reforms of 1990 had created tremendous opportunities for small consumer-oriented firms in Poland. However, Sportis had been dependent on the centralized State distribution system for the bulk of its orders, so with the collapse of that system it was in a perilous position. Although it had begun some subcontracting for Western companies, it was fundamentally in no position to compete with the West, with no marketing experience, poor efficiency and grossly inadequate accounting and control systems. Its response, in early 1991, had been to enter a joint venture in the Soviet Union, but that too was fraught with difficulties and uncertainty. In this environment Sportis could only survive by accomplishing major strategic and organizational changes. But what were those changes, and were they practically feasible?

Storehouse plc

Storehouse – with a £1200 million turnover – is a British-based clothing and furniture retailing group. The group was created by the designer and entrepreneur, Terence Conran, through a combination of organic growth, mergers, and acquisitions. This growth has never been smooth, even at the best of times, but by the late 1980s the company seemed to be moving from crisis to crisis – remaining in profit but under perpetual threat of takeover as its main business persistently under-performed. The case study provides an opportunity to look at the relationships of leadership and corporate culture to the strategy process, and to critically analyse the formulation and implementation of an acquisition-based growth strategy. It presents the students with major unresolved issues of corporate strategy and the role of the centre, together with some 'live' business unit strategy issues that can be further researched by students in Britain through visits to some of Storehouse's 900 shops and those of its leading competitors.

Taurus Hungarian Rubber Works: implementing a strategy for the 1990s

Formerly Hungary's national, state-owned rubber company, Taurus is now a public shareholders' company with over 8000 employees and a turnover of 20 000 million forints. Though a large company in Hungarian terms, it is a very small player in the world rubber industry. Following a major strategic review in 1988, it responded to the economic opening up of Eastern Europe by entering on a strategy of diversification and international joint ventures. The problem presented by the case study is how, in 1990, to implement that strategy. This case can be used either to explore the particular problems facing companies in Eastern Europe or as a general case on strategy implementation.

THE CASE METHOD

Strategic management is not an exact science, and cannot be learnt from textbooks alone. The strategic problems which managers face are typically complex and multidimensional, characterized by high levels of uncertainty and involving issues not only of markets and economics but also of personality and cognition, social psychology, politics, and organizational culture. As such they are both organizationally and situationally specific. Their effective handling requires clarity and creativity of thought, but also — and critically — the judgement that is born of experience. The analysis of case studies provides a type of vicarious experience. It is no substitute for the real thing, but is an essential complement to textbooks and lectures, through which theories and frameworks can be tested against real life situations.

In some business schools, strategic management is taught primarily by intensive case study analysis, with textbooks and readings taking very much a back seat. In others the teaching is more traditional, with the case studies used more as illustrations. Most leading business schools take a middle line, making ample use of textbooks, readings, and lectures or seminars, but also allowing for substantial periods of intensive case study analysis and discussion.

The cases in this book are all designed for, and will all repay, a thorough and intensive analysis. They are rich studies, each one of which is capable of supporting at least an hour of class discussion, and many of which can profitably sustain far longer periods of debate. Such debate can only be profitable, however, if it is adequately prepared for by both students and teacher. Where possible, students should thoroughly analyse a case study both individually and in small groups before it is discussed in class. There is no 'correct' way of proceeding in this analysis, but the following steps will need to be included:

1. Read the case twice through, thoroughly and carefully. The first reading is to get your bearings. The second is to note down or

highlight what seem to be the key features discussed, in the light of any questions that may have been set by the teacher.

2. Read carefully any other readings that have been assigned, including textbook chapters, articles, and so on, and note any readings from earlier in the course that may be relevant to the current case study.

3. Go through the financial data and any other quantitative information, calculating key ratios and looking for any unusual or noteworthy features. Even if the questions do not appear to be concerned with the financial performance it is still wise to include this step. A change in stock ratio or debt, for example, or an exceptional item in the accounts, may prove to be critical to your analysis.

4. Determine what appear to be the key strategic issues facing the company, and how these appear to relate to the questions that have been asked. In the later stages of a course, the case studies may be used to explore specific themes, but these cannot be addressed in isolation from the fundamentals of the company's strategic position or strategy-making processes.

5. Ask what other information, not included in the case, you need to carry out your analysis. Many students assume that if information is relevant it will be included in the case, and that it is somehow unfair if it is not. Most case studies are, to a large degree, compilations of information relevant to the issues addressed, and students are not normally expected to undertake further research into the companies involved. (This, of course, is where the case study method most obviously falls short of real management experience. A manager faced with a real strategic issue will have no case study to refer to for guidance, and an enormous amount of information to take into account, as well as enormous uncertainties. He or she may not even know that there is an issue to be addressed.) However, case studies do not normally include more general information, for example on the state of the economy or of the stock market, or on the general social, economic, and political environment. This information is readily obtained if not already to hand, and may be critical to the analysis of a case issue.

6. Prepare a case analysis, addressing the questions that have been asked, and test out its robustness to criticism within the study group. There are many 'wrong' answers in strategic management, but very few 'right' ones, and in a case study discussion it is the strength of the argument that matters, not what answer is reached. The objective of an analysis should be to use whatever concepts or frameworks are relevant in order to structure an argument that is clear, rigorous, and creative, while at the same time being sensitive to the practicalities of the specific situation concerned.

Good preparation on the part of the teacher is equally important. The table on page 2 gives some indication of the issues covered by the cases in this book, and the support package for teachers gives further guidance on course construction and on the use of the cases in conjunction with standard texts, as well as teaching notes for the individual cases.

Just as there is no 'correct' way to prepare a case, there is no 'correct' way to structure a course. Some teachers structure their courses around textbook chapters while others devise their own thematic structures. Some base their structure on the stages in the strategy process, others on industry context, and others on key strategic issues. Whatever structure is adopted, the teacher should approach a case session with a clear idea of the specific learning objectives of that session: what precisely the case discussion is intended to achieve. He should then conduct his own exhaustive analysis of the case, studying the materials in the support package and undertaking any additional research required. He should then determine the supplementary readings to be assigned with the case, and redo the analysis from a student's perspective. In class the teacher should be in a position to lead the case discussion gently but firmly to the desired conclusion within the time available, ensuring that all aspects and approaches receive a proper hearing, and that as many of the class as possible are brought into the discussion. It is always a good idea to write up the students' thoughts and suggestions on flip-charts or boards, and many teachers find it helpful to have in their heads a picture of what these charts or boards are likely to look like by the end of the session. The writing-up process can then be used not only to recognize the students' contributions, but also to structure the debate and provide a visual basis for the concluding discussion.

1

Amstrad plc (A)

Case written by John Hendry

ENTREPRENEURIAL BEGINNINGS

Alan Sugar was a born entrepreneur. As a teenager in London's East End, his ventures ranged from boiling beetroots for a local greengrocer to cutting up rolls of 35 mm film for resale. On leaving school he became a trainee statistician at the Ministry of Education but soon left to work for a small electrical firm. He continued to do work 'on the side' as well, selling car radio aerials and other accessories from the back of a minivan in a street market. In 1968, at the age of 21, he set up his own company, AMS Trading Company (General Importers) Ltd, later shortened to Amstrad.

In 1970 Sugar saw an opportunity to go into manufacturing. One of the key selling points of hi-fi turntables was their plastic dust covers, most of which were made by an expensive vacuum-forming process. Sugar manufactured them by injection-moulding, which was a much cheaper process providing you could get sufficient volume, and he cornered the market. Soon after this he moved into hi-fi units themselves, as well as clock radios, cassette recorders, and car radios and cassette players, assembling products from sub-units and components sourced in the Far East. By 1980 turnover had reached £8.8 million and profits £1.4 million, and in April 1980 the company was floated on the Stock Exchange. By 1983 turnover had soared to over £50 million and profits to £8 million. A small Hong Kong company had been formed to monitor and co-ordinate subcontracted manufacturing throughout the Far East.

From hi-fis to personal computers

In the financial year 1982–83 Amstrad's sales were dominated by racked hi-fi systems, for which it had over 35% of the UK market. That year also saw the introduction of its colour televisions. In 1983–84 colour

Exhibit 1   Amstrad: 10-year record.

	1980	1981	1982	1983	1984	1985	1986	1987	1988	1989
Turnover (excluding VAT) (£m)	8.8	14.1	28.1	51.8	84.9	136.1	304.1	511.8	625.4	626.3
Profit before taxation (£m)	1.4	2.4	4.8	8.0	9.1	20.2	75.3	135.7	160.4	76.6
Profit after taxation (£m)	1.1	1.2	2.6	5.3	5.7	14.0	52.0	93.4	105.1	51.1
Dividends pence/share (including tax credit)	0.06	0.11	0.14	0.16	0.19	0.27	0.49	0.97	1.87	1.87
Dividend cover (times)	5	3	6	10	8	14	27	24	14	6
Retained profit for the year (£m)	0.8	1.1	2.4	5.1	5.0	12.9	47.2	89.6	93.0	43.1
Earnings pence/share after tax	0.22	0.26	0.54	1.12	1.17	2.57	9.54	17.13	18.99	9.01
Share capital and reserves (£m)	3.7	4.8	7.2	12.3	29.2	42.2	88.1	179.5	256.2	310.8
Key ratios	(%)	(%)	(%)	(%)	(%)	(%)	(%)	(%)	(%)	(%)
Turnover growth over prior year	56.5	61.2	98.6	84.6	64.0	60.2	123.5	68.3	22.2	0.1
Profit before tax over prior year	49.9	74.6	100.8	68.6	13.3	121.1	273.5	80.3	18.2	−53.2
Profit before tax as a percentage of sales	15.5	16.8	17.0	15.5	10.7	14.8	24.8	26.5	25.6	12.2

televisions accounted for over 90% of turnover, and Amstrad also introduced video cassette recorders. In June 1984 it also delivered its first home computer, and for the year 1984–85 computers comprised nearly two-thirds of turnover, with televisions and video recorders making up most of the balance. The introduction of computers was also responsible for taking its exports up to 53% of total turnover, from just 13% the previous year. Thereafter, though both audio and video products continued to sell well, sales were dominated by computers. In August 1985 Amstrad introduced the CPC6128 personal computer with integral disk drive and monitor, and the PCW8256 word processor – computer, software, monitor, and printer all for £400. In April 1986 Amstrad bought the computer business of Clive Sinclair for just £5 million, giving it 75% of the UK home computer market. In September 1986 it introduced the PC1520, an IBM-compatible PC, the base model of which was also priced at just £400. In 1987 this was followed by the more powerful PC1640, and in 1988 by portable versions of both the 1520 and 1640. In the year 1987–88, professional computers (the IBM compatibles) accounted for about 55% of the £625 million turnover; home computers (rationalized into a small Sinclair range) about 20%; video recorders about 15%; and audio and computer printers less than 5% each.

THE PROBLEMS BEGIN

It was in about 1988 that things started to go wrong. Amstrad had run into trouble with its products before. An early launch into citizens' band radio and the initial launch of video cassette recorders were both failures, but in both cases the company was able to cut its losses quickly and move on to other products. The hard disk version of the PC1520 encountered overheating problems, leading to delays while a revised model was launched incorporating a fan, but this proved to be only a minor hiccup in Amstrad's rampant growth. The problems of 1988, however, were more serious.

Up to this time, Amstrad products had been targeted firmly at the consumer. The PC1520 and PC1640 were described as business computers, but sold principally to individuals working or studying at home, the self-employed, or very small businesses. In 1987, however, it announced the PC2000 range; a new range of up-market personal computers using fast 286 and 386 chips, which were supposed to take the company firmly into the corporate market. This range was originally due to be launched in late 1987, but design problems delayed the launch until September 1988. A chronic shortage of memory chips severely limited the early production, losing an estimated £50 million of sales, and a design error resulted in 7000 machines being recalled in July 1989 at a cost of about £6 million. Demand was also much weaker than had been anticipated, and in September 1989 the range was relaunched at lower prices.

The chip shortage lasted for much of 1988 and 1989, and reflected the notorious cyclical nature of the silicon chip market. Despite press comment about a pending chip shortage as the electronic industry boomed in the late 1980s, Amstrad failed to act until it was too late. Then in October 1988 it rushed into paying £45 million for a small minority shareholding of a chip manufacturer, Micron Technology, in an effort to secure supplies. As Sugar commented some months later, 'It was a lousy deal'. The shares were worth, at most, £30 million.

In this same period, problems with a Taiwanese subcontractor led to a break in audio supplies in the crucial pre-Christmas selling period in 1988, and in the autumn of 1989 Amstrad pulled out of the audio market. An attempted move into the supply of satellite aerial dishes, seen as a major new market, suffered both from technical design problems and from delays in the launching of UK satellite TV. The launch of another major new product – a low-priced fax machine – was also delayed.

Finally, Amstrad ran into difficulties with its European subsidiaries. Throughout most of the 1980s it had only two overseas subsidiaries: a distribution company in France and the Hong Kong company. By the late 1980s the Hong Kong company employed 500 people: 100 managing the Far East subcontracting operations; the remainder working in a printer factory which acted as a testbed for production innovations, and provided a benchmark for assessing subcontractors' production. Faced with the prospect of European Community import controls, however, as

Exhibit 2   Amstrad: consolidated profit and loss account (year end 30 June).

	£ thousand				
	1985	1986	1987	1988	1989
Turnover	136 061	304 150	511 798	625 426	626 323
Change in stocks and work in progress	1 686	4 298	52 222	(14 541)	173 766
Other operating income	512	348	858	1 838	1 524
Raw materials etc.	(103 539)	(207 130)	(399 998)	(382 046)	(599 791)
Other external charges	(7 316)	(18 924)	(20 470)	(47 175)	(67 922)
Staff costs	(3 594)	(4 672)	(7 261)	(15 781)	(24 338)
Depreciation	(1 047)	(1 168)	(1 645)	(2 759)	(4 824)
Other operating charges	(2 364)	(3 851)	(3 783)	(9 488)	(26 198)
Interest receivable	449	4 198	5 174	10 120	9 542
Interest payable	(691)	(1 965)	(1 183)	(5 188)	(11 475)
Profit before tax	20 157	75 284	135 712	160 406	76 607
Taxation	(6 147)	(23 279)	(42 313)	(55 258)	(25 517)
Profit after tax	14 010	52 005	93 399	105 148	51 090
Ordinary dividends	(1 027)	(1 893)	(3 816)	(7 903)	(7 957)
Extraordinary items	(42)	(2 954)	—	(4 287)	—
Retained profit	12 941	47 158	89 583	92 958	43 133

well as with a need for shorter lead times and greater flexibility, it decided to move some of its production to Europe. In 1988, rather than simply subcontracting, it set up a joint manufacturing venture. However, it underestimated the problems of start-up, and the ensuing delays added to its existing supply shortages. Meanwhile, again in 1988, Amstrad also sought to increase control of its overseas distribution – previously contracted out – by setting up a series of distribution subsidiaries. Over an 18-month period 10 of these were set up, but the head office support needed was underestimated, and the firm quickly found itself carrying unwieldy inventories.

An end to rapid growth

The cumulative result of these and other problems was that Amstrad's turnover for the year 1988–89 was almost identical to that for 1987–88, bringing to an abrupt end its long history of rapid growth. At the same

Exhibit 3   Amstrad: consolidated balance Sheet (year end 30 June).

	£ thousand				
	1985	1986	1987	1988	1989
Fixed assets:					
Intangibles	160	379	284	469	382
Tangibles	6 883	7 219	11 620	22 949	44 428
Associated company			980	1 125	
Listed investments				42	44 574
	6 993	7 598	12 884	24 585	89 384
Current assets:					
Stocks	25 173	33 277	95 687	122 142	325 155
Trade debtors	23 660	38 325	54 809	130 629	100 432
Other debtors	1 418	3 523	9 343	12 115	22 740
Prepayments	614	333	601	931	1 299
Deferred taxation		3 755	1 934	1 336	6 422
Overseas taxation			1 833		1 409
Investments	257				
Cash	13 519	62 467	107 630	186 673	44 681
	64 641	141 680	271 837	453 826	502 138
Creditors (due within one year)	(28 614)	(61 175)	(105 202)	(222 232)	(276 792)
Net current assets	36 027	80 505	166 635	231 594	225 346
Total assets less current liabilities	43 020	88 103	179 519	256 179	314 730
Finance lease obligations					(3 920)
Provision for taxation	(850)				
Net assets	42 170	88 103	179 519	256 179	310 810
Capital	5 452	27 260	27 260	27 812	28 419
Share premium account	12 327			12 612	13 806
Revaluation reserve					9 848
Profit and loss account	23 785	60 235	151 055	214 551	257 533
Other reserves	606	608	1 204	1 204	1 204
Shareholders' funds	42 170	88 103	179 519	256 179	310 810

time profits collapsed by over 50% as operating margins fell from the company's traditional 25% to much nearer the industry average of 10%, while the share price dropped from over 200p in the summer of 1988 to under 50p in late 1989.

By the end of 1989 Amstrad was the dominant supplier of satellite

Exhibit 4 Extract from the *Amstrad Annual Report 1985.*

We are experts in design and engineering – one of our talents is to engineer products with all the specifications and facilities the market demands and delete those unusual facilities that are only enjoyed by the minority. In short we produce what the mass market customer wants and not a 'Boffins ego trip'. We have identified trends and opportunities in the market and applied our philosophy of engineering, outstripping the competition on price and specification and, more importantly, on quality. The relationship with our Engineering Team ... is quite unique. We have a team of people who can understand the commercial side as well as the technical side of product innovation.

Our other talents are in the procurement of component parts and in the understanding and reading of the semiconductor market.... We are also very flexible concerning the manufacturing territory for our products and in selecting the area most suitable for the item in question to be made. Our marketing skills and understanding the seasonable nature of our business is one of the main reasons for our success. Having the right inventory at the right time is important.

Alan Sugar

dishes for the UK market, and the PC2000 range of computers was at last making a significant contribution to turnover. But inventories, though declining, were still high, and with personal computer product cycles shortening dramatically any out of date stocks were not going to be easy to shift. The new fax machine, though imminent, was not yet in the shops; sales of home computers were declining; and the PC2000, on which the company's prospects largely depended, was not making an impact on the main corporate market. It was selling well to small firms, but the primary reason for its development had been to take Amstrad out of this market, in which margins were being squeezed, and into the less price-sensitive mainstream business market. This move was still perceived as critical for Amstrad's future growth.

FACING THE FUTURE

Where had Sugar gone wrong? Comments in the press suggested that the problem was primarily one of management structure. Alan Sugar had built up the company with a minimal structure, keeping tight personal control over everything that went on and taking all the important decisions himself. The view was, however, that it had grown to a size where such an entrepreneurial approach was simply not feasible. Most of the problems of 1988–89 could, it was claimed, be traced back to over-stretched management, and if Amstrad was to recover its stability and start moving forward again it would have to 'join the adults' and become more professional. Sugar noted other reasons, including an undisciplined chase for profits to keep the stock market happy, but basically he seems to have agreed. In the autumn of 1989 he introduced a new and greatly extended corporate structure, reinforcing his top management team with several key new appointments and relinquishing some of his own executive power. He also strengthened considerably his new product development team, noting that Amstrad relied heavily on its stream of new products and could no longer risk expensive mistakes. His overall strategy, though, remained the same: to move into the corporate market; to continue to take control of overseas distribution; and to bring manufacturing increasingly into Europe and into the company, rather than relying on subcontractors.

'The truck driver and his wife, the people I'm selling to, he associates a computer with those things he sees when he checks in at the airport on his way to Costa del wherever – it is, things with a keyboard and a screen.

'I think when this type of average man goes to a shop and sees possibly what Sinclair and Acorn call a computer, to him – with respect – it looks like a pregnant calculator – he can't associate with it.'

Sugar says the first generation of electrical, computer-type objects gave mum and dad a bit of a pain at home. 'What was happening was that the kids were occupying the television, there were loads of wires all over the place – and then, the kids couldn't be bothered to set up the computer or game after a while, and a lot of the first generation of computers ended up with their cables wrapped around them and thrown under the staircase.'

And with Amstrad's everything-with-chips, all-in-one box approach? 'Mum and Dad say "**that's** the computer, it goes in Johnny's bedroom – and it stays there".'

Sunday Times, 27 January 1985

Alan Sugar, founder and chairman of hugely successful Amstrad Consumer Electronics, is living proof that charm is not a necessary requisite to get along in business.

His manner is disconcertingly direct and the only obviously mild thing about the 38 year old entrepreneur are the 'extra mild' cigarettes he smokes with some ferocity. One of his favourite sayings is 'cut the crap', which could be seen as the motto that has sped him, in under 20 years, from street-market trader to head of a public company worth around £150 million.

'Sure he's abrupt,' says an employee, 'but people are loyal to him because of his track record. He's fought his way up from nothing and he's not superior. If there's a box to be shifted while he's around, he'll do it himself.'

Sugar doesn't like talking about himself and prefaces most personal statements with 'I don't want to sound big-headed.' But his Rolls Royce and shirt cuffs bear his initials and he's quick to identify the personal reasons for his success.

'I seriously believe that I have got an in-born talent. Some people are born with the talent to be a musician, others with a brain to be an engineer or programmer or doctor. I just have an aptitude towards business, trading and dealing. It's something you can't learn at university, it's just in you.'

Employees say it is difficult to identify ranks within the organisation. But Sugar notes: 'I'm very important to Amstrad. I think businesses in our sector need a spearhead. There are other businesses that have boards padded out with the right honourable lieutenants and flight marshals or whatever. But deep down, when you cut the crap, there is some spearhead there. In an industry like ours there is a prime motivator and that's me.'

The simple philosophy that produced Amstrad's word processor and home computers is the same that brought success in audio equipment. Sugar put the amplifier, tuner, tape-deck and turntable into a neat glass-fronted cabinet, called it the Tower, priced it low and sold thousands.

'There's no innovation there. All we've done is taken a logical step. And there's a lot more of these steps that can be taken,' he says.

Amstrad's products are made in the East, either bought-in or manufactured under contract. And in its past financial year, over 50 per cent of the company's revenue came from sales abroad with Amstrad risking little by selling direct to distributors who are responsible for marketing the product.   *Observer*, 27 October 1985

The design of the PCW8256 illustrates Amstrad's emphasis on the useful, and its impatience with the superfluous.

In the first place, it uses an 8-bit processor which is really yesterday's technology. The standard microprocessor these days is 16-bit, as with the IBM PC, and most manufacturers are now moving towards designs based on the 32-bit chip.

Sugar takes the view that, as far as the customer is concerned, the number of bits the processor can address is quite beside the point: '8-bit, 16-bit, 1-bit', he says, 'who cares, so long as it works.'

And it does work. Indeed, it works faster than some famous-name 16-bit machines, thanks to the dedicated word-processing software.

The Z-80 chip may be old hat, but it's proven and reliable, and is perfectly adequate to the task. Above all, it is dirt cheap, because of the huge volumes in which it is produced.

Sugar says the inherent limitations of 8-bit chip design have not held up development at all. He is, as usual, realistic about the PCW8256. If it has a two-year life, he'll be happy. But he expects it to last longer than that.

Amstrad's ability to create mass market products lies in its pricing strategy. The company has, until recently at any rate, left the trail blazing to others – to the Japanese in the audio and video markets and to the likes of Sinclair and Acorn in the computer market.

Sugar's trick is to extract from those pioneering products the key design and engineering elements, to apply his version of Occam's razor to the 'illogical' bits and pieces, and then to re-package the device in ways that permit extremely aggressive pricing.

In his words, 'We look at the competition, take it to bits, and see if we can engineer something similar or better – usually better, and cheaper. We identify the facilities that aren't useful and we ditch them to reduce costs.'

It would be misleading to regard the result as a no-frills version of the original. 'Techno-cosmetics' (as they are sometimes called) are as evident in Amstrad products as they are in those of the competition.

Amstrad was first to introduce the controversial double-cassette deck in its racked stereo products (a move that has infuriated the British Phonographic Industry), and the company also pioneered remote control for audio systems.

In Sugar's book, there are frills, and frills. He is merciless with those that are merely the product of some boffin's ego trip, but he is swift to incorporate those that are 'useful' in the sense that they appeal to his customers. Perhaps his greatest skill is his remarkable feel for such things. He, more than any other player in the customer electronics market, has a sense of what consumers want.

The 'realism' that Sugar sets such store by is evident in Amstrad's remarkable agility when confronted by changes in the marketplace, and also in the company's uncanny sense of timing.

Growth over the past five years, which have seen annual sales multiply almost 16-fold, has not been accompanied by a corresponding increase in the size of the planning team. Sugar and half-a-dozen senior lieutenants, specialists in design, engineering, and finance, run the company from the ninth floor of Amstrad's headquarters in Brentwood. Sugar himself sits in the middle of an open-plan office, at a desk distinguished from all the others only by the presence of a large, leather, Chesterfield-type armchair.

From this modestly-appointed eyrie in north east London, Sugar and his assistants monitor and regulate a £136m a year company operating in markets stretching from Hong Kong to Chicago. It is a classic example of a small group decision-making system and it works just fine.

A new product or, more rarely, a new market idea, normally begins in Sugar's mind, the product of his feel for what his customers, people between 17 and 35 in the BC1C2D socio-economic groups, are yearning for.

The key criterion and normally the basis of Sugar's insight, is price.

He decides that if Amstrad can market a shelf-mounted audio system for £300, including speakers and incorporating a compact disc (CD) player, a twin cassette deck, a radio tuner, and a conventional record player, it will sell like hot cakes.

He convenes a meeting and asks his experts whether, by pruning any illogical and useless facilities, such a product can be produced at a cost sufficiently below £300 to show an adequate profit. The engineers go away and do their sums.

They re-convene and report their findings. If Sugar likes what he hears, the 'go' button is pressed.

The marketing department (or at least that part of it outside Sugar's head) is not consulted. As Sugar puts it, 'We go ahead with production as soon as we know we've got a winner.'

Usually, they know they have such a winner when Sugar's gut feeling tells them so. He has a favourite metaphor to explain the point: 'If we found a way of making £1 notes for 50p, marketing wouldn't be the problem. The problem would be doing it.'

The decision about where to make the new product is based on the physical size and shape and on the sourcing of components. If 90% of the components come from Japan, then the Far East is the logical place to manufacture. If, as in the case of the audio products, it is more of a belt and braces operation, perhaps involving substantial UK sub-contracting, then the product is as likely as not to be made at Amstrad's manufacturing and warehousing complex at Shoeburyness.

It is the product that defines the territory of manufacture, not marketing considerations or any idea of a proper balance between 'in house' manufacture and sub-contracting.

Once launched, the sales performance of the new product is carefully monitored. The process begins with detailed sales forecasts and is backed up with a high-speed reporting system. New sales are immediately chalked up on blackboards in the office at the top of the Brentwood headquarters.

Sugar is realistic about sales reports: 'We're not blinded by the odd extraordinary result or by a seasonal down-turn in sales.

'Some of our competitors were dazzled by their initial success. We're always a bit pessimistic.'

The small decision-making group can react very swiftly to a genuinely surprising trend. Better than expected sales may lead to an increase in production, though this is not always possible. Worse than expected sales invariably lead to a reduction in production budgets or, when appropriate, to a complete withdrawal from the market.

The City appears not to have fully appreciated this agility. When it was concerned about the general level of computer sales earlier this year, it marked down Amstrad's shares. It should have known that the surest and earliest sign of disappointing sales at Amstrad is the company's prompt withdrawal from the market.

It's not as if there aren't any precedents. Amstrad pulled out of clock radios when the market collapsed; it withdrew from the CB radio market with a pocketful of profit when that business failed to match up to expectations; it ceased production of 22-inch colour TVs; and it stopped ordering video cassette recorders when quota agreements between Europe and Japan seriously undermined Sugar's pricing strategy.

The same pragmatism has characterised Amstrad's approach to export markets. Sugar pursues a zero-exposure export policy. Amstrad first finds an importer, and then he, the importer, puts up the finance. All sales to importers are irrevocable, and all are made on the basis of irrevocable letters of credit.

'If you have a good product,' says Sugar, 'people beat a path to your door.

'Most people seek us out. We just choose from the bunch.'

Financial Weekly, 17 October 1985

Amstrad has two notable strengths. One is the way in which it puts together and markets very low cost products such as its recently launched word processor complete with printer for £459 including VAT. The other is the speed with which it gets itself out of problematical markets like colour television, video and of course CB radio.

Amstrad products are always aimed at the mass market, are usually very basic with no frills and are remarkably cheap. Sugar's favourite description of his typical customer is 'the lorry driver and his wife'.

'Amstrad's key strength is Alan Sugar's ability to identify a price-point at which a volume of product can be shifted. The company then aims for that price point in the whole design of the product, by working backwards and allocating the margins', says Robert Miller-Bakewell, analyst at stockbrokers Wood Mackenzie.

'We take our leaf out of the Japanese book. Only we do what they do quicker', says Sugar, founder major shareholder and chief executive. 'They are good at identifying volume markets, studying the available products and seeing how they can make them better and cheaper.'

Like Amstrad home computers the attraction of the new word processor is not just that it is very cheap but that it is sold as a complete unit which only needs a plug.

When Amstrad first moved into the home market in Summer 1984 rivals typically sold just the computer with some software and a heavy emphasis on technology and power. But in order to make them work you had to buy and assemble all the peripherals like screen, cables, and cassette or disc drive.

Amstrad entered the market with a computer that came complete with all those necessary peripherals. There was nothing stunning about the technology but it was an important repackaging of the product. Suddenly home computing was accessible to all those people who could not – or did not want to bother – with the trouble of assembling a 'system'.

Similarly, the new word processor is a personal computer with printer, the screen, a disc drive and a generally acclaimed word processing program. No other company offers a serious product at such a low price nor sells as a complete assembled package something which is attractive to the non-expert buyer – although extra blank discs must be purchased before it can be used. 'We keep the product very simple,' says Alan Sugar. 'It comes in one box, with one power cord. You plug it in and it works.'

The packaging of the product is not just a good marketing ploy, it is also an important key to Amstrad's pricing and applies equally to the audio equipment, the home computers and the word processor. By linking all the constituent parts Amstrad can avoid duplicating many components from cardboard boxes to microchips.

Obscure

Costs are cut further by keeping the product as basic as possible and not offering extra facilities, which Sugar believes very few people need or would use. On the computer side he is particularly contemptuous of reviewers who seem more interested in obscure functions than in the basics of the machine.

The third element which enables Amstrad to keep its costs low is its small company structure. Founded in 1968 by Sugar to sell tinted plastic covers for record players, the company is still very closely run by him and greatly depends on his instinctive entrepreneurial and managerial flair. There is very little middle management and most of the decisions seem to be made by Sugar – although he accepts this will have to change as the company grows.

The fourth reason for Amstrad's low costs is its willingness to subcontract work wherever possible. The most obvious and most important is manufacturing, which is largely done in the Far East. The home computers and the new word processor are both assembled by the subsidiary of a Japanese company in Korea.

Amstrad also subcontracts a number of other activities such as distribution. It does not want the overhead of a fleet of lorries during the quiet summer period.

The level of subcontracting has also helped Amstrad maintain its reputation for being fleet-footed. Indeed Sugar values this highly: 'It is better to accept a lower margin, but have the flexibility to get out of something.'

Amstrad has shown it can make mistakes but get out of trouble with little apparent difficulty. CB Radio was one business which Amstrad entered with enthusiasm. But the day CB Radio was legalised Sugar decided – correctly – that the widely-held projections for demand would not be met and sold his entire stocks. Amstrad was one of the few companies to make a profit out of CB.

Financial Times, 23 October 1985

Malcolm Miller, Amstrad's sales and marketing director, gave a hint of the speed culture. 'We're doers' he said. 'We get on with things. If you have a good idea, every day you waste talking about it is a day's lost profit.'

And there are speed structures as well as a speed culture. Finance director Ken Ashcroft recalled what it was like when he joined the company: 'It was a revelation to me to see the simplicity of decision-making.'

Amstrad is built for speed from the bottom up. It has unbundled the traditional industrial package and turned manufacturing into a sub-contracted activity that can be used like a tap, to be turned up or down and on or off depending on market conditions and product development schedules.

Just as Amstrad lacks commitment to its products, so it lacks commitment to its manufacturing arrangements and component sourcing. The achievement Sugar takes most pride in over the past year is the change in the 'bill of materials' for computer production from 95% Japanese to 50% Japanese since last January.

The wholesale flight from yen-priced components as the Japanese currency soared in foreign exchange markets required only a modest increase in the Amstrad purchasing department.

Managers of corporate treasury departments (Amstrad has one now) are used to shifting surplus cash in and out of currencies at short notice but to change the whole currency mix of a manufacturing company's materials purchasing in so short a time is remarkable.

'It was natural to us,' said Sugar, 'because it was necessary for the survival of the margin.'

Speed and agility are important secrets of Amstrad's success. The third essential ingredient is what might be called the company's vision system: its ability to identify market niches and – using its inner eye – to dream up the right products to fill them. Sugar himself makes a major contribution here.

Amstrad uses outside firms like MEJ Electronics (hardware) and Locomotive Software for product development (though the 'in-house' r&d facility has been strengthened recently) but product ideas and associated marketing strategies come from Amstrad.

Sugar on customers: I'm realistic and we are a marketing organisation so if it's the difference between people buying the machine or not, I'll stick a bloody fan in it. And if they say they want bright pink spots on it I'll do that too: What is the use of me banging my head against a brick wall and saying, 'You don't need the damn fan, Sunshine'?

Financial Weekly, 1 October 1987

So while Amstrad notched up pre-tax profits of £90.12m on sales of £351.06m in the first half of this financial year, its own workforce is small. In Hong Kong, Amstrad's Asian base, the company employs less than 500 people, around 400 of whom work in its small factory making printers.

Amstrad's cramped Hong Kong office hardly looks like a nerve centre for one of the most successful British companies of the decade. Shared with a textile concern and tucked away in Kowloon's jewellery quarter, about 70 engineers and administrators control the company's web of sub-contracting, purchasing and shipping arrangements in the Far East.

At the heart of these is Amstrad's network of major sub-contractors manufacturing the company's computer, audio and video products. Amstrad depends on them for its most fundamental requirement – products at the right price and quantity for the high streets of Europe. This explains the care with which a new sub-contractor is chosen.

In one recent case, says Stan Randall, Amstrad's head in Hong Kong, the company was impressed by the product coming out of a Taiwanese factory which it had not used before. Amstrad's Hong Kong engineers took the factory's products apart, studying the techniques used by their Taiwanese counterparts. They worked out a price and quality specification for a large quantity of a particular Amstrad product. 'At that stage, the factory didn't even know we were interested in them,' Randall says.

When Amstrad knew what it wanted and the price it was prepared to pay, its team visited the factory. They spent four days crawling over its procedures. Satisfied with what they found, they began negotiating an order for 200 000 of the products.

Amstrad keeps tight control over its sub-contractors. Randall, one of only two people from Britain employed by Amstrad in the Far East, insists on up to five of his Hong Kong engineers working full-time in a sub-contractor's factory when a new product is being introduced. Amstrad supervises and pays for the installation of new tooling for its products. Once a sub-contractor is bedded down, Amstrad maintains pressure on quality through a team of 20 inspectors, based in Hong Kong, who are constantly visiting the sub-contractors.

Randall, who was Amstrad's purchasing manager in the UK before setting up the company's subsidiary in Hong Kong in 1981, says Amstrad uses its printer factory there as a testing ground for innovative production ideas. Sandwiched into four floors in Kowloon, the plant will be churning out 50 000 printers a month by the end of the year. Printers were chosen as the sole product for Amstrad itself to make in the Far East because Amstrad's direct competitors own the other printer factories in the region.

Randall aims for a stable set of sub-contractors so that they learn to take Amstrad into their confidence about their future plans. Amstrad has been dealing with the Japanese company which makes its computers and word processors in a Korean plant for 14 years. 'It's a long-term relationship. We have had some companies get very big on the back of Amstrad business,' Randall says.

But he tries to remain highly flexible within his stable bedrock of sub-contractors and major suppliers. 'You always have to keep your options open to move your production round the region.' says Randall, a workaholic never far from his cellular phone.

Financial Times, 1 August 1988

Last year Amstrad's operating margins were a huge 25 per cent. That is more than double those of competitors such as Compaq, which like Amstrad is young and fast growing but unlike Amstrad sells premium-priced computers.

'The reason Amstrad earns so much is that the machines are underengineered and the company understaffed (last year Amstrad's 1400 staff brought in sales of almost £1/2m a head). Margins could come all the way down to 10 per cent,' declares Keith Woolcock of CIBC Securities. At that level Amstrad would have made just £60m, profit last year, not £160m.

One way Amstrad is attempting to maintain its margins is by moving into the corporate computer market where buyers are less concerned with price than with hastle-free reliability.

The new range is the key to this strategy. Some Amstrad watchers believe it may have missed the boat. Others are more sanguine. The truth is no one really knows how successful the new range will be. No one doubts its importance. The existing machines still have plenty of mileage in them, particularly overseas. But like a shark Amstrad needs to keep moving. And with computers now accounting for around three-quarters of Amstrad's sales, it is hard to see how the consumer side could take up the slack if computers flag.

Investors Chronicle, 23 April 1989

Alan Sugar saw £52m clipped from his personal fortune in two days last week, after the second profits down-grade of the year for his troubled Amstrad consumer electronics group. The shares closed down 21p at 141p on Friday, as analysts forecast that profits would be £110m this year, compared with £164m in the year to June 1988.

But Sugar is not facing poverty; his stake in Amstrad is still worth £351m. However, he does need to recapture the City's confidence and to this end he is recruiting 10 financial and technical executives.

'Our problems are very simple,' Sugar told the *Sunday Times*. 'We have had such phenomenal growth over the past few years that we are still operating with a management team you would expect to be running a company a fraction of our size.

'From an engineering point of view we have too small a team to take on too big a task, and we are now paying the penalties in terms not only of our ability to design new products, but to maintain our existing ranges.'

Sugar admitted failing to keep a tight hold on the financial reins. 'There is nobody to blame but ourselves. It was entirely our own naivety in thinking we could take on products as advanced as the new business personal computers so quickly. They represent a much bigger dimension in technology,' he said.

'We must strengthen ourselves in engineering and design,' he said, 'especially in our method of checking, testing and bringing products to the market so that they are rock solid as soon as they go into production.

'We've also got to get a team of heavy hitters on the financial side, to improve our product planning and take much more firm control of inventories, especially in our overseas subsidiaries.'

Sugar said that a top priority must be 'continuing to design a stream of products and bringing them swiftly to market. We can't take two years to design products; it must continue to be other companies copying us two years later.

'I don't mean that we should hire a vast force of design people, but we could do with more engineering foremen to manage the technical team.'

Sunday Times, 23 April 1989

His management style is not so much hands-on as hands-in. In 1984, when Fraser was settling in at Microsoft, Sugar rang him up. 'He wanted to sell some piece of software on a volume deal with his new computer,' Fraser says. 'I quoted him our standard price, 60 pence a copy. He blew his top. "I don't buy anything on that basis," he roared. "Don't you know the business I'm in? I sell yesterday's technology at tomorrow's prices. If people want Dolby [hi-fi noise reduction], I give them Dolby B, not Dolby C." [Dolby B was introduced in 1968, Dolby C in 1980.] He said he wouldn't take the product. Boom. End of conversation. Over the years I had many thundering conversations down the phone with him about various things. It was always very abrupt, very blunt.'

There is little escape from observation if a job is not done well. 'In Amstrad you either last three weeks or you last for ever,' Sugar told his student audience. Stan Randall, after 18 years Amstrad's longest-serving employee says: 'He walks constantly from department to department, from finance to marketing to sales to dispatch, spending five minutes here, 10 minutes there, finding out what people are doing, helping out or pushing people along.' (The same applies when he visits the Hong Kong offices, where he knows many of the indigenous senior staff by first name.)

At least once a week Sugar sees the heads of a foreign subsidiary. The R&D departments are used to having him stomp into their impromptu meetings and sit listening to the discussion before throwing in a question to stir them up. Keeping Amstrad alert in spirit and structure has been crucial to his success. 'Every day you spend sitting around talking about an idea is a day of wasted sales,' says Malcolm Miller, group sales and marketing director.

To push prices down, the company plays suppliers off against one another. 'It's attention to detail,' Sugar explains. 'Say the power cord on a unit costs £1.50. If we use 50 000 per month, in a year we spend on that one item alone, £900 000.' Armed with that, the company looks to see if it can reduce its specification and at the same time searches for other suppliers.

'We may get the price reduced by 25 pence,' Sugar continues, 'and you may say – why waste your time? But 25 pence multiplied by 50 000 per month by 12 months is £150 000. As you can see, a good day's work for one bloke.'

The early products contained some interesting touches from the Amstrad philosophy of providing the absolute minimum at the lowest price. One person who took the facia off an early Amstrad hi-fi found the button for 'chrome/normal' cassette tapes was not connected. A hi-fi reviewer recalls an Amstrad speaker that appeared from the front to have two speaker cones, like high-priced rivals. When he took the front grille off, he found only one cone. The other had been painted on.   *Business*, July 1989

SUGGESTED QUESTIONS

1. What generic strategy or strategies has Amstrad pursued in the past, and what strategy is it pursuing now?
2. How appropriate is this strategy to its resource base and competitive environment?
3. What are the sources of its competitive advantage, and how is it exploiting these?
4. On what do you blame its recent difficulties, and what actions should it take to overcome them?

Andersen Consulting (Europe): entering the business of business integration

Case written by Sumantra Goshal with Mary Ackenhusen

A partner in Andersen Consulting defined its business as 'helping clients manage complexity'. As information systems technology progressed over the decades, Andersen emerged as the world's largest information systems consulting company through 'analyzing and then systematizing business's current information requirements into commodity products and then quickly proceeding to the next tier of complexity'. According to Terry Neill, head of services in the UK practice:

> Andersen's greatest challenge is constant commodization of its products and services. Our success depends on our ability to stay ahead of the commodization envelope.

In the 1940s Andersen's expertise lay in designing the complex and manual accounting processes required in corporations to meet the in-creased reporting demanded by the Securities and Exchange Commission (SEC) in the United States. The business had become routine by the 1950s with many companies able to do the work as efficiently and cost-effectively as Andersen, but by this time Andersen had moved on to the next emerging business system requirement which had never been done before: payroll systems. These had become commonplace by the 1960s and the firm had proceeded on to the development and integration of computerized accounting and payroll systems. Likewise, with the intro-

© 1992 by INSEAD, Fontainebleau, France
This case was prepared by Mary Ackenhusen, Research Associate under the supervision of Sumantra Ghoshal, Associate Professor at INSEAD. It is intended to be used as the basis for class discussion rather than to illustrate either effective or ineffective handling of an administrative situation. Reprinted with the permission of INSEAD.

duction of personal computers, networks, and fast-paced change in the capability of hardware and software, the 1970s and 1980s offered a constant stream of new opportunities as the company's clients struggled to exploit these new technologies to manage the increasing complexity of their businesses.

The emerging business integration market, described by Andersen as the clients' need for an integrated business, information and people strategy, was the company's target for the 1990s. Building on its unequalled strength in systems integration, Andersen sought to broaden its capabilities so as to be able to help clients formulate and implement strategic thrusts that encompassed all activities and functions on an integrated basis.

This new business vision presented an enormous challenge for the company. While there was broad agreement among the senior partners on the need for pursuing the business integration market, there were considerable differences of opinion on how to implement the strategy without sacrificing the strengths inherent in Andersen's traditional organizational values and management processes. There were also some significant differences in the market structures in different countries that called for a delicate balancing between the need for a coherent worldwide business integration strategy and the demand for different implementation approaches to suit the context of different national operations. Further, the thrust into the business integration market also required the development of two new skill areas – namely, **strategy** and **change management** – and the seamless integration of those skills into the existing organizations which supported Andersen's unique strengths in systems integration and information technology. To integrate the client's business, Andersen needed first to integrate its own business, which could prove to be the most difficult task the company had faced yet.

ARTHUR ANDERSEN AND COMPANY

In 1913 Arthur Andersen, the son of Scandinavian immigrant parents, purchased a small audit firm in Chicago which had since grown into the major accounting and consulting firm of Arthur Andersen. Andersen's vision was to establish 'a firm that will do more than routine auditing . . . a firm where we can measure our contribution more by the quality of the services rendered than by whether we are getting a good living out of it'. For more than three-quarters of a century, his philosophies have continued to influence the firm's culture as well as the profession of accounting as a whole.

Andersen wanted to build a practice with intelligent, well-trained people, but he could not find them through the profession's traditional method of hiring high school and commercial school graduates. At this time he was also teaching accounting at Northwestern (a major US business school) and he began recruiting his brightest students. This meant he had to pay more for his staff, but he found that the extra productivity and the comprehensive understanding of business they brought with them were worth the higher cost. Andersen also started the – then unheard of – practice of paying his employees during their training period. In other accounting firms, the employee paid the firm during this period of apprenticeship.

Andersen ingrained in his company the concept that the client always came first, regardless of personal sacrifice – evenings and weekends were not sacred. 'The client deserves our best, regardless.' To help support this philosophy, Andersen initiated the practice of paying overtime to his employees in the face of strong criticism from the major accounting firms of the day.

Extensive professional training, which became a well-known distinguishing feature of the company, had its roots in the 1920s. Training was strongly advocated by Andersen, beginning with mandatory lectures given by him and by other senior partners several times a week in the office and expanding to a rigorous course developed in the 1940s, designed to teach common standards to all US Andersen employees. From the onset, these courses were taught by insiders. It was Andersen's feeling that 'lectures should be given by men in our own organization who have pedagogical inclinations because these men [understand] our methods and procedures'.

The culture built by Andersen was one of inscrutable professional honesty even at the cost of losing a client. He always said that if the staff 'thought straight and talked straight' they would earn the respect of clients. According to former CEO Duane Kullberg, 'Those remain words we live by – not simply a hand-me-down slogan'.

The firm outpaced market growth in the 1950s and 1960s, expanding internationally and domestically through a mixture of a few high-quality acquisitions and the establishment of new offices. This period also saw the beginnings of the consulting arm of the business which helped fuel growth in the 1970s when the market for audit began to stagnate. The consulting business continued to be the major impetus for growth through the 1980s.

ANDERSEN CONSULTING

The origins of the Andersen Consulting practice lay in the industrial engineering function sponsored by the firm's founder, the purpose being to '. . . show the strong or weak points in company position or management, and seek to correct such weak spots'. This function was given second priority to the audit business through the 1940s until, in 1951, Joe Glickauf, an influential partner, built a copy of an advanced design computer which had been developed at the University of Pennsylvania. When he presented it to the partners with his vision of what it could mean for the future of business systems, they voted to give full support to the development of the area. The implementation of an automated

Exhibit 1   Andersen Consulting: financial summary.

Year	Worldwide			EMEAI		
	Net revenues ($m)	Partners	Professionals	Net revenues ($m)	Partners	Professionals
1991	2256	755	21 668	908	191	7751
1990	1850	692	18 188	663	172	6263
1989	1433	586	15 373	465	143	4974
1988	1106	529	12 009	360	123	3743
1987	828	469	9 231	236	108	2858

Exhibit 2   Andersen Consulting: worldwide organization.

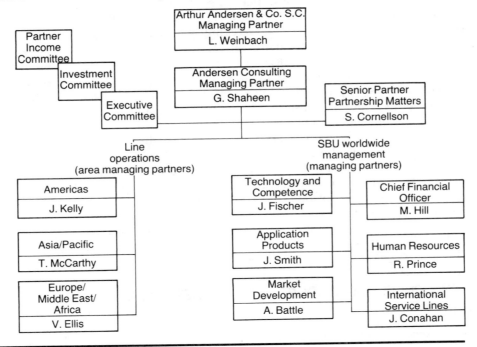

payroll system at GE in 1952 was Andersen's first computer-based project – it is believed to be the first commercial application of a computer.

Since the 1950s Andersen's consulting business has grown quickly with the advancement of information technology and its capabilities. The strong culture and training infrastructure established by Arthur Andersen for the accounting practice have also proven to be key strengths in this business. Initially, clients came from the customer base in the audit business but by 1990 their share had declined to less than 20%. By 1990 Andersen Consulting had emerged as the largest player in information systems consulting and was, in fact, the largest consulting company in the world, with over 20 000 professionals, operating in more than 50 countries. Worldwide revenues of $1.9 billion represented a compounded annual growth rate of 30% between 1985 and 1990 (see Exhibit 1). The company designed and implemented large-scale information systems and provided all associated services including programming and training of client personnel. Andersen also developed and marketed its own proprietary software and was an increasingly active player in the business of facilities management (i.e. managing computer operations outsourced by its clients).

Andersen, the man, always stressed homogeneity within Andersen, the firm, with his maxim, 'one firm, one voice'. Continuous reinforcement of this principle through standardized training and extensive formalization of work procedures positioned the firm for consistent service and methods across all offices and all countries. By the late 1980s, maintenance of the 'one firm' concept became increasingly difficult as Andersen began to branch off into two distinctly different businesses – audit and tax on the one hand, and consulting on the other – with vastly different professional norms, market structures, business approaches, and compensation levels in the two activities. Matters came to a head with the increasing demand of consulting partners for remuneration consistent with the significantly higher profitability and growth of the consulting practice, and in 1988 the two businesses were formally separated into two divisions. The consulting arm was renamed Andersen Consulting and was given the freedom to develop its own compensation system and management structure (see Exhibit 2). While a 24-member board of partners retained responsibility for providing oversight of the company as a whole, both business units now had significant strategic and operational autonomy so that each could respond most effectively to its own market and business needs.

ANDERSEN CONSULTING (EUROPE, MIDDLE EAST, AFRICA AND INDIA)

Andersen Consulting in Europe, the Middle East, Africa and India (EMEAI) emerged as a separate entity when the management of the tax/audit and consulting businesses was divided. In 1990 Andersen EMEAI had offices in 18 countries staffed with 6500 professionals who generated total 1990 billings of $695 million. This made it the largest consultancy in Europe in terms of gross revenues. The EMEAI practice had been growing at a rate of 28% per year in people terms over the preceding five years.

Exhibit 3 Andersen Consulting: EMEAI organization.

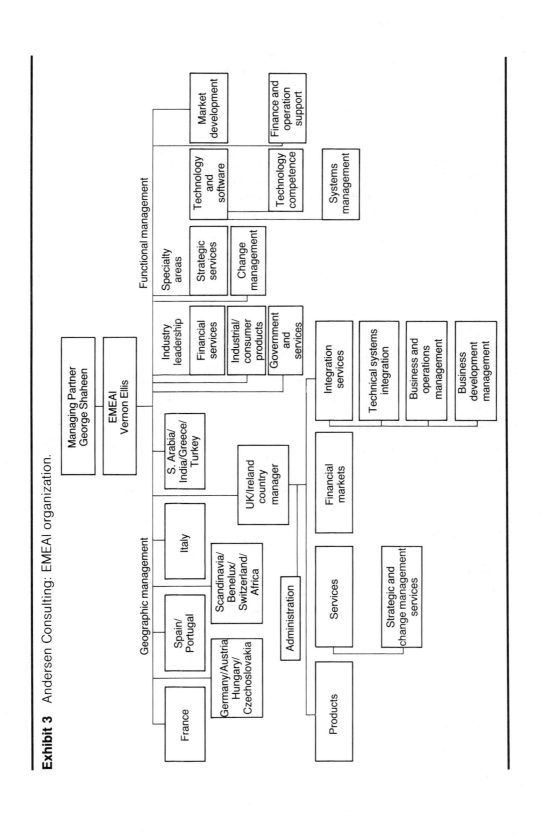

The Andersen organization was built around a geographic base of country practices (see Exhibit 3 for the EMEAI organizational structure). A matrix structure including industry functions, specialty skills, and functional skills was overlaid on top of this legally autonomous aggregation of national practices, creating an organization of considerable complexity.

Each country or country group was managed by a country managing partner who had reporting to him or her three industry sector heads and several heads of specialty skill or functional areas. The three industry sectors were **financial services**, **industrial and consumer products**, and **government and services**. The number and types of specialty and functional heads depended on the size and expertise of the office and included strategy and change management. Every professional in a country reported to either an industry, specialty skill, or functional head. Additionally, larger countries often had a varying number of industry subsector heads (e.g. oil and gas) and functional managers (e.g. logistics). These partners had no direct reports and reported into one of the industry sectors.

Each country was responsible for effectively utilizing its professionals to meet annual, and multi-annual, fee and productivity targets. A country managing partner's most important job was the management of his or her people resource to ensure they were either utilized within the country practice or loaned out to support a job outside the country practice and therefore still effectively utilized.

Vernon Ellis, the managing partner of EMEAI, was based in the UK. Each country managing partner reported to him as did the European heads of each of the three industry sectors and the heads of the specialty and functional skill areas. These regional sector or functional managers were responsible for practice leadership which included setting strategy and assisting in the staffing and execution of projects in their respective areas, and were linked to their counterparts in the country offices through what were referred to as 'dotted line relationships'.

THE ANDERSEN WAY

While all professional service firms assert that people are their key asset, at Andersen Consulting this assertion was translated into a set of institutionalized practices that lay at the core of what was often described both within and outside the company as the 'Andersen way'. The company invested heavily in building the capabilities of its people and the systems which supported them. These assets were then effectively leveraged through the project team structure to provide value to the client.

Building capabilities: developing people

The training infrastructure was one of the key distinguishing features of Andersen. Every new employee worldwide was required to take a six-week Computer Application Programming School (CAPS) course, taught in Andersen's luxurious St. Charles (Illinois) Education facility which was referred to, not inappropriately, as 'the university'. This rigorous course taught the fundamentals of computer applications and programming through intensive work sessions designed to simulate project work at a client site. With 80-hour weeks and the requirement of business attire throughout the programme, the simulation was realistic and emphasized that 'At Andersen, training is serious business'. The same methods were used to teach liberal arts majors and engineers alike in the Andersen methodology of systems design and implementation. As one senior partner described:

> CAPS is a real shock at first . . . you wonder how you'll be able to keep up, it is very intense . . . but then you find that everyone is in this together and you begin working as a team helping each other to pull through. And since then, this group has been my main network within the company. The experience created a career-long bond with these cohorts.

Andersen Consulting educated all its professionals in a uniform approach to each aspect of a job, whether it was systems design, programming, project management or writing a proposal for new business. The tools were designed to eliminate any ambiguity in the nuts and bolts of a project. This common tool set, embodied in numerous and thick reference manuals, was used worldwide to ensure consistency in firm performance and to enhance the ability of consultants from different countries and disciplines to work together. In combination, the uniform training programme at St. Charles, with the immense documentation tools, provided the core of Andersen's success in management information consulting: the ability to hire new undergraduates and in six weeks turn them into productive programmers.

Training continued throughout a professional's career with a standardized system that required everyone to spend nearly 1000 hours over a five-year period in training, undertaking a pre-specified set of courses at pre-designated intervals (see Exhibit 4). All training still conformed to Andersen's original contention that the best teacher came from within, allowing the more senior professionals to impart their learning to the new recruits. All offices of the company around the world were allocated a fixed number of hours of training they had to provide for staff, and faculty roles were allocated within the office among partners and other experienced staff. The internal faculty members were supplied with standard material for teaching their classes, but were also encouraged to embellish their sessions with examples from their most recent assignments. These new case stories were then incorporated into the teaching material that was provided to the next faculty for the same sessions. Approximately £35 000 were spent on a new employee in the first five years and an extraordinary 10% of Andersen's revenue was allocated to professional training. Internally, training was emphasized as an important

Exhibit 4   Training and experience in the progression from graduate to manager.

	Month										Minimum training hours
Mandatory experience	6	12	18	24	30	36	42	48	54	60	
Orientation/SFC/CAPS	•••										240
Basic accounting course	••										24
Programming/testing	120 days										
Introduction to financial and management information	••										24
Business practices		••••									72
Systems installation			•••								138
Programming supervision			50 days								
Detailed design			100 days								
System testing			50 days								
Conversion preparation				20 days							
Hardware/software evaluation				20 days							
Systems design					•••••						118
PSD – technical design					150 days						
– functional design					150 days						
Installation planning, organisation and cost benefit analysis					20 days						
Elective schools/courses					••••••••••••••••••••••••••••••						280 approx
Special study					100 days						
Client service school								••••••••••••••			63
Information planning											
											959

Note: 1 Start and finish points are the earliest and latest respectively
2 Number of days is the minimum requirement
3 This sets out the guidelines for the minimum path to manager
4 Training programmes are set out in bold; others represent professional work experience

benefit of working for Andersen: 'Your skills aren't just good news for the client. After training with Andersen Consulting, you could work for anyone, anywhere or you could work for yourself.'

The majority of Andersen's recruiting had historically been targeted at young undergraduates directly out of university. Each recruit had to undergo extensive interviewing, and the objective was to seek out bright achievers who could best be 'moulded' into the Andersen pattern with the expectation of a long career in the firm. Recruiting was a major activity for all professionals at Andersen's, including the partners.

Likewise, the development and nurturing of new recruits was an important part of upper management's role. Andersen partners were involved in subordinate development through a formal counselling pro-gramme. Each new employee was assigned a counselling partner upon arrival and met with this partner every six months to discuss performance, career interests, and other pertinent topics. Each partner counselled 20–30 professional personnel.

The typical career path with Andersen Consulting began with 1–2 years as an assistant consultant working mainly on large systems integration projects as a programmer, with regular formal and informal training in information technology and business skills. The next 3–5 years as a senior consultant were spent broadening technical and business skills in client engagements with more specialized training. In 5–8 years a professional could be expected to take on the role of project manager and, in 9–12 years, most recruits still with the firm would be expected to become a partner.

Like universities, Andersen followed the up or out principles of a meritocracy: each individual either performed well and moved up the ladder, or left the firm, opening up opportunities for those behind in the queue. The evaluation process was tough: only 50–60% of new professional recruits would become a manager and perhaps 10% would ever become a partner.

Assistant and senior consultants were evaluated on their performance every three months by their project managers. The evaluations were taken very seriously by both sides and were a valuable tool for performance improvement. Theoretically, project managers were evaluated themselves every six months by their project partner, but these often turned into self-evaluations due to limited partner time for the process.

Consultant and manager compensation was strictly based on merit, though the range between an outstanding performer and a satisfactory performer was less than in other comparable companies. There was no bonus or profit sharing below the partner level.

To facilitate personal development and professional contacts, Andersen Consulting prided itself on its vast and varied methods of communication within the firm. Every industry, functional, and country group had at least one newsletter which helped the fast-paced professionals stay on top of new projects, successes, and issues in their areas of interest. Likewise, these groups often sponsored conferences and circulated files of interesting papers on current issues. For those consultants with a wide area of interest, oversaturation – not lack of communication – was the problem.

The ongoing training at St. Charles and the European centre in Eindhoven in Holland provided professional and social stimulation. To help retain a 'small-firm feeling', personnel groups of 100–200 people were formed solely for the purpose of regular social gatherings. Upward communication with the partners was also facilitated through informal partner/manager dinners held on a regular basis.

The end result was a strong 'cultural glue' which helped Andersen employees to understand each other's objectives, methods, and motivations across offices and functions. They grew up together after college with the same experiences and values. As one manager remarked:

Exhibit 5   The economics of a typical professional service firm.

	Relative number of professionals by level	Relative net billings per head by level	Relative compensation of professionals by level
Associate	100	100	100
Manager	40	156	250
Partner	20	208	633

Key assumptions: 1 Target utilization: associate (90%), manager (75%), partner (75%)
2 Relative net billing per head = relative billing rate/hours × utilization rate × available hours; relative billing rate/hours: associate (100), manager (187), partner (250)
3 Relative compensation = salary + bonus
Source: Professional Service Firm Management, Maister, D (1985).

It's hard for outsiders to work at Andersen. They just don't know our vocabulary, our systems. While those who grow up in Andersen can carry out a task based on one sentence directions, an outsider will be lost. Andersen's can think alike.

Other firms in the industry expressed both their envy and their scorn for this strong internal homogeneity by the label 'Andersen Androids' which was almost a source of pride within the company.

Leveraging capabilities: managing project teams

The project team was the main organizational unit of Andersen for leveraging the capabilities of its people to deliver value to the client. Each team was made up of at least one partner, one manager, and a number of junior level consultants, and utilized the worldwide network of experts to participate on the team or advise. The ratio of partner time to consultant time attributed to the project determined the economics of the project and, therefore, of the firm. At Andersen, the partner to consultant ratio was very low with, for example, only 180 partners out of 6500 professionals in EMEAI, which resulted in high compensation for the partners leveraged off the large base of associate and senior consultants. Somewhat offsetting the favourable economics of a high consultant to partner ratio, target utilization rates were lower than the industry norm due to the emphasis on training and other forms of personnel development. Target rates for partner, manager, and consultant levels were 50%, 75%, and 80%, respectively. Nevertheless, this ability to leverage the expertise of partners across a large base of consultants was why Andersen partners were among the most highly compensated in the industry (see Exhibit 5 to review the economics of a typical professional service firm).

A project manager was chosen by the partner managing the case, according to skills, past experience, and availability. The company had a data base detailing each professional's skills and experience by industry and client, as well as his or her current assignment and availability. Partners complained, however, that it was too hard to codify all the important characteristics of a team player and the data base was typically used only as a last resort. The personal networks of the partners were often more important for selecting project managers and later staffing the teams.

With the partner's guidance, the project manager built the team and provided day-to-day management in the execution of the project. To staff a project, the manager would call on the worldwide resources of Andersen to get the proper fit. For example, for a project at Jaguar, the UK office, which had done relatively little work in the automotive field, borrowed personnel from the Paris office which had worked extensively with Renault and Peugeot. The manager was also responsible for meeting budget and time commitments and for the professional development of team members. People management was a very important part of this job.

Availability was the key to forming a team and therefore the scheduling data base, which detailed who was available and when, was the most utilized formal data base within Andersen. Each consultant was expected to be 80% utilized on client projects with the other 20% of his or her time being spent in training, other personal development activities, or downtime. The Andersen culture would rarely allow someone to be pulled from a case before its completion: the client's needs came before the business's. There was, therefore, a relatively limited pool of available talent to be placed on a team, and there were considerable pressures to utilize anyone not currently on a team. Though Andersen professionals had some latitude in choosing projects which met their own career development needs, most conceded that the system did not – and probably could not – be expected to support this objective fully.

Providing stewardship: the role of partners

Partners at Andersen spent 50% of their time on case work, 25% selling new projects, and 25% on development of subordinates. The partners were seen as the entrepreneurs of the business because they traditionally developed their own portfolio of business based on their own contacts and interests.

Each partner owned a piece of the firm and participated in the management of the firm on a one-person, one-vote basis. According to one partner, 'This is how we challenge sacred cows. Ownership is a great driver of arguments and strong opinions'.

Partners shared costs on a worldwide basis. Partner income was determined by a distribution formula based on the number of his or her units. Unit allocations were set by a partner committee which evaluated business generated, business performed, development of personnel, teamwork, practice leadership, unique skills, and other areas. Practice management partners evaluated all partners working for them and other partners could contribute to the review process as they felt appropriate. All management partners were evaluated by a comprehensive process of upward evaluation which was set up to be non-attributable, though many partners chose to discuss their feedback with the management partners they were evaluating. All partners received a listing of the unit allocations of every other partner in the world. Though there was an appeal process, it was rarely used. In general, the partners approved of the fairness of the evaluation and compensation systems. As described by one, 'It may not be perfect every year, but over a period of time, everyone seems to get what they are due'.

The partners saw themselves as the stewards of the firm who should continue to strengthen the firm for those who would follow. Sacrificing immediate personal income for the long-term benefit of the firm was a cherished norm. The first international expansion of the company in 1957 provides a good example. The proposal to open new offices in Paris, London, and Mexico was brought to the partners' meeting after the profits for the year had already been disbursed to them. Client needs required immediate opening of these offices, and the partners decided to pay back 40% of their income so that the firm could expand, even though many of them would not serve in the company long enough to reap the benefits. Likewise, year after year the partners continued to approve the tremendous investment in the training of future generations of Andersens. When a partner retired he took with him only his initial capital investment in the firm, and no appreciation or goodwill accumulated over his period of partnership. One partner reflected: 'The style of the organization is set by high quality people with high values which we pass on to the next generation. It's a strong cultural influence.'

THE BUSINESS OF BUSINESS INTEGRATION

The information technology (IT) consulting business could be divided into two broad segments. The first segment – the larger and the more traditional of the two – was the IT professional services market that included custom software development, consulting, education and training, and systems operations. The other more complex segment was the systems integration market, which was when one company took the technical and administrative responsibility for tying together information networks potentially involving multiple hardware and software vendors and multiple corporate functions. Systems integration projects usually ranged from $1–10 million in the commercial sector, but could go as high as $100 million for large-scale government projects.

In 1989 the IT professional services market for Europe exceeded $15 billion and was growing at the rate of 20% per year. The 1994 market size was expected to approach $39 billion of which 68% was attributed to custom software development. The systems integration market was only

Exhibit 6 IT professional services and systems integration (Europe): key competitors.

Company	1988 European prof. services est. revenue ($m)	1988 European prof. services market share (%)	1988 European systems integr. est. revenue ($m)	1988 European systems integr. market share (%)	1989 World revenue ($m)	1989 World profit ($m)	Revenue CAGR (%) 1986–89	Profit CAGR (%) 1986–89
IBM	660	5.3	190	9.9	62 710	3758	6.3	−7.8
Cap Gemini	590	4.7	180	9.4	1 202	89.4	34	40
Volmac	245	2.0	[1]	[1]	283	53	12[2]	4.1[2]
Finsiel	225	1.8	[1]	[1]	625	n/a	n/a	n/a
Sema	220	1.8	80	4.2	478	18	55	44
Bull	220	1.8	35	1.8	5 890	−48	23	n/a
Olivetti	200	1.6	45	2.3	7 406	166	7.3	−29
Unysis	180	1.4	55	2.9	10 097	−639	11	−145
Digital	140	1.1	[1]	[1]	12 742	1073	19	20
SD-Scicon	140	1.1	85	4.4	462	5	66	3
Andersen	105	.8	155	8.1	1 442	n/a	31	n/a
Logica	75	.6	65	3.4	280	20	29	42
Siemens	80	.6	65	3.4	32 398	836	8	2
Others	9 470	75	962	50.2				
Total	12 550	100	1917	100				

[1] Market share is insignificant and included in 'others'.
[2] CAGR (compound annual growth rate) is 1987–89.

$1.9 billion in 1989 but was expected to grow to $6 billion by 1994 (over 30% per year), with over half of this revenue coming from associated consulting services. In comparison, the systems integration market in the US had grown to $8.8 billion by 1990 and was expected to grow to $20.5 billion by 1995.

Both the size and growth rate made the systems integration and professional services markets very enticing to most key competitors in the information field. The high growth rate was attributable to the decentralization of in-house information systems departments, fast-paced technological changes with the associated new product introductions, the externalization of in-house corporate services, and the ongoing restructuring of major industrial markets.

European competition in such attractive markets was stiff and was continuing to attract new entrants. In professional services, the market was quite fragmented, the key competitors being IBM (5.3%), Cap Gemini Sogeti, the French software multinational (4.7%), and Volmac, a Dutch software company which received 90% of its revenues from the Netherlands (2.0%). Andersen was ranked number 13 with a 0.8% market share. The top three competitors in systems integration and their European market shares were IBM (12.5%), Cap Gemini Sogeti (11.8%) and Andersen Consulting (10.2%) (see Exhibit 6 for other competitors).

Many of these companies also competed in the related businesses of facilities management and packaged software. Facilities management was an important market because it could often be an entry into a systems integration project; likewise it helped systems integration firms hone their technical skills. Packaged software was important because many clients demanded standardized solutions from a vendor before they would consider a later purchase of professional services. Andersen Consulting had become quite active in both markets.

From systems integration to business integration

The systems integration market had been experiencing serious quality problems as projects fell short of client expectations in functionality, cost and completion deadlines. It was increasingly believed that the potential of IT could not be realized until a firm had a clear business strategy to direct the use of IT and had made the necessary organizational changes for IT to support a new way of doing business. Overlay of new IT capabilities on existing business practices rarely yielded the potential or expected benefits: the real pay-off lay in utilizing the new technology to support fundamental redirection of business strategy and management processes. This realization was the driving force behind the need for an integrated business philosophy and hence the potential of a business integration consulting market as the next level of complexity beyond the systems integration market.

According to Andersen's preliminary market research, only a few European clients recognized the need to better integrate their functional consulting requirements to produce an integrated business strategy through the engagement of one firm. Nevertheless, the company felt confident the market was going that way and had decided to build the competencies and infrastructure to exploit what they expected to be the new opportunity of the 1990s.

Key competitors in the emerging business integration market were potentially the same as in the systems integration market, with the addition of the general consulting firms. The traditional software and hardware companies such as Cap Gemini, IBM, and DEC were considered to be strong competitors with perhaps unequalled technical expertise but lacking in project management skills. Systems integrators such as SD-Scicon and Sema, two European-based companies specializing in software services and integration, were also seen to be technically strong and farther along in the task of building the needed project management skills. The large accounting firms were serious competitors in terms of project management skills, with less perceived competence in technical areas. Lastly, the general consulting firms, McKinsey, PA Consulting, and others, had excellent reputations for their ability to develop and implement corporate strategies, with easy access to corporate boardrooms and some experience in systems design, but they had minimal systems implementation experience.

Many of these companies had already begun to prepare for an expanded business integration market by taking action to broaden their skill base or geographic scope through mergers, acquisitions, and alliances. IBM had taken minority positions in numerous companies with large European market shares, and Andersen had developed numerous strategic alliances with companies such as DEC, IBM, and Sun Microsystems. Sema and SD-Scicon were both results of recent mergers.

Andersen's entry into business integration

The need to link an IT project to the rest of the business was not a new concept to Andersen, though it was not formally recognized as Andersen's strategic thrust under the name of 'business integration' until 1988. Even before formal recognition of the strategy, specialists were being groomed in two key areas where Andersen did not yet have a reputation and skill base, namely **strategy** and **human resource change management**. In 1987 these became the separate practice areas of **strategic services** and **change management**. Shortly thereafter the formal concept of business integration with its associated four-bubble graphic (see Exhibit 7) was adopted by Andersen Consulting, who described business integration as:

> A seamless combination of skills from each of the four areas: strategy, technology, operations and people. In developing business solutions it [is] necessary to consider all four areas and select in the appropriate balance, using different proportions in different situations. [This requires] people who are not narrowly based in a single discipline but who combine knowledge and understanding of each of these different areas.

In support of the four functions, four **centres of excellence** were formed: Strategic Services, Change Management, Operations, and Information Technology. The Strategic Services group worked with clients to develop and implement successful strategies in all areas of corporate activity. The Change Management group worked with organizations to position their people, processes, and technology to master change with maximum benefits. The Operations group helped clients develop effective day-to-day processes including implementation of just-in-time (JIT) systems, plant re-layouts, quality assurance systems, etc.; and the Information Technology group contained very specialized hardware and software experts to assist in implementing state-of-the-art customer solutions. For most country organizations, only Strategic Services and Change Management were distinct skill sets: Operations and Information Technology were still located within other functional or industry groups.

These specialty areas were geared to building up repeat and continuous experience in their respective areas of a world-class nature. The IT generalist background of a standard Andersen consultant was deemed unsuitable to efficiently support these specialty areas to the level needed

Exhibit 7 The business of business integration.

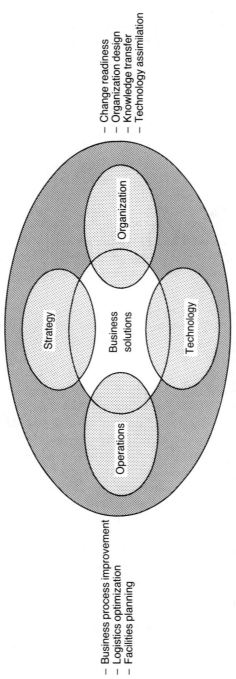

- Strategic planning
- Buyer values/customer focus
- Product/market strategy
- Financial strategy

- Change readiness
- Organization design
- Knowledge transfer
- Technology assimilation

- Business process improvement
- Logistics optimization
- Facilities planning

- Technology assessment
- Information technology planning
- Systems integration
- Computer systems management

to compete in the emerging business integration market. As described by Vernon Ellis:

> You could try to produce a complete Renaissance man but it is impossible these days. The business world is too complex . . . We need both generalists and specialists. Some people will be in just one bubble, some in the middle of all the bubbles, and some at specific intersections.

In numbers, these specialists were few compared to the rest of Andersen. In 1989/90, there were 170 strategy specialists and 290 change specialists within EMEAI. The majority of Andersen professionals were the IT generalists (the 'engine room', as described by one consultant) in the middle of the graphic bubble chart – although the vast majority of these 'IT generalists' specialized in an industry or industry sector. IT generalists were the people doing the execution and had a 'delivery mechanism' skill set. They were expected to have a good general business understanding of each of the specialist areas as well as a thorough knowledge of the IT area – Andersen's traditional strength. The project manager's challenge was to glue the expertise of the specialists and the business understanding of the generalists together into a successful project team.

The experience at National Power

A business integration case often developed through an evolutionary process. As described by Vernon Ellis, 'Usually we start with one aspect of a project and hopefully it broadens into a business integration project. Our aim is not to sell more work but to make sure the end result is better implementation'.

National Power in the UK was recently given the mandate to privatize, and called on Andersen Consulting to assist them in this major operational, organizational, and cultural change. Tim Forrest, who was also the industry head for oil and gas/energy in Europe, served as the partner on the initial engagement.

The team was composed of 15 Andersen consultants and included specialists from each of the centres of excellence. Forrest estimated that the project fell into the four areas of business integration, as follows: Strategy (10–15%), Information Technology (40–50%), Operations (25%), and Change Management (15%).

The first three months were spent deciding on the new mission of the company. The objectives articulated by National Power upon engaging Andersen were: 1. to become a cost-effective supplier of electricity; 2. to take advantage of market opportunities; and 3. to diversify into new businesses to optimize revenue.

Tim Forrest gave his view on what Andersen offered as strategic input to this mission:

> It was really to make the strategy work. It was partly to flesh out the ideas they had, because they were very conceptual. Within each area,

there were myriads of things that needed to be done in every part of the organization. The Strategic Services people talked to a variety of National Power managers at different levels to get some specific definitions of what the company would do differently in the future and to ascertain what it would take to do those things differently.

In evaluating the contribution of the Change Management personnel, Forrest commented:

> Initially they were focused on IT because the IT department had been 1200 people two years ago. At the beginning of the year it was split three ways . . . 300 was all that was left . . . Basically they were in a very depressed state, they didn't know what the company was trying to do . . . They didn't understand the IT strategy or the business strategy, so initially the Change Management people were very much focused on talking to as many senior people as they could within the IT department to find out what their concerns were . . . Once they got these people reasonably motivated and fired up, they then started to optimize the communication the other way [to the user community].

The technology and operations content of National Power was the type of work that Andersen had specialized in for many years. After developing strategic objectives, critical success factors, and key performance indicators for each area, elaborate IT systems and operational systems were designed in the areas of Work Management, Inventory Management, Operational Information, and Project Management Systems.

In evaluating the relationship between the various centres of excellence and the generalist practice, Tim Forrest stated:

> The core of the business is still the same [the IT/Operations concentration]. Change Management helps us to do lots of things we've done for the last 20 years, only we now do them very much better. There's nothing particularly new about Change Management . . . they're extremely good at forcing us to think more about cultural change and the impact of technology on people . . . quite honestly, the strategy input is a bit the same, or at least on many projects it is like that. Strategy is forcing the project team to think, well what are we really trying to do with this system? . . . In relation to our main practice, it is the discipline that helps us do our main job better.

THE CHALLENGE OF MANAGING COMPLEXITY

By 1990 the strategy of business integration had been well-communicated and widely accepted within Andersen, though there were some different internal views on how the company was pursuing the market. Vernon Ellis recognized this lack of clarity:

> There are still conferences and debates on the strategy, which reflects an emerging understanding with no clear answer yet. We may be

actually facing dichotomies to a certain extent which are not capable of resolution.

Balancing conflicting demands

At the core of these dichotomies lay the conflicting needs for building best-in-class capabilities in each of the skill areas needed to support the business integration strategy, and the demand for integrating those skills internally in a manner that would provide Andersen with some competitive advantage over the scores of other companies targeting the same opportunity. As described by Terry Neill:

> We are the best in the business systems piece. What goes with strategy or change is that we have to be the best in each piece. In strategy, there are established leaders like McKinsey and our challenge is to develop a reputation as good as theirs. The change management business is still fragmented, just like the IT marketplace in the 60s and 70s, with small 'guru' style firms and individuals. We are doing the same thing in change management that we did there.

Gerard Van Kemmel, Managing Partner of France agreed:

> I don't believe clients will buy a business integration project unless the supplier is the most skilled and best value in each area. Otherwise, a customer will hire the best firms and integrate themselves.

The other internal viewpoint stressed the importance of integrating the functional pieces of a customer solution.

> I don't think we want our strategic services practice to be the same as McKinsey's. We want the market to accept that we do strategic services work, but if that was all we had, we would be no better than McKinsey. I think that's why the integration bit, the fact that we can talk readily across into the other areas, and that we offer the portfolio, is a very strong message. Otherwise, we could just divide the building into four wings and put McKinsey down one wing, Andersen down another wing, someone who was good at change in another wing, and then some technology experts down the fourth wing.

And, while the two perspectives were not necessarily contradictory, their operational implications were not easy to reconcile. As described by an external industry analyst:

> If you want to be the best in each piece, you have to grow each activity separately – specialize each group with the most challenging assignments dedicated to its particular area. If you want to really integrate, you need to develop a different model of what strategy and change is all about, redefining them from the perspective of integrated delivery. Best-in-class specialization and effective integration require not just different structures and management processes,

Exhibit 8   Andersen Consulting: UK and Ireland.

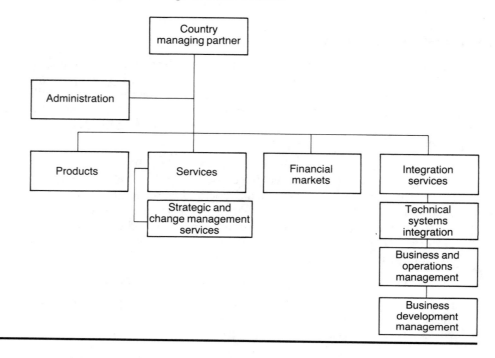

Exhibit 9   Andersen Consulting: France.

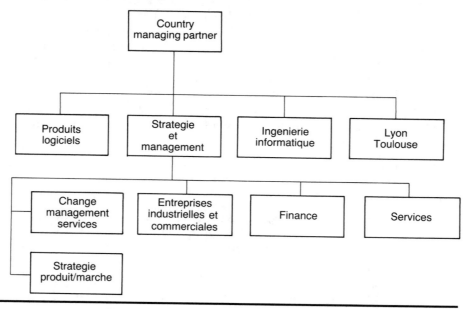

but even different definitions and visions of what each bubble represents.

Further, some differences of views still lingered on the right balance between allowing individual partners and local practices the freedom to develop their businesses entrepreneurially, identifying and exploiting local opportunities, and the need for pursuing a coherent worldwide business integration strategy. As described by Ellis:

> Historically, our partners have been entrepreneurs and that is how Andersen has been so successful. Partners built their own practices based on their skills, interests and contacts. They managed the projects start to finish. Now we need a different approach. A worldwide strategy requires that the partner finds the best person for each job, and often that person may not be him. We need a change in the partner mindset.

Terry Neill also suggested that perhaps there was a need to consider some fundamental organizational changes to adapt to the new strategic approach:

> Everyone here is a doer – that's our style – but sometimes we don't have enough people fully dedicated to thinking things through and that, sometimes, shows up. We have had occasional false starts. Perhaps we need a dedicated internal strategy and planning group – with young partners spending two or three years in the role – in much the same way as officers in the military spend short periods in staff roles as a key part of their career development.

Responding to national differences

The corporate vision of business integration was not always mirrored at the country operating level. For example, the UK and French offices pursued the business integration market with varied implementation strategies due to the competitive and cultural differences of the two markets and historical differences in the two practices.

The French information technology market was the most developed in the world in terms of percentage of gross national product (GNP) spent on IT and was also the largest market in Europe. The market structure reflected a much clearer dichotomy between IT and business consulting. In the IT area, the market had several large world-class competitors such as Cap Gemini and Sema who were able to compete successfully with Andersen on a cost basis. From this 'IT only' view of the French market, Andersen was sometimes seen as a small player. In contrast, it was historically very strong in the sector of management consulting.

By some measures, the UK was the third largest IT market in Europe and also very competitive. Andersen was very successful in the UK because the market was willing to pay a relatively high rate due to the perception of extra value being added when performed by an 'integrator'.

This meant that Andersen could often command significantly higher rates in the UK than France for IT work. On the other hand, Andersen's UK competitors would often try to position Andersen as IT consultants so as to undermine the market perception of Andersen's strengths in the business consulting area.

Culturally, in France, the corporate IT function was perceived to be of lesser stature than in the UK. In the UK, the top IT job was a key management position charged with helping the company integrate its business and information technology strategies. In France, the position of IT director was not seen to be the way to the top – top positions in corporations were reserved for the graduates of the elite 'grandes écoles' system, a group to which the IT directors did not typically belong. The IT director had little or no voice in corporate strategy and top management issues. The result was that IT directors ran a relatively insular and controlled world without top management interference. When they hired consultants they looked for firms who were cheap, had a flexible workforce, and most importantly would allow them full control of the project. A successful consultant in France would never go around the IT director to top management.

These market differences led to very different recruiting and development systems in the two countries. To develop and maintain the French strength in management consulting, the French office had always recruited from the 'grandes écoles' educational system. These individuals were trained in the fundamentals of IT through the traditional Andersen course work (CAPS, etc.) but were only required to work in IT for a very limited time period (6–12 months) after which they were assigned to the management consulting practice.

The majority of Andersen employees in the French office focused on the IT business were not recruited from the 'grandes écoles'. They were on different pay scales – although these were significantly in excess of their French IT competitors. One career track within this organization did draw from the 'grandes écoles' system; these were the employees who helped integrate the IT business with management consulting when needed and who were the future partners of the IT business.

In contrast, the UK had always been much stronger in the IT business and recruited to develop and maintain this skill. Recruits came from the top British schools, were trained in the Andersen methodology, and were then required to work in systems design and programming for 3–5 years.

Because of these competitive, cultural, and historical differences, the French and UK national organizations pursued some very different approaches in implementing the business integration strategy. The UK implementation replicated the corporate vision as laid out by Ellis. The four centres of excellence were integrated at the country level to present a 'seamless combination of skills' to the clients. The Strategy and Change Management areas were distinct organizations reporting into the Services industry subsector. The professional development infrastructure was the same for all professionals in terms of training requirements, salary structure, and promotion opportunities.

The French model maintained separate organizations for the information technology business – Ingénierie Informatique – and the management consulting business – Stratégie et Management. Within Stratégie et Management, there was a very successful stand alone practice in Change Management. The Strategic Services function was not a separate area within the management consulting arm because the French management felt their professionals were well-schooled in strategy, making it unnecessary to develop this expertise in a separate group. Although the two organizations sometimes sold their services separately, more than 80% of their work was for common clients.

While recognizing that the French model was very different from the corporate blueprint, local management strongly believed that their approach was better suited at least for the French market. Firstly, a distinct IT organization showed a commitment to Andersen's core expertise in information technology with a focus on productivity and skills. Secondly, the structure recognized the French market's IT-business dichotomy and made IT directors more comfortable because they could deal with a separate consulting group as they always had in the past. Thirdly, the structure allowed for recruitment of people with different profiles and expectations, and made it possible for the company to remain as a cost-effective competitor in the traditional IT business while protecting the high-quality image necessary for success in the management consulting and business integration fields. Lastly, it allowed clients to easily buy only one service from Andersen (just IT or just consulting) as a stand-alone piece of work and to do the business integration themselves.

The long term vision of how Andersen's strategy should be developed also varied between the two country offices. The UK was organized by three main industry groups: Financial Markets, Products, and Services. A fourth division, Integration Services, housed specialist technology, software, and systems management skills. The UK practice had three further centres of excellence – Strategy and Change Management, housed in Services, and Operations/Logistics, housed in Products. The French vision planned for a centre of excellence structure within each of the three industry groups (Financial Services, Products, and Services) as soon as each area had enough critical mass to justify the organization.

Developing new capabilities

Of the four centres of excellence, the newly formalized areas of Strategic Services and Change Management were still establishing themselves both internally and externally. Change Management was challenged to establish a distinct skill set for itself. Its historical roots were to provide training to clients in support of large complex systems being installed by Andersen. However, since 1988, Change Management's scope had expanded rapidly to reflect the cultural and organizational challenges of major transformational change in large organizations. Change Management was defined in three practice areas: Technology Assimilation which supported the training and education needed to ensure that the expected benefits of major IT investments were fully delivered; Knowledge Transfer which covered training in all its aspects, including the use of training technologies; and Organization Change which included the strategic and tactical aspects of process and organizational change.

Much of Andersen's Change Management work in 1988 and 1989 was still in the training area (Knowledge Transfer) but the balance was rapidly changing as partners recognized the key role of the people and change dimensions in executing Andersen's business integration strategy. Because the Change Management market subsector was very fragmented with few large players, cost was an important element of competition.

Strategic Services marketed the following services in support of business integration: strategic management studies; competitive/industry analysis; market and sales planning; operational planning; information technology strategy; and organizational strategy and change management. In reality, most Strategic Services work seemed to have an operational bent. As one partner described the practice:

> Most of the strategy work, after all, is concerned with sorting out strategies to optimize a business, rather than what company should I go and acquire in the marketplace. In other words, it's what I would call internal strategic consulting, rather than external strategy consulting.

Some partners had expressed concerns about the potential overlaps between the Change Management and Strategy skill sets as Change Management moved into organizational change work. Others shared Terry Neill's view:

> Executing our business integration vision requires that we be able to mobilize project teams with a portfolio of skills in systems, strategy, process and change management. We need world class skills in each dimension and the ability to bring them together for a client without the client having to concern himself about divisions which could be created by the internal structures of Andersen Consulting. We now have a dozen large high quality UK clients where we are making business integration a working reality. These companies are seeing the value of the skills portfolio and that will accelerate the removal of internal barriers. We are winning with those organizations who see the skills of strategy and execution being inextricably intertwined.

To fill the specialist needs, Andersen broke with its tradition of hiring recent graduates and 50% of the centre of excellence hires were brought in as experienced 'outsiders' at senior and manager levels, while the other 50% came from within the firm or were recruited at an MBA level from the outside. In general, Strategic Services recruited MBAs from top business schools, and Change Management brought in experienced individuals from the fields of organization change, industrial psychology, and education. Though Andersen prided itself on growing organically and not through acquisition, a small manufacturing consulting firm was acquired in 1988 in the UK to enhance the skill base of the Operations specialty practice.

The new recruiting model and acquisition strategy required a rapid build up of expertise and internal training. Some partners felt that Andersen made a slow start in this area. Nevertheless, good progress was made in 1990 and 1991 in building training and methodologies for the emerging Change Management and Strategy skill sets. Andersen's ability to roll out and deploy new training and approaches quickly and effectively was seen by several partners as the key to success in delivering on the business integration vision. On-the-job-training was somewhat hindered because project opportunities for inexperienced, newly trained specialists could only grow at the rate at which Andersen was succeeding in taking its business integration strategy to the market.

Absorbing a large number of outsiders was a significant challenge for a firm whose strong cultural roots were passed on from one generation of recruits to the next through the institutionalized mechanisms represented in the 'Andersen way'. Normally, similar training, work tools, experiences, and ways of thinking made a team work smoothly. With the development of specialists within the centres of excellence, some of the common parameters were diluted. These outsiders came in at middle management levels with different ideals and methods, weakening the cultural glue that had traditionally bound together a team of Andersen consultants.

The more experienced professionals hired from the 'outside' did not view the traditional Andersen training programme as an appropriate initiation for a senior employee. A recent MBA from a top institution recruited into Strategic Services was required to take the full six-week CAPS course at St. Charles and then work for several months on a systems project – the typical progression for an undergraduate recruit. His view was that the requirement added no value, and he did not think it compared favourably to the first few months of strategy work that his counterparts at the strategy boutiques experienced. Likewise, a newly hired senior manager in Change Management who had refused to participate in the six-week course said, 'I would quit before I would take the CAPS course!'.

Furthermore, there was a concern within the Strategic Services practice that the Andersen compensation/development philosophy was hampering their ability to recruit and retain top individuals. They felt there was a need to at least approach some of the benefits which were found at their competitors' shops. Base compensation was on par with the competition, but in the boom times for strategy consulting in the 1980s, some partners felt that Andersen's unwillingness to have bonuses might have put the firm at some disadvantage in recruiting. On the other hand, Andersen grew by nearly 40% in the UK in 1991 while most of its competitors were laying off large numbers of people. Most felt that its approach was thus vindicated – especially since so many strategy consultants from other firms applied to join Andersen, partly because of its rapidly growing reputation in the strategy area.

The generalists, in contrast, complained that the recently recruited specialists did not know how to do things in the 'Andersen way' and did not want to take the time to learn. The opinion of a member of the Change Management group who had come through the traditional Andersen career path was, 'If you change the infrastructure and make it different than the rest of Andersen, the result will be a loss of trust'. Another generalist consultant agreed, 'We're somewhat suspicious of the Strategic Services and Change Management types, especially if they are an external hire but even if they were moved from the IT area of the practice'.

A specialist in the Change Management field saw the tension between the groups differently; 'Although less than 50% of our consulting practice is now in the US, our origins in the Midwest leave strong cultural values. We tend not to appreciate gurus or luminaries. Apartness, or individual aggrandizement, is neither revered, rewarded, or encouraged.'

The result of these difficulties was that the turnover in Strategic Services and Change Management was higher than for the firm in general. Consequently, Andersen had begun to fine-tune the profile of a successful outside hire to more closely match the characteristics of an Andersen undergraduate recruit and the traditional Andersen culture. Additionally, the mandatory computer-based training that all Andersen recruits had been required to take in the past at St. Charles was shortened, and in some cases waived, for outside manager-level recruits. There was no formal policy in this area, but increasing flexibility seemed to be the direction in which Andersen was heading.

Integrating the multinational network

Andersen saw one of its competitive advantages to be its ability to serve a multinational client, or a client who would like to become multinational, through its own network of multinational offices to provide an integrated, pan-European, or even worldwide, solution. This service created a need within Andersen for professionals who embodied a multinational perspective in terms of language, culture, and business knowledge. As one partner explained:

> There are very few [companies] who can pull into a project the resources from around the world. I've got over 20 000 people, and somewhere in the world we can find that somebody who really does understand a particularly difficult problem.

But as Andersen grew in size and organizational complexity, the firm was finding it increasingly difficult to take advantage of its enormous people resources to develop, identify, and effectively utilize this multi-national specialist. As expressed by Terry Neill:

> A key impediment could become our ability to share knowledge quickly. In the past we have done it entirely by the personal network . . . now we're too big to do this. We need to improve our own IT network. But we also need to protect and improve our informal human network. Both are difficult, but both are challenges we must respond to urgently.

After an individual was identified as needed on a project team, the country manager had to agree to release the individual. Because the country manager was responsible for his or her own profits, and these specialists tended to be very effective on national cases, deployment of people to regional or worldwide project teams was becoming more and more a source of conflict. There were incentives within the partnership evaluation system which measured how well each partner supported the multinational practice needs, but in reality, it was recognized that country interests came first.

Andersen was also finding it hard to hire and develop enough consultants who wanted and had the ability to participate in multinational cases. Language and cultural differences were difficult to overcome and many consultants preferred not to work outside their local area.

In 1991, a pilot programme was introduced in the Strategic Services area to try to better develop and manage the valuable multinational specialist resource. Breaking from the traditional structure in which all professionals reported within a geographic region, a multinational specialist team was formed, which had a small centralized core in one country and a network of specialists located in various other countries, all reporting directly to the head of the team. As expressed by Bill Barnard, the partner in charge of market development for Europe who developed the programme:

> In areas where we have very few specialists, we can't afford to have them only work in one country. We need to move them into different countries to work multinationally which causes conflicts with the country managers. Some conflict is good but we need to protect these people and to help them get repeat experience and develop their skill sets. Otherwise, their experience gets lost.

Andersen also attacked this problem by trying to hire and develop people who liked multinational activity and by stressing in the education process that international relocation was part of the job. A human resource programme introduced in 1990 supported a small group of individuals for development through exchange programmes across Europe. Nevertheless, Bill Barnard predicted that it would take until the end of the century before Andersen worked as a truly integrated European operation.

SUGGESTED QUESTIONS

1. What are the key elements of the Andersen Consulting (Europe) strategy for the 1990s?
2. What are the firm's existing sources of competitive advantage, and how appropriate are they to the new strategy?
3. In what ways has the firm's competitive advantage been reinforced by its organizational structure and corporate culture? How appropriate are these to the new strategy?
4. How can Andersen Consulting (Europe) best implement this strategy, what problems (internal and external) is it likely to face, and how might it address these problems?

3

Benetton SpA (A)

Case written by José-Carlos Jarillo and Jon I. Martínez

I should say the new strategy relates to our intention of structuring Benetton as a proper multinational company. That means we plan to create a complex global manufacturing system to advance our mission to reach the two-thirds of the world where we do not have a presence. It is in this light that our recent choice to diversify into the field of financial services must be interpreted. The financial services companies that we operate – generally in partnership with important banks and financial institutions – have to be considerate and provide the necessary support for Benetton's new development policy. In addition, the new and more sophisticated system that we are going to build in the field of services (not only financial services but the service industry overall) may help us in our attempts to implement the entrepreneurial formula that I have tried to explain to you.

With these words, Mr Aldo Palmeri, General Manager of Benetton, SpA, outlined the strategy for the future development of Benetton; a strategy designed to keep the outstanding rate of growth the company had enjoyed since its inception.

HISTORY OF THE COMPANY

The Benetton story was a tale of huge success built from humble origins. Started some 25 years ago, the company had reached $1 billion in world-wide sales, building from its strengths in one of the most mature, labour-intensive industries in labour-expensive Western Europe.

© 1988 by the President and Fellows of Harvard College
Harvard Business School Case 9-389-074
This case was prepared by Jose-Carlos Jarillo and Jon I Martínez as the basis for class discussion rather than to illustrate either effective or ineffective handling of an administrative situation. Reprinted by permission of the Harvard Business School. The casewriters gratefully acknowledge the assistance of Mr Franco Furnò, manager of Organizational Development at Benetton SpA, in the preparation of this case.

The firm was a typically Italian family concern, with four siblings – Giuliana, Luciano, Gilberto, and Carlo – involved from the beginning in the company operations. The eldest brother, Luciano, was born in 1935, and spent his childhood through the harsh times that the Second World War brought to north-eastern Italy. Upon his father's death, he had to leave school at the age of 15 to take a job in a men's clothing store. In 1955, Luciano, who had just turned 20, told Giuliana he was convinced that he could market the bright-coloured, original sweaters she used to make as a hobby, so why shouldn't they leave their jobs and start a business?

With 30 000 lire, obtained from the sale of Luciano's accordion and Carlo's bicycle, Luciano and Giuliana bought a knitting machine, and soon afterward Giuliana put together a collection of 18 pieces. Luciano was immediately able to sell them to local stores. Sales increased steadily over the next few years, until Giuliana had a group of young women working for her and Luciano had bought a minibus to carry these employees to and from a small workshop the Benettons had set up near their home.

In the early 1960s, Luciano Benetton put into practice several innovative ideas that helped turn the company from a small enterprise into a giant. The first idea was to sell only through specialized knitwear stores (as opposed to department stores and boutiques selling a wide range of clothes), whose owners would presumably be more interested in pushing sales of his particular product. Luciano made use of another idea which was unusual at the time: to offer retailers a 10% discount if they paid in cash on delivery of his product. At that point, Benetton sweaters did not bear the family name (they used names, such as 'Lady Godiva' or 'Très Jolie'), but they already had the Benetton characteristics of medium–high quality and stylish design at a very reasonable price.

Two more new ideas emerged, this time for lowering production costs. The first was a novel technique for making wool soft, like cashmere; it was based on a method Luciano had observed while visiting factories in Scotland, where rudimentary machines with wooden paddles beat raw wool in water. The other idea was to buy and adapt obsolete hosiery-knitting machines, at a price of $5000 apiece – a fraction of the cost of a new machine. The refurbished machines did their new job perfectly.[1]

Benetton was formally incorporated in 1965 as 'Maglificio di Ponzano Veneto dei Fratelli Benetton'. The small enterprise consisted of Luciano, Giuliana, and their younger brothers, Gilberto and Carlo. Gilberto was placed in charge of financial issues, while Carlo headed the production system. In the same year, the first Benetton factory went up in the village of Ponzano, a few kilometres outside Treviso, in north–eastern Italy.

In 1968 the company opened the first independent outlet in the mountain village of Belluno, not far from Venice. With its appealing merchandise and its spare, intimate interior, the store was an immediate success. The store occupied only about 400 square feet, in part because of the limited

Benetton product range at the time, but it set the pattern for the stores to follow. 'It was conceived on the idea of the specialized store, the desire for an alternative to the department store,' said Luciano Benetton to an American journalist. He added: 'From the beginning, we wanted to create an image – the right people to open our stores, the décor, the colours.'[2]

Through the late 1960s and early 1970s the Benettons concentrated their efforts on capturing the domestic market. By 1975 the distinctive white and green Benetton knitting-stitch logo had become the symbol of a phenomenon in the Italian commercial scene. Approximately 200 Benetton shops had opened in Italy; many of them, but not all, bore the Benetton name. The idea of having other names – Sisley, Tomato, Merceria, 012 – with a different decoration and selection of Benetton clothes, grew out of the intention of appealing to different segments of the market and of avoiding mass flops: if one Benetton store was a failure, others in the same area would not bear the stigma. Over the years, however, none of these names had achieved much importance, and many of them were being folded back into the Benetton brand.

In spite of the early opening of their first foreign outlet in Paris, in 1969, international sales had remained negligible for the company for most of the 1970s. In 1978, 98% of the company's sales of $80 million were in Italy, where opportunities for continued high growth were diminishing. Consequently, the firm launched a major expansion campaign into the rest of Europe, always following their system of only selling through specialized, Benetton-named outlets. Sales boomed as the network of shops spread north into France, West Germany, Britain, Switzerland, and the Scandinavian countries. In the early 1980s, most young women in Europe seemed to be buying Benetton sportswear, including Princess Caroline of Monaco and Diana, Princess of Wales, which gave Benetton worldwide publicity. By 1982 sales had grown to roughly $311 million. In 1983 Benetton had sales of $351 million, from 2600 stores in Europe.

Though the Benettons still expected some growth in Europe, they saw greater opportunity farther afield. By the end of 1983 the company had already placed 31 shops in department stores throughout Japan, and 27 shops in major cities of the United States. Interviewed by an American magazine, Luciano Benetton confessed: 'Being in America is like a dream – it is so big, so prestigious. If we do well, it will help us in Japan because they like whatever is big in the US.'[3] Progress in both countries had been difficult at the beginning, however. Instead of opening European-style shops, 18 of the 27 US shops were in department stores, such as Macy's, where Benetton had small boutiques from which it obtained a percentage of the profits. The 'joint-venture' was short-lived, perhaps due to the Macy's practice of quickly marking down prices on slow-moving items, which went completely against Benetton's philosophy.

The company set up some manufacturing units outside Italy. The existing factories in France, Scotland, and Spain were joined by an American facility in North Carolina in 1985. However, production outside Italy was not started for economic or technical reasons, but to bypass protectionism in those countries.

The complexity of handling an ever-expanding network of shops, production volumes, materials flows, and employees kept increasing. By the late 1970s, everybody in the company felt that something had to be done. The decision was made in 1981 to recruit professional managers. Aldo Palmeri, a highly regarded 36-year-old executive at the Bank of Italy (Italy's central bank) in Rome, was hired as a consultant and after a year became the new Managing Director. Although he had several ideas for reorganizing Benetton, his limited experience in industrial companies obliged him to recruit an experienced manager to put them into practice. This man, in charge of personnel and organization, was Mr Cantagalli, who joined Benetton in 1983 from a similar position with 3M, a large American multinational, in Italy.

They proceeded to recruit experienced managers from other large companies to form a 'professional team'. The newly created organization department had to implement an organization development programme to bridge the old 'handshake management' culture with the new and more formal one. This process of creating new functions and written procedures lasted three years and finished in October 1986.

The Board of Directors was composed of the four members of the Benetton family and Aldo Palmeri. However, the Benettons did not play the conventional, distant role of members of the board and took part in many day-to-day decisions. Although it did not appear in the organization chart, most of the senior functional managers had two reporting relationships: a formal one to Aldo Palmeri, and an informal one to a member of the Benetton family. Hence, two different groups of young adults had to coexist at the top: the self-made Benetton siblings, and the well-educated ex-multinational executives. The main task of the organization development department was to join both cultures. According to Franco Furnò, manager of this department, 'there has been a lot of improvement in this mutual understanding process in the last three years, but the job is not finished yet'.

Until July 1986 the four Benetton siblings shared 100% of the company's equity. After reporting strong 1985 results (see Exhibit 1), the company offered a total of 15.6 million common shares to the public. Some 11 million were listed in the Milan and Venice stock exchanges, 4.48 million in the Euromarkets, and the rest offered to Benetton's employees, agents, and clients. The total stock issue represented about 10% of the company. In addition, the company sold lira- (L70bn) and Deutsche Mark-denominated bonds (DM200m) with warrants. It was estimated that the whole financial operation represented about 20% of the company's equity, bringing in around $200 million.

THE COMPANY IN 1987: AN OVERALL DESCRIPTION

Benetton was a vertically de-integrated company, not only in manufacturing, but also in the three other main activities that constituted its

Exhibit 1   Financial highlights.

Consolidated balance sheet as of December 31 (millions of Italian lire) ($1 equals approx. 1400 Italian lire)

Assets	1986	1985
Current assets	833 192	494 891
Investments and other non-current assets	5 431	6 372
Fixed assets (net)	134 636	80 335
Intangible assets	15 548	10 215
Total assets	988 807	591 813
Liabilities and stockholders' equity		
Current liabilities	373 663	317 203
Long-term liabilities	251 148	76 730
Capital gains roll-over reserve		130
Minority interest in consolidated subsidiaries	2 437	4 742
Stockholders' equity	361 559	193 008
Total	988 807	591 813

Consolidated statements of income (millions of Italian lire)	1986	1985
Revenue	1 079 060	879 535
Cost of sales	701 818	558 501
Gross profit	377 242	321 034
Selling, general, and administrative expenses	169 303	150 653
Income from operations	207 939	170 381
Other income (expenses)	1 878	6 368
Gain from disposal of treasury stock		3 198
Income taxes	(87 008)	(69 788)
Deferred income taxes	(5 468)	
Income before minority interest	113 585	97 423
Income to minority interest	(556)	(1 226)
Net income for the year	113 029	96 197

value chain: styling and design, logistics and distribution, and sales. The company relied on external people and companies for the major part of these crucial activities. It employed some 1500 people at the end of 1987.

The styling or design of the garments was done outside the company by a number of international freelance stylists. Giuliana Benetton, with a staff of about 20 people in the product development department, interpreted the 'look' created by the stylists and performed the modelling phase.

More than 80% of manufacturing was done outside the company, by 350 subcontractors employing about 10 000 people. In-house production accounted for the remaining less than 20% (mainly dyeing) and was performed by 700–800 people.

Logistics and distribution activities were also performed mainly by outsiders. For storage the company used a single, huge warehouse for finished products. In addition, the logistics department at Benetton was in charge of delivering the finished garments to the stores all over the world.

Finally, the company utilized an external sales organization of almost 80 agents to take care of a retailing system of nearly 4000 shops spread all over the world. The internal part of this activity was performed by seven area managers who co-ordinated the selling system as a whole, divided by territories.

The operating cycle

There were basically two fashion seasons: spring/summer, beginning in February and ending in July, and autumn/winter, beginning in September and ending in December. The large volume of company business required that production planning for woollen and cotton articles began far in advance of shipment to the stores. Roughly, 21 months elapsed from the preparation of clothing designs for a particular selling season to the final payment of commissions to Benetton agents.

There were a number of basic steps in the operating cycle. Firstly, the preparation of final designs; then the assembly of a few samples of each of the 600 items in the total collection. A 'pre-presentation' meeting was then held between Giuliana Benetton, the manufacturing managers, and some of the company's 80 agents, which eliminated about a quarter of the models; the remaining were then produced in small quantities for presentation by area managers to agents and by agents to store owners. Upon receipt of the first orders, the planning department 'exploded' a rough production plan for the season, by fabrics and styles; purchases were made according to this plan, and capacity with the subcontractors negotiated; finally, production was started and deliveries begun just in time for the selling season. They were scheduled so that each store could present 80–90% of all items (fabrics, styles, and colours) in its basic collection to its customers at the outset of the selling season.

Although shops committed orders seven months before the selling season, giving Benetton time to schedule, produce, and deliver, the production plan did allow some flexibility for the retailer in three ways. Firstly, from August through to early December, as they gathered more information about colour preferences, shop-owners were allowed to specify colours for woven items that had been held in 'grey' up to that point, with a limit of 30% of the total orders for woollen items on such orders. Given the popularity of colourful weaves and jacquards in the previous three to four years, 'grey' stock had only represented about 15–20% of all orders. This trend was expected to change in the coming years, which would mean a return to more 'grey' orders.

The basic production plan was also adjusted through the presentation of a 'flash collection' just before the season. The flash collection corrected styling mistakes in the basic product line and usually included about 50 new designs based on 'hit styles' presented by fashion houses (competitors) during the two main seasonal shows.

Finally, orders could be adjusted through 'reassortment', which was the most critical phase in the production plan, requiring great coordination and follow-through by retailers, agents, and producers. Reassortment occurred during the last third of each selling season, when retailers were allowed to add orders to their original ones based on sell-through of popular items. Juggling retail orders to match manufacturing capacity for thousands of shops in a five-week period was not an easy task. There was a minimum economical production batch, so sometimes when the reassortment order was not enough to fill the minimum batch, the marketing people would get in touch with shop managers to propose some alternatives. As Benetton moved into new geographic areas, the complexity of reassortment grew incessantly, because the best sellers for different areas tended to vary widely.

Payments to subcontractors, representing a major cash outflow, were made 70 days after the end of the month in which production occurred or, in the case of the spring-summer collection, in October. Collections from retail stores were based on a season beginning date of March 30 for the spring/summer season, with one third of payment due 30, 60, and 90 days after that date or the date of actual receipt of merchandise. This was designed to minimize retailer's investment in inventories.

Manufacturing activities

The company was divided into three divisions: wool, cotton, and jeans. In 1983 Benetton had seven plants in Italy. In 1985 the number of plants decreased to five, and in 1987 the company owned just three production units; one for each division. The reason for this reduction in the number of plants was simply a matter of the company's philosophy of vertical de-integration and external production as a mode of organization. All those divested plants acted in 1987 as Benetton subcontractors.

As shown in Exhibit 2, Benetton utilized three different kinds of raw materials. In the wool division the raw material was basically thread, no matter whether it was acrylic, cotton, or actual wool. In the other two plants, the raw materials were basically fabrics. The wool division's technology was mainly knitting, while the other two divisions' technology was essentially cutting.

Benetton was the biggest purchaser of wool thread in the world. It purchased about 9 million kilos of thread per year. The other two divisions bought raw materials (fabrics) from 80–90 different suppliers. The company centralized all the purchasing activities as this was perhaps the main source of economies of scale in the industry. In 1987, 37 tons of yarn and 40 tons of fabrics entered the production system daily, to be transformed into 180 000 garments, adding up to 40–45 million garments per year.

Exhibit 2   Flow of materials.

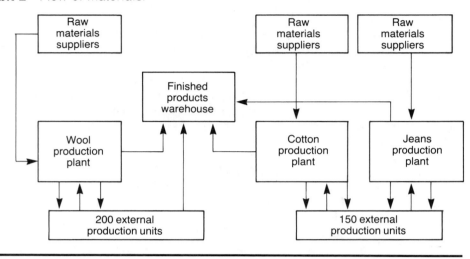

The wool division worked with 200 external production units. Benetton owned a percentage of the equity of the largest of them. The cotton and jeans divisions worked with another 150 external production units.

Benetton gave the external contractors the exact quantities of raw materials (calculated by computer), technical documents, an idea of the time needed to perform each single production activity, etc. Therefore, although these production units were external, Benetton provided much of the technical ability needed to run them, as most of them worked exclusively for the company. In addition, Benetton advised subcontractors about the required machinery to buy, and offered them financial aid through its own leasing and factoring companies. The contact with the subcontractors was also facilitated by the fact that, according to an Italian journalist, it could be said there was no manager at Benetton who was not at the same time owner, president, or director of a leading sub-contracting company in the Lombardia–Veneto area.

Although most of the manufacturing activities were externally performed, some were centralized at headquarters in Ponzano Veneto. Among these were all purchasing, production planning, technical research, product development, acquisition and exploitation of patents and rights, cutting by computer, and dyeing.

Even allowing for the added costs of shuttling raw materials and semi-finished products among subcontractors and Benetton's factories, the savings brought by decentralization resulted in total production costs for woollen items almost 20% below those of garments of comparable quality made in Europe and on a par with those made in the Far East.

Table 1   Summary chart of the manufacturing process in the wool division

Production phase	Performed internally (%)	Performed externally (%)	Number of contractors	Degree of exclusiveness (%)
Knitting	1	99	70–80	90
Assembling	–	100	100	100
Chemical treatment	25–30	70–75	3	100
Dyeing	100	–		
Finishing	5	95	20	100

The following pages explain in detail how the wool division worked to achieve those results.

The wool division

The wool division consumed 55% of all raw materials used by the company, and woollen garments represented about 47% of total sales in units. Three out of four woollen garments (i.e. 15 million garments) were sold in the autumn/winter season. The remaining 25% were sold during the spring/summer season. They were manufactured following a process made up of four sequential phases: knitting, assembling, dyeing, and finishing.

Knitting   Once the agents had collected the orders from the stores and sent them to headquarters, the technical department prepared the order portfolio for each of the three divisions. Thus the manager of the wool plant received an order portfolio that only included the articles to be manufactured in that plant.

The proportion of internal work in the knitting phase had decreased in the last five years. In 1982 only 40% of the knitting of wool had been performed externally. As shown in Table 1, just 1% of the knitting phase was done internally in 1987, and 90% of that 1% was concentrated in a very specific type of knitting machine. Benetton had decided to keep that kind of machine in-house because it had a lot of problems finding such machines in external companies. The machine was very expensive and, therefore, risky for external contractors. The company also used its internal production to have first-hand information on the productivity and costing of the knitting phase.

Benetton worked with 70–80 subcontractors in the knitting phase, and nearly 90% of them worked exclusively for Benetton. Mr Morelli, plant manager for the wool division, argued that there were pros and cons to that exclusivity: 'The main advantage is that the company can count on them to plan its production, as it knows their production capacity, kind of machines, number of shifts, etc. But the main disadvantage is that the company has to assure the saturation of their machines, which is risky for both Benetton and the external contractors.'

Assembly   This phase of the manufacturing process was performed completely outside the company by more than 100 external contractors, who worked exclusively for Benetton. In 1982 only 60% of this activity had been done externally. Most contractors had less than 15 employees, for Italian law imposed many regulations on larger companies. Approximately 14–15 was also a good number to set up an assembly chain.

According to Mr Morelli, Benetton did not perform the assembling phase internally because 'first of all, it goes against the philosophy of the company, that looks for de-integration and flexibility. Secondly, there are some economies in doing this job externally because these small subcontractors have to pay less in terms of social costs according to Italian law, although the salary level is almost the same'.

Dyeing   The early 1970s saw the development of Benetton's perhaps most widely publicized production technique: the dyeing of assembled garments rather than yarn, for single-colour garments. Up to then, it was the yarn that was dyed, and then the parts knit and the sweater assembled. The Benettons discovered that, to some extent, the critical fashion factor was colour, not shape. They decided, therefore, to knit and assemble a large part of their production undyed ('grey') and wait until fashion trends for colours became clearer to make the final colour decision. They thus avoided overproduction of sweaters in non-appealing colours and ensured they could meet demand for the 'best hits' of the season. The process was slightly more expensive but had the advantage of allowing production to respond quickly to public demand. It also allowed the company to maintain almost no inventory, and to produce mainly to order.

The company kept 100% of the dyeing phase internally. In 1982 half this phase had been performed outside the company. The whole process was concentrated at home because of the great importance of the dyeing phase for a company whose main distinctive product characteristic was its colourful style, and the ability of its garments to produce colour-co-ordinated sets of clothing. In addition, dyeing was both the most complex and the most capital-intensive process, which made it risky for external subcontractors.

Before the dyeing phase, every article had to pass through a chemical treatment to soften and de-wax the wool. The pieces that used already-coloured threads had to pass through this chemical treatment, too. This phase was also a capital intensive one but, technically speaking, was not as sophisticated as dyeing. The main part of this chemical process (70–75%) was performed outside the company by three external companies. Two of these plants had belonged to Benetton until 1985, when it sold them to their plant managers. These plants became joint ventures between these new entrepreneurs and Benetton. These plants employed about 100 people each.

Finishing   Only 5% of this phase was performed in-house, in contrast to the 80% done internally in 1982. The 20 subcontractors that performed the other 95% worked exclusively for Benetton. This phase was labour-intensive and did not require particular machinery. It was split in two parts: quality control of each single garment, and packaging.

Some problems in the Benetton-subcontractors relationship

Luigi Muzio, Managing Director of one of the largest external firms in which Benetton had an important equity position, commented: 'The main problem in working for Benetton is the great number of changes in articles, colors, etc., they do in a very short time. We have to adjust the machines weekly or even nightly to follow all these changes. This means a large number of different articles produced in small batches each, which, from a manufacturing point of view, is very inefficient.' This subcontractor also complained about the machinery suggested by Benetton. In his opinion, they had a 'final product orientation' instead of a 'process orientation', not taking into account the productivity or the suitability of the machinery to the subcontractor's characteristics. Thus he maintained that the machinery suggested by the company was often more suitable to a craftsman than to an industrial concern.

Subcontractors ran a big risk when they decided on the purchase of a certain type of machine. The key factor that decided the usefulness of the knitting machines was the thickness of the thread. Fortunately, this did not vary so rapidly as styles, colours or fashion in general. However, the company had experienced some problems of this type in the past, for some subcontractors had been stuck with machines that were useless for the current fashion trends. The firm had facilitated the change of the machines both by buying them or by allowing the contractors wide margins on some orders so they could reinvest this money in new machinery. For this reason, Benetton tried to concentrate in-house the most expensive and fashion-dependent activities.

Mr Muzio realized that working exclusively for Benetton involved a risk, but on the other hand it had the advantage of allowing them to dispense with a sales and marketing department: 'The constant work provided by Benetton enables this company to concentrate in manufacturing, with just a few people in charge of administrative and financial tasks. Working only for Benetton means one invoice per month, fixed payment conditions, etc. We often receive requests from potential clients, but I'd rather work this way.' Mr Morelli, head of the wool division, pointed out that 'one of the main problems in working with external firms is to achieve the required flexibility in them. They have to completely adapt to Benetton demands in terms of working periods, vacation, etc.' Another Benetton executive voiced this concern: 'This is neither a "just in time" system nor a very scheduled one.'

Subcontractors worked normally eight hours a day, but when the company was in a hurry they had to work over the weekend, and 12 or more hours a day. Nearly 10% of all subcontractors were released every year because they failed to meet quality standards.

One of the highlights of the company's network of subcontractors was described by Mr Morelli: 'Benetton maintains a sort of "umbilical cord" with external contractors. They are considered part of our family, and feel confident in telling us their problems.' Plant managers knew personally each subcontractor and some of them became friends, to the point that they talked about their personal problems and asked for advice. Manufacturing people visited subcontractors very often. In addition, they were permanently in touch by phone. This daily communication allowed them to work in real-time, solving little problems and making production adjustments.

According to the firm, the less experienced the subcontractor in the clothing industry, the better it would adjust to Benetton's philosophy. It was more difficult to create this 'umbilical cord' with people who had previously worked for other clients. The experienced contractor tried to impose conditions before starting the relationship.

Finally, there was a strong identification with Benetton, not only within the company, but also among subcontractors' employees. Luigi Muzio said: 'Workers in my company are fully identified with Benetton. They feel very proud of belonging to a worldwide-known group born in an ignored province of Italy. It is the first time that an apparel producer of this region develops into a world-class company, and this means a lot for this people.'

High-tech production processes

Many experts in the clothing industry agreed that the Benetton success formula was based on the company's ability to combine fashion with industry, using advanced technology. Luciano Benetton confirmed this to an American business magazine: 'There are many elements to our success, but the real point is that we have kept the same strategy all along – to put fashion on an industrial level. Most of the rest of Italian fashion is still on an artisan level.'[4]

For production, Benetton used numeric control knitting machines linked to Apricot (a British firm) computer-aided-design (CAD) personal computer terminals. Designers using the 10 CAD terminals could play around with knitwear colours and patterns on a video screen. Once a designer decided on a particular pattern, the computer prepared a tape that would direct the knitting machine to automatically produce the fabric, in an easy-to-assemble form of pieces. Since 1980 they had also used a Gerber Camsco CAD system that they had connected to a Spanish-made Investronica automatic cutter, turning the system into a CAD–CAM (computer-aided design and manufacturing) unit. The CAD–CAM system's automatic cutter followed pattern pieces stored in the computer's memory, which turned out 15 000 full garments every eight hours, wasting less than 15% of the cloth.

Logistics

Logistics played an important role in the Benetton strategy. Stores carrying Benetton products were designed with limited storage space for back-up stocks. Upon arrival at the store direct from the company, merchandise was often checked and placed directly on the display shelves. This required both a carefully prepared schedule of shipments to stores, and a large and efficient warehouse to store finished products at headquarters.

The new robotized warehouse in Castrette was the main symbol of Benetton's high technology; it became fully operational in February 1986. With a cost of over 42 billion lire (about $32 million) to build and outfit, the warehouse was a huge automatic box run by a DEC minicomputer that directed several robots via remote control. The robots could read bar codes on boxes, and then sort and store them. The operation of the warehouse was totally automatic and there was no human handling in the whole process. A staff of five specialists just monitored the movements via computer.

Selling activities

There were three groups of 'actors' involved in selling activities: the company, the agents, and the shop owners and managers. Although his only formal position was as a member of the board, the real marketing manager was Luciano Benetton, who in the past had formally occupied this position many times. Under him, the commercial director and the area managers comprised the marketing department. Nearly all the members of the commercial organization had been hired by him, and were used to working directly with him. Area managers were company employees in charge of territories run by a number of agents. There were seven area managers for nearly 80 agents. All the area managers were Italians.

Riccardo Weiss, the area manager in charge of the US, Canada, Japan, and countries of the Eastern block, described one of the tasks of an area manager: 'He does every month what agents do every day: have a look at each shop and its problems. We are always watching the movement store by store. Sometimes we talk directly with shop-owners, although agents don't like that. But they need to hear the voice of the company from time to time.' Mr Weiss went once a month to the US and talked almost daily with every agent by phone.

Another important task an area manager performed, was the collection of the money from the shops. On average, an area manager devoted

Exhibit 3   Distribution network.

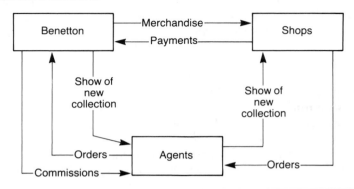

30–35% of his time to follow payment problems. His rush periods were May–June for the spring/summer collection, and October–November for the autumn/winter one.

Agents

As shown in Exhibit 3, the agents constituted the interface between Benetton and the shops. They were not Benetton employees, and had exclusive rights over a sales territory. Luciano Benetton had personally hand-picked most of the 80 agents. Right from the start, Luciano looked for a new kind of agent, who could fit with the particular philosophy of the emerging company. He wanted 'personal attitudes, rather than business experience'. As an executive put it, 'the thing that really strikes Luciano is the entrepreneurial spirit in an agent, rather than anything else'. The company's relationship with its agents was managed largely on a verbal basis of trust: only in 1984 had formal contracts begun to be written between Benetton and the agents. Only rarely had agents had to be replaced for failure to meet expectations.

Twice a year, all agents had to spend one week at headquarters getting to know the new collection for the season and selecting a sample of 30–40% of the 600 items of the total collection. After this, every agent went back to his territory and took about 30–40 days to present the sample collection to each shop owner. Then the agent helped the shop owner in selecting the most suitable articles for each particular shop, and asked for orders. At the end of each day, the agent sent the orders collected in that day to headquarters. Articles were shipped directly to the shops from the central warehouse, without passing through the agent. During the season, the shop owner sent the money directly to Benetton, dividing the total payment in three quotas, which were paid 30, 60, and 90 days from the date of actual receipt of the merchandise. After this, the company payed the agent a 4% commission on the value of goods shipped from the factories.

Manlio Tonolo was the agent for the north-east region of Italy. He had joined the company in 1969 as the manager of the second shop opened by the company in Padova. He had worked with Luciano Benetton in a men's clothing store when they were teenagers. Mr Tonolo explained the criteria for selecting an agent at that time: 'The candidate had to have an enthusiastic predisposition towards the work itself. Luciano was looking for people who could be potential consumers rather than agents, who could understand the product – the multicolored sweater, which back then was completely unconventional – and believe in it.'

The main responsibilities of the agents were to: a) select the location of new shops; b) find and select potential investors for new shops; c) help new clients in starting shops and train them, usually in the agent's stores; d) look after the shops and help owners to manage and control their shops; e) present the collection to shop managers and help them in choosing goods; f) collect orders and transmit them to headquarters; g) encourage image competition among shops.

Agents were also encouraged to reinvest part of their commissions in opening new shops, thus becoming clients themselves. This mechanism produced a 'self-multiplying effect' in the retailing network. This policy of encouraging agents to have and run their own shops helped them to get a first-hand knowledge of the retail business and its problems in practice. For instance, Mr Tonolo owned 35–40 shops out of the 200 he supervised in north-eastern Italy. More than competitors, the shops owned by him served as examples to other shops recently opened in such aspects as window dressing, products display, overall image, etc. Besides this, according to Mr Tonolo, the concentration of shops in an area of a town, instead of reducing the sales of each one, tended to increase them.

Agents normally had a small organization to perform their multiple activities. Although agents visited the shops regularly, they usually hired young assistants who controlled the shops' overall image and problems on a weekly basis. In addition, the assistants helped the agent in the task of monitoring the new trends in young people's culture. They had to visit the places where they met (discotheques, bars, etc.) and see how they behaved, not only what they wore.

The majority of European agents were Italians, as were almost 50% of the US agents. Some of these had started in Europe and then moved to America. Benetton had found it difficult to find agents with the 'right mentality' in America, so they had to replace them with Italians, already familiar with the firm. These had had their share of difficulties in attempting to penetrate the American market, because of their ignorance of laws and regulations. 'They had too much of the Italian mentality,' as one executive pointed out.

Table 2   Stores in operation at year-end

Year-end	1982	1983	1984	1985	1986	1987★	1988★	1989★	1990★
Stores	1917	2296	2644	3200	3893	4650	5300	6200	7000
Change	n/a	379	348	556	693	757	650	900	800

★ Morgan Stanley Research Estimates

Shops

Fewer than 10 of the Benetton stores worldwide were owned and operated by the company. These were located in key cities such as Milan, New York, Rome, and Düsseldorf. The rest were set up by independent entrepreneurs, who often owned several shops in the same area. Benetton approved location of the shops and Luciano personally oversaw the more strategic sites.

Shop owners were not retail experts. As Luciano Benetton put it: 'We have caused a new type of retailer to become important who until the day before was perhaps a florist or a hairdresser. His prior career was of no importance, but he had to have the right spirit to work in a Benetton shop.' Mr Weiss, area manager for North America, Japan, and Eastern Europe, commented: 'Experts in retailing are not good shop owners (and managers) because they don't understand very well the particular Benetton system.' When asked about this 'shop philosophy', he mentioned the following characteristics:

- new window display every week;
- good sales people in stores; good service;
- competition among Benetton shops in the same area based on image (window decoration, garment diversity, and display);
- no price competition: prices were set directly at the factory or at least 'strongly suggested', as in the US. In addition, markdowns could not be taken before discussing them with the agent.

The 'turnover' among shop owners was low. For example, of the 200 shops controlled by Mr Tonolo in the north-east of Italy, which were owned by 50–60 people, only five or six shop owners had been replaced in a period of 10 years.

The growth of the network of shops had been enormous, as can be seen in Table 2.

Retailers did not sign franchise agreements (Luciano Benetto hated bureaucracy and found that the current arrangement 'stimulates the full capacity of the owners'). They were neither required to pay Benetton a fee for use of its name nor a royalty based on a percentage of sales or profits. In this respect, the term 'franchising' in describing the Benetton retailing network was a misnomer.

All Benetton outlets were required to follow basic merchandising concepts, the most important among them being that all merchandise must be displayed on open shelves accessible to customers, who could touch it and try it on. The open displays in an otherwise undecorated space create an impression of great colour and fashion to the window-shopping customer. Important also was the selection of salespeople: they must be young and very customer-oriented. They had to be able to advise the customer on which garments co-ordinated well, and what were the best colours to wear for a particular person. Benetton used five mechanisms to control its 'identity' in spite of the dramatic increase in the number of shops:

- Standardization of the shop image. Retailers had to choose among 12 basic layouts and fixture selections. This furniture must be provided by only three Italian suppliers, located near headquarters.
- Central supply of advertising material, which was produced at headquarters and shipped to the shops all over the world. Shops were allowed to do some advertising in local media (mainly newspapers) after the company had checked the advertisement.
- A strict pricing policy. The computer back at Benetton printed the price in local currencies in each tag attached to every article. For the US market it was a 'suggested' price.
- Benetton shops could only sell Benetton products.
- Strong initial training of shop owners by the agent.

Many people had called Benetton 'the fast food of the fashion industry', a comparison Luciano Benetton did not disagree with: 'I like the idea that we are similar to fast food in the sense of organization, the efficiency, the cleanliness of image, the publicity.'[5]

Promotion strategy

Employing one agency in Paris for France (Eldorado) and another in New York (J Walter Thompson) for the rest of the world, the company had co-ordinated its advertising worldwide. Since the product was the same all over the world, the company had been able to maintain the consistency and international character of its advertisements. The themes, 'Benetton – All the Colors in the World,' in 1983–84; and 'United Colors of Benetton,' from 1985 on, had appeared on outdoor billboards and in numerous magazines all over the world, always in English. These campaigns were the results of brainstorming sessions held by Luciano Benetton and several friend/consultants including photographers and designers, such as Oliviero Toscani.

About 4% of Benetton's sales was spent on direct advertising. Additionally, the company sponsored sports events, including rugby and basketball teams, and a Formula 1 motor racing team.

Global outlook

When Luciano Benetton was asked if he wanted Benetton to become another McDonald's, he commented:

> Not McDonald's for the same level of goods, the same consumer, but, yes, for the distribution all over the world. I would like us to be everywhere. Another company we might compare ourselves to might be Coca-Cola or Pepsi-Cola, since we aim our product at young people. The idea behind Benetton – which was basically that of mass-produced, medium priced fashion that moves with the trends yet maintains something classic – had not changed since our clothing started to become not just a strictly European product but a product for the whole world. In America, in Australia, in Japan – where we envision having two hundred shops – it has been consistently accepted. In all these countries, the prototype client remains the same – young and female. Naturally, there are regional differences. In America, for example, we reach a public a little different from that in Europe – a more sophisticated public, which travels, and might have seen the product first in Europe.[6]

In spite of their general success entering new markets, there were certain countries where the company had found serious difficulties due to tariffs, import quotas, and other protectionist barriers. Benetton decided to invest in local facilities in order to avoid current or potential protectionism. Benetton Sarl, in France; Benetton SA, in Spain; Tabando Ltd, in Scotland; and Benetton USA, Inc, were the four foreign manufacturing subsidiaries set up by Benetton International NV, based in Holland. There was no international manufacturing network at Benetton: these manufacturing units outside Italy produced only to satisfy local needs, and they did not supply all the goods needed in those countries. For example, the plant located in North Carolina produced only about 5% of what was sold in the US market.

In other countries – where Benetton could not enter through exports and was not interested in building manufacturing facilities or in developing joint ventures with local partners – licensing agreements to use the Benetton trademarks were signed. Thus, local companies in Brazil, Mexico, Japan, Portugal, India, and Argentina payed royalties to Benetton for each item they produced and sold. There were a total of 183 licensed operations in these six countries. Although these operations generated only a 5% licence profit for the firm, they must adhere to Benetton standards. The range of products and the manufacturing technology were exactly those of Benetton's, because all these licencees visited Ponzano Veneto's factories, bought the machinery under the firm's supervision, and so on.

Information systems

The company had committed itself to using the best information systems available and to improving them when they could. Benetton spent about

1.2% of its annual turnover on this, including hardware, software, and personnel. As the company was growing at a rapid rate each year, the information systems were always being restructured to cope with the new demands.

The most important of these systems was the connection between the agents and the firm. They had started with a dedicated network of minicomputers located in seven European cities, that acted as nodes, connected to the company's mainframes in Italy. As retail operations had grown, this dedicated network became increasingly expensive. Then, after a successful test in North America, agents were connected to the Mark III General Electric Information System's value-added network service available round the clock in 250 cities in 25 countries. The service provided network access and data-filing software. All application software was Benetton's own. Mark III replaced the need to operate the information system centre at headquarters 24 hours a day and relieved the burden of long-distance, often transcontinental, telephone charges for data transmissions. Use of Mark III was indispensable during reassortment.

'Keeping track of the financial information of each one of the 4000 shops in the world is completely mad and useless,' argued Bruno Zuccaro, the manager of information systems at Benetton, and former executive of Zanussi and Honeywell. This had been an information systems project in the past, but had failed due to administrative and technical problems. The project consisted of having a cash register in each single shop to keep track of the shop's sales and financial situation. This would have allowed the company to know the cash-flow of each shop and the money it had. However, it was neither accepted by shop owners nor by the Italian law that specified a certain type of cash register for tax purposes.

The information systems department was working on a project to connect a sample of a few representative shops all over the world. The sample contained shops that started selling early in each season due to their condition of international centres where trendy people went, such as up-market ski resorts. By installing a computerized point of sale (POS) system in each of these shops, the company could gather information about fashion trends in design, colours, etc., well in advance of the season, which was critical for planning and producing the reassortment articles. This project was being tested in five Italian shops to see how it worked and how well it was accepted by shop owners and agents.

Each shop owner was free to manage his or her shops as he or she pleased, but the information systems staff had developed a software package for retail shop management which they planned to encourage retail shops to buy. The software ran on an IBM personal computer equipped with a bar-code reader, since all garment tags came from the factory with critical information printed in bar code. The system processed sales, inventory, orders, and receipt of goods.

The information systems department had not done much to connect the subcontractors network. The firm felt that they were too many and most of them too small for attempting this task. The company knew the production capacity of every subcontractor, but the production scheduling and the allocation process of the production plan to each contractor was not done by computer. Therefore, Benetton did not know the exact amount of work that each subcontractor had in a given moment.

IDEAS FOR THE FUTURE

Changes in the subcontractors' network

Benetton was working with a constellation of 350 subcontracted production units. The idea was to simplify the complex problem of being in touch with so many external firms, and deal only with the 9 or 10 largest subcontractors. These, in turn, would be in touch with all the medium-sized and small contractors. To better control those big contractors, the Benetton family – not the company itself – would own shares in all of them. It was also planned to integrate those large subcontractors into the company's own information systems.

The US subsidiary

Benetton was planning to increase the production volume and the range of products in the US subsidiary located in North Carolina. It was currently making T-shirts and classic trousers there, which only accounted for 5% of the total US consumption of Benetton products.

There were two main reasons to manufacture in this overseas facility: to avoid protectionism problems; and the fact that some Americans preferred garments 'made in USA'. Other reasons for producing locally rather than importing from Italy were the wild gyrations of exchange rates, and the tariffs and transportation costs the company had to bear. As a result of this last factor, final prices to consumers were 35–40% higher in the US than in Europe. Benetton had to pay 24–25% in tariffs, and 7–8% in transportation.

Financial matters

The company was planning to go public in the New York Stock Exchange. It wanted to reinforce its international image and to secure funds for a planned diversification process, although the company had already accumulated a substantial amount of financial resources in the last years.

Diversification of the Benetton Group

In December 1985 the holding company changed its name from INVEP SpA to Benetton Group SpA and increased its capital stock from 8 billion lire to 70 billion lire by capitalizing reserves.

The INVEP holding, created in 1981, encompassed all the business activities controlled equally by the four Benettons. The main business of the group had traditionally been Benetton SpA, accounting for about two-thirds of the group sales. In December 1985, the three different companies named Benetton Lana SpA, Benetton Cotone SpA, and Benetton Jeans SpA, were merged into Benetton SpA, becoming its three manufacturing divisions.

The group invested from the beginning in related business activities, such as the 50% share in Fiorucci SpA, the Milan-based design firm acquired in 1981, and the 70% of Calzaturificio di Varese, an Italian shoe manufacturer bought in 1982. The first investment allowed the company to enter into the more rarefied realms of European fashion, and the second provided them with shoes for sale along with sweaters and shirts in Benetton shops around the world.

However, both investments were only marginally profitable. At the end of 1983, Luciano Benetton commented about Calzaturificio di Varese: 'As an experiment it has been quite interesting, but the factory is old and there have been many problems.'[7] However, after two or three years of operations, this company began to show positive results and it was considered a success. On the other hand, the investment in Fiorucci SpA was sold in 1985. At the time of that sale, Benetton purchased 5% of Nolan Norton Italia Srl, a company in the computer industry.

Benetton had taken advantage of its well-known trademark in licensing agreements covering a wide range of consumer products, for example cosmetics, perfumes, socks, toys, household linen, etc. It had also arranged successful alliances with Bulova to sell watches with the Benetton name, and with Polaroid for the manufacture of Benetton sunglasses.

The diversification process of the company had gone beyond related business activities and entered into the financial services sector. Some of these investments were: a 70% of In Factor SpA, a factoring subsidiary with a capital stock of 5 billion lire; a 50% stake in two leasing companies, Leasing SpA and Finleasing Italia SpA; 20% of the private Banco di Trento e Bolzano in northern Italy; and a 10% stake in leasing companies in France and West Germany, which were run by Banca Nazionale del Lavoro, Italy's biggest bank.

Luciano Benetton had announced new projects for the coming years: 'The future will include diversification in retailing, financial services in banking and elsewhere, in Italy and abroad.'[8] According to Aldo Palmeri: 'Benetton's plan to develop financial services will call for the company to achieve, within two years, a 50–50% mix in group turnover between industrial and financial revenues.'[9] Benetton was planning to:

- Expand its factoring and leasing subsidiaries both in Italy and abroad. It had received authorization from the Ministry of Foreign Trade in Rome to operate in the factoring business outside of Italy.
- Form a financial services and venture capital company in Milan that would engage in currency swaps, syndicated loans, corporate finance, underwriting, and other investment banking activities for the clothing

and textile sector, in partnership with another big Italian clothing manufacturer.

Carlo Gilardi, Benetton's finance director, admitted that 'although we have a handful of Citicorp specialists in currency swaps, factoring and leasing, it will be necessary to enlarge our human and managerial resources substantially to reach our goal.'[10]

NOTES

1. The biographical notes in the preceding paragraphs are adapted from 'Profiles–Being Everywhere', *The New Yorker*, Nov. 10, 1986, pp. 53–74.
2. *The New Yorker*, op.cit., p. 58.
3. 'Benetton: Bringing European Chic to Middle America.' *Business Week*, June 11, 1984, p. 60.
4. 'Benetton Takes on the World', *Fortune*, June 13, 1983, p. 116.
5. *Wall Street Journal Europe*, June 24, 1986.
6. *The New Yorker*, op.cit., p. 63.
7. *Fortune*, op.cit., p. 119.
8. *Financial Times*, May 23, 1986.
9. Ibid.
10. Ibid.

SUGGESTED QUESTIONS

1. How would you describe Benetton's strategy? What is distinctive about this strategy and on what does it depend for its success?
2. What are the critical elements of Benetton's structure, and how do they contribute to its success?
3. How can this success best be maintained in the future? What are the main dangers, and how should they be addressed?

4

Cadbury Schweppes plc (A)

Case written by Tony Eccles with Martin Stoll

INTRODUCTION

1986–88 were three busy years for Cadbury Schweppes as its management sought to stave off an unwelcome investor and to reassure the market about its own managerial ability. In 1986 the British-based food and drinks group restructured its business to concentrate on what it saw as the group's strengths in confectionery and soft drinks. For £97 million it sold its Beverages & Foods Division to a management buyout company, Premier Brands, headed by the Cadbury Schweppes Planning Director (a 36-year old Wharton MBA). As a result, Cadbury Schweppes parted with such well-known British brands as Typhoo tea, Hartley Chivers jam, Marvel milk powder, Smash mashed potatoes, and Kenco coffee (later sold by Premier Brands). Premier also took over Cadbury's drinking chocolate and Cadbury's chocolate biscuits, both of which continued to use the Cadbury name (and Cadbury chocolate as an ingredient) under licence.

Just as decisively, in Britain, Cadbury Schweppes changed sides in the 'Cola War', dropping its long-time partner Pepsi in favour of Coca-Cola. Schweppes, which had held the British Pepsi franchise for 32 years, took a 51% stake in a new joint UK company with Coca-Cola which handled all Coke and Schweppes brands.

Internationally, Cadbury Schweppes made large-scale changes, most notably through buying Canada Dry which doubled Cadbury Schweppes' worldwide drinks market share. It also took a 30% stake (later 34.4%) in the US soft drinks maker, Dr Pepper. As a result of these acquisitions, Cadbury Schweppes became the third largest soft drinks company in the world.

Explaining these moves, the Chairman of the company, Sir Adrian Cadbury, emphasized that it had bought and sold businesses 'with the sole objective of building up its brand strengths in line with the Group's declared aims'. He suggested that, in judging bid and merger activity, 'The test to apply to acquisitions and divestments is what they do for the ability of the companies concerned to compete successfully in international markets'.

In the Chairman's view, the restructuring of Cadbury Schweppes into what he called the 'leading British branded food and drink company' had met that test.

Even so, as the Company entered 1987, it still found itself the subject of unwanted attention, when the US holding company, General Cinema Corporation, acquired an 8.5% stake in Cadbury Schweppes. Following the market crash in October 1987, General Cinema raised its holding to 18.1%, which it still held in 1989, some of its stake being tied up in GC's elaborate financing structure.

HISTORY

In 1969 Cadbury and Schweppes agreed to merge. Each company was strong in its own markets. Schweppes was well regarded for its carbonated soft drinks and mixers. Cadbury was mainly known for its chocolate products. There was little overlap between the two companies' products, but there was a close affinity in terms of markets, price levels, and a commitment to strong branding. The merger aimed to create a robust international company capable of facing large competitors such as Coca-Cola, Pepsi and Mars. The Cadbury and Schweppes operations were to be integrated in order to benefit from the stronger financial, marketing, and distribution functions which would result.

These benefits were to prove elusive. Prospective scale economies were difficult to capture. The two companies sold discrete items to similar outlets in similarly sized packs, yet neither production nor distribution were amenable to amalgamation. The production processes of chocolate making and filling of bottles had few shared features. Bottling required local manufacture to keep down the cost of transporting glass and water. Chocolate making had scale economies which encouraged centralization. Distribution thus started from different points and went via different distribution chains in different manners – even when the products eventually arrived at the same retail outlet.

The cultures of the two companies were also dissimilar and there was rivalry for top management positions in the merged enterprise. This was to some extent resolved in 1974 when Adrian Cadbury, a great grandson of the founder John Cadbury, became Chairman and Basil Collins, from Schweppes, became the new Managing Director. (In 1984 Collins retired and was replaced as Managing Director by Dominic Cadbury, who was chosen in preference to the group's Finance Director, Michael Gifford. Gifford became Chief Executive of the Rank Organisation.)

Strategy

As Cadbury Schweppes began to redefine its strategy under Collins, many of its 1969–74 acquisitions were sold. Cadbury Schweppes had spent £70 million buying into health food, brewing, and veterinary products, but after a thorough review of operations and markets a top management gathering in 1977 affirmed its support for:

A concentration internationally on the major Cadbury and Schweppes brands to produce volume growth from a narrower product range, based on a consistently higher level of marketing, production and quality standards and so a better return on assets.

The drinks business would be developed mainly by further franchising (which is a typical feature of the soft drinks industry) and geographical priority would be given to developed countries, notably the United States, the world's largest market for both confectionery and drinks.

The company set itself the goal of achieving a 5% annual increase in real earnings per share and a 25% return on operating assets; that is fixed assets and working capital, excluding other funds such as investments, stakes in associated companies, and items such as brand values and restructuring provisions. This was quite an ambitious target given that in 1977 the pre-tax return on assets was only 13%.

The 1977 conference was seen as a key step on the road to improvement, but as a director said later: 'The real achievement was to make the analysis stick. Anyone can analyse, it is getting commitment and action.'

Action included a programme of acquisition and investment. Duffy Mott (apple juice, Clamato, etc.) and Holland House (cocktail mixers) were purchased in the USA as well as Peter Paul, the third largest US chocolate firm. £97 million was invested in the Bournville chocolate factory, cutting 37 production units to 12 and halving its 6000 workforce whilst expanding production capacity to 1500 tonnes per week (1.6 million bars and 50 million individual items such as Hazelnut Whirls and Creme Eggs).

In 1982 trading profits outside Britain exceeded UK profits for the first time. Cadbury Schweppes' sales, capital employed, and pre-tax profits rose by 50% between 1979 and 1983. However, increases in tax payable and a series of extraordinary rationalization costs had eroded the benefit of profit improvements, and the 1983 post-tax profit attributable to Cadbury Schweppes (£42.4m) had risen little above the 1980 level (£41.1m) although the dividend (£24.2m) had risen 60% compared to 1980 (£15.3m). However, Adrian Cadbury was able to report that the return on operating assets had reached 19.6% in 1986 and that they 'hoped to close the gap further in 1987'.

In 1987 the return on operating assets reached 26.1%; in 1988, 29.9%; in 1989, 31.7%; and in 1990, 31.6% (see Exhibit 2).

Exhibit 1 Cadbury Schweppes: sales and profits, and summarized balance sheets, 1986–90.

		1990 (£m)	1989* (£m)	1988* (£m)	1987* (£m)	1986* (£m)
Sales and profits	Sales					
	United Kingdom	1,476.0	1,257.5	1,024.4	941.9	735.4
	Europe	638.0	479.7	391.3	344.0	306.0
	Americas	403.7	372.4	387.0	423.1	419.8
	Pacific Rim	495.5	545.7	460.8	319.8	294.1
	Africa and Others	132.9	121.4	96.9	94.5	73.7
		3,146.1	2,776.7	2,360.4	2,123.3	1,829.0
	Trading profit					
	United Kingdom	148.5	100.2	91.9	81.9	64.6
	Europe	68.0	58.6	46.5	39.7	28.1
	Americas	43.3	37.7	24.1	21.2	8.4
	Pacific Rim	58.6	61.1	50.1	35.2	29.8
	Africa and Others	15.5	15.0	13.5	9.6	7.9
		333.9	272.6	226.1	187.6	138.8
	Interest payable less investment income	(57.2)	(31.1)	(17.1)	(10.3)	(14.6)
	Associated undertakings	2.9	2.8	4.6	4.4	5.7
	Profit before taxation	279.6	244.3	213.6	181.7	129.9
	Taxation	(78.0)	(69.5)	(51.1)	(55.5)	(44.8)
	Profit attributable to minority interests	(22.2)	(17.0)	(22.8)	(14.2)	(9.7)
	Extraordinary items	—	15.2	28.8	1.7	26.0
	Profit attributable to shareholders	179.4	173.0	168.5	113.7	101.4
	Dividends	(83.6)	(76.3)	(55.6)	(47.3)	(37.6)
	Profit retained	95.8	96.7	112.9	66.4	63.8

* Prior year comparatives have been re-stated using average exchange rates.

		1990 (£m)	1989 (£m)	1988 (£m)	1987 (£m)	1986 (£m)
Summarized group balance sheets	Assets employed					
	Stock	328.2	334.8	253.4	257.4	237.1
	Debtors	554.1	548.2	434.5	398.2	308.9
	Cash, loans, and deposits	180.6	90.7	242.0	139.9	177.4
		1,062.9	973.7	929.9	795.5	723.4
	Short-term borrowings	(136.3)	(133.7)	(114.1)	(163.1)	(79.9)
	Other creditors and provisions	(934.3)	(933.2)	(736.8)	(569.9)	(497.1)
		(7.7)	(93.2)	79.0	62.5	146.4
	Fixed assets	1,299.5	1,155.1	727.2	680.0	639.6
		1,291.8	1,061.9	806.2	742.5	786.0
	Financed by: Capital of Cadbury Schweppes plc	174.7	173.6	153.7	151.7	142.9
	Reserves	593.2	421.7	436.6	401.5	404.5
	Perpetual subordinated loan	118.9	—	—	—	—
	Long term loans	289.0	381.4	124.7	112.9	185.6
	Minority interests	116.0	85.2	91.2	76.4	53.0
		1,291.8	1,061.9	806.2	742.5	786.0

Exhibit 2   Sales, trading profit, and operating assets analysis.

		Total (£m)	United Kingdom (£m)	Europe (£m)	Americas (£m)	Pacific Rim (£m)	Africa and others (£m)
1990	**Sales**						
	Confectionery	1,322.7	715.4	195.6	30.2	290.3	91.2
	Beverages	1,823.4	760.6	442.4	373.5	205.2	41.7
		3,146.1	1,476.0	638.0	403.7	495.5	132.9
	Trading profit						
	Confectionery	163.0	83.3	19.3	8.9	42.3	9.2
	Beverages	170.9	65.2	48.7	34.4	16.3	6.3
		333.9	148.5	68.0	43.3	58.6	15.5
	Operating assets[†]						
	Confectionery	547.7	320.4	81.1	5.9	102.1	38.2
	Beverages	565.3	259.9	167.1	51.1	77.8	9.4
		1,113.0	580.3	248.2	57.0	179.9	47.6
1989	**Sales***						
	Confectionery	1,118.4	571.2	156.3	18.3	289.8	82.8
	Beverages	1,658.3	686.3	323.4	354.1	255.9	38.6
		2,776.7	1,257.5	479.7	372.4	545.7	121.4
	Trading profit*						
	Confectionery	127.4	53.9	18.4	8.2	37.7	9.2
	Beverages	145.2	46.3	40.2	29.5	23.4	5.8
		272.6	100.2	58.6	37.7	61.1	15.0
	Operating assets[†]						
	Confectionery	530.6	288.7	71.2	0.6	135.2	34.9
	Beverages	468.4	212.7	101.7	72.2	73.1	8.7
		999.0	501.4	172.9	72.8	208.3	43.6
		(%)	(%)	(%)	(%)	(%)	(%)
	Return on assets						
	1990	31.6	27.5	32.3	66.7	30.2	34.0
	1989	31.7	23.3	39.5	60.9	33.5	41.0

* These have been re-stated using average exchange rates.
[†] Operating assets represent tangible fixed assets, stock, debtors, and creditors after excluding restructuring provisions, borrowings, taxation, and dividends.

ORGANIZATION STRUCTURE

With 60% of its sales coming from outside the UK in the early 1980s, Cadbury Schweppes chose to organize itself primarily on a geographical basis. The multi-business territories were then split down further into 'product streams', that is individual companies each engaged in an identifiably separate product market.

The form each business took varied a lot, with Cadbury Schweppes

Exhibit 3   Cadbury Schweppes: financial ratios, 1986–90.

			1990	1989	1988	1987	1986
Trading margin	Trading profit / Sales	%	10.6	9.8	9.6	8.8	7.6
Return on assets	Trading profit / Average operating assets	%	31.6	31.7	29.9	26.1	19.6
Return on equity*	Earnings / Average ordinary shareholders' funds	%	29.1	27.4	24.7	20.0	15.0
Interest cover	Trading profit / Net interest charge	Times	5.8	8.8	13.2	18.2	9.5
Fixed charge cover	See below	Times	4.7	6.9	8.9	10.3	6.9
Dividend cover	Earnings per ordinary share / Dividend per ordinary share	Times	2.2	2.3	2.5	2.4	2.1
Gearing Ratio*	Net borrowings / Ordinary shareholders' funds + minority interests	%	49.7	62.4	(0.5)	21.6	14.7
Operating asset turnover	Sales / Average operating assets	Times	3.0	3.2	3.1	2.9	2.6
Working capital turnover	Sales / Average working capital	Times	20.3	18.8	14.6	13.6	12.1
Earnings per share – net basis		p	25.29	24.22	23.35	19.53	14.16
Dividends per share		p	11.50	10.70	9.20	8.00	6.70
Net assets per share*		p	88.29	85.74	97.56	92.60	97.44

These ratios have been re-stated to reflect the change in accounting policy in respect of the translation of the profit and loss account at average exchange rates.

Operating assets represent tangible fixed assets, stock, debtors, and creditors after excluding restructuring provisions, borrowings, taxation, and dividends.

Fixed charge cover, which shows the cover for total financing charges, is defined as follows:

$$\frac{\text{Trading profit} + \text{Dividends from Associates} + \tfrac{1}{3} \text{ operating lease rentals}}{\text{Net interest charge} + \text{preference dividends (gross)} + \tfrac{1}{3} \text{ operating lease rentals}}$$

* These ratios exclude preference shares at their redemption value.

products being sold by subsidiaries, associated companies, and by franchisees. Thus Schweppes products were sold by a subsidiary in West Germany, by a franchisee in Italy, and Cadbury Schweppes products were sold by a company with 30% local ownership in Australasia (100% Cadbury owned since late 1988).

The criteria for separation or amalgamation into companies, divisions or regions were primarily those of:

1. Size of sales.
2. Source of sales (export, franchise, associate, subsidiary).
3. Separate identity of markets/products sold.

Four regions – the UK, America, Australia, and Europe – accounted for the bulk of Cadbury Schweppes operations. The regions were not precisely geographical since the European region had responsibility for Schweppes in Latin America as well as for Schweppes-Asahi in Japan. (Asahi, Japan's third largest brewer, is part of Sumitomo.)

Cadbury Schweppes had no subsidiaries or major associates in South America or in countries operating the Arab boycott. However, it did have soft drink franchisees in more than 40 countries and exported confectionery products directly to more than 90 markets through Cadbury International.

In 1985 Cadbury Schweppes reorganized to provide a global perspective for the two main businesses – chocolate and soft drinks – with the exceptions of Australasia and North America where the regional structure continued. The UK regional structure was dropped and its chief, Terry Organ, became Managing Director of international confectionery. Reporting to him were Neville Bain, the Managing Director of UK confectionery and Jim Schadt, the Chief Executive of Cadbury Schweppes North America for confectionery. Schadt also reported on drinks and overall North American region matters to the global head of the drinks business, Dominic Cadbury, as did the head of Schweppes in the UK, Derek Williams.

The UK drinks division was divided into three main elements: 'operations' and two trading units – 'licensed and catering' which included dispensed drinks and wines, and 'take-home' which included all the advertising.

Main Board Director Mervyn Blakeney co-ordinated the use of Schweppes' brands worldwide in addition to his role of managing Europe/Asia/Africa region, in future to be known as Schweppes International Ltd (SIL).

With the retirement of Terry Organ in 1986, Neville Bain became Managing Director of group confectionery. In 1987, when Bain became Managing Director of the world confectionary stream, Jim Schadt was appointed Managing Director of the world beverages stream and so Mervyn Blakeney began to report to Schadt. In 1988 Blakeney resigned, believing that it was inappropriate to run Schweppes' European interests out of North America. In the years 1981–87, Schweppes' trading profit in Blakeney's territories had risen from £1 million to £50 million per year via a combination of organic growth, renegotiated partnership arrangements, and acquisitions. The worldwide beverages stream, which negotiated partnership arrangements and acquisitions, would now be managed by a management team based in Connecticut charged with 'delivering more innovative, skilful and single-minded direction of our beverages brands globally'. The 1988 group structure is shown in Exhibit 4.

Exhibit 4   The group structure of Cadbury Schweppes plc, 1988.

```
                    ┌─────────────────────┐
                    │      Chairman       │
                    │  Sir Adrian Cadbury │
                    └─────────────────────┘
                              │
                    ┌─────────────────────┐
                    │   Group Chief       │
                    │    Executive        │
                    │   N.D. Cadbury      │
                    └─────────────────────┘

┌──────────────┐  ┌──────────────┐  ┌──────────────────┐  ┌──────────────┐
│ Group Finance│  │ Development  │  │ Group Secretary/ │  │Group Personnel│
│  Director    │  │  Director    │  │Chief Legal Officer│  │  Director    │
│  D.P. Nash   │  │ R.J. Elliott │  │   M.A.C. Clark   │  │  A. Gozzard  │
└──────────────┘  └──────────────┘  └──────────────────┘  └──────────────┘

┌──────────────┐  ┌──────────────┐  ┌──────────────────┐  ┌──────────────┐
│Managing Director│ │Managing Director│ │ Chief Executive │ │Managing Director│
│  Coca-Cola & │  │Group Confectionery│ │Cadbury Beverages│ │ Sodastream UK │
│  Schweppes   │  │  N.C. Bain   │  │   J.P. Schadt    │  │  M. Duguid   │
│  Beverages   │  └──────────────┘  └──────────────────┘  └──────────────┘
│ D.R. Williams│
└──────────────┘
```

CONFECTIONERY MARKETS

The UK

The confectionery market was divided broadly into chocolate (£2380m), up 3% in value and volume on 1988, and sugar confectionery (£1070m in 1989), up 3% in volume on 1988. Sugar confectionery accounted for 31% of the market by value and 38% in volume. The confectionery market represented about 8% of the overall food market. Cadbury Schweppes had been mainly concerned with the chocolate sector and, while it had just over 32% of the UK chocolate market, it had only 3% of the sugar confectionery market compared to Trebor's 15%, Rowntree's 10%, and Bassetts' 11%. In March 1989, following a hostile bid for Bassetts by Procordia of Sweden, Cadbury Schweppes bought Bassetts for £91 million including its manufacturing plant in Holland, thus raising its share of the UK sugar confectionery market to 14%.

Sugar confectionery manufacture had few economies of manufacturing scale compared to chocolate and as a result the market was fragmented with no dominant supplier. The chocolate market, by contrast, was heavily concentrated and dominated by three companies – Cadbury, Rowntree, and Mars. Cadbury and Rowntree were estimated to each have about 25% of the chocolate market by volume and about 30% (Cadbury) and 26% (Rowntree) by value. The American private company, Mars, was thought to have 30% of the market by volume, but only 24% by value. Imports were below 10% in volume, but growing slowly.

Market share	(% value) UK	1988 Europe (including UK)
Cadbury	30	9
Rowntree (Nestlé)	26	11
Mars	24	17
Nestlé	3	9
Suchard	2	13
Ferrer Rocher	2	10

Source: Henderson Crosthwaite.

The UK chocolate market grew in volume terms by about 25% between 1980 and 1985. Some of that increase came from an increase in chocolate bar size and per capita consumption rose from 122 grammes to 157 grammes a week. In 1988 volume grew 5.5% (in 1987, 1.4%; in 1986, −2.4%).

The major segment of the market was 'countlines', that is chocolate bars, often filled with cereal, caramel, and nut-based centres, and sold for individual consumption. The countline sector, worth over £1000 million in 1988 (£710m if you excluded chocolate biscuit countlines) and where Cadbury remained weaker than Mars, had been growing at the expense of the moulded bar sector, where Cadbury had been strongest with nearly half this £335 million market. Mars had almost half the chocolate countline market compared to Cadbury's one-third. The remainder of the chocolate market consisted of 'assortments' (worth about £330m a year), novelties (such as chocolate eggs), and 'selflines' (for example a box, bag or tube of identical chocolates such as Maltesers) as well as more specialist items such as liqueur-filled chocolates. The Easter novelties (predominantly eggs) market was worth £150 million in 1989 and the Christmas market (predominantly assortments) was worth £350 million.

Confectionery continued to be the UK's largest packaged food market, as indicated below.

	1988 sales (£m)
Cereals	650
Biscuits	950
Savoury snacks	1150
Tea/coffee	1200
Bread	1925
Carbonated drinks	2375
Milk	2825
Confectionery	3285

Chocolate accounted for 80% of spending. Cadbury, Mars, and Rowntree accounted for 80% of the total spend on chocolate. Confectionary spending represented £1.10 per head per week (33p sugar; 77p chocolate) in 1988 (in 1989, £1.16). About 60% of purchases were on impulse, not always by the ultimate consumer.

The consumer	Population (%)	Buyers (%)	Eaters (%)
Women	41	63	40
Men	38	29	26
Children	21	8	34

Source: Gordon Simmons Research.

COMPETITOR ACTIONS

In the late 1970s, Cadbury's was being outpaced by both its rivals. In response to rises in raw material prices, Cadbury had thinned the chocolate bars of its major brand, Cadbury's Dairy Milk, and had reduced advertising expenditure. Meanwhile Rowntree's research had shown that people preferred the taste of thicker chocolate bars. Thus when Rowntree introduced a new chunky chocolate bar – Yorkie – with heavy advertising, it quickly achieved a 20% market share of the chocolate block market. To make matters worse, Mars started to compete in the UK, as it had in the US, by increasing the size of its chocolate countlines, while holding prices constant.

New brands

Cadbury responded to the increased competition in three ways. First, it invested heavily in new machinery, spending £97 million at its Bournville plant. Secondly, it restored Cadbury's Dairy Milk and other lines to their earlier thickness and spent heavily in advertising support. Finally, it produced its own successful solid chocolate countline 'Wispa'. Unfortunately for Cadbury, Rowntree launched a chunky version of 'Aero', which quickly grew to £50 million per annum sales, showing that brand growth was still possible in the solid block market. As Cadbury commented about Wispa: 'There is still an astonishing appetite by people for just good chocolate. They don't need great new tastes brought in.'

Since 1980 Cadbury had launched 13 new brands, such as Wispa, Biarritz, Spira, Twirl, and Applause. In 1989 it launched three new brands: Tribute, a chocolate assortment aimed at men; Inspirations, fruit-flavoured chocolates for women; and Heritage, a high-quality, low-volume prestige gift box.

Building new brands took time. Many of the leading products had long pedigrees. Cadbury's Dairy Milk had been sold for 84 years; Cadbury's Flake since 1920; Kit Kat for 50 years. Mars also introduced many of its best sellers decades ago.

Mars brands	
Mars Bar	1932 (Milky Way in USA, launched in 1923)
Maltesers	1936
Bounty	1951
Galaxy	1960
Topic	1963
Twix	1967
Snickers	1968 (Previously Marathon in the UK)

Fry's Turkish Delight was launched in 1914; Fry's Chocolate Cream in 1866. The top 20 confectionery brands represented half the UK market (nine from Cadbury; seven by Mars; and four by Rowntree).

NORTH AMERICA

Cadbury Schweppes boosted its small presence in the North American chocolate market in 1978 with its purchase of the third largest US chocolate maker, Peter Paul. The acquisition brought it two strong brands – the chocolate covered coconut bars 'Mounds' and 'Almond Joy' – and greatly expanded its US operations, previously accounting for less than 10% of its total sales. In 1986 the Peter Paul bars, together with York Peppermint Patties, still remained the company's major product brands, though Creme Eggs had been successfully introduced from Britain (the Bournville plant can turn out over 4 million Creme Eggs per week).

Cadbury-Schweppes did not follow Rowntree's example in franchising its products, such as Kit Kat and Rolo to Hershey in USA and Kit Kat and Golden Toffee wafer to Fujiya in Japan. Cadbury's view of Rowntree's approach was to ask: 'How will they ever get into the States like that? We'd never sell our major brands; they're our birthright.'

Great American Disaster

Cadbury learnt a hard lesson about the differences between the UK and US markets in 1985. Cadbury had been operating through food brokers who had responded to Cadbury Schweppes' incentives with massive orders, but the orders were unmatched by sales. Cadbury had lost direct touch with its customers despite spending $50 million on marketing (about 20% on sales – double the market average.) The US confectionery division sales slumped from a near £40 million profit in 1984 to a £6 million loss in 1985, pulling down group profits by 25%.

The result of the 'Great American Disaster' was a dramatic shake-up in Cadbury Schweppes US operations – half the top executives were sacked, seven different operating companies were merged into two, seven layers of management were reduced to four, and manufacturing facilities were reduced by a third. The rationalisation process continued through 1986 when Cadbury Schweppes took the decision to sell its Canadian confectionery business and to return to licensing its products in the Canadian market.

Analysts were impressed by the forthright way in which Cadbury had shaken up its North American confectionery business, but were still waiting to see how it would perform in 1987. As one analyst said: 'The company's greatest unknown and major determinant of profitability in 1987 will be the US confectionery side. So far the signs there are very good, but it's early days . . .'

1987 saw the North American confectionery operations increase market share to 8.5%, with sales up 12% and a £3 million trading profit. However, its position in the US market has been very different from its leading position in the UK. In the US, Mars and Hershey together held about 70% of the market.

Rowntree had also bought into the North American market by acquiring Tom's Foods, Laura Secord Chocolates, Sunmark, and the Original Cookie Company. In 1987 Rowntree sold its snack food interests both in the UK and the US.

Falling world cocoa prices were expected to assist Cadbury's profitability in 1988. However, in August 1988, having yet to achieve satisfactory results from its US confectionery assets, Cadbury sold the business to Hershey for $315 million and franchised its brands to Hershey in the US market. This reduced Cadbury-Schweppes' operating assets and secured future income from the franchise agreement, thus enhancing return on operating assets significantly.

WORLD

The world chocolate market shares were as follows:

Mars	13%
Nestlé	7%
Hershey	6%
Rowntree	5%
Cadbury Schweppes	5%

The world market was about 4.5 million tons annually, with Europe accounting for almost one-third. The European market (worth £5.25 billion annually) was less concentrated than North America, though Suchard, Mars, Nestlé/Rowntree and Ferrero-Rocher jointly held over 60% of the German, French, Italian, and Benelux markets. The rest was largely held by smaller companies.

Neither Cadbury Schweppes nor Rowntree had done well in the European chocolate market, partly because tastes were different and partly because of the difficulty of creating a foothold. Whilst Cadbury focused on expanding in North America, Rowntree concentrated on

Europe, acquiring a German company as early as 1964. Nevertheless, losses were persistent and, in 1987 it only made profits of £11 million on £300 million sales in Europe, compared to Cadbury's £5.5 million trading profit on £61 million sales.

However, after purchasing Beatrice Foods' Australian confectionery interests for £56 million in 1987, Cadbury turned its attention to Europe and, in January 1988, bought Chocolat Poulain of France for £94 million. Poulain became the distributor for Cadbury's chocolate products in France.

Jacobs Suchard of Switzerland had also been active, since Jacobs – a family-owned German coffee company – took over the Suchard/Tobler chocolate businesses in 1982. (It was the leading European coffee roasting business and ranked third in the world after General Foods and Nestlé.) In 1986 it paid $730 million for the large US confectionery firm E J Brach and, after a tussle with Nestlé, took over Belgium's biggest chocolate maker, Cote d'Or in 1987, as well as Du Lac of Italy. Having developed its cross-border distribution network to raise sales of brands such as Toblerone and Milka, Jacobs Suchard sought to increase its brand strength in the growing area of countlines, to complement its base in chocolate blocks.

In 1988 Jacobs Suchard, having quietly acquired 3% of Rowntree, bought a further 11.9% of Rowntree in the market at a cost of £162 million, and announced its intention to raise its holding to 25%. Suchard, already Europe's biggest confectionery producer (£2.4 billion sales) would obtain 24% of the UK chocolate market and 11% of the sugar confectionery market if it were to add Rowntree's £1.4 billion sales. After a protracted battle, Rowntree was instead bought by Nestlé in June 1988 for £2.55 billion, an exit price–earning ratio of 23 for a company with £409 million of net assets.

Suchard profited by nearly £200 million in selling its 29.9% stake to Nestlé, which had now displaced Mars as the largest chocolate company in the world (£2.5 billion sales) and overtaken Suchard as Europe's largest chocolate firm.

European confectionery consumption (kg/head/year)

	Chocolate	Sugar	Total
UK	8.0	5.0	13.0
Germany	6.7	6.3	13.0
Holland	6.8	4.9	11.7
Ireland	5.7	5.8	11.5
Belgium/Luxembourg	6.8	4.2	11.0
Denmark	5.6	5.2	10.8
France	4.2	2.6	6.8
Italy	1.2	2.2	3.4

Note: Consistent data is not available for Spain, Greece and Portugal.

SOFT DRINKS MARKETS

A global market

The world carbonated drinks market, which takes in 177 countries, is now well over 100 billion litres a year and is growing at 5% per annum. US consumption is still way ahead of any other market (38% of world volume; 50% of world value at about $30 billion in 1986) with Americans drinking more carbonated water than natural water.

World consumption, 1986 (billion litres)		Per capita consumption (litres/head)	
North America	39	USA	169
Latin America	18	Canada	75
Western Europe	15	West Germany	68
Far East	15	Spain	55
Eastern Europe	10	UK	46
Asia	4	Italy	30
Africa	3	France	20
Australasia	2		
Caribbean	1		
	107		

Although there are great differences between national markets, the world's carbonated drinks markets are dominated by Coca-Cola and Pepsi; Coke with about 40% of the world market and Pepsi with about 12%. Outside the US, Pepsi is strong in Venezuela, the Philippines, and Saudi Arabia. (Coca-Cola was on the Arab blacklist).

SCHWEPPES IN THE US MARKET

In January 1986 the Pepsi Corporation announced plans to acquire 7-Up from Philip Morris for $380 million. This would have created a combined group with 34% of the US soft drinks industry. A month later, Coca-Cola announced plans to acquire Dr Pepper for $420 million. Both bids quickly ran into anti-trust difficulties because the Coca-Cola group already had about 40% of the US market and PepsiCo about 30%.

Because of the anti-trust ruling, a new player in the soft drinks market – the Dallas based investment firm Hicks and Haas – was able to buy 7-Up's domestic operations and the major stake in Dr Pepper, which had 7% of the US carbonated drinks market compared to 7-Up's 6%.

Coca-Cola and PepsiCo, having thus failed to acquire new brands at home, looked overseas, with PepsiCo acquiring 7-Up's international operations for $246 million and both companies realigning relationships in the UK. Both companies also bought some of their largest franchised bottling operations, thus becoming a major force in the production and distribution of soft drinks. Coca-Cola then floated off its expanded bottling operations as Coca-Cola Enterprises, a company with a turnover of $3 billion. By 1989 Coca-Cola Enterprises and PepsiCo controlled about a third of the US production and distribution of their respective products.

In 1986 Cadbury Schweppes paid RJR Nabisco $230 million for Canada Dry and Sunkist, immediately selling the Canadian bottling part of Canada Dry to Coca-Cola. Later in the year Cadbury Schweppes spent $17.5 million on buying 30% of Dr Pepper. A further 4.4% of Dr Pepper was bought in January 1987 for about $2.5 million.

Schweppes (1.2%) and Canada Dry (3.0%) together had 4.2% of the total US soft drinks market. But two-thirds of their sales were in adult lines, such as fruit-based drinks, mixers, and club soda. Their market share in this high growth area was over 6%, but was projected to rise to 10% by 1990, building on a market platform of 'distinctive drinks for discerning tastes'.

The shape of the US market had been changing with the expansion of the diet/health sector (about 25% in 1989). Sugar-free, salt-free, caffeine-free drinks; fruit-based, still and carbonated beverages; mineral waters and now, originating from Australia, fruit-flavoured mineral waters; all increased sales. For counter-culturalists, a cola with double the normal caffeine was available – called 'Jolt'.

Cadbury Schweppes reversed the long-term decline of Canada Dry sales and Schweppes also raised its own North American sales by 14% in 1987. Globally, the Cadbury Schweppes beverage business increased sales by 42% and trading profit by 34% in 1987, with a further increase of 18% volume and 22% trading profit in 1988, when sales reached £1.3 billion.

In April 1988 Dr Pepper merged with 7-Up, and Prudential Bache Interfunding bought 49% of the merged company. Cadbury Schweppes received $108 million whilst retaining 8% of Dr Pepper/7-Up.

Market share	Volume (%)	Market share	Type (%)	Top 10 Brands	Volume (%)
Coca Cola	40	Colas	62	Coca-Cola Classic	18.2
Pepsico	30	Lemon-lime	12	Pepsi-Cola	17.4
Hicks & Haas	13	Orange	7.5	Diet Coke	8.8
Royal Crown	6	Other fruits	8	Dr Pepper	4.7
Schweppes/C–D	4	Root beer	5.5	Diet Pepsi	3.9
Others	7	All others	5	Sprite	3.3
				7-Up	3.3
				Mountain Dew	2.6
				Coke (new)	2.3
				Royal Crown Cola	2.1
				All other brands	33.4

Source: US Market Data, 1986.

Despite the introduction of diet colas, the cola sector has been losing share, particularly to lemon and lime flavoured products.

SCHWEPPES IN THE UK MARKET

The UK carbonated drinks market was worth £1.8 billion in 1988, with sales of Coca-Cola accounting for £270 million and Pepsi for £90 million. The total UK soft drinks market in 1988 was some seven billion litres worth almost £3 billion. Schweppes, with 14% of the carbonated drinks market in the UK, was already the leading brand in the UK mixer market before its takeover of Canada Dry. Schweppes' sales grew by 5% volume, 10% value in 1988. The whole market was completely restructured between 1986 and 1989 with the formation of two new companies – Coca-Cola/Schweppes Beverages (CCSB) and Britvic Corona, representing Coke and Pepsi respectively in alliance with new trading partners and providing each group with a much wider product range.

UK PRICES

Schweppes switched its allegiance from Pepsi to Coke when the opportunity arose due to Coke's dissatisfaction with its previous franchisee arrangements. Pepsi was not only outsold in the UK by Coke but was believed by Cadbury Schweppes to be typically sold at a 5% discount ex-bottler – a claim denied by Pepsi's new franchisee, Britvic Corona, which asserted that price parity was normal.

Britvic Corona

With such a major shake-up in the market by Coke and Schweppes, it was inevitable that the other major players in the market would realign. As Schweppes had given up its Pepsi franchise, Pepsi was looking for a new franchisee. This coincided with Beecham's decision to rationalise its own product lines. Beecham, which had been a Coca-Cola franchisee in the UK, decided to sell its non-health soft drinks to Britvic, a company jointly owned by Bass, Whitbread, and Allied Lyons. Beecham retained its health drinks, including Ribena, PLJ, and Lucozade.

Britvic paid Beecham £130 million in October 1986 for Corona, Idris, Hunts, Tango and Quosh brands. PepsiCo then took a 10% stake in the new company, Britvic Corona, in exchange for bringing Pepsi and 7-Up to the product range which now included Britvic juices and Whites lemonade. Ironically it also included Cadbury Schweppes' Canada Dry, for which it was the UK distributor. The new company was estimated to have about 20% of the UK soft drinks market.

Coca-Cola and Schweppes Beverages

Coca-Cola and Schweppes Beverages (CCSB), in which Cadbury Schweppes held the controlling 51% stake, claimed to already sell a third of carbonated drinks in the UK. Selling Fanta, Lilt, Quattro, Roses Lime Juice, and Kia-Ora, as well as Coke and Schweppes brands, the management of the new company was very optimistic about the strength of its approach:

> Instead of fragmented organisations competing with each other to sell the same brands, we now have one company which can sell the acknowledged market leaders in every major sector.

Manufacturing and distribution

On the manufacturing and distribution side, CCSB had been making substantial investments in plant, as well as rationalizing operations. Before the link with Coca-Cola, Schweppes had already closed eight out of 14 bottling plants and halved the number of distribution depots to some 25, reducing its workforce by 50%.

Following the link-up, 41 depots were cut to 20; nine plants reduced to eight; and joint CCSB volume grew 15% in 1987 with accompanying gains in market share to a claimed one-third of the UK market. CCSB then built Europe's largest soft drinks plant at Wakefield (£60m) which opened in September 1989. It later sought to build a similar large plant at Northampton.

EUROPE

In 1988 Schweppes had 12% of the Spanish carbonated drinks market through its Rioblanco subsidiary and also had 8% of the French market, where its main competitor was Orangina. In Italy, Schweppes operated through a franchisee, San Benedetto. Schweppes still had links with Pepsi (and in Australia) and with 7-Up in France. More Schweppes tonic water is consumed in Spain than in the UK.

GENERAL CINEMA AND THE THREAT OF TAKEOVER

General Cinema Corporation was the largest independent bottler of soft drinks in the US. It bottled both Schweppes and Sunkist products, though Pepsi was its major customer, and was also involved with soft drinks as a manufacturer, developing Sunkist in 1977 before selling it to R J Reynolds in 1981.

Richard Smith, the company Chairman, had a record of buying substantial stakes in other companies – 'investment with involvement'. In 1982 it bought 18% of Heublein (now part of Grand Metropolitan) which took refuge in a takeover by R J Reynolds. General Cinema agreed to accept stock in Reynolds for its Heublein stake, which brought it an annual $20 million dividend income. In 1984 General Cinema acquired a minority stake in the US retailer Carter Hawley Hale to help fight off an unwanted takeover by The Limited. When the Limited renewed its takeover bid for Carter Hawley Hale in 1986, a business restructuring followed which left General Cinema with majority control of the specialty stores division, which included Bergdorf Goodman in New York and the Dallas-based Nieman Marcus Group. Although smaller than Cadbury Schweppes, General Cinema had been more profitable ($90 million net earnings on $998 million revenues).

To fend off unwanted attention, Cadbury Schweppes, whose Chairman, Sir Adrian Cadbury, was a Director of the Bank of England, ran an expensive corporate advertising campaign based on the slogan 'Management proven in the market place' which described the actions Cadbury Schweppes' managers had taken to win wider markets for the Company's brands.

Cadbury Schweppes, wrote Sir Adrian Cadbury in the 1986 annual statement, offered shareholders an exciting portfolio of international brands with internationally experienced managers committed to their development. He stressed that: 'Our brands are unique properties – assets in which we invested nearly £200 million in 1986 alone in advertising and marketing support.'

He went on to explain the Board's approach to providing for the profitable growth of the Company as follows:

> The most difficult decisions which the Board has to take are those involving the balance between profit now and profit in the future. It would for example have been possible to have tackled our marketing problems in North America less vigorously than we did, so spreading the costs of action but delaying the return from it. Equally your Company's profits should be considerably increased in the short term by cutting the investment in marketing, in innovation and in management. What guides the Board's judgement in these matters is the need to provide for the continued profitable growth of the Company into the future.

Capital investment duly rose 48% from the 1987 level to reach £148 million in 1988. In France, Chocolat Poulain doubled its profits compared to 1987.

Cadbury Schweppes had not yet embraced the new fashion for capitalizing the value of its brands in its balance sheet despite investing £268 million worldwide in brand marketing in 1988 (in 1987, £227m).

SUGGESTED QUESTIONS

1. What are the key strategic issues facing Cadbury and Schweppes?
2. How should Cadbury-Schweppes balance the forces for global integration with the requirements of local markets?
3. Should Cadbury manufacture 'own-label' products? Should Schweppes enter the main Cola markets?

5

Csepel Machine Tool Company

Case written by Joseph Wolfe and Jozsef Poor

1989 seemed to have been a good year for the Csepel Machine Tool Company. More importantly, it had been a tumultuous yet basically successful decade. Since 1985 sales had increased an average of 7.5% a year and the company had successfully weathered the financial crisis which had hindered its managerial freedom in the early 1980s. More recently, management had been able to lessen the firm's dependency on domestic sales, doubly important because of Hungary's stagnant economy, and it had increased its vital hard currency sales by 23% in just one year. Moreover, it appeared that the firm's strategy of customizing its products as much as possible to suit the unique needs of various customer groups, especially those in the People's Republic of China, was a viable way to operate in an industry which had been only marginally profitable in other advanced industrial countries.

Something, however, was seriously wrong as numerous fears and misgivings were held in various quarters within Csepel. Profits were falling and the company's sales had been erratic for the past four years. Yet, even allowing for Hungary's double-digit inflation, many felt sales revenues were actually falling. Accordingly top management was forecasting that 1990 revenue would range from 2.05 to 2.19 billion forints, and that profits would run between −55.6 and 66.6 million forints for the three alternative pro forma income statements developed by top management (see Table 1). Various managers questioned whether Csepel should continue pursuing its customizing strategy, with its attendant high manufacturing costs and operations, within a market easily accessed by

© 1990 by Joseph Wolfe and Jozsef Poor
This case was prepared by Joseph Wolfe and Jozsef Poor as the basis for class discussion rather than to illustrate either effective or ineffective handling of an administrative situation. The casewriters gratefully acknowledge the use of materials and consulting reports created by Maria Roboczki Bordane, Eva Tihanyi, Andras Farkas and Anna Jakab Baane.

Table 1 Csepel Machine Tool Company: 1990 pro-forma income statements under three scenarios (millions of forints)

	A	B	C
Revenues:			
Domestic	407.0	430.0	450.0
Exports			
CMEA ruble market	648.0	231.4	130.0
Hard currency	993.2	1428.0	1610.0
Total	2048.2	2089.4	2190.0
Manufacturing cost:			
Direct	1124.1	1145.2	1182.6
Overhead	900.0	900.0	900.0
Total	2024.1	2045.2	2082.6
Other income:			
US dollar support	–	–	32.2
Ruble export	−86.3	−30.0	−13.0
Profit before taxes	−55.6	34.2	66.6
Less taxes	–	17.1	33.3
Profit after taxes	−55.6	17.1	33.3

Source: Company internal forecast.

superior Japanese machine tool technology, without instituting strict cost controls and modernizing the company's ageing product line. As the 1990s began, Csepel's top management faced a number of thorny issues and problems and a clear course of action did not seem to exist.

MACHINE TOOLS AND THE MACHINE TOOL INDUSTRY

While the lathe is still today's most widely used machine tool, other tools mill, drill, bore, plane, cut, and shape steel and castings into their final form. Demand for these tools was highly dependent on the amount of metalworking activity in both heavy and light industry. The machine tool industry's largest customers were the automobile manufactures and their parts and sub-assembly suppliers, followed by the aircraft industry and all others which involve finishing, grinding, or stamping metal. Accordingly, the demand for machine tools was quite high in Western Europe and Japan and amongst Japanese automobile manufacturers, regardless of the location of their plants. Alternatively the demand in Detroit and in the Big Three's – Chrysler, Ford, and General Motors – plants scattered throughout the United States, Canada, and Mexico had been relatively low during the past decade. In the short term experts believed that the American automobile industry would defer its purchases of the larger, more sophisticated, flexible manufacturing systems due to

Table 2   American machine tool industry performance

Measure	1985	1986	1987	1988	1989	1990	1993
Sales ($ billion)	3.2	3.3	3.4	3.7	4.0	4.3	5.6
Operating margin (%)	8.5	9.3	9.2	9.6	9.5	9.0	12.0
Net profit ($ million)	28.8	80.9	31.3	76.4	105.0	185.0	300.0
Net profit margin (%)	0.9	2.5	−0.9	2.1	2.6	4.3	5.4

Notes: Results for 1989 and 1990 are estimates; performances for 1993 are mean estimates of the years 1992–94.
Source: Brophy, T 'Machine Tool Industry', *Value Line Investment Survey*, November 17, 1989, p. 1336.

the losses incurred by both Ford and General Motors in 1989, and the plant closings at Chrysler, as it tried to reverse its sagging fortunes.

Statistics for the American machine tool industry are presented in Table 2. Sales growth had been less than GNP growth in the US and net profit margins had only been 2.03% of sales during that period. A number of firms, such as Cross & Trecker, Acme-Cleveland, and Cincinnati Milacron restructured themselves, while others attempted diversifications out of the industry. Certain Japanese machine tool manufacturers, such as Yamazaki Mazak Corporation, Okuma Machinery Inc, and Toyoda Machinery USA, were very bullish about the industry's prospects. Yamazaki Mazak planned to enter a variety of world markets with innovative cost-cutting machine tool stations which enhanced end-user value by justifying their purchase as an investment in efficiency and higher end–product quality. Okuma, Toyoda, and other Japanese manufacturers were broadening the product lines being exported to the US to include grinders and screw machines which were machine tool categories not included in the industry's 1986 voluntary restraint agreements. Exhibit 1 outlines the nature of the machine tool industry's technology and the degree to which its technology had been diffused in most technologically advanced nations. Table 3 presents data on the dollar value of worldwide production of machine tools by selected capitalist and socialist countries.

THE CSEPEL MACHINE TOOL COMPANY

Today's Csepel Machine Tool Company started manufacturing military ordinance in 1889 and shortly thereafter an iron and steel plant was built. Bicycle and automobile production began in 1925 and airplane engine production was added to its industrial empire in 1927. The firm was nationalized in 1946. Various Soviet industrial organizational concepts were quickly introduced over the years. Rather than continuing the Taylorism which had been used since its introduction in the 1930s by consultants from the German Method Time Measurement Association

---

Exhibit 1   Two decades of technological progress in the machine tool/production engineering industry.

By the early 1980s extensive software had been developed which fully automated and optimized all steps in the manufacture of a component. These programmes select the machining sequence, selection of machine tools, clamping, selection of the operation sequence, tool selection, choose the optimum cutting conditions, and numerically control the entire machining operation. Programmes and machines of this type were in wide use in many industries.

By the mid-1980s fully self-optimizing adaptive control of machine tools had been developed, and on-line process identification and optimization were in general use in manufacturing plant. Work preparation in the form of machine loading and scheduling was being accomplished by computers in over 75% of all American factories.

In the 1990s standardized computer software systems would be commercially available. About 70% of manufacturing would be using group technology in its manufacturing processes The machine industry's traditional lathes, boring mills, and broaching machines were being rapidly replaced by plastic machinery, flexible manufacturing machinery, and advanced composite machinery to reflect the new materials which were being introduced as replacements for iron and steel.

Adapted from Merchant M E (1971) 'Delphi-type Forecast of the Future of Production Engineering', *CIRP Annuals*, Vol. 20, No. 3, p. 213; and Kearney, A T, Inc. (1989) *US Manufacturing Competitiveness – Profiles in Competitive Success*, p. 10, Chicago.

(REFA), a planning orientation comprising a series of three- and five-year national plans was strictly applied. Beginning in the 1950s, workers were encouraged to over-produce, shops were given greater autonomy through the addition of staff support, and a new management level was added to monitor the company's conformity to the centralized plan. The government assumed control of the company's import/export effort through its Ministry of Commerce, and its research and development (R&D) function was removed to the Institution for Mechanical Industry Research in Budapest. From 1946 until 1968 the company quadrupled its number of shops while adding 112 800 square feet of factory space and a new office building to its manufacturing complex. Table 4 demonstrates that the company's general product mix became more diversified after a heavy period of concentration in drilling and milling machines in the 1960s.

Its machine tool business began in 1979 as an in-house supplier for its own needs, but one year later the firm began to sell its tools to outside firms in both Hungary and abroad. Over the years it developed a solid reputation by offering a series of innovative, high-precision products.

In 1983 the company reorganized itself into an independent, state-owned company called the Machine Tools Factory of the Csepel Works. Its debut was inauspicious as the new entity was burdened by nearly 700 million forints worth of debt, and delinquent account receivables of

Table 3 *World production of machine tools (selected years in millions of dollars)*

Country	1975	1980	1984	1985
United States	2 451.7	4 812.3	2 423.2	2 575.0
West Germany	2 403.6	4 707.6	2 803.7	3 123.1
Japan	1 060.6	3 826.1	4 473.3	5 268.7
Italy	873.1	1 728.1	996.0	1 056.4
Great Britain	728.3	1 395.8	674.9	722.9
Switzerland	535.9	994.1	759.2	956.7
France	678.6	957.9	465.5	468.5
Total	8 731.8	18 421.9	12 595.8	14 172.3
Soviet Union	1 984.4	3 065.0	2 776.4	3 015.0
East Germany	585.1	891.5	789.1	789.3
Rumania	106.0	590.0	353.0	324.1
Czechoslovakia	305.4	331.5	325.2	334.4
Poland	422.8	605.0	120.7	97.3
Yugoslavia	65.0	231.8	225.9	238.6
Hungary	50.0	421.3	198.1	160.0
Bulgaria	25.5	43.0	192.5	192.5
Total	3 544.3	6 179.1	4 980.9	5 151.2
World total	12 276.1	24 601.0	17 576.7	19 323.5

Source: Cited by Istvan Nemeth (1987) 'Machine Tools Export for the Hard Currency Market' (unpublished dissertation), University of Economics, Budapest.

Table 4 *Production by general machine tool groups*

Product	1946	1960	1970	1980	1989
Drilling machines	110	500	700	500	172
Milling machines (including NC and CNC)	100	660	295	100	67
Lathe machines (including NC and CNC)	n/a*	n/a	40	240	93
Grinding and other high precision machines	n/a	1	29	160	36

* Product not manufactured at this time.
Source: *90 Years of the Csepel Iron and Metal Company* (1982) Csepel Iron and Metal Company, Budapest.

500 million. The company's resulting low working capital forced it to abandon its ambitious modernization programme and to find new sources of cash in an effort to stabilize operations. A manufacturing building was sold in 1986 and, more importantly, the company obtained equity financing by transforming itself into a publicly-held shareholders' corporation. In this regard Csepel became a pioneer within the Hungarian economy, and this action became a model for others to emulate. The

Table 5   Major Hungarian machine tool manufacturers (1987)

Company	Employees	Revenue (million forints)	Fixed assets (million forints)
Csepel Machine Tool Company	2 500	2 500	1800
SZIM Machine Tool Company	15 000	10 000	2590
DIGEP Mechanical Factory	3 000	300	910

Source: Istvan Nemeth (1987) 'Machine Tools Export for the Hard Currency Market', p. 27 (unpublished dissertation), University of Economics, Budapest.

Exhibit 2   Csepel Machine Tool Company: sales and profits, 1985–89.

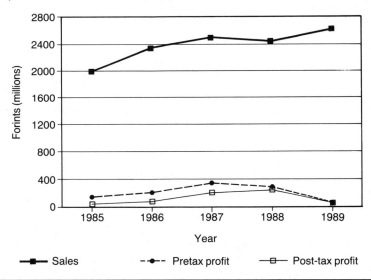

company split itself into two stock corporations in October 1988 – the larger of the two was capitalized at 860 million forints and became known as the Csepel Machine Tool Company while the smaller one, called the Csepel Fixture and Tool Corporation, was capitalized at 160 million forints. In making this division, the Csepel Machine Tool Corporation retained its original interests in manufacturing and providing parts for its lathes, machining centres, and drilling and milling machines, while the Csepel Fixture and Tool Corporation manufactured small fixtures, tools, and parts. Within the Hungarian economy, Csepel was only one of three manufacturers. As shown in Table 5, the company was much smaller

Table 6 Planned sales compositions, 1988 v. 1992 (in billions of forints)

Product or service	1988	1993
Finished products	2.38	2.63
Services	0.08	–
Tools	0.05	–
Parts production	–	0.70
Other	–	0.18
Total	2.50	3.50

Source: Consultant's report and company interviews.

Exhibit 3 Csepel: sources of sales, 1985–89 (million of forints).·

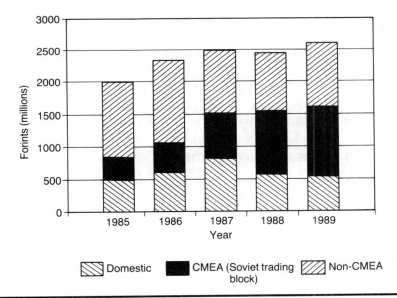

than the SZIM Machine Tools Company while DIGEP (Deutsche Industrieanlagen GmbH) had a minor claim to the market.

Although the Csepel Machine Tool Corporation was able to retrench and stabilize its operations, Exhibit 2 shows that the firm's profits peaked in 1987 while sales continued their upward climb to about 2.6 billion forints in 1989. Over the next three to four years Csepel expected to boost its sales to over 3.5 billion while simultaneously changing its sales composition to that displayed in Table 6. The 700 million forint sales in parts contracts were planned as joint ventures with Western companies and as a revival of the once-flourishing businesses the firm had with the

Exhibit 4   Csepel: product mix and product prices by geographic market, 1989.

Machine type	Model number	Product price (in 000's of forints)			Annual production	Life Cycle position	Competitive strength
		Hungarian	US dollar	CMEA countries			
Radial	RF-50	747.7	577.5	577.9 ⎫	200 for	All very late	All are weak
Drilling	RFh-75	1 449.4	1 116.4	909.6 ⎬	entire		
Machines	RFh-100	2 015.7	2 056.1	1 558.2 ⎭	group		
CNC	Yasda	n/a*	23 951.4	n/a	30 to 40	Early	Average
Machining	MK-500	11 683.4	9 460.0	12 072.9	35 to 55	Early	Average
Centres	MV16	10 903.6	n/a	n/a	10 to 15	Relatively late	Weak
	MV110	11 989.6	13 294.9	n/a	6 to 8	Relatively early	Average
CNC	SDNC 610						
Lathes	1000	8 951.5	10 581.9	6 566.2	35 to 50	Relatively early	Strong
	SDNC 610						
	1500	n/a	4 742.4	8 464.1	35 to 50	Relatively early	Strong
	RS-100	5 516.3	9 258.8	n/a	15 to 25	Very early	Average
	TCFM-100	1 616.2	n/a	2 047.2	25 to 30	Very early	Strong
High-	FKP-326-10	7 315.5	10 851.5	7 259.4	35 to 40	Mature	Weak
precision	UP-1	15 726.0	n/a	n/a	5 to 10	Very early	Strong
Systems							
Special-	PTC-71-180	n/a	n/a	4 431.7	10 to 15	Mature	Weak
Purpose	SMC-71-180	n/a	n/a	5 539.8	10 to 15	Mature	Weak
Systems							

West in the 1970s. A large slump in demand in the early 1980s had caused this market to diminish significantly. Exhibit 3 displays the source of Csepel's sales by general market areas for the past five years.

Products and new product development

The Csepel Machine Tool Corporation produced the finished products listed in Exhibit 4. Its product line consisted of five basic types of equipment – radial drilling machines, computer numerical controlled (CNC) machining centres, CNC lathes, precision equipment, and special-purpose machinery. The radial drilling machines came in three different sizes with a movable column and varying operating lever lengths. Ten years earlier these units had annual sales of about 1000 per year. Csepel's CNC machining centres consisted of four different models. The first was the Yasda model which came in three different sizes; the design was purchased in 1979 from the Yasda Company. The next model, the MK-500, was created by Csepel itself and was a small machining centre. The third set of models in the 'M' family consisted of the model numbers MV1-6-11 and MV1-10-11. These models came in both horizontal and vertical versions.

Csepel made four different kinds of lathes. The first was a tailor-made shaft and pulley lathe made under a licensing agreement with Heid. The next was designed by Csepel and met the needs of the precision instrument industry. The third model in this group was the TCFM-100 which was used for training purposes as well as being able to produce both revolution solids and box-shaped parts.

Table 7 Csepel R&D expenditures (in millions of forints)

			Year		
1985	1986	1987	1988	1989	1990*
37.4	27.1	81.2	55.7	18.7	15.0

*Planned.
Source: Company records.

The company's next set of products was a high-precision gear-cutting system which came with a twist–drill attachment and programmable logic control, and the UP-1 which was a small precision lathe. The last two products, the PTC-71-180 and SMC-71-180, were special-purpose systems exported solely to the Soviet Union.

The company's R&D expenditure for 1985–89, in addition to its budget for 1990, is presented in Table 7. In commenting on the number of Csepel products in the late stages of their life cycles as well as the general lack of new products coming on-stream, Levente Godri, the central plant's Chief Designer explained:

We don't have enough engineers in the first place and those we do have get too involved in daily operations – so much so they don't have any time to do new product development. We could hire some good people from the Technical University in Budapest and they would staff a new R&D Department but I don't know if that would really solve our problem.

I see two ways to get more new products for us. We could use a project manager approach. We could pick out two to three projects to be pursued for the next year and we'd select project leaders who could hire personnel from those that are available within the company. These leaders would stay in charge of the project as long as they stayed within the budget. Another way would be to set up an independent engineering bureau to operate on its own or jointly with another firm.

Whatever we're doing we have to do a better job than we're doing now. Unfortunately our bonus system is based on the on-time delivery of machines so our R&D people spend time in the shop helping to get orders delivered instead of spending time developing new products.

As if to underline Godri's observations about being saddled with plant production problems, the leader of the NC assembly and machining shop interrupted the conversation by telephone demanding that an engineer be sent immediately to the production unit to make a substitute part which had not been delivered by a supplier. This call was made even though each shop had an on-duty technical assistant to handle these minor crises.

Table 8 Proportions of special order work by product line

Product line	Proportion
Radial drilling machines	2% to 3%
CNC machining centres	30% to 50%
CNC lathes	20% to 40%
High-precision systems:	
FKP-326-10	5% to 10%
UP-1	100%
Special-purpose systems	100%

Source: Consultant's report.

Godri later explained these problems could be completely avoided if substitute parts could be identified and used, but Csepel's part numbering system did not disclose or cross-reference part substitutions.

In addition to producing machines for its finished goods inventory, Csepel willingly worked to special customer specifications. As shown in Table 8, the proportion of these special orders varied by product type. Overall, the firm had little trouble obtaining equipment orders as it attempted to satisfy each customer's unique requirements. It also obtained a reputation for quality products and low prices.

Factories and manufacturing operations

The company manufactured its machine tools and parts in two factories. The central plant, which also housed its executive offices, was in Budapest while its second plant was in Nyirbator, a countryside city of about 30 000 inhabitants in the north-eastern section of Hungary's Great Plain. Because of the high degree of specialization existing within the company, neither plant could make an entire machine tool. While the Nyirbator facility featured a better plant layout because it was relatively new, outside experts generally agreed that Csepel's factories left much to be desired. About 15% of its production equipment was less than 10 years old, another 37% was 11–20 years old and almost half was over 20 years of age. The firm had only 24 numerical control machines of its own and about 59% of its equipment had been depreciated to scrap value. It was believed that an investment of $4.7–6.0 million would be needed to modernize Csepel's production equipment while an additional $12.0 million would be needed to introduce extensions to its current product lines and to acquire and introduce advanced production control and information systems. Table 9 displays a repair status summary of the company's equipment.

Despite using technology which was frequently 20–25 years old, the technological gap had often been bridged by engineering know-how and exceptionally skilled and dedicated workers. In recent years, however, the

Table 9 Production equipment state of repair

Repair state	Proportion of equipment
Good	46.3%
Average	48.0%
Poor	5.7%

Source: Consulting report.

central plant had begun to lose both its highly-qualified and cross-trained senior factory technicians, as well as its younger trainees, to local private sector machine shops and small factories. This was due to their superior working conditions and freedom from forced overtime work near the end of the business year. Ironically, they often worked with old equipment sold to the private sector machine shop by Csepel itself. Because of the lack of alternative employment opportunities in the Nyirbator area, a similar loss of blue collar workers had not occurred at that facility.

Central plant operation

Due to the nature of the products being manufactured and the availability of various types of equipment, the manufacturing process in the central plant, as shown in Figure 1, was more complex than that found at Nyirbator. The central plant's formal organization, which also included the firm's headquarters personnel, was also more elaborate. See Figure 2 for Csepel's central plant organization chart at Budapest.

A conversation with Arpad Koknya, Deputy General Director in charge of the central plant's manufacturing operations, revealed both the complexity of the production control process and certain problems that had not been resolved.

> Every quarter for each month and each shop my department produces a production plan. We also do this for Nyirbator. On the basis of this plan our department assembles a portfolio of shop cards, raw materials requisitions, and time and labour charges by order number. If everything is alright the portfolio goes to the production department. The department then launches a new shop order. When the shop manager gets the portfolios he assigns them to various foremen who have the workers get the tools and raw materials bill. That's the normal process.
>
> When his assignment is completed each worker signs-off on the bill. But we have a stupid quality control system that works well for simple, small things, but for complicated sub-assemblies like ours it doesn't work so well. It can really cause big problems if the assembly is produced in a number of steps.
>
> Our quality control system is a mixture of worker self-inspection

110

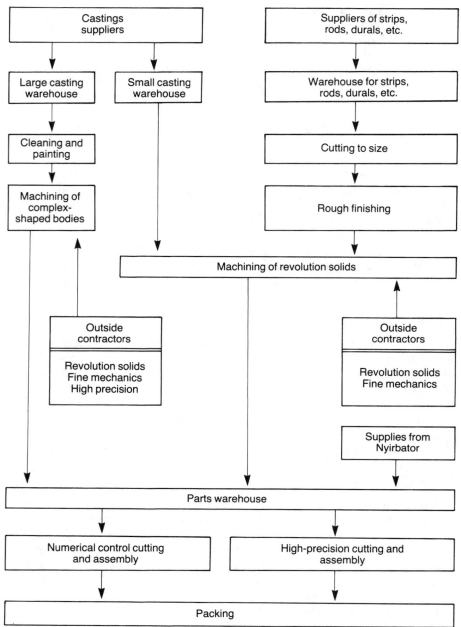

Note: About 5% of the company's 24 000 parts and subassemblies are manufactured in the central plant. The plant handles parts requiring extreme accuracy and/or state-of-the-art technology. Its layout is not very rational although efforts are being made to create a more orderly plant configuration.

Fig. 1 Central plant manufacturing sequence.

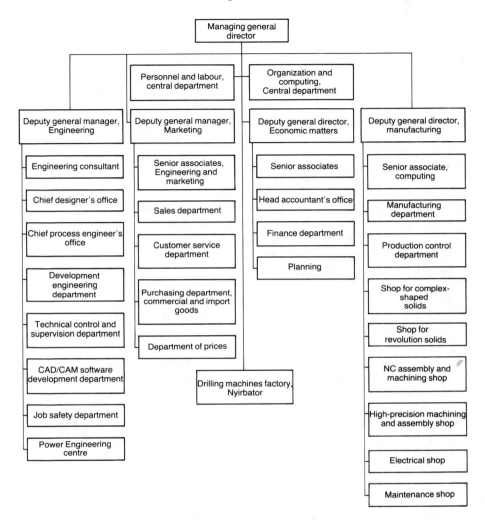

Fig. 2   Organization chart for Csepel Machine Tool Company.

and staff department quality control inspection. Under worker self-inspection, that worker himself says whether the work is good or not, while the quality control department looks at the entire sub-assembly when it's been completed. Many of our workers sign-off that this work is up to standard but it isn't and we don't find out about it until it shows up in the final sub-assembly. Or what's worse, after it's been delivered and we have to field service it ourselves. We should really punish these guys but the present employment situation doesn't allow us to do this. We also have a quantitative bonus system in the production of parts and this also adds to our problems.

Table 10   Csepel Machine Tool Company inventory levels (in thousands of forints)

Inventory type	1985	1986	1987	1988	1989
Purchased stocks and raw materials	450.6	578.0	610.9	551.8	777.5
Goods in process	185.5	139.8	171.6	192.3	216.5
Finished goods	15.5	17.4	31.8	36.3	23.4
Total	651.7	735.2	814.3	780.4	1017.4

Source: Internal company records.

Another part of our production problem also has something to do with parts. Each month our department sets up a so-called parts shortage list (PSL). The PSL has a list of final products on the left side and on the right side the number of missing parts for that product with the part's identification number. This list is a key input into the parts manufacturing operation. They have a production schedule which deals with making parts for the PSL and parts for things currently being assembled. Those items on the PSL get a higher priority. Unfortunately, our computer system can't handle it, so a lot of parts searches show 'out-of-stock' messages even though they're really in stock. Too often we're making parts we don't need and their higher priority slows up our regular production runs.

The creation of our production plan for assembly operations isn't so complicated, but it's co-ordinating the production that's difficult. Because of how our sales orders come in we only have to deliver about 20 units per month in the first part of the year but about 60 to 100 units a month in the last part. Because we have a limited number of assembly workers they get very overworked by the end of the year – sometimes our best workers get sick from stress. But life isn't so easy for management either. These swings in production cause headaches for everybody. If the sales department could just forecast sales better we'd have fewer problems down the line.

Table 10 presents data on the various inventory levels carried by Csepel within various stages of production.

Nyirbator plant operations

The Nyirbator plant was originally created to manufacture parts for all Csepel products, as well as serving as part of the Hungarian government's plan to bring industrial economic development to the country's rural areas. Accordingly the original labour supply was drawn from unskilled agricultural workers who had to be intensively trained in company-run technical training programmes. Over the years Csepel had been a strong supporter of the city's technical school which became the

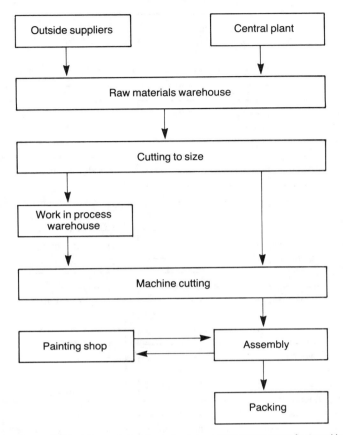

Notes: Almost 90% of Csepel's parts and subassemblies are manufactured in this factory. The process technology is simpler compared to that used in the central plant. Nyirbator's products are easier to assemble than those produced in the central plant but their unit value is significantly lower. Except for high precision parts, the plant is self-sufficient.

Fig. 3 Nyirbator manufacturing sequence.

firm's major source of skilled labour. In 1989 the plant employed about 740 people and it generated sales of 649 million forints.

The plant moved from producing parts only to manufacturing both parts and the company's basic drilling machines. (See Figures 3 and 4 for presentations of Nyirbator's manufacturing systems and organization chart.) Although the plant was more modern in its layout, various Nyirbator managers felt that constraints placed on them by headquarters robbed them of their chances to be more profitable. The drilling machine plant's Director of Economic Matters, Janos Fazekas, expressed it in the following manner:

First of all our plant has to manufacture Csepel's low profit items. As bad as that is, many times we get urgent orders by fax from the

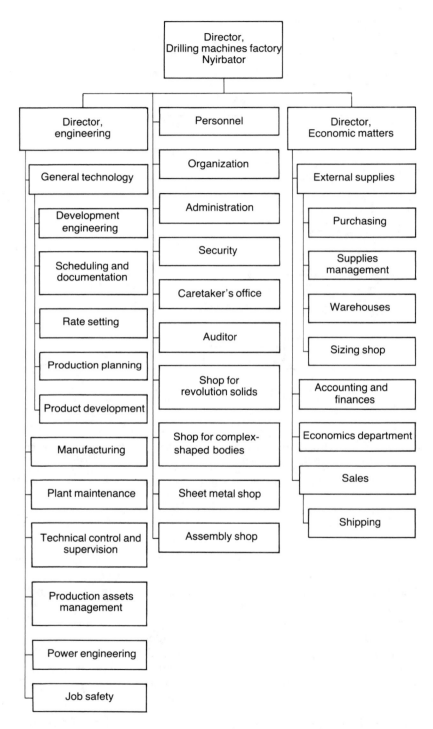

Fig. 4 Organization chart for Nyirbator factory.

central plant which forces us to shut down our machines to supply them. We argue about these things all the time.

We want to be more independent and to have more power in these discussions with production control and planning. These departments consider us to be their slaves and don't consider our specific bottleneck problems and they continue to bother us with their special orders which overuse our special machines.

Also headquarters' sales operations are very slow in processing domestic orders. We could do a faster job on these sales if we could set up our own sales department.

Nyirbator's Engineering Director, Istvan Szatmari, also thought that the plant should have more freedom if only to develop a line of more profitable products for the facility.

In recent years we've brought in new engineers for new product development but all their time is spent in operations. They want to design new tools but can't. We're also in conflict with the central plant's R&D operations because they won't give us the freedom to operate on our own.

As much as Nyirbator's management felt shackled, they had occasionally taken advantage of the poor telephone communications between their two cities and the lack of tight internal auditing control existing at headquarters. By falsely listing desired equipment as production parts they were at times able to purchase non-authorized office equipment. In one instance they obtained a prized Xerox machine.

Headquarters operations

Csepel's headquarters was staffed predominantly by people who had been promoted from within and they all had graduated from production operations after many years of service. The one exception was Istvan Rakoczy, the head of the company's computer services. Top management's pace and style appeared to be dictated by that practised by Gabor Hajnoczy, Csepel's Managing General Director. Two or three mornings a week, beginning just after the shift opened, he toured the central plant's shops with Arpad Koknya. These rounds, which were conducted both there and occasionally at Nyirbator, could last up to three hours and could occur more often should problems be plaguing a particular production run. Hajnoczy was very familiar with plant operation, and its workers, and he knew many employees on a first-name basis. Should he see something that appeared to be wrong he would immediately order a change in either the production method or the order's schedule. Observed while holding a two-hour discussion in Gabor Hajnoczy's office, he was interrupted many times by short telephone calls from plant personnel and brief conferences with his secretary. He also had to sign a number of technical orders as well as sign a request for computer supplies. Several

Exhibit 5   Csepel Machine Tool Company: income statements (unaudited; in millions of forints).

	1985	1986	1987	1988	1989
Revenues:					
Domestic	484.7	605.8	814.2	567.0	542.5
Exports					
CMEA ruble market	352.8	466.4	694.7	981.4	1058.9
Hard currency	1151.0	1263.6	982.2	898.1	1016.9
Total	1988.6	2335.8	2491.1	2446.5	2618.3
Direct manufacturing cost	1044.4	1173.7	1277.8	1294.7	1385.8
Operating profit	944.2	1162.2	1213.3	1151.8	1232.5
Overhead cost:					
Factory overhead	351.2	478.0	478.4	282.0	352.6
Admin. overhead	325.5	293.8	299.2	505.8	689.8
R&D expense	37.3	27.1	81.2	55.7	18.7
Customer service	11.3	16.2	12.5	22.1	17.0
Land rent	4.0	3.7	–	–	–
Miscellaneous	53.4	64.9	70.4	97.1	8.1
Total	782.7	883.7	941.7	962.7	1086.2
Additional expenses	156.3	129.8	107.4	62.9	137.2
Other income:					
Export support	123.0	16.0	60.7	–	–
Ministry support	2.1	35.7	79.1	129.2	35.1
R&D subsidy	5.0	–	51.2	35.7	5.9
Vendor penalties	6.1	2.4	2.4	–	3.4
Other	2.5	5.7	3.0	–	8.3
Total	138.7	59.8	196.4	164.9	52.7
Profit before taxes	143.9	208.4	360.6	291.1	61.8
Taxes	109.6	133.1	151.4	49.3	0.3
Profit after taxes	34.1	75.3	209.2	241.8	61.5

very lengthy telephone calls dealt with decisions about where pieces of shop equipment should be placed for a shop-floor layout change that was underway.

Although some appreciated top management's intimate working knowledge of plant operations and its accessibility, others saw it as 'always having someone breathing down our necks' or showing too much concern for production and the bonuses attached to on-time production deliveries. The head of the central plant's sales department, Gabor Nagy, commented that:

> Top management's manufacturing bias is the company's major problem – it keeps us from being flexible. This company doesn't

Exhibit 6   Csepel Machine Tool Company balance sheets (unaudited; in millions of forints).

	1988	1989
Assets		
Current assets:		
Cash	1 139	3 230
Bank account	32 646	16 276
Additional accounts	13 896	−32 949
Bonds	—	—
Domestic Buyer	203 731	192 807
Foreign Buyer	666 332	978 162
Total	917 744	1 157 526
Employee fund	657	—
State budget fund	—	2 882
Total	870 720	1 173 851
Inventories:		
Goods in process	192 216	216 533
Finished goods	36 315	23 362
Total	229 687	239 895
Raw material	428 644	678 293
Purchased stocks	123 201	99 229
Total	551 845	777 522
Total	781 532	1 017 417

(cont.)

have its own selling rights because it must trade through Technoimpex. This was all right at one time because Technoimpex had traditionally been machine tools orientated. Now Technoimpex wants to buy and sell a whole range of products so it doesn't represent us as well as it once did – their representatives can't emphasize us like they did before because they have so many other companies to represent and they really don't want to emphasize our machine tools any longer. To cover ourselves on this we now have service representatives, who can also help us with our sales, in such places as Rumania, West Germany, and the United States. Where we don't have our own people we use Austria's Intertrade which specializes in steel and machine tools.

The General Manager's plant tours not only disturbed many production workers, they also appeared to interfere with the operations of other company functions. As an example, Nagy observed that:

Sometimes our General Manager gets orders on his own when he's out in the field . . . and when he comes back he simply gives these orders directly to the production department. This is bad for us in sales because we can't tell how effective we've been. We don't

Exhibit 6   *continued*

	1988	1989
Contingency fund	—	—
Other active accounts	257 231	45 158
Temporary account	—	—
	257 231	45 158
Shares held	6 000	228 000
Assets held	—	—
Foreign investments	6 000	228 000
Fixed plant and equipment	928 097	1 091 681
Less depreciation	735 634	786 716
Plant additions	22 559	82 249
Net book value	215 022	387 214
Total assets	2 177 030	2 838 030
Liabilities		
Accounts payable	—	840 399
Domestic deliverer	812 413	188 014
Foreign deliverer	24 962	12 935
Factoring	30 000	113 810
Creditors	308	36 144
Salaries payable	10 511	17 933
Social security payable	21 747	34 077
Prepaid taxes	−125 762	−33 389
Other accounts	200 270	262 972
Total	1 063 519	1 694 405
Paid-in capital	835 000	835 000
Retained earnings	−99	323 344
	834 901	1 158 344
Income tax liability	−35 910	−53 613
Profit account	−3 716	−22 428
Profit	318 236	61 489
Total liabilities	2 177 030	2 838 197

know if we got the order because of him or because we had been developing the same customer over the past few months. By doing things this way we can't tell why the sale was ever made.

Looking to the future

For the head of the organization and computing department, 1990 and beyond were going to be exciting years. Istvan Rackoczy was proud to say:

I've recently convinced top management they should buy the MAS–MCS (Management Accounting Systems – Management Control

Exhibit 7   Hungarian economic deflators by activity segment.

Market	1985	1986	1987	1988	1989*
Domestic[1]	100.0	104.4	112.1	111.2	117.4
CMEA[2]	100.0	107.2	110.1	110.1	110.0
Non-CMEA[3]	100.0	116.5	137.3	157.5	177.0

*Preliminary estimate by Central Statistical Office.
[1] Domestic Sales Price Indices – Machine Tool and Machine Equipment Industry, *1988 Statistical Yearbook for Industry*, p. 134, Central Statistical Office, Budapest.
[2] Sales in CMEA Relations – Machine Tool and Machine Equipment Industry, *1988 Statistical Yearbook for Industry*, p. 130, Central Statistical Office, Budapest.
[3] Non-CMEA Foreign Trade Price Indices – Machine Tool and Machine Equipment Industry, *1988 Statistical Yearbook for Industry*, p. 132, Central Statistical Office, Budapest.

System) integrated software package from the British software firm Hoskyns. It's being introduced at the Hungarian firms VIDETON, BHG, and SZIM and it's a system that can manage the MIS problems for a company our size – production planning, all the paperwork controls, operations scheduling, and operations finance.

We bought a used IBM 4361 from a German firm late last year, and 70 workstations, as well as some in Nyirbator, are being installed right now. It's the first time we've tried to implement a real integrated management system. It'll cost the company nearly 100 million forints but it should be completed in 1991. If this implementation is successful I'd like to make the department into a separate money-making operation. This would allow us to serve Csepel, keep our people busy, and help them earn more money.

For Peter Toth, General Manager of Economic Matters, the future was a bit more cloudy. As for Csepel's current situation he noted the order book was very low in general and even more so for domestic clients. Overall prices were rising, the government was cutting its support for CMEA exports, and optimal production lot sizes have not been established. His suggestions for improving 1990s company performance entailed the following:

- Dismiss 15% of all personnel (or about 200 employees).
- Raise the salaries of all remaining personnel by 20%.
- Reduce costs in general including the stock level of various finished goods.
- Investigate opportunities for new ruble exports.
- Maintain the company's traditionally good relations with its creditors.
- Accelerate the rate at which products are delivered to customers.
- Find a joint venture partner.

SUGGESTED QUESTIONS

1. Csepel's most recent financial operating results contain both good and bad news. What is the good news? What is the bad news?
2. What common elements seem to flow from the observations of Csepel managers, and what differences? Why might such a diversity of opinion exist in the same company?
3. How is MBWA (Management by Wandering Around) working or not working at Csepel?
4. What generic strategy is being pursued by Csepel? To what extent is the choice of strategy proactive or reactive? Does Csepel possess those elements which will make the pursuit of the chosen strategy successful?
5. What is the nature of Peter Toth's list of things to do, and to what degree are his attentions correctly focused?
6. What organizational form and control systems should Csepel adopt?

Digital Equipment Corporation International: competing through co-operation

Case written by Per Jenster with Francis Bidault and Thomas Cummings

On the afternoon of 19 February 1986, David Stone, Vice-President of International Engineering and Strategic Resources for Digital Equipment Corporation International, sat in his Geneva office looking out across the Rhone valley. Eight months earlier he had briefed senior officers at corporate headquarters in the United States about an effort to try out a new customer relationship. It was supposed to be based on a collaborative software development project between DEC (Digital Equipment Corporation) engineers and ITT Telecoms engineers located in four European countries. The DEC–ITT project was seen as an opportunity to try out a radically new approach to business partnerships in the information technology business. But how far could he let the 'experiment' run?

Rumours were coming in from the financial department and from the central engineering group at headquarters, as well as from different country managers and their account executives. Everyone seemed to have a different understanding of the DEC–ITT relationship. With income from the project not even coming close to matching costs, David Stone knew that he should reassess his original strategy.

He logged on to his electronic mail system, skipped the 38 new messages and accessed his E-mail archive to reread the eight-month-old

© 1990, 1991 by IMD, Lausanne, Switzerland

This case was prepared by Research Fellow Thomas Cummings under the supervision of Professors Per Jenster and Francis Bidault as the basis for class discussion rather than to illustrate either effective or ineffective handling of an administrative situation. Reprinted by permission of IMD, Lausanne, Switzerland.

The casewriters gratefully acknowledge the contribution of Michael Horner, Digital Europe.

message from DEC International's European Chairman which had been the catalyst leading to the 'co-operative activities' with ITT:

To: D Stone   July 15, 1985
Fr: P C Falotti
Status: Urgent

David – news from the front . . . our courtship with ITT seems to have gotten off the track. Insider tells me that Apollo has a European (Brussels ITT) confirmation for 40 workstations. Don't know if ITT is looking for a counteroffer, but we need to act fast. We might be able to make something of our 'strategic relationship thinking' and link it to the recent work done by your Metaframe group. What can we do?

BACKGROUND

Eight months earlier, Stone had asked a multi-functional team led by Michael Horner, part of the Metaframe 'think tank', to work with ITT on a partnership arrangement. Rather than simply sell hardware and software to ITT, Mike had assembled a team to build an engineering relationship. The team would rely on DEC's new workstation and computer-assisted software engineering (CASE) technologies to transfer software development methodologies and project management know-how to ITT. Because of the potential partnership, some of the people involved believed that DEC had sold several million dollars worth of hardware. This rumour could neither be confirmed nor simply linked to this joint software engineering project. Nonetheless, David had committed some of his best people in the hope that a significant, long-term relationship with ITT would materialize, leading to major sales increases and useful new software tools. This activity had raised a lot of questions, both from inside the organization and from other customers with pressing needs.

DIGITAL EQUIPMENT CORPORATION INTERNATIONAL (EUROPE)

Digital Equipment Corporation had established overseas sales and distribution in the late 1960s which eventually led to the founding of Digital Equipment Corporation International (Europe) as a wholly-owned operating company in 1979.

DEC Europe's mission was to import, develop, manufacture, and market networked computing systems for customers in Europe. The first Chairman and founder of Digital International was Jean-Claude Peterschmitt, a polished European statesman and businessman from Switzerland. He contributed much of his time and energy to breaking down technical and economic barriers among the European States, and between the US and Europe. Petterschmitt believed that the computing industry was moving quickly from its US origins to an international computing and communications environment, and that Digital had a role to play, both as a vendor and as a developer of new technologies.

DEC worldwide and European sales and personnel, 1978–85

Year	Worldwide		Europe (with % of worldwide)			
	Sales ($)	People (thousand)	Sales ($)	%	People (thousand)	%
1985	6686	89	1945	29	18	20
1984	5584	86	1462	26	14	16
1983	4272	73	1074	25	11	15
1982	3381	67	1006	30	10	15
1981	3198	63	935	29	10	16
1980	2368	56	687	29	9	16
1979	1804	44	486	27	7	16
1978	1437	39	377	26	6	15

Wherever possible, Digital International had adopted a management structure similar to that of Digital US. The parent company had been a pioneer in organizational design and development. The company structure, known as the matrix, was built around key managers, who were responsible for core product groups. In Europe there was a matrix between the core product groups and geographic regions. The core product groups were built on Digital's product and technology expertise, with country managers responsible for meeting regional quotas. A major addition to the matrix was that of the country managers, who had overall responsibility for co-ordinating Digital's business activities in and among different countries (see Exhibit 1a).

Digital's structure worked well during its period of rapid growth in Europe, protecting its product base in two major market segments (engineering and scientific computing). At the same time, the strength of its product range ensured strong growth in nearly all geographic segments (see Exhibit 1b).

PRODUCT/MARKET ISSUES

Throughout the early 1980s, new competitors had reduced Digital's lead in scientific computing. In the high-end mainframe segment, IBM had recently streamlined its products into four key product groups and was offering networking capabilities. In the low-end microcomputing segment, IBM had captured Apple's early lead by introducing the personal computer (PC and PCAT) products in its traditionally strong business computing segments (see Exhibit 2). DEC's strength had traditionally been in the mid-range minicomputer market, where it ranked second behind IBM. Competitors such as Sun Microsystems (founded in 1982) and Apollo were moving fast in a new segment – **technical workstations**. Digital realized the early possibilities of technical workstations and saw

Exhibit 1A Digital International: country management under European area management.

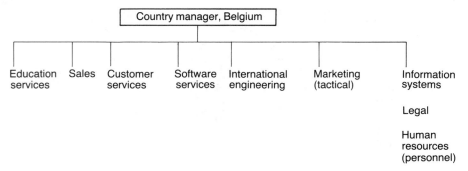

Exhibit 1B Digital International: European area management team.

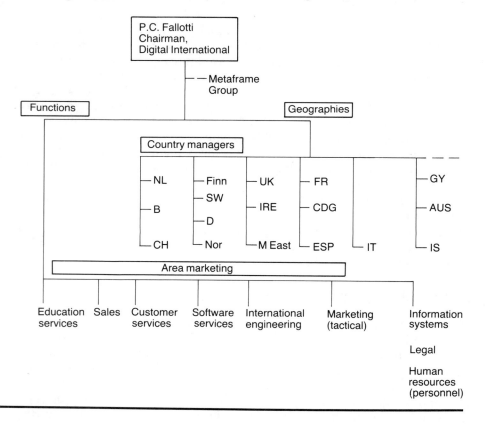

them as a way to incorporate new features and technological developments into high-performance, multi-task desktop computer configurations that would sell for less than $100 000 (see Exhibit 3). Conflicting internal product development paths hindered Digital's ability to lead in this new

Exhibit 2 Faced with sluggish demand for their traditional products, mini-computer makers are banking on cheaper models... but competition in this market is fierce.

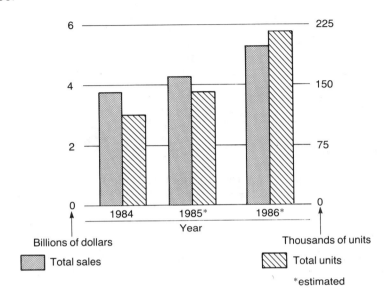

Billions of dollars

▨ Total sales

Thousands of units

▨ Total units

*estimated

Company	Market shares	
	1984	1985*
IBM	24.1%	24.5
Digital	18.4	19.2
Wang	8.4	6.7
HP	5.0	4.3
Data General	4.5	3.6
Texas Instruments	3.3	5.6
Convergent Tech.	2.1	5.7
AT & T	1.9	2.5
Burroughs	1.5	2.1
Prime	1.5	2.1
Other	28.8	26.7

*estimated

segment, but two bright lights were on the horizon: 1. the company's answer to the workstation market, the Microvax II and DEC's increasing share in the emerging software development; and 2. computer assisted software engineering (CASE) markets.

In addition, the company was ready to announce a second generation VAX system, resulting from a three-year investment of over $2 billion in research and engineering. With the announcement of several new hardware, software, and service products, Digital entered what industry experts called a new product transition phase. This meant that the new hardware and software products were not quite 'in sync' with the existing orders for equipment. This factor was felt in the marketplace, offering

Exhibit 3   The top 10 companies in minicomputers, 1984 and 1985.

Company	1985 Units	1984 Units	Change (%)
IBM	3500	3500	NC
Digital Equipment Corporation	1600	1527	4.8
Hewlett-Packard	1050	950	10.5
Wang Laboratories	870.9	970.5	−10.3
Data General Corporation	799.7	840.0	−4.8
Prime Computer Inc.	563.7	479.1	17.7
Tandem Computers	533.1	477.1	11.7
Harris Corp	470.0	410.0	14.6
Fujitsu Ltd	439.0	383.9	14.4
Nixdorf Computer	407.9	340.0	20.0

The top 10 companies in microcomputers, 1984 and 1985.

Company	1985 Units	1984 Units	Change (%)
IBM	5500	5500	NC
Apple Computer Corp	1603	1747	−8.2
Olivetti	844.5	496.9	78.0
Tandy Corp	796.8	573.5	38.9
Sperry Corp	742.8	503.4	47.6
Commodore Int'l	600	1000	−40.0
Compaq Computer	503.9	329.0	53.2
Hewlett-Packard	400	500	−20
Convergent Tech.	395.2	361.7	9.3
Zenith Electronics	352.0	249.0	41.4

Source: Datamation, 1985.

further possibilities for competitor encroachment on Digital's traditional customers.

THE COMPETITIVE ENVIRONMENT FOR ENGINEERING WORKSTATIONS

Workstations were one segment of the general computing market. Industry analysts often identified the other segments as mainframes, minicomputers, and personal or microcomputers. Minicomputer prices ranged from $30 000 to $100 000; workstations were from $15 000 to $60 000, and personal computers from $1500 to $20 000.

The workstation market had emerged in the early 1980s with Apollo's introduction (in 1981) of its technical workstation. Sun Microsystems soon followed in February 1982 with the introduction of the Sun 1, a product that included a CPU printed circuit board, a video board, a power supply, and a high-resolution monitor. Its typical customers were universities and sophisticated end users who followed technological developments. By 1984–85 the customer base broadened to include users in Fortune 1000 companies. Digital and Data General had both entered the market with proprietary CPUs in the workstation market, but it was still not clear whether the products would be accepted by users. Rumours of an IBM workstation were rampant, but had not yet materialized.

A key feature of the newly-defined workstation segment was rapid change. The life of a workstation design was short – 18 months at best – because the base technology of the workstation, the microprocessor, was continually improving in speed and performance.

Apollo Computer Corporation had a keen interest in redefining the market to include the new workstation segment. IBM had a virtual lock on the mainframe segment and, by then, 60% of the microcomputer market. The fuzzy middle ground included minicomputers, superminis, and workstations, all with shifting price/performance characteristics. Domination of this segment was still undetermined, but workstations were taking the early lead.

It was still early in the game for engineering workstations, and sales would continue to hinge on price performance specifications of the various machines, as well as software development. One way to push software development would be to form networked engineering partnerships.

TECHNOLOGICAL INNOVATION IN DIGITAL: THE ROLE OF CENTRAL ENGINEERING

At the heart of Digital's technology development process was a high-level group in the US known as Central Engineering. This team, established by Kenneth Olsen, the founder of DEC, provided the platform for developing the base technologies of the company. Central Engineering relied on current technical developments in the field and feedback from the product marketing groups to decide on its portfolio of technologies. Once Central Engineering had agreed on a five-year technological trajectory for the company's products and services, the product groups were responsible for getting the base technologies into product/market areas.

David Stone saw, early on, that the Digital–ITT relationship would not easily fit into the technical development process and plans of Central Engineering. Under normal circumstances it should fit into one of the product/market areas – **software services and applications services (SWAS)**. But the Digital–ITT relationship had both a market intent and software engineering mandate. It was working across Digital's product/market areas, trying to create its own expertise in software tool development for telecommunications companies.

Fortunately, David Stone could point to a history of joint technical development projects that his International Engineering Group had carried out in Europe. Differences in engineering approaches had given

Exhibit 4　The convergence of computer and communications technologies.

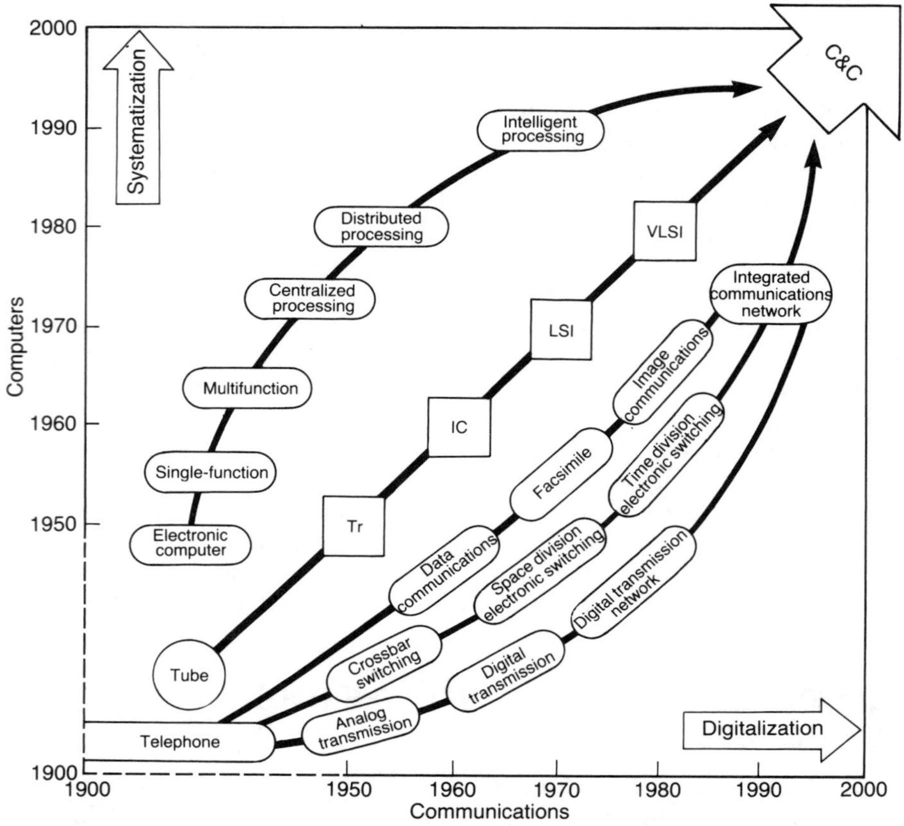

Source: 'Perspective on C&C Vision', courtesy of NEC Corporation, K. Kobayashi, 1985.

Digital Europe some leeway in its joint engineering approaches. The engineering group of Digital Europe had written the company manual on university–industry partnerships. But university links were different from working with customer engineering groups. Sharing early knowledge with the customer in exchange for a clearer view of their current problems and future needs required a different management approach. David Stone knew that joint technical development with ITT would require having the project fit into one of the existing technical pipelines, but at the same time that it called for a creative market/technology approach.

FORMING POLICIES ON STRATEGIC ALLIANCES IN EUROPE

The period of 1984–85 had been turbulent for the world computer industry. Market growth was beginning to slow down from a 25%

Exhibit 5 Partnership approaches from European companies and national groups.

UK
British Telecom
Plessy

Scandinavia/Benelux
LM Ericsson
Televerket
Philips

France
CGE-Telic
Thomson
Matra

Italy
Olivetti
Fiat
Stet/Italtel

Germany
Siemans
Nixdorf
Kienzle
Bosch

Pan-European
Esprit
EC12 interconnect standards
National government signals in
UK, D, FR, ESP, SW

average compound growth rate to a more docile 10–15% per annum. Industry experts spoke of two central issues: 'convergence of technologies' between computing and other industrial segments such as telecommunications (see Exhibit 4) and 'strategic alliances' that ranged from simple technology and market exchanges to industrial megadeals.

In Europe Digital had received more than 10 offers to form so-called strategic alliances (see Exhibit 5). In the emerging spirit of European integration, Digital had even been approached about participating in Eureka, Esprit, and other joint technology development programmes.

Digital Europe's top engineering people felt that the company was well positioned in an era of converging technologies. DEC had maintained its own proprietary hardware and software, and had migrated from scientific and engineering applications to a broader customer base. Digital had led the computer industry in several areas of its technical development. Ethernet networking software, an early product designed for networked computing systems, was one such technology. Digital engineers had also become experts at using their network technologies to carry out development projects simultaneously at several geographical locations.

Exhibit 6   Statement of principles: the Metaframe Group.

Vision of the ideal – metaframe group, 8 April 1986

To become more productive, organizations must have a consistent philosophy of organization which empowers their employees to fulfill the company's mission. Below is Digital's vision of the ideal philosophy to achieve productivity (and high employee morale).

We believe in the dignity of the individual, the increase in his productivity which comes from associating freely with others in his organization accessing the information required by his job, and his obligation to provide information to others as he receives it. We want to help to increase the effectiveness of interpersonal communication. These beliefs lead to the peer-to-peer style of networking we produce, as well as to the management style we use: computer mediated information (notes, files, . . .) is an appropriate implementation of this style. Interestingly, this style is applicable also to computers interfacing with machines; on the shop floor we could use the slogan 'liberate the Robots' to identify the power which we can add to the manufacturing process when the parts of the process are appropriately connected.

We look forward to the evolution of the business world to the 'one corporation' concept, in which the information flow between departments of two different companies is as easy as that between equivalent departments in the same company. This interaction would make clear that the primary long-term added value of a company is the processes which it has; if those processes are not clearly superior to those available externally, then the company should seriously consider using the external processes instead of its internal ones. This style of management would quickly lead to the distribution of processes to the place where they can be done best, just as distributed computing moves the computation to the place where it can be done best. Examples are just-in-time manufacturing which moves your inventory outside your company or external manufacturing which moves the whole process outside.

We define the mission of Digital as the production of quality information systems, products and services; where information systems are defined as 'the way in which a company acquires, shares, integrates and uses data to fulfill its mission, optimize its productivity and competitiveness and plan its evolution'.

The final stage of our relationship to other companies occurs when we take the risk of agreeing to do new things together as partners. Previous to this stage, we sell products, services, architectures and then processes which we already have. The partnership commitment is to make things which both parties agree are necessary, but which were not previously part of the repertoire of either company.

We recognize that a major part of our perceived added value lies in the Digital Computing Environment (DCE), which allows high productivity in applications development, flexible restructuring of information flows to adapt to organization and mission changes, and enhanced capability for effective information management and exchange. We should therefore be developing programs to make the use of the DCE as attractive as possible to OEMs, software houses and internal company applications developers.

Yet, partly because of Digital's proprietary technology path, a number of managers viewed strategic alliances as an overly complicated approach to business and technology development. Under Kenneth Olsen, Digital had become known as a 'go it alone' company. In the history of the company, Digital had made several acquisitions, but all were informal agreements and true joint ventures were a new development.

Falotti argued convincingly that Digital Europe would have to develop a systematic process for evaluating the offers of potential European partners, and that such a process would require a major shift in corporate values. David Stone had asked Michael Horner and Tony Setchell to form a low-key group that would build a framework for considering partnership proposals – one that would recommend how to act. The multidisciplinary team, known as the 'Metaframe Group', took their mandate seriously. As Michael Horner often stated, 'We were working on an industry level, seeking industry solutions'. Over the next several months, they wrote a policy statement (see Exhibit 6) and carried out analysis that considered the following issues:

- partnership approaches;
- future competition;
- future technology trends;
- market evolution;
- how Digital provides solutions for customers.

The group developed a visual mapping exercise that would juxtapose the competitive and technological positions of various companies across information technology industries. The mapping tool was also used to define Digital's strategic and technical position on the map, and suggest various possible partnering combinations (see Metaframe, Exhibits 7a and 7b).

Potential partners were mapped according to their competitive positions in the information technology sectors. If a company looked promising, the Metaframe team would go to the next level of analysis and discussion. A detailed segmentation of a partner's core competences and geographic coverage revealed – through visual mapping – the degrees of overlap and points of convergence between Digital and virtually every other company that the team chose to map (see Exhibit 8). These maps later proved useful before and during management discussions with potential partners. Segmentation and analysis was the first major step toward partner identification and opening discussions, but the Metaframe team also used the mapping to reveal a deeper understanding of Digital's own market and technological capabilities.

The Metaframe Group's work revealed that Digital's top management faced a difficult challenge: The company would have to sustain its current customer relationships, while developing new frameworks for identifying and building partnerships. Joint technology development and engineering with customers was highly recommended by the team. The Metaframe process also confirmed the value of visual presentation of communication

Exhibit 7A Metaframe: the competitive positions of possible partners.

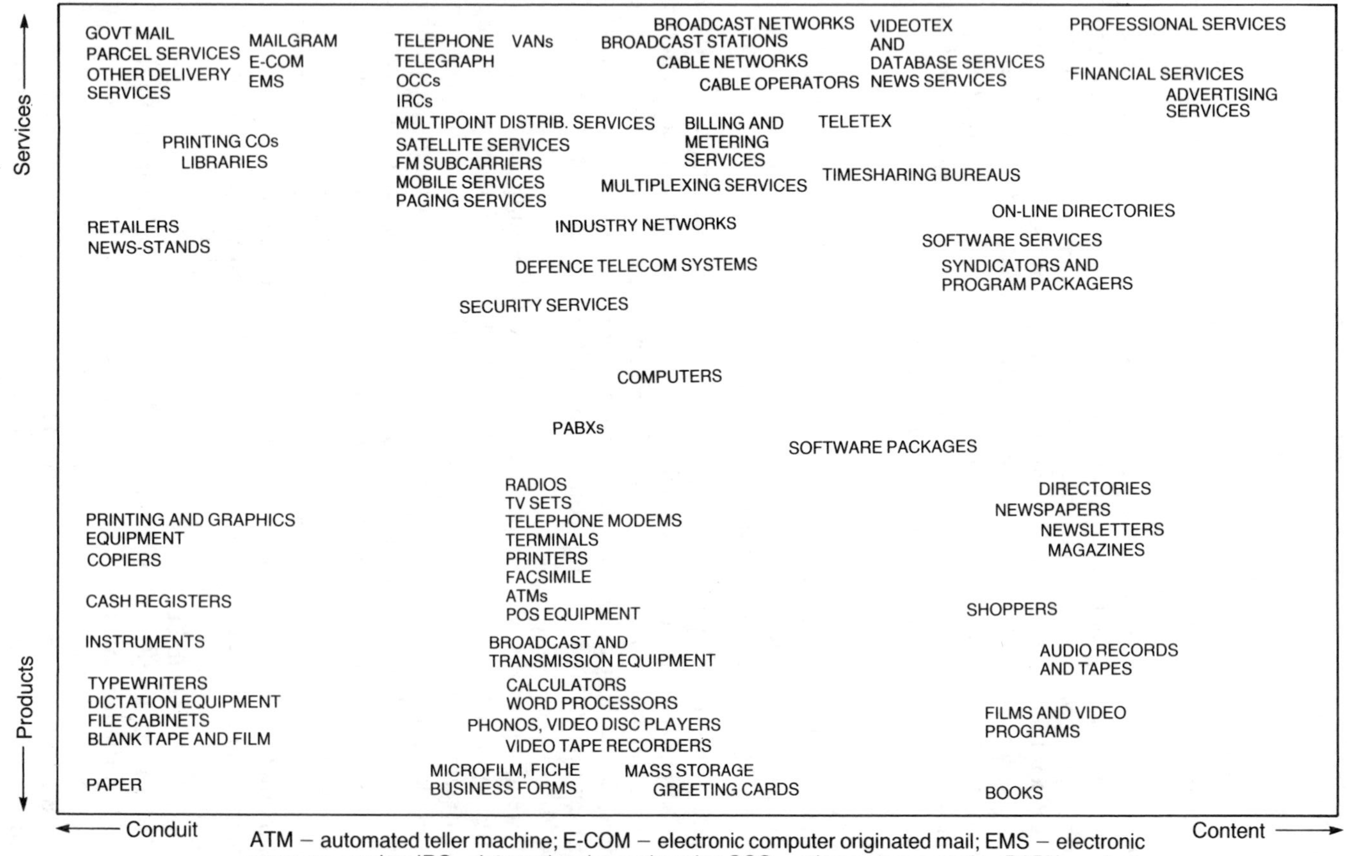

Services ←

Products →

← Conduit

Content →

GOVT MAIL
PARCEL SERVICES MAILGRAM
OTHER DELIVERY E-COM
SERVICES EMS

PRINTING COs
LIBRARIES

RETAILERS
NEWS-STANDS

PRINTING AND GRAPHICS
EQUIPMENT
COPIERS

CASH REGISTERS

INSTRUMENTS

TYPEWRITERS
DICTATION EQUIPMENT
FILE CABINETS
BLANK TAPE AND FILM

PAPER

TELEPHONE VANs
TELEGRAPH
OCCs
IRCs
MULTIPOINT DISTRIB. SERVICES
SATELLITE SERVICES
FM SUBCARRIERS
MOBILE SERVICES
PAGING SERVICES

INDUSTRY NETWORKS

DEFENCE TELECOM SYSTEMS

SECURITY SERVICES

PABXs

RADIOS
TV SETS
TELEPHONE MODEMS
TERMINALS
PRINTERS
FACSIMILE
ATMs
POS EQUIPMENT

BROADCAST AND
TRANSMISSION EQUIPMENT

CALCULATORS
WORD PROCESSORS
PHONOS, VIDEO DISC PLAYERS
VIDEO TAPE RECORDERS

MICROFILM, FICHE
BUSINESS FORMS

BROADCAST NETWORKS
BROADCAST STATIONS
CABLE NETWORKS
CABLE OPERATORS

TELETEX

BILLING AND
METERING
SERVICES

MULTIPLEXING SERVICES

COMPUTERS

MASS STORAGE
GREETING CARDS

VIDEOTEX
AND
DATABASE SERVICES
NEWS SERVICES

TIMESHARING BUREAUS

ON-LINE DIRECTORIES

SOFTWARE SERVICES

SYNDICATORS AND
PROGRAM PACKAGERS

SOFTWARE PACKAGES

PROFESSIONAL SERVICES

FINANCIAL SERVICES
ADVERTISING
SERVICES

DIRECTORIES
NEWSPAPERS
NEWSLETTERS
MAGAZINES

SHOPPERS

AUDIO RECORDS
AND TAPES

FILMS AND VIDEO
PROGRAMS

BOOKS

Source: Compaine, B. (1985) *Understanding New Media.*

ATM – automated teller machine; E-COM – electronic computer originated mail; EMS – electronic message service; IRC – international record carrier; OCC – other common carrier; PABX – private automatic branch exchange; POS – point of sale; VAN – value added network

Exhibit 7B Metaframe: mapping the competitive positions of possible partners.

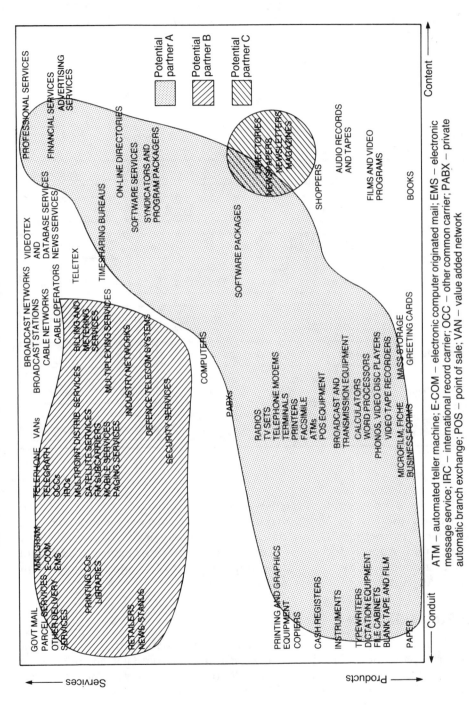

Source: Compaine, B. (1985) *Understanding New Media.*

Exhibit 8   Metaframe Group: Detailed Segmentation for Partnering Process
An Illustration of DEC'S – U.S. Patent 4 936 778

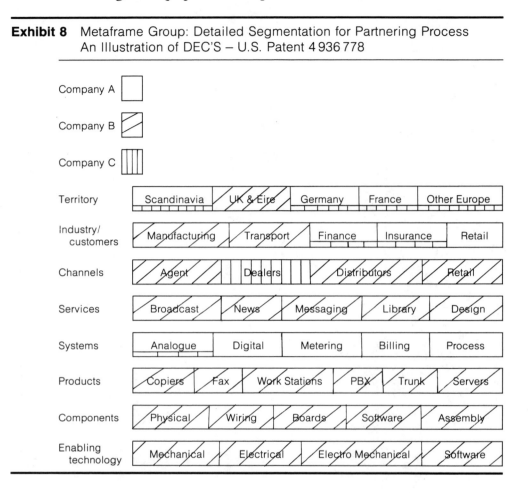

tools. By overlaying the strategies of various companies, the group could surface critical issues before making choices about new technologies and business partnering. The Metaframe Group remained an invisible task force until August 1985 when a request from ITT Europe provided David with an opportunity to take the group's abstract ideas and test them with a major customer of long standing.

ITT CORPORATION

ITT was a conglomerate multinational corporation that had grown enormously under the 23-year stewardship of Harold Geneen. In 1979 he stepped down as Chairman of the Board, having made more than 250 acquisitions and having built ITT into a vast confederation of companies comprised of 2000 working units. During the same period, revenues had gone from $800 million to $22 billion, and earnings from $30 million to $560 million. The Geneen legacy was inherited by Rand Araskog on 1 January 1980. Unfortunately for Araskog, Geneen left behind a $5 billion debt, accrued, in part, by his merger and acquisition activities. It was partly as a result of ITT's heavy debt burden and partly due to the restructuring of several ITT units, that ITT was targeted and subjected to hostile takeover bids during the early 1980s. Even *Fortune Magazine* took some stabs at ITT, calling it 'a museum of the investment and management ideas of the sixties'.

Araskog took a number of steps to reduce the size of ITT's corporate debt. Between 1980 and 1983, ITT sold 61 companies in order to generate proceeds of $1.3 billion. He streamlined the holding into five 'product' areas and four service areas:

Product areas	*Service areas*
Automotive products	Insurance operations
Electronic components	Financial services
Fluid technology	Communications and information services
Defense and space technology	
Natural resources	Hotels and community development

ITT Telecommunications was part of the communications and information services area, but relied on technical know-how, especially from the eletronic components group.

ITT TELECOMMUNICATIONS AND THE SYSTEM 12

The telecommunications industry was rapidly shifting from analog to digital switching systems, and virtually every major player wishing to compete in the global telecommunications business had reoriented their R&D strategies to move from electro-mechanical to digital switching technologies. Success in this technological shift had come at a price: an Arthur D Little study estimated that, given the shortness of the digital system technology lifecycle (5–8 years compared to 25–30 years for electromechanical systems), developers of new telecommunications switches would have to obtain 8% of the world market share in telecommunications switching equipment in order to break-even on development costs. ITT engineers were also aware that 75% of digital switch development costs would be software- and not hardware-related (see Exhibits 9 and 10).

ITT had embarked on its own ambitious development project in the late 1970s: the System 12. The company had developed its own technical protocols, including the CCITT development platform – a hardware architecture and software language intended to protect the company's investment, and establish a new telecommunications standard. The development project grew from the company's Connecticut laboratories to several key technology development sites in Europe.

Exhibit 9   Telecommunications switch development: technology life cycles.

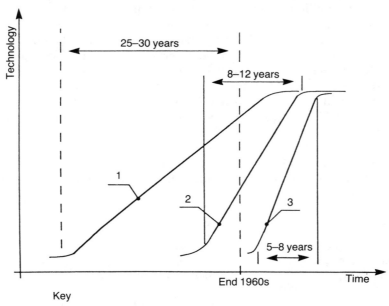

Key

1 Electromechanical systems
2 Analog stored program control (computer)
3 Digital systems

Source: Ferdinand Kuznick, IMD Lecturer.

Exhibit 10   Telecommunications switch development: hardware vs. software development costs.

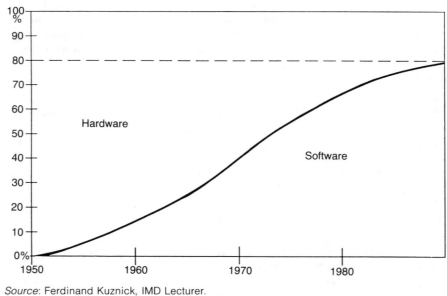

Source: Ferdinand Kuznick, IMD Lecturer.

Exhibit 11   ITT Europe: organization chart.

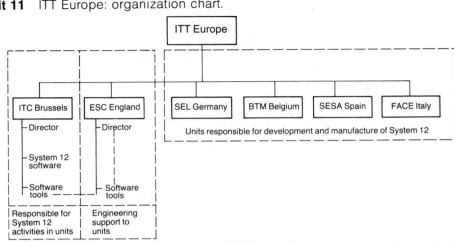

From Digital's perspective, ITT was confronting one of the most demanding software development projects in the history of telecommunications – its System 12 (S-12). Over 2500 software engineers in four European locations had been working on the project for seven years, and there was no end in sight (a printout of the source code was said to fill two rail cars with paper).

The groups responsible for S-12 functional activities and engineering support were ITC Europe in Brussels and ESC in Harlow, UK. Those responsible for the development and manufacture of the S-12 were SEL in Stuttgart, Germany; BTM in Antwerp, Belgium; SESA in Spain; and FACE in Italy (see Exhibit 11).

In the first phases of the S-12 project, it had been relatively easy to port software across programming languages and hardware configurations. As S-12 development grew in size and complexity, subtle changes became major events in which each engineering group had to consider the changes of another group before proceeding.

When different groups attempted to work with several million lines of code, modifications became inevitable, and engineers had to overcome bugs by inserting a 'patch'. One engineer noted, 'By the mid-eighties, we were putting new patches on top of old patches'. To remedy the situation, ITT hired Tony Kenny, an ex-IBM engineer. Tony had been keen to spread the risks of any major changes in ITT's software development procedures. His solution to the slowdown in the S-12 development project was to use CASE tools.

Various factors led to questioning the potential value of ITT's long-term switch development project. These included:

1. Lack of support for technological development

In the race to develop telecommunications hardware, little thought had been given to developing software processes and tools for the ongoing modification of products and services. Two presumptions proved to be false: that computer companies could provide off-the-shelf software tools to system developers, and that the cost of software development would increase at a slower rate than hardware development costs.

2. Questionable market share for the System 12

The major world market for telephony, the US, was shaken in 1983 by a consent decree which resulted in breaking up AT&T's regional telephone business into eight independent companies and splitting Bell Laboratories in two: AT&T Bell Labs and BellCorp. Despite the break-up, AT&T was moving fast in developing a digital switch and would be ensured a significant market share after its introduction. The AT&T break-up created eight new competitors on the world telecommunications scene. In October 1984, Rand Araskog noted that, given the cost of the project and the increasing number of competitors, 'there are doubts about the S-12's viability in the United States'.

3. ITT as a potential takeover target

During the early 1980s, ITT was the target of several hostile takeover attempts, each one proposing to split the company into several companies that would bring greater value for the shareholders. While Araskog succeeded in beating back each attempt, he was also required to dispose of several businesses.

THE REQUEST FROM BTMC AND ITT (EUROPE)

In July 1985 the Belgian subsidiary of ITT (BTMC in Antwerp) sent a request for a tender to Digital's Belgian office (see Exhibit 11). In simple terms, the offer focused on engineering workstations. Under normal circumstances, the Digital country manager would hear about the bid request in advance. But this tender ofter puzzled him. Given Digital's long-standing customer relationship with ITT (dating back to Digital's first minicomputer purchase in 1968), the request had been hastily made, suggesting that BTMC was jumping at another new workstation offer. He was also aware of recent discussions about engineering workstations between Apollo Computer Corporation and ITT.

The country manager, being close to ITT headquarters in Brussels, had heard rumours of a 'strategic agreement' being forged between Kenneth Olsen and Rand Araskog, the Chairman of ITT. Since the BTMC request referred to specific hardware, and because ITT was a strategic customer in several national markets, the country manager contacted David Stone in Digital's European headquarters. The ITT country manager decided to get clearer signals from senior management before proceeding.

Indeed, BTMC's request coincided with several ongoing discussions between ITT and Digital managers. Senior managers in two other ITT companies (ESC in Harlow, UK, and ITC Brussels, Belgium) had been talking with Digital about the development of software tools for the

S-12. CASE tools were high on their list of needs. ITT's European headquarters (ITT Brussels) was at the centre of the various proposals to work with Digital.

It was the hardware request from BTMC (ITT Belgium) that led to Pier Carlo Falotti's E-mail message to David Stone. The country manager's hunches were correct. Over the previous months, there had been several informal discussions between top-level DEC and ITT personnel about hardware, software, and strategic collaboration. Digital's European Chairman Falotti knew that ITT was going through a strategic and technological transition. In the US the company had successfully fought off several acquisition attempts by corporate raiders. In Europe the S-12 telecommunications switch development project was taking significantly longer than expected. David remembered how thoroughly the Metaframe Group had reviewed ITT's situation. He wondered, 'Was Digital courting a four-headed monster?'

By late summer and early autumn 1985, the trade journals were full of news about an overall computer industry slump. Kenneth Olsen had announced to shareholders: 'The marketplace is in turmoil. Much of the industry has been devastated in just the past two years.' The main hardware vendors, IBM, Digital, Hewlett Packard, Apollo, Prime, and Data General, were repositioning their products and services in the mini-computer segment. Digital's profit level was below that of one year earlier, yet it had outperformed most market analysts' expectations, thanks to cost controls and revenue growth, particularly in Europe. Apollo Computer had reported an after-tax operating loss of $4 million and a $14.4 million inventory write-down, resulting in a net loss of $18.4 million. Prime Computer posted a 7% profit increase in a 19% revenue gain that went from $165 million to $196 million. Data General saw its pre-tax earnings plunge 98% to $800 000. More than 60% of the companies had lower rates of return than in the previous quarters. Most experienced wide swings in stock prices, and a number of smaller competitors either merged, formed alliances or disappeared from the market.

Despite the overall industry downturn, there was growth in a few key segments, most notably the emerging CAD–CAM and workstation markets. While some industry analysts pointed to the workstation as an exciting new development in computing, others played down its development, noting that workstations were only a reconfiguration of technologies from higher (mainframe) and lower (microcomputer) performing segments.

Apollo Computer Corporation was the founder of this segment and, along with Sun Microsystems, was one of the most aggressive marketers of engineering workstations. Their presence was only beginning to be felt in Europe, but this firm had caught the eye of ITT's S-12 software development engineers.

DEC'S RESPONSE TO THE ITT TENDER OFFER

David Stone had called Michael Horner, head of engineering strategy, to discuss ITT's tender offer to purchase workstations and related software products. David wanted to evaluate whether ITT might consider a joint technology development effort. He also saw it as a way to take the Metaframe Group's work into practice. Together, Michael Horner, the Metaframe Group, and David Stone had reviewed ITT's proposed shopping list of hardware, software, and support services. As David Stone had been aware of the high-level discussions between the two companies, he advised Michael Horner to co-ordinate a meeting with some of ITT's European managers before they responded with a bid. In the back of his mind he was intrigued by the complex software engineering problem facing ITT. If Digital could form a joint software engineering team that would help ITT solve its problems, there would be other customers facing similar challenges.

Horner co-ordinated the first meeting between ITT and Digital Europe management. The primary goal of the meeting, from Digital's perspective, was to explore how the two companies might consummate a broad agreement that would lead to joint technology development. Since the top management of both companies had called for a closer strategic relationship, David Stone's proposal would be to define the boundaries of a new strategic and technical relationship. Within a few days a hardware sale had been delicately placed on the back burner, and strategic engineering groups had been assigned from both companies.

During the initial Digital–ITT meetings, two clear camps of managers emerged on the ITT side: those who sought to purchase equipment and know-how from a computer vendor; and those who saw the opportunity to solve some larger software challenges through the newly created partnership. The ITT Engineers from ESC Harlow and SEL Stuttgart were particularly intrigued with a possible joint development effort. Michael Horner remembered the strong response from Gunter Endalee, the Chief Systems Engineer from SEL:

> Gunter was one of the brightest developers in ITT. He knew that the S-12 was a major undertaking, requiring multi-site engineering co-ordination. Except for announcing formal changes in software, he had given up trying to co-ordinate his efforts with the other ITT development groups in Europe. Digital's offer to review ITT's software development practices and propose new tools was an exciting possibility for Gunter. He never considered specific hardware and software to solve his problems. Digital had offered the conceptual breakthrough he sought.

Even after the Digital–ITT meetings in the autumn of 1985, ITT's BTMC division in Antwerp had continued to push for a range of computer hardware and software products that would help the company streamline and facilitate the S-12 software development process. In

Exhibit 12   Digital Europe

Metaframe Group
David Stone, Chairman
Mike Horner, Technology Specialist
Tony Setchell, Telecommunications Strategist
Haskell Cehrs, Telecommunications Specialist
Lutz Reuter, Organizational Specialist
Eric Sublet, Contracts
Renato Rattore, Italy
Jean Paul Myeller, France
Peter Kohlhammer, Germany
Bill Strecker, Corporate Strategy USA
Skip Walter, Consultant (US based)

ITT project team
Mike Horner, Project Manager
Bob Wyman, Consultant
Patrick Scherrer, Software Engineer
Alex Taylor, Communications
Gerard Zarka, User Representative
Theo de Jongh, Project Manager Designate
Etienne Bossard, Technology Specialist
Specialist in Antwerp
Specialist in Harlow
Specialist in Stuttgart

their eyes, a Digital–ITT agreement would not prevent a multi-vendor solution. The computer industry press had recently focused on two new developments in computing which were particularly promising for ITT engineers: the specialty engineering workstation, and CASE tools. The heart of ITT's tender offer had concentrated on these new tools.

Michael Horner organized Digital–ITT meetings for the top 20 ITT engineers and then for each major software engineering group in Europe. Digital showed how its software tools specialists in Valbonne, France, working with ITT engineers at several locations, could redesign ITT's software development approach. But with each successive discussion, Digital also learned about ITT's lack of a common strategy for the S–12 technology development. Key S–12 engineers at the different development and engineering sites had each been independently responsible for purchasing hardware and for S–12 development. Whole teams of ITT software engineers had developed separate components of the S–12 with different hardware and software standards. As one Digital engineer from Brussels, Etienne Bossard, put it: 'ITT is not a company. It is a confederation of companies. As a result, technical groups do not normally communicate across the confederation, which makes for chaos when they make changes.'

APPLYING METAFRAME TO THE DIGITAL-ITT PROJECT

The initial meetings with ITT went well. Digital and ITT engineers had agreed that a team would be assembled with the top echelons of ITT software engineers participating in introductory meetings. Michael Horner became the European corporate sponsor of the Digital–ITT project for David Stone. Horner assembled an ITT project team that would implement discussions between ITT and the Metaframe Group (see Exhibit 12). He brought in Bob Wyman from the US, one of Digital's leading software engineering experts. Bob Wyman had worked on Digital's most successful software development program to date: **All-in-One**. He also had an interest in extending his knowledge about CASE and saw the Digital–ITT project as a serious applied engineering challenge. Michael Horner and Bob Wyman agreed to meet ITT's European managers and engineers to persuade them that DEC could assist ITT as it redefined its software development processes. From Michael Horner's perspective, the first meetings with ITT engineers were successful. He recounted one meeting called to discuss hardware priorities:

> I simply began to describe how we went about developing software. I could see they were getting excited and wanted to hear more. For the next three hours, they questioned me about Digital's approach to software development. It was clear that I was describing a brave new world.

Over a two-month period in the autumn of 1985, Michael Horner and Bob Wyman travelled to all of ITT's S-12 development sites in Europe. As Michael observed:

> It was a process of getting buy-in from ITT's top management and then moving through the ranks. We targeted the first 20 people and prepared a road show. Each time, we made the following points.

- Buying more equipment would not solve ITT's long-term S-12 problem.
- DEC's knowledge of CASE tools and networked computing would be valuable if applied to telecommunications software development and, since it was a generic problem, would serve the interests of both companies.
- If ITT worked with Digital, it would be considered a privileged customer, and the S-12 engineers would be introduced to Digital's emerging technologies.
- As a result of a strategic agreement, Digital would provide equipment to key engineering sites and eventually assign a Digital engineer to work with the customer's engineers at each site.

Bob Wyman estimated that it would require around 8000 man-years to redefine and complete the software development for the S-12. This task had to be managed among 2500 engineers working in three to four parallel sites. As Wyman put it: 'We had to network the sites and get them working together. But before ITT ever used CASE tools and workstations, we had to crash through the cultural and technical barriers.'

Following the initial visits, the key sites were confirmed, and Digital began to establish network links between ITT sites: ESC Harlow, ITC Brussels, SEL Germany, and BTM Belgium. Digital, Valbonne, would serve as Digital's link to the network. Michael Horner had asked Gerard Zarka to find and configure the latest hardware and software, and to get it to several ITT European locations. Cost was not an initial consideration. Zarka was known throughout Digital Europe for his ability to get the latest equipment to the right place at the right time. He was also known less fondly by some country managers as someone who would jump the equipment delivery queue. Zarka described his efforts in Digital-ITT:

I agreed wholeheartedly with the metaframe concept. ITT was asking for boxes. We refused. We focused on building their human/technical links through networked computing. Why? Because we knew that more machines were not going to make them more productive. Their problem had reached a too high level of complexity.

The first step had been to build and demonstrate a network. We located some of Digital's state-of-the-art equipment: five Microvax 2-Q5 (fully loaded and networked) hardware configurations. They were the first ones shipped to Europe. The sales managers on the DEC side objected initially. We were shipping about $1.4 million of the latest technology to four countries, free of charge, and contributing who knows how many hours to the Metaframe cause. Since every country has its own budget in Digital, if a country sales person objected, we were stuck. In one case, two machines sat in customs for two months until the sales manager agreed to let us install the box at an ITT site.

The Digital Metaframe team realized that better co-ordination through a network was necessary for such a large and complex software development organization. Once the network was more or less in place, the teams had started to work on defining software tools that would integrate information, time, and project management protocols based on Digital's early experience with CASE tools. All of the engineer-to-engineer discussions focused on streamlining the S-12 software development process.

The team had succeeded in 'championing' this approach at some of ITT's sites, but some ITT engineers and managers continued to drag their feet. They wondered if Digital were trying to take over their project and how a networked software development approach would affect different sites. How would Digital react when ITT exposed its internal processes? Bob Wyman was the recognized technical 'champion' of the project at Digital, but attaining the role and status of project champion across companies remained inaccessible to him. Some ITT people had simply not accepted a genuine proposal coming from, in their eyes, an outsider (developers from other sites were also considered outsiders).

Michael Horner became increasingly convinced that the Digital–ITT relationship provided special opportunities for both companies. He convinced many people that his small group had developed a new approach to working with customers and business partners. Instead of focusing on 'getting the sale', they discussed how to solve ITT's long-term software development problems. The group had even coined the term 'representative target customer' to describe and define engineering specifications for a future set of customers who would have different price/performance requirements.

He viewed their work at ITT as a prototype for future engineering-to-engineering relationships. But as an active participant in the ITT process, he was becoming aware of the differences between the two engineering cultures. He had recently asked David for more time to see whether the model would work. David remembered Michael's emphatic words: 'Look, if we can get them to believe in what we do and in our approach, it is basically the same as an OEM sale. Inject the right people early on, inspire them, fund them, and wait a year for things to happen.'

By the following February, eight months after members of the Metaframe Group had been assigned to ITT, the project was adrift. The tools developed by Digital were not being integrated into the ITT development process at many of the sites – different sites continued to use their own software development techniques. The network was in place, but could not seem to overcome ITT's cultural barriers.

Digital's Central Engineering in the US was asking questions about the new software development project. From their perspective it had three problems. First, it was somewhat disconnected from Digital's Central Engineering strategy; second, the development project itself involved a customer, requiring Digital to share proprietary software technologies and next generation hardware; and third, there were similar software tool developments going on in other parts of the company that had received approval from Central Engineering.

The partnership became increasingly complicated when the country management teams, who were closely linked to software services, started to hear about the project from their customers and field people. One manager contacted David Stone to find out why Digital's most advanced workstations were being shipped free of charge to ITT development labs, when his best customers were on a six-month waiting list for the same hardware.

Time for action

David Stone had discussed the Digital–ITT relationship with his staff during the previous week, knowing that the product–market issues would have a bearing on what DEC could do with ITT. There was always a strong pull from headquarters in Maynard, Massachusetts, to keep technical developments and product/market segmentation close to home. Digital Europe's limited manufacturing capabilities reinforced this point. But at the same time, Digital Europe was doing comparatively well and had an expanding customer base. The country managers were generating a lot of business, and there were several advanced engineering projects and university–industry partnerships in the pipeline.

David Stone had still other reasons for being concerned about the Digital–ITT project. Very few customers had ever been in direct contact and worked together with people in Digital's engineering area. In addition, Digital's general management voiced a concern that Digital might be sharing its core technical competences with its partners. David Stone had had to build a strong case for developing a software engineering link with ITT Europe. Perhaps he would find new ways to justify the merits of the project.

David picked up the phone to call Michael Horner. Together they would decide how to proceed. As the dial tone sounded, he thought back to early 1985 when everyone was talking about alliances. He was surprised at how often he had been called to establish 'customer relationships'. Yet ITT Telecom had some serious engineering challenges to overcome. As soon as David Stone heard Michael Horner pick up the telephone, he said, 'Michael, we'd better meet tomorrow at 8.30 to decide what to do about the Digital–ITT project.'

SUGGESTED QUESTIONS

1. What is David Stone's current challenge?
2. What were Digital's objectives regarding the partnership?
3. What are the potentials and limitations of each objective?
4. Can we decide on an overall priority of the partnership? What about secondary priorities?
5. How should David Stone proceed?

7

DRG Plastic films: the European stretch film industry (A)

Case written by Peter Williamson with Darron Brackenbury

In 1987 DRG Plastic Films was the second largest producer of polyethylene stretch film in the UK and the fourth largest in Europe. Under the leadership of Hugh Ellis, the Managing Director, DRG had achieved a successful record of profitability and growth since its entry into the stretch film industry five years previously, and had emerged as a significant force in the European industry.

During those five years, DRG had concentrated on improving quality and growing sales as the market for stretch film expanded rapidly. DRG also led the development of new materials because it was concerned that stretch film might become a commodity. By 1987, however, Ellis was concerned that the market was becoming more complex as the range of applications for stretch film proliferated and national markets within Europe were developing in different ways. There were also concerns about what would happen when the industry began to mature and whether or not this would result in an industry shakeout. Having built the core of a successful business, was it now time for a change in strategy, or would Ellis's formula continue to guide the business successfully through the next few years?

To explore these questions, this case looks at the stretch film industry, DRG Plastic Films' strategy and position in the industry, and the nature of the problems facing the company in 1987.

© 1988, 1989 by Peter Williamson and London Business School
This case was prepared by Peter Williamson and Darron Brackenbury as the basis for class discussion rather than to illustrate either effective or ineffective handling of an administrative situation.
The casewriters gratefully acknowledge the asistance of DRG and its staff.

THE PLASTIC FILMS INDUSTRY IN 1987

Altogether there were 26 producers of stretch film in Europe and a variety of applications in which the product was used. There were also many smaller businesses emerging which bought the large 'mother-rolls' of film from the producers and slit and rewound them into smaller roll sizes for distribution to the customer. These companies were in competition with some of the producers.

The product

Polyethylene stretch film was used in a number of packaging and wrapping applications. It was first used as a medium for constraining and protecting products on wood or metal pallets during distribution and transportation. This application constituted the vast bulk of stretch film sales in 1987.

The peculiar property of the film which made it so suitable for this purpose was 'memory'. The film was stretched, typically between 30–40%, during the wrapping process, and retained its elasticity or memory afterwards. The effect was that a stack of products on a pallet was held tightly in position and would not move or spill in transit.

Wrapping products for distribution in this way had many advantages over pallets with side restraints, plastic strapping, shrink wrapping, and large board containers – methods used before the advent of stretch film. Stretch film was less expensive for many applications, resulted in pallets which were easier to load and unload, and because the film was transparent and had to be torn off before unloading it made pilferage easier to detect. Furthermore, stretch film medium was suitable for use in automated wrapping equipment, thus giving users the opportunity to reduce the total costs of the packaging process.

Stretch film was produced by either of two basic processes: the **cast process** or the **blown process**. In both of these the starting point was to prepare a mixture of different grades and types of polyethylene, EVA and PVC resins which were purchased from suppliers in the form of small granules. The mixture was fed into a screw extruder from a large hopper and heated and mixed into a molten state. The molten mixture was then extruded through a die.

The blown process used a circular die. The basic idea was that air was blown up through the centre of the die, solidifying the melt and forming a continuous bubble of film. The bubble appeared in the shape of a continuous cylinder of film which was closed at the top by being passed between two rollers. The layflat tube was then drawn off through a series of rollers and slit into two rolls of film simultaneously.

The cast process produced the film by extruding molten resin through a flat die onto a rotating metal cylinder called a chill roll. The molten resin solidified on contact with the roll and was then drawn off through a series of rollers before being wound onto a mother-roll. The latest cast

Exhibit 1A   Stretch film: evolution of shipments.

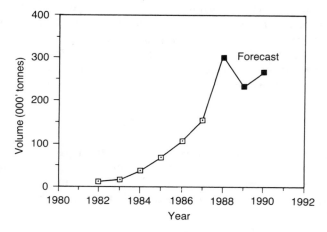

Exhibit 1B   Stretch film: evolution of growth rate in sales, European market.

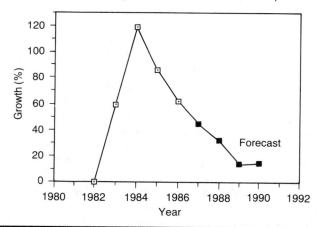

equipment was capable of slitting the film and winding it onto smaller sized rolls sold to customers in one continuous process.

Each production process had a slightly different effect on the properties of the finished film. Cast film was almost perfectly transparent and had inherent 'cling' on one side. Blown film had a misty transparency but was more resistant to puncture in certain applications. Blown film cling was produced by the addition of a chemical 'tackifier'. Cast film could be produced in thicknesses down to seven microns, and both blown and cast film could be produced in thicknesses ranging from 15–50 microns for different applications. The vast majority of film tonnage sold was around 20 microns thick.

With both blown and cast film, the film properties and quality were dependent on a number of factors. Control of temperature, speed, and tension of the film throughout the production process was critical. These factors were controlled by the equipments' accuracy and reliability, and the skill and experience of engineers and machine operators. Film properties were also significantly influenced by the design of the resin mixture, and this in turn had a substantial effect on raw material costs due to the different costs of each grade of resin. Producers sought to optimize film properties and raw material costs by improving the design of the resin mixture. Some producers were making film which had two or three layers, produced by using a screw extruder/resin mixture for each layer, and running these separate molten resins together in the extrusion die without mixing. This helped the optimization of properties and costs. Film design was further complicated by the fact that some resin mixtures allowed the machinery to run faster and more productively than others. For the same total film cost, the blown process generally involved lower raw materials cost and higher proportion of processing costs compared with the cast process.

Industry growth

Between 1982 and 1986 sales of stretch film grew rapidly. The producers were hard pushed to keep up with demand over this period, and consequently prices and margins were high. As shown in Exhibit 1A and 1B, forecasts aggregated from several industry sources were optimistic, showing continued revenue growth up to 1990. In spite of this, many people in the industry were concerned that growth would tail off sometime in the early 1990s. The most worrying problem in such a dynamic growth market was uncertainty about when this would happen.

In 1987 sales of new (as opposed to replacement) cast film extruders were forecast steady in the short term, and unit sales of stretch film wrapping machines were forecast to grow by 5% in the next three to four years.

Industry structure

In 1987 the European stretch film industry was dominated by three major manufacturers. The two largest producers, Mobil and Manuli, together made up 40% of European production, having market shares of 27% and 13% respectively. Teno, the third largest company, had a market share of 9.5%. DRG and Bonar were also significant forces with market shares of 5.2% and 6.7% respectively.

Equipment

A typical cast extrusion line cost around £1 million and had a capacity of 5000 tonnes of 21-micron film per year. Because the equipment was complex and had to be built to order, it could take between a year and 18 months from placing an order to start up of a new line. This was followed by up to six months shakedown to get the new equipment debugged and running at capacity.

A typical blown line cost from £200 000 to £250 000 and could produce 1000 tonnes of 21-micron film per annum. The equipment was simpler than a cast line and consequently delivery time and shakedown were quicker. Most of this equipment was specific to stretch film and could not be easily converted to production of other film products.

In addition to a number of cast or blown lines, some producers needed equipment to slit and rewind film. This process converted a large mother-roll of film produced on a line into smaller roll sizes required by customers. A typical rewinder cost £60 000 and could process well over 6000 tonnes of film a year.

Pricing

Pricing varied depending on product quality and order size. In 1987 a good quality film was priced at £1100 per tonne. The rapid growth of the industry and high demand meant that companies had been able to set prices at relatively high levels and not worry about price competition. However, there were signs that this situation might change as some companies were offering heavily discounted bulk orders to customers outside their normal regional markets. Also, when the market eventually began to mature, price competition could be expected to become more intense.

A few years before, customers had been prepared to pay a premium to the few producers capable of making high quality film. Now, however, most producers had solved the technical problems in production and made reasonable quality products.

Raw materials

The film producers bought polyethylene resins in various grades and types. The key ingredient in stretch film was linear low density poly-ethylene (LLDPE). LLDPE was available in two basic grades, octene and butene. The film producers optimised film properties and raw material costs by blending the more expensive high quality octene grade with the less expensive butene grade. In addition to LLDPE, the producers bought ordinary low density polyethylene (LDPE) grades which made up the bulk of the raw material used in stretch film. LDPE was much less expensive than LLDPE.

Nearly all resin purchases were bought from four large suppliers: Dow Chemical, DSM, Exxon, and BP. Between them these companies supplied over 80% of all polyethylene resin sales in Europe. The resin industry was very capital intensive. A typical polyethylene cracking plant had an annual capacity for 140 000 tonnes of various resin grades.

There were two different processes used to make LLDPE. Dow used a proprietary process which produced octene grades thought to give better performance than those of the other suppliers; consequently, all stretch film producers bought some of Dow's branded octene grade, Dowlex.

Customers

The stretch film market was undergoing a complex evolution. Individual European country and regional markets were developing at different rates, and new applications for the product were appearing.

In 1987 there were four basic applications for stretch film:

- Pallet wrapping – packaging goods for distribution.
- Bundle wrapping – collations of identical products such as canned foods or cartons of detergents.
- Reel wrapping – for protection of newsprint and paper mother-rolls.
- Silage wrapping – for sealing of silage (winter cattle fodder) bales during fermentation.

Pallet wrapping was the first application to be exploited with stretch film and, consequently, the market was relatively mature, although still growing. In 1987 it constituted most of the demand for stretch film.

Typically, a pallet (usually about a metre square) was stacked with a picked order in a distribution warehouse by hand up to a height of two metres. Stretch film was then wrapped around the pallet in several layers until the sides of the pallet and stack were completely covered. The film could be applied either by hand – 'hand-wrap' – or semi-automatically by purpose-built equipment – 'machine-wrap'.

Hand-wrap users applied the film with a simple device which let out film under tension from a small roll. The operator tied the end of the film to the pallet and then walked around it applying a continuous overlapping length of film until the stack was covered. He then cut the end off the reel and tucked it under the film layer. The film's cling and tension held the stack firmly in place.

Machine-wrap users built the stack on a turntable. The operator tied the end of the film to the pallet and then set the machine in motion. As the stack spun round on the turntable, the reel of film moved up a column applying a consistent amount of film under tension. Finished stacks could then be moved around by forklift truck.

Hand-wrap users were usually small companies distributing a diverse range of goods. They were generally unconcerned with the finer details of film performance and quality, and tended to buy on price.

Machine-wrap users tended to vary from medium size to very large establishments. The range of goods they dealt with was often much smaller but in much greater volume, which facilitated the use of semi- and fully-automatic equipment. They were much more concerned with film performance and quality. A film break on an automated wrapping line was troublesome and expensive, and in some operations could stop factory production. Buyers tended to opt for reliable quality films, and traded off film cost per tonne against 'yield' (i.e. the area of film yielded from a given weight after stretching). They were also concerned with the performance of film on the pallet, since sharp corners and jostling in transit might result in a spilt pallet load. The recipient of such an inconvenience would always complain loudly about it.

The largest machine-wrapping operations for stretch film had fully integrated wrapping lines at the end of factory production lines. One such example was a washing machine manufacturer: the final production line operation was a completely automated film wrapping line which encased the finished product in stretch film for protection during delivery to distributors and retailers. This was a departure from the normal method of packaging white goods in board containers.

Bundle wrapping

In 1987 bundle wrapping was in its infancy. This application involved completely automatic wrapping of small, high-volume products as the final stage of production line operations. Typical products suitable for packaging in this way were canned foods, packets of detergent, cigarette cartons, and cartons of toothpaste, to name but a few.

Bundle wrapping was performed by expensive equipment which took individual items of product and arranged them into a rectangular collation. The collation or bundle was then held and manipulated by the machine whilst being totally encased in stretch film. The wrapping operation was a development of fairly well-established principles used in overwrapping machines which, for example, applied cellulose film to cigarette cartons and shrink film to trays of drink cans.

The established methods of packaging collations were board containers (cardboard boxes), shrink wrapping with polyethylene shrink film (often on board trays), or overwrapping with any one of a number of films. Stretch film bundling had advantages over these methods for many types of product collation. It was less expensive than board containers as the material cost per unit was lower. It eliminated the expensive heating process required on a shrink film wrapping line. Also, stretch film was much less expensive per unit in materials than many of the other films used in overwrapping lines.

There were, however, concerns about how effective the process was vis-à-vis the established alternatives. For example, would the collations be adequately protected in transit, and would a stretch-wrap line be capable of matching the higher operating speeds of shrink-wrap lines?

Pressure to introduce bundle-wrap was being exerted from several quarters. Large supermarket chains were interested because of the time and cost involved in disposing of waste packaging materials from established media. Stretch film was extremely light and could be compressed into very compact bales in comparison. Also, several innovative packaging equipment manufacturers had developed machines capable of stretch-wrapping collations, and were concentrating their sales effort on this new product.

The small number of companies bundle-wrapping their products in 1987 were primarily concerned with film quality and reliability, since a film break could literally shut down a plant until it was repaired. Because of the relatively large quantities of film that they used, however, they also negotiated hard for bulk purchase discounts.

Reel wrapping

Reel wrapping was also a very new application in 1987. It was a method of packaging and protecting large mother-rolls of newsprint and paper in transit from paper mills. Stretch film offered protection against damage to the outer layers during handling. It also helped to prevent either ingress or egress of moisture during transportation on open lorries in order to maintain a stable moisture content until use. Excessive drying out of the reel was just as bad as getting it wet. Stretch wrap was seen as an acceptable replacement for the usual wax or plastic impregnated paper wrappings currently in use. Unit costs for wrapping were considerably less due to the lower material cost.

Reel wrapping used relatively thick film, between 60 and 80 microns. Because thicker films cost much less to produce than thinner ones, and were priced roughly the same per tonne, reel wrapping was a very profitable application market to be in.

The wrapping process was fairly simple. Finished paper reels, roughly a metre in diameter and a metre long, and weighing in the order of one tonne, were placed on a machine which rotated the reel in two axes simultaneously. The reel was completely encased in film led off a roll at the side of the machine.

In 1987 only a few film producers were supplying the paper mills. Buyers were mainly concerned with quality, even though this was much less important in thick film use than in thin films.

Silage wrapping

Silage wrapping was a peculiar market for stretch film. At first sight there seemed to be no advantage to wrapping bales in stretch film rather than bagging them in large polyethylene sacks, because the film cost was similar for a given tonnage of silage production. In addition, stretch wrapping required a mobile wrapping machine, which, although simple and costing only a few thousand pounds, was nevertheless a substantial investment for most farmers and contractors. However, experience had shown that bales wrapped tightly in stretch film produced substantially better quality silage with less waste than bagging. Stretch wrapping excluded more air from the bale allowing the anaerobic fermentation to work more efficiently. Also, since stretch film was a much tougher material than LDPE which the bags were made out of, punctures and the resultant silage wastage occurred much less often.

Exhibit 2   Application markets for stretch film.

Application	Estimated potential market size (Kilotonnes pa)
Pallet wrap	150
Collation	100
Silage wrap	15
Reel wrap	3

Source: DRG.

The silage-wrapping market had been developed almost solely by a Norwegian agricultural equipment manufacturer, Underhaug, who sold the mobile wrapping machines and in the early days had distributed film. Stretch film for silage wrapping had to have additional properties such as an ultra-violet (UV) barrier, otherwise UV light inhibited the fermentation process. Various colours had also been experimented with in an effort to reduce bale temperature in bright sunlight, although no real answers had emerged to this problem in 1987. Farmers and contract balers were difficult people to deal with. They would often buy the cheapest film they could find at the start of a season, only to have problems with the wrapping process and be forced to buy a more expensive film recommended by Underhaug. The potential market size of each application was not known with any accuracy, but some industry estimates were available which indicated roughly the order of magnitude of each (see Exhibit 2).

THE EUROPEAN MARKET

Geographically there were marked differences in the stage of market development reached by different countries and regions in Europe. There were also obvious differences in potential market size in individual country markets and their degree of maturity. The predominant applications in countries varied, as did customer characteristics. For example, the majority of film sold for silage-wrapping was in Scandinavia and the UK; the French market placed more emphasis on price than others (see Exhibits 3 and 4).

COMPETITORS

The 26 competing firms in Europe were active in different regions and countries. Many of the smaller stretch film producers confined their activities to national domestic markets. The larger firms were active in several national markets (see Exhibit 5).

Exhibit 3   Regional markets for stretch film.

Region	Relative potential market size	Current market size (est. kilotonne)
UK	1	40
West German	1.95	20.8
France	0.97	15
Spain	0.16	5
Italy	0.78	31.2
Scandinavia	0.32	12.8
Netherlands/Belgium	0.52	20.8
Austria/Switzerland	0.11	4.4

Source: DRG.

Exhibit 4   Estimated market maturity (existing applications).

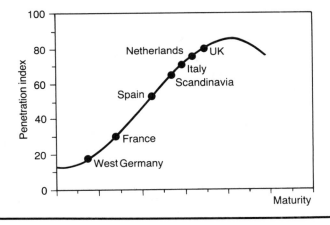

Mobil

Mobil was the market leader. In Europe it was by far the largest producer of stretch film and had substantial investments in the production of other types of film, notably oriented polypropylene (OPP), in which it was also the market leader.

Mobil's business had traditionally been based in the oil exploration, production, refining, and marketing fields. In 1987 approximately 90% of its revenues still came from petroleum operations. For a number of years it had been building and acquiring a range of diversified businesses. Starting in petrochemicals, it now had substantial interests in the packaging industry in operations such as plastic films, paperboard, box-

Exhibit 5   Regional market shares.

Region	Main competitors	Estimated market share (%)
UK	Mobil	25
	Bonar	21
	DRG	20
	BCL	13
	Teno	11
	Manuli	4
West Germany	Mobil	22
	Hamb' Unt'	14
	Fardem	9
	Teno	6
	Dickel	6
	Lakufol	6
	AOE	5
	Manuli	4
	DRG	3
Italy	Manuli	30
	Crocco	25
	Mobil	25
	Derifaw	n/a
	IPAC	n/a
Netherlands/Belgium	Mobil	60
	Fardem	20
	Sidac	10
France	Cofra-Charfa	n/a
	Fayard	n/a
	Semo-Ogen	n/a
	Silvalac	n/a
Austria/Switzerland	Hamb'Unt'	30
	Pavag	n/a
	Afex	n/a
Scandinavia	Teno	35
	Ranimuovi	n/a
	Borden	n/a
	Nyborg	n/a

Source: DRG.

board, boxes, and cartons. In had investments in timber and pulp production, and was the largest supplier of plastic grocery bags in the US. Mobil also had interests in retailing, having acquired Montgomery Ward, and was experimenting in other retail areas with prototype stores for automotive parts, home electronics, and appliances. The company's annual reports stressed its 'bold business strategies and aggressive invest-ment programme'.

Mobil announced first-quarter results for 1987 showing revenues of $12.7 billion and net income of $252 million. Its assets were estimated at $40 billion. Its annual total capital expenditures had averaged over $2 billion in recent years, running at around $150 million a year in paper-board and packaging, of which $25 million was in Europe.

Mobil had begun producing stretch film in Europe in 1982 along with the other top four producers, and had invested heavily in cast extrusion equipment, with plants first in Belgium and then in Italy. Production operations were considered to be some of the most efficient in the industry, producing top quality film. Because Mobil sold such large tonnages, it was considered to be the industry standard in terms of quality.

Mobil sold its stretch film output through distributors, and backed this with a relatively large spend on advertising and promotional literature. The company was also thought to have spent large sums of money on R&D in stretch film.

Manuli

Based in Italy, the Manuli group of companies was privately owned by the three Manuli brothers, Mario, Antonello, and Sandro, who held a majority stake in Dardanio Manuli, the group holding company. The brothers were aggressive and successful entrepreneurs who had built the group up with a variety of interests resulting in a listing on the Italian Bourse in 1986. Subsidiary companies were in energy cables, tele-communications, and opto-electronics, packaging, protection, and rubber industrial products.

Early in 1987 it was rumoured that Manuli were interested in acquiring Coverplast-Italiana and Coverfilm, which would make Manuli the largest Italian producer of protective film and polyethylene film.

Manuli's 1986 results showed a turnover of $263 million and pre-tax profit of $20 million. The net worth of the business was $126 million. The packaging business made 33% of turnover and contributed 45% of the cashflow.

Manuli's stretch film operation used cast extrusion technology in modern, efficient plants. However, quality was generally considered to be poor by industry standards and Manuli often sold large bulk orders of film at a substantial discount, particularly outside Italy. Perhaps because of this, Manuli had a reputation for competing aggressively on price. Most of Manuli's stretch film sales were through distributors, with some large orders sold direct.

Teno

Teno AB, based in Sweden, was the largest manufacturer of LDPE film products in Scandinavia, as well as being the largest stretch film producer. Turnover in 1987 was expected to reach £90 million. Although ostensibly a relatively small company, Teno was part-owned by Neste OY, the Finnish state oil corporation, through a 24% shareholding. It was generally thought that both Teno and Neste wanted this holding increased as part of the development of closer relations between the two companies.

Neste had assets of FIM 20bn and had invested FIM 2.2bn in 1986. Neste activities included petroleum, petrochemicals, and downstream operations in polyethylene, PVC, and polystyrene, as well as industrial chemicals and shipping. The business had weathered substantial inventory losses in oil trading resulting from its dependence on fixed-price trade agreements with the Soviet block. Neste's investment programme seemed to be aimed at reducing the impact of oil price related fluctuations, and included the acquisition of diversified operations.

In April 1987 Teno opened a new sales office at Aylesbury in the UK. The office was to sell all types of polyethylene film and intended to consolidate Teno's position in the UK – its largest export market. It was rumoured that Teno might open a manufacturing plant in the UK before the end of the year.

Teno's stretch film was widely regarded as top quality, and was produced almost entirely by the blown process. Sales were through distributors. Teno had invested in R&D selectively and had pioneered both silage-wrapping and reel-wrapping applications from a film design and marketing standpoint. It was the market leader in both these applications which constituted a relatively large proportion of sales in Scandinavia.

Bonar

Bonar Polyethylene Films, part of the Low and Bonar industrial group, had recently completed a £5 million investment programme, and press reports indicated that substantial sums had been invested in a blown, coextruded, polyethylene film facility at Leominster.

Low and Bonar, based in Dundee, had undergone a period of change and were now seen as an aggressive company seeking high growth, high profit industries. A doubling of turnover and trebling of profits over five years confirmed this. Half-year earnings for 1987 were forecast at £8 million (pre-tax) on a turnover of £143 million. The packaging business was 28% of group turnover in 1986.

The annual report had identified 'nine technologies in which we have particular technological and product strengths. Mainly applied in polymer related industries'. Activities included packaging, plastics, textiles, and electronics.

So far as stretch film was concerned, Bonar quality was regarded as reasonable, although not as good as Mobil. Sales were mainly through distributors.

Other competitors

Although there were many other competitors in Europe, most were comparatively small and little was known about them other than where they produced and approximately what tonnages. Many had entered the business only recently; and published data on the industry tended to be out of date almost before it was in print.

The quality of the film produced by these companies varied considerably, with very few able to compete on quality and performance with the big producers, although continuing experience might change this situation.

DRG PLASTIC FILMS

Company history

DRG Plastic Films was a business unit in the packaging business group (PBG) of DRG plc. This major packaging, paper, and stationery group was best known through some of its branded products, such as Sellotape and Basildon Bond. DRG plc enjoyed a strong position in the UK and had operations throughout Europe, North America, Australia, and New Zealand. The DRG group turnover was around £650 million in 1987, with roughly a third of this coming from the PBG.

DRG Plastic Films was created in 1980 in response to the increasing commercial pressure on non-resin packaging solutions. It was formed by splitting off part of the DRG plastics packaging unit which produced such diverse products as confectionary wrappers and medical drip bags. The new unit was to produce films for the packaging unit as before, but could also concentrate more sharply on the plastic films market.

The man chosen to head up the new unit was Hugh Ellis, an experienced former salesman with the packaging unit. Under Ellis's guidance, the films unit grew steadily and profitably, and in 1982 began producing stretch film.

STRATEGY

Products and markets

Ellis recognised that DRG was one of the smaller producers in an industry dominated by giants. He was convinced that product quality and performance, the traditional strengths of DRG's business, provided the most effective means of competing against such large concerns. He was also aware of the greater flexibility of a small operation and built up DRG's reputation as a company which could respond to rush orders. This ability gave DRG the opportunity to bid for sales on a follow-up basis and contributed significantly towards growth.

DRG Plastic Films initially served two markets: food and medical. It was not until 1982 that the company entered the stretch film market. The food market consisted of many different types of customer, each with their own requirements. Products ranged from clingfilm, sold as a consumer product and to food producers and supermarkets, to specialized coextruded multilayer films for food packaging. Coextruded film was also used in many packaged food applications from biscuits to bacon. The very specific performance requirements of these applications had resulted in considerable film design expertise being built up by DRG, and confirmed the value of providing a quality product. The medical market consisted mostly of sterilizable wraps for instruments and dressings along with bags for intravenous drip solutions. Quality was all important in medical applications.

Customers in both the food and medical markets mostly used heavily automated plants to produce their products. Ellis's commitment to quality and performance paid dividends, because the performance of the end product was directly affected by the packaging. For example, a burst drip bag found by a hospital meant that the whole batch became suspect. To avoid risk of failure when in patient use, the whole batch had to be retested, which was an expensive operation. If the batch ultimately failed the contents had to be destroyed. The quality of the plastic film used in this type of package was therefore of prime importance.

Stretch film

It was from this background that DRG began producing stretch polyethylene film in 1982. Ellis saw stretch film as another facet of the revolution in packaging technology, one which was a new high-growth opportunity for companies who could get in on the ground floor. The next five years was to prove this vision correct.

Manufacturing

DRG began stretch film production in its existing plant in Bristol. Stretch film was initially produced on a cast coextrusion line which had ample spare capacity to run stretch film in addition to coextruded films. Ellis made a decision early on to use the cast process for all stretch film production, on the grounds that the company was already familiar with it and it better satisfied quality requirements. Customers associated quality with clarity and the cast film had noticeably better clarity than blown film. Quite apart from this, underutilized cast equipment was already available for stretch film production in the plant.

DRG quickly established a reputation as a quality producer, simultaneously achieving recognition as one which could respond rapidly to rush orders. Customers quickly began to associate Mobil, Teno, and DRG as the three top-quality producers in the industry. This perception was reinforced by bad experiences with poor quality film from other,

Exhibit 6 Stretch film: industry cost structure.

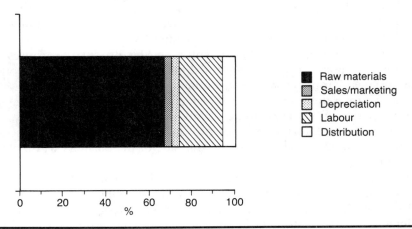

smaller producers in the early days of the industry. Most producers found quality problems were the most significant issue to overcome in establishing themselves in the market.

DRG steadily improved its product performance and quality, carefully nurturing its reputation as a top-quality producer. It introduced a number of innovations in stretch film. One such innovation was the introduction of 'one-sided-cling'. A combination of the properties of cast film and experience with clingfilm had produced a stretch film with inherent cling on one side only. This was preferable to two-sided cling because it eliminated the problem of adjacent pallets sticking together during transit. This often resulted in spilt loads due to the film tearing whilst pallets were unloaded. Another advantage of one-sided cling was that it wound off the roll silently compared to two-sided cling films which produced high noise densities whilst unwinding. In machine wrap applications this was an important consideration.

The decision to produce solely cast film was further justified when some of the blown film producers experienced problems with tackifiers. Under certain conditions of temperature and humidity, the tackifying agent tended to ooze out of the end of the film roll. Customers were concerned about this, particularly if they were packaging foodstuffs.

In 1986, with market growing strongly, DRG invested in a cast extruder dedicated to stretch film production. The new equipment was more productive than the existing machine, and was by that time a necessity as the old equipment was running at capacity purely on stretch film.

The new plant came on stream in 1987, by which time Ellis was already considering where to site the next investment in plant and equipment. It made sense to invest in a site on the Continent, although exactly where was as then undecided.

Marketing and service

DRG's marketing effort capitalized on the foundation of quality and innovation in the company. The pallet-wrap film was branded as 'Astraflex' and used an eye-catching theme: 'Astraflex – the silent film'. Charlie Chaplin appeared prominently on the product brochures and customer response to the promotional literature seemed good. As one of the salesmen commented, 'the customers just love Charlie!'

The major selling effort was directed at pallet-wrapping applications, and more specifically at customers with machine-wrapping facilities. This comprised approximately 80% of turnover. Hand-wrap customers made up the remainder of sales, although this side of the business was regarded very much as a sideline.

DRG's ability to respond quickly to customer demand was backed up by a willingness to assist customers with wrapping problems on site. DRG's wealth of experience and product knowledge could be of considerable help to customers in getting the best performance out of their wrapping facilities.

Sales and distribution

In contrast to the other main producers, DRG sold the vast majority of its stretch film output direct. The salesforce concentrated solely on stretch film. Ellis believed that this arrangement was much more responsive to customer needs than selling through a distributor. Although this strategy was more expensive than using distributors, it had paid off over the years. Also, Ellis thought that he could achieve better delivery times than a distributor.

DRG Plastic Films had two sales offices, one based in Bristol and another near Frankfurt in West Germany. Apart from this it sold small quantities of film in France through a DRG subsidiary company.

Research and development

DRG's R&D effort was focused on making improvements to existing products. Ellis saw little value in spending large amounts of money on fundamental research, and preferred to concentrate instead on steadily improving the performance and quality of Astraflex. One reason for this was that the major producers were usually quick to emulate each other's innovations with seemingly little difficulty. It was relatively easy to examine a competitor's film and adjust the design and processing to produce similar properties if one had the know-how. This was exactly what had happened with 'silent film'; less than a year after DRG had introduced it all three of its largest competitors had incorporated the same properties into their stretch film.

Future outlook

Ellis's main concern was what was going to happen in the stretch film industry when the market began to mature. The producers were investing in plant and equipment heavily, and sooner or later it looked like there would be overcapacity in the industry. At the same time many of the smaller producers were starting to catch up on quality, and these two factors combined might precipitate a price war.

On the applications front, DRG had recently introduced a silage wrap-film grade, and Ellis was considering introducing film grades suitable for other applications.

Another concern was the 'Completion of Europe' set for 1992. This programme, initiated by Brussels, intended to complete the Treaty of Rome and make the EEC internal market free of trade restrictions. This would involve setting standards for many industrial products, including plastic films. Ellis wondered how this would affect his business.

SUGGESTED QUESTIONS

1. How do you foresee competition in this industry changing over the next five years across Europe?
2. What are DRG's sources of competitive advantage relative to its competitors in the industry? What disadvantages does it suffer?
3. How might DRG improve its future position by targeting particular segments as the market develops? Are the appropriate segments defined by product type, customer type or region?
4. Outline the main elements of the strategy you would recommend DRG should follow. Why?

8

Note on the major appliance industry in 1988

Note written by Sumantra Ghoshal and Philippe Haspeslagh with Dag Andersson, Nicola De Sanctis, Beniamino Finzi, and Jacopo Franzan

In 1988 the major appliance industry consisted of a fairly large number of products including kitchen appliances such as cooking ranges (both gas and electric), refrigerators, freezers, microwave ovens, and dishwashers; and laundry products such as washing machines and dryers. The basic technologies and designs for most of these products, except for the microwave oven, were developed before the Second World War. Over the last four decades, technological advances in this business had primarily focused on the development of new features, improving energy efficiency, product standardization, and the exploitation of new materials. Given the consistently low or even zero rate of growth in the overall industry in recent years, competition had been particularly fierce and average profitability had been poor. Producers who were unable to achieve competitive cost positions or specialty niches had found it difficult to survive. An additional feature of the industry had been the increasing importance of distribution in the total cost structure, resulting from increasing concentration in distribution channels and a general shift of bargaining power from the manufacturers to the distributors and retailers.

Initially characterized by a high level of fragmentation, the industry was evolving towards increasing concentration with seven companies accounting for over 50% of the global market (see Exhibit 1). Over 70% of the worldwide demand for household appliances was concentrated in three markets: the United States, Europe, and Japan. Each of these

This case was prepared by Dag Andersson, Nicola De Sanctis, Beniamino Finzi and Jacopo Franzan, Research Assistants, under the supervision of Sumantra Ghoshal and Philippe Haspeslagh, Associate Professors at INSEAD. It is intended to be used as the basis for class discussion rather than to illustrate either effective or ineffective handling of an administrative situation. Reprinted with the permission of INSEAD–CEDEP.

Exhibit 1 The seven global appliance producers and their sales in 1987.

Company	Sales in 1987 (US $ billion)
Electrolux/Zanussi/White	5.10
General Electric	4.35
Matsushita	4.18
Whirlpool	3.95
Bosch-Siemens	2.20
Philips	2.00
Maytag-Hoover	1.58

markets had developed along similar lines but had remained relatively isolated from the others due to differences in customer tastes and preferences, divergent technical standards, and the relatively high cost of transportation for most products of the industry except for a few items such as room air-conditioners and microwave ovens.

THE NORTH AMERICAN MARKET

In 1988 the North American market for household appliances was valued at approximately $12 billion. Whereas strong consumer spending and favourable pricing had allowed for a unit growth of about 3% during the period 1986–88, industry observers were expecting a decline in total industry shipments over the next two to three years. Indeed, replacement demand (accounting for over 75% of industry shipments) had been above normal levels, implying some borowing of future business.

Overcapacity in the US market had already resulted in a wave of mergers and acquisitions in the 1980s. Of some 230 mostly single-product-line manufacturers operating in the late 1940s, less than 10 remained of which four – GE, Whirlpool, Maytag, and White, a subsidiary of Electrolux – accounted for 80% of the business. In 1986 Whirlpool completed its purchase of KitchenAid, White Consolidated was acquired by Electrolux, and Maytag merged with Magic Chef – all within six months. By now most of the survivors produced and sold all the major appliances.

Only one of the US producers – Whirlpool – had started to position itself as a global appliance manufacturer. In contrast to companies like GE and Maytag who had limited their operations to the US and its adjacent markets such as Mexico and Canada, Whirlpool believed that significant presence in all the key regional markets was essential for its long-term survival in this business. As a result, it had pursued an aggressive strategy of geographic expansion. In 1985 it took a majority interest in Inglis, Canada's second largest appliance company. In 1986 it acquired a 65%

interest in Aspera, an Italian compressor manufacturer, and raised its equity interest in three Brazilian companies. Finally, in 1988, it bought into a strong presence in Europe by acquiring a 53% stake in Philips' major appliance business, with an option to buy out the remainder.

Besides increasing concentration, two other trends characterized the present situation in the US major appliance market: a push toward full line marketing to growing inter-firm sourcing, and increasing competition in the high price segments.

Strategic components such as compressors had a significant weight in the cost structure of domestic appliances. Their production is a scale-intensive activity: for example, doubling compressor production can reduce unit costs by about 15%. Strength in component production, therefore, was a vital source of competitive advantage in this business. The resulting search for volume in component production had led to a widespread practice of private labelling and cross-sourcing among the US manufacturers.

Simultaneous to their search for cost reduction, companies attempted to improve profitability by focusing on the relatively stable and profitable high-end segment of the market. GE's monogram line and White's Euroflair lines – both introduced in 1988 – were developed specifically for this segment. Maytag traditionally served this niche and had recently announced its commitment to further upgrade its product lines to strengthen the company's image among the more sophisticated and less price-sensitive buyers. Whirlpool – historically strong in the mid-price segment but weak at the high-end – had also made a determined effort to overcome this weakness through its acquisition of KitchenAid and its more expensive product lines.

One special case in the industry was Sears, which held a dominant position in the distribution end of the household appliances business in the US, controlling some 25% of the retail trade. In order to preserve its bargaining power, the company actively influenced the structure of the supplier industry. The formation of Whirlpool, for example, was the result of a Sears initiative to merge two existing companies so as to create a single viable rival to GE. During the last three years, Whirlpool had distributed more than 50% of its US sales through Sears. Montgomery Ward, another large department store chain, had similar ties with manufacturers who supplied it with private label products.

Recently specialized appliance and/or consumer electronics chains had made inroads against both the department stores and independent dealers on the basis of aggressive pricing. Industry observers regarded this development as leading not only to increased price pressure on the manufacturers, but also facilitating eventual entry by foreign manufacturers.

THE JAPANESE MARKET

With a population of 122 million people, Japan was second only to the United States as a single national market for household appliances.

Exhibit 2 Market shares (%) of leading Japanese manufacturers in 1984.

	Refrigerators	Microwave ovens	Laundry machines	Electric ranges
Matsushita	27.0	28.5	25.1	27.6
Toshiba	18.1	10.9	15.7	18.1
Hitachi	14.7	13.2	17.5	15.3
Sharp	13.0	31.9	9.0	8.3
Mitsubishi Electric	10.0	4.4	9.6	14.8
Sanyo Electric	9.2	2.9	13.0	10.2
Others	7.9	8.2	10.0	5.7

Exhibit 3 Distribution networks of leading Japanese appliance manufacturers in 1984.

Company	Number of sales companies in Japan	Number of company-owned retail shops in Japan
Matsushita	101	27 000
Toshiba	22	12 000
Mitsubishi Electric	14	5 500
Sanyo Electric	11	4 500
Sharp	1	3 800

Matsushita was the market leader in nearly all product categories. Hitachi and Toshiba were fighting for second position while Sharp, Mitsubishi, and Sanyo competed in the third tier. Exhibit 2 shows the market shares of the leading Japanese manufacturers for the main product categories.

Distribution of household appliances in Japan continued to be very complex and fragmented, involving a host of small and large 'actors' such as trading companies, producer-owned sales companies, several layers of wholesalers, and different types of retailers. Most wholesalers carried the brands of a single manufacturer. The leading appliance producers had tightly controlled distribution networks with their own sales companies and a large number of company-owned outlets that sold a diverse range of consumer products produced by the company, including household appliances. Exhibit 3 shows the number of sales companies and retailers that were owned or controlled by the five leading Japanese competitors. This distribution system was, however, slowly changing, with the emerging independent supermarkets, specialty stores and discount chains gradually increasing their share of the retailing market at the cost of the company-owned retail outlets.

In contrast to their own actions in other businesses such as consumer electronics, Japanese producers had been relatively slow in internationalizing their domestic appliance business. So far their international activities had been limited to the neighbouring Asian and Pacific markets and, except for microwave ovens and air-conditioners, they had made little efforts to develop market shares in Europe or the US. However, this was expected to change soon since many of the largest companies had now given explicit warning of their intentions to build up strong global presence. The following statement by the general manager of Matsushita's corporate overseas office reflected this commitment: 'Foreign makers are right to expect that Matsushita and other Japanese companies will enter the US and European markets soon enough. The traditional makers won't be number 1 and number 2 forever.' Even more direct evidence of the emerging Japanese vivacity was manifest in the words of John Bennigsen, Director of Marketing and Sales of Toshiba consumer products in the UK: 'Every time I go to Japan, I lick my lips over the prospect of bringing some of our products to Europe. I think it is fair to say that we are seriously considering the European market.'

THE EUROPEAN MARKET

The overall market for household appliances in Europe was characterized by very low or, in some instances, even negative growth. As shown in Exhibit 4, the penetration levels for most products were extremely high in most key markets. There were significant differences among the various products, however, and while annual demand growth for washing machines was −0.4% between 1978 and 1983, that for microwave ovens was as high at 40% during the same period. Similarly, while demand in countries like the UK and Holland had been stagnant, others such as Spain had registered significant growth.

In 1970 there were 695 producers of household appliances in Europe. By 1988, while some 300–350 fringe producers continued to survive, six companies – Electrolux Zanussi (25%), Philips Bauknecht (13%), Bosch-Siemens (12%), Merloni-Indesit (10%), Thompson (6%), and AEG (4%) – controlled 70% of the market. Currently, there was a manufacturing overcapacity of 20–40% in Europe for the different product categories and most companies had to struggle with low or even negative profitability in this business. AEG, Thompson, and some of the Italian manufacturers had survived only because of direct and indirect government subsidies. Lately, East European producers had vigorously attacked the low-price segments for products such as refrigerators and cooking ranges. Except in the microwave oven market, Japanese imports had not yet made any major inroads. As a production platform, Italy held the number one position with 39% of total European production, West

Exhibit 4   Penetration levels in selected European countries in 1981* and 1985 (% of households).

Country	Washing machines		Dish washers		Refrige- rators		Freezers		Microwave ovens
	1981	85	1981	85	1981	85	1981	85	1985
Germany	90	95	25	33	95	98	52	61	4
France	81	84	19	28	96	97	30	39	2
Belgium	80	83	16	19	93	95	45	51	2
Netherlands	87	91	11	13	98	98	44	52	n/a
Italy	88	95	16	18	89	95	28	35	n/a
UK	80	87	3	8	94	98	31	43	15
Sweden	65	72	21	25	94	98	66	76	n/a

* 1978 figures for The Netherlands, Italy and United Kingdom; 1979 figures for Sweden.

Germany was second with 22%, France third with 11%, followed by the UK with 10%.

Major European competitors in the household appliances business could be categorized into three broad groups:

1. Companies that produced and sold in single national markets (national players).
2. Companies that produced primarily in a single country, but marketed in many countries through exports (exporters).
3. Companies that produced and marketed in several countries within Europe and outside (global or regional players).

GEC's Hotpoint division was a typical example of a national player. It was the leader in the washing machine and dishwasher markets in the UK and probably one of the most profitable appliance producers in Europe with an operating margin of over 12%. Hotpoint only competed in the UK market, where it had a niche as a low-cost producer with a strong marketing organization. Managers of Hotpoint supported the company's nationally focused approach by pointing out the very limited penetration of international brands in the different European countries. Although these brands were often available in all major national markets, they typically commanded very small market shares in comparison to the brands of the local producers. To some extent this was due to differences in customer tastes and national technical standards which had made product standardization difficult. In the case of washing machines, for example, spin-speed and method of loading were two features for which different national customers had traditionally expressed very different preferences. High transport costs of the bulky finished products, high and fixed costs of advertising required to develop and support pan-European brands, the difficulty of obtaining shelf-space in the retailers' showrooms, and the need for a fairly extensive after-sales service network were among the other factors that had so far helped the national players at the cost of the exporters and the global players.

A clear example of the exporter strategy was provided by Merloni, a manufacturer based in central Italy. Between 1984 and 1986 Merloni doubled its production and reached an output level of 1.6 million units, achieving the highest level of worker productivity in Europe (741 units per worker per year). Merloni believed that, in the long run, its formula of centralized high-scale production in low-cost Italy with decentralized and differentiated marketing efforts in the different national markets would prove superior to both the national player and the integrated global producer-marketeer strategy. To support this strategy, in 1987 Merloni acquired Indesit, a large but financially stretched Italian producer, who had strong marketing presence in a number of neighbouring countries.

Electrolux provided a good illustration of the global players' strategy. The company believed that global-scale volume was absolutely vital for long-term survival in this business, and that local or regional production was necessary to build and maintain adequate market shares in all the major markets. While acknowledging the need to respond to the differences in tastes and preferences of national customers, they believed that those differences were narrowing and that the market characteristics would converge. They also believed that, by developing the ability to transfer and leverage product concepts, components, and manufacturing techniques from one market to another, they could develop insurmountable advantages over others with more new product launches and shorter development cycles. In the words of Anders Scharp, Electrolux's CEO: 'Even if national differences persist for some years to come, there are many other ways of benefitting from economies of scale. For example, co-ordination of component production, such as compressors, motors and pumps can quickly produce cost benefits ... Besides, even at the finished product level, the trend is quite clear: new products are more international.'

9

Electrolux: the acquisition and integration of Zanussi (A)

Case written by Sumantra Ghoshal and Philippe Haspeslagh with Dag Andersson, Nicola De Sanctis, Beniamino Finzi, and Jacopo Franzan

In recounting the story of Electrolux's acquisition of Zanussi, Leif Johansson, head of Electrolux's major appliance division, had reasons to feel pleased. Through financial restructuring and operating improvements Zanussi had, in only three years since the acquisition, gone from a massive loss of L.120 billion in 1983 to a tidy profit of L.60 billion in 1987★ – a turnaround that astounded outside analysts and was perhaps more impressive than the expectations of even the optimists within Electrolux. More important was the progress made in integrating Zanussi strategically, operationally, and organizationally within the Electrolux group, while protecting is distinct identity and reviving the fighting spirit that had been the hallmark of the proud Italian company. Having been the first to suggest to President Anders Scharp that Electrolux should buy financially troubled Zanussi, Johansson had a major personal stake in the operation's continued success.

By early 1988, however, the task was far from complete. Not everything was going well at Zanussi: the company had recently lost some market share within Italy to Merloni, its arch-rival. Merloni had taken over domestic market leadership following its acquisition of Indesit,

★ $1 = L.1170 = Skr.5.85 (International Financial Statistics, December, 1987)

© 1989, 1990 by INSEAD–CEDEP, Fontainebleau, France
This case was prepared by Dag Andersson, Nicola De Sanctis, Beniamino Finzi, and Jacopo Franzan, Research Assistants, under the supervision of Sumantra Ghoshal and Philippe Haspeslagh, Associate Professors at INSEAD. It is intended to be used as the basis for class discussion rather than to illustrate either effective or ineffective handling of an administrative situation.
Reprinted with the permission of INSEAD–CEDEP.
The casewriters gratefully acknowledge the co-operation of the Electrolux company and its executives, and financial support from the INSEAD Alumni Fund European Case Programme.

another large Italian producer of household appliances. There had been some delays in Zanussi's ambitious programme for plant automation. Moreover, a recent attitude survey had shown that, while the top 60 managers of Zanussi fully supported the actions taken since the acquisition, the next rung of 150 managers felt less motivated and less secure. It was not clear whether these problems were short-term in nature and would soon be resolved, or whether they were the warning signals for more basic and fundamental maladies.

Though Leif Johansson felt it useful to review the integration process, his concerns focused on the next stage of the battle for global leadership. The industry was changing rapidly with competitors like Whirlpool and Matsushita moving outside their home regions (see Chapter 8 'Note on the Major Appliance Industry in 1988'). At the same time some local European competitors, for example GEC–Hotpoint in the UK and Merloni (Ariston) in Italy, were making aggressive moves to expand their shares in a relatively low-growth market. The Zanussi takeover and the subsequent acquisition of White Consolidated in the United States, catapulted Electrolux to the top of the list of the world's largest producers of household appliances.

The challenge for Johansson now was to mould all the acquired entities into an integrated strategy and organization that would protect this leadership role and leverage it into a profitable worldwide operation.

ELECTROLUX

In 1962 Electrolux was on a downward curve. Profits were falling and the company had not developed any significant in-house research and development capability. Compared with other appliance manufacturers such as Philips, Siemens, GEC, and Matsushita, it had a limited range of products: the core business was made up of vacuum cleaners and absorption-type refrigerators. These refrigerators were increasingly unable to compete with the new compressor-type refrigerators developed by the competitors, and sales of the once highly successful lines of vacuum cleaners were rapidly declining.

That same year ASEA, a company in the Wallenberg network (an informal grouping of major Swedish companies in which the Wallenbergs – the most influential business family in Sweden – has some equity shares) sold Electro-Helios to Electrolux for shares and thereby became a major shareholder. Electro-Helios was a technological leader in compressor-type refrigerators and a significant producer of freezers and cooking ranges. This led to a major expansion of Electrolux's role in the Swedish household appliance market, but the company found itself in financial difficulty again due to rapid expansion of production capacity during a period of severe economic downturn.

In 1967 Hans Werthén was appointed CEO of Electrolux. In the next two decades he and the other two members of what was known as the 'Electrolux Troika', Anders Scharp and Gösta Bystedt, would manage to develop the company from a relatively small and marginal player in the business into the world's largest manufacturer of household appliances.

Growth through acquisitions

At the core of the dramatic transformation of Electrolux was an aggressive strategy of expansion through acquisition. At the beginning, Electrolux concentrated on acquiring firms in the Nordic countries, its traditional market, where the company already had a dominant market share. Subsequent acquisitions served not only to strengthen the company's position in its household appliance activities, but also to broaden its European presence and open the way to entirely new product areas. Exhibit 1 illustrates Electrolux's major acquisitions between 1964 and 1988.

With more than 200 acquisitions in 40 countries, and 280 manufacturing facilities in 25 countries, the Electrolux group had few equals in managing the acquisition and integration processes. The company generally bought competitors in its core businesses, disposing of operations which either failed to show long-term profit potential or appeared to have a better chance of prospering under the management of another company. In addition, Electrolux always tried to ensure that there were sufficient realizable assets available to help finance the necessary restructuring of the acquired company. Thus, from the beginning of the 1970s up to 1988, the group made capital gains from selling off idle assets of more than Skr.2.5 billion.

At the same time, flexibility had been maintained in order to pick up new product areas for further development. A typical example of this was the chain-saw product line that came with the acquisition of the Swedish appliance manufacturer, Husqvarna, in 1978. By developing this product line through acquisitions and in-house development, Electrolux emerged as one of the world's leading chain-saw manufacturers with about 30% of the global market. Another example was provided by the new business area of outdoor products (mainly forestry and garden products), which had grown from the small base of the Flymo lawnmower business through the acquisition of firms like Poulan/Weed Eater in the US and Staub/Bernard Moteur in France.

The two most notable departures from the strategy of buying familiar businesses had been the 1973 acquisition of Facit, a Swedish office equipment and electronics manufacturer, and the 1980 purchase of Gränges, a metal and mining company. Both companies were in financial trouble. Electrolux had difficulty in fully mastering Facit; after bringing the profit up to a reasonable level, it was sold off to Ericsson in 1983. The borrowing necessary to buy Gränges, combined with the worldwide economic downturn and rising interest rates, pushed Electrolux into a sobering two-year period (1981–83) when profit margins declined. However, through the Gränges takeover Electrolux also acquired new businesses for future growth. An example was the manufacturing of seat

Exhibit 1 1987 turnover by product line, 1987.

1987 turnover by product line
Million Swedish kronor

Sales billion Swedish kronor

70
65
60
55
50
45
40
35
30
25
20
15
10
5

1962 63 64 65 66 67 68 69 70 71 72 73 74 75 76 77 78 79 80 81 82 83 84 85 86 87 88

Major company acquisitions and divestments since 1962

White goods 28,476
Aluminium products 5,853
Vacuum cleaners 5,571
Food-service products 2,394 (of which)
Forestry products 2,356
Building materials 1,810
Cleaning machines 1,761
Garden products 1,756
Sewing machines 1,739
Garden equipment and vending machines 1,717
Air-conditioners 1,711
Components protection 1,619
Car safety and laundry products 1,296
Leisure bath and industrial handling 1,132
Kitchen areas and industrial handling 1,128
Material refrigeration 1,074
Commercial refrigeration 1,068
Laundry services 1,040
Commercial cleaning equipment 760
Sterilisation and disinfection equipment 633
International Mining 360
Agricultural implements 236
Home electronics 211
Food-service equipment and vending machines 211

ElektroHelios, white goods

Getinge, sterilization equipment

Atlas, white goods Elektra, ranges

Flymo, garden products ASAB, cleaning services

Kent, commercial cleaning equipment Quatfass, food-service equipment

Euroclean, commercial cleaning equipment

Kreft/Siegas, kitchen & bathroom cabinets Växjö Rostfritt, disinfection equipment

Eureka, vacuum cleaner Emerson Quiet Kool, air-conditioners

Facit, office machines Wascator, industrial laundry equipment
Ballinsgslöv, kitchen & bathroom cabinets

Martin, kitchen ranges Tornado, vacuum cleaners

Therma, white goods, commercial appliances Tvättman, laundry services
Husqvarna, sewing machines, white goods, chainsaws Partner, chainsaws

Jonsered/Pioneer, chainsaws Tappan, household appliances

Columbus Dixon, commercial cleaning equipment Gränges, metals
Océanic, radio/TV Voss, kitchen ranges Paris-Rhône, vacuum cleaners

Hugin, cash registers Norlett, garden products Progress,
vacuum cleaners Lequeux,
sterilization products Völund, industrial laundry equipment

Klippan, safety belts Sümak, commercial refrigeration equipment
Zanussi, household & commercial appliances, industrial products
Camping Freeze, caravan refrigerators ZK Hospital, disinfection
products

White, household appliances, industrial products Gotthard, scrap recycling
Poulan/Weed Eater, forestry & garden products
Zanker, washing machines Beijer Bygg, building materials
Duo-Therm, air-conditioners Staub Bernard Moteur, garden
products

Tricity/Stott Benham, white goods, food-service equipment
Design & Manufacturing, dishwashers

*Corberó/Domar, white goods Alpeninox, food-service equipment
Britax/Kolb/Coldrive, safety belts Alfatec, vacuum cleaners
A & E Systems, caravan enhancements
Bruynzeel, materials handling equipment Unidad Hermética,
compressors*

Gränges Kraft, hydro electric power

**Facit, office machines Hugin, cash registers
Platzer (Gränges division), contractors
Emerson Quiet Kool, air
conditioners**

**Metallverken/Wirsbo
(formerly Gränges division),
metals, tubes**

*Océanic,
radio/TV*

Electrolux Corp., vacuum cleaners

belts, now concentrated in the subsidiary Electrolux Autoliv. Nevertheless, the acquisition of Gränges would be the last diversifying acquisition.

Even though Electrolux had dealt with a large number of acquisitions, specific companies were seldom targeted. In the words of Anders Scharp, 'You never choose an acquisition, opportunities just come'. The company made it a practice to simulate what the merger combination with other companies would result in should they come up for sale. The financial aspects of an acquisition were considered to be very important. The company usually ensured that it paid less for a company than the total asset value of the company, and not for what Electrolux would bring to the party.

Based on their experience, managers at Electrolux believed that there was no standard method for treating acquisitions: each case was unique and had to be dealt with differently. Typically, however, Electrolux moved quickly at the beginning of the integration process. It identified the key action areas and created task forces consisting of managers from both Electrolux and the acquired company in order to address each of the issues on a time-bound basis. Such joint task forces were believed to help foster management confidence and commitment and create avenues for reciprocal information flows. Objectives were clearly specified, milestones were identified, and the first phase of integration was generally completed within three to six months so as to create and maintain momentum. The top management of an acquired company was often replaced, but the middle management was kept intact. As explained by Anders Scharp, 'The risk of losing general management competence is small when it is a poorly performing company. Electrolux is prepared to take this risk. It is, however, important that we do not change the marketing and sales staff'.

Electrolux prior to the acquisition of Zanussi

The activities of the Electrolux group in 1984, prior to the acquisition of Zanussi, covered 26 product lines within five business areas, namely: household appliances, forestry and garden products, industrial products, commercial services, and metal and mining (Gränges). Total sales revenue had increased from Skr.1.1 billion in 1967 to Skr.34.5 billion in 1984. The household appliance area (including white goods, special refrigerators, floor-care products and sewing machines) accounted for approximately 52% of total group sales in 1984. Gränges was the second largest area with nearly 21.5% of total sales. The third area, industrial products, provided heavy equipment for food services, semi-industrial laundries, and commercial cleaning.

By the 1980s Electrolux had become one of the world's largest manufacturers of white goods with production facilities in Europe and North America, and a small presence in Latin America and the Far East. The Group's reliance upon the Scandinavian markets was still considerable. More than 30% of sales came from Sweden, Norway, and Denmark.

European sales, focusing mainly on Scandinavia and Western Europe, constituted 65% of total group sales. The US had emerged as the single most important market with 28.9% (1987) of total sales.

Electrolux's household appliances were manufactured in plants with specialized assembly lines. Regional manufacturing operations were focused on local brands and designs and established distribution networks. Sales forces for the various brands had been kept separate, though support functions such as physical distribution, stocking, order taking, and invoicing might be integrated. With increasing plant automation and product differentiation, the number of models and the volume produced in any given plant had risen sharply. As described by Anders Scharp, 'We recognized that expansion means higher volumes, which create scope for rationalization. Rationalization means better margins, which are essential to boost our competitive strength'.

One important characteristic of Electrolux was the astonishingly small corporate headquarters at Lilla Essingen, six kilometres outside the centre of Stockholm, and the relatively few people who worked in central staff departments. The size of headquarters was a direct outcome of the company's commitment to decentralization. 'I believe that we have at least two hierarchical levels fewer than other companies of the same size,' said Scharp, 'and all operational matters are decentralized to the subsidiaries.' However, most strategic issues such as investment programmes, and product range decisions were dealt with at headquarters. The subsidiaries were considered to be profit centres and were evaluated primarily on their returns on net assets as compared with the targets set by the corporate office. Presidents of the diversified subsidiaries reported directly to Scharp, while others reported to the heads of the different product lines.

The acquisition of Zanussi

In June 1983, Leif Johansson, the 32-year-old head of Electrolux's major appliance division, received a proposal from Mr Candotti, head of Zanussi's major appliance division in France, from whom he had been 'sourcing' refrigerators for the French market. The proposal called for the investment of a small amount of money in Zanussi so as to secure future supplies from the financially troubled Italian producer. The next day Johansson called Anders Scharp to ask, 'Why don't we buy all of it?', thereby triggering a process that led to the largest acquisition in the history of the household appliance industry and in the Swedish business world.

ZANUSSI

Having begun in 1916 as a small workshop in Pordenone, a little town in northeast Italy, where Antonio Zanussi produced a few wood-burning cookers, Zanussi had grown by the early 1980s to be the second largest

Exhibit 2   Consolidated financial statements for Zanussi Group.

Consolidated income statement for Zanussi Group (in million Skr.)

	1980	1981	1982	1983
Sales	3826	4327	4415	5240
Operating cost	−3301	−3775	−3957	−4654
Operating income before depreciation	525	552	458	586
Depreciation	−161	−98	−104	−130
Operating income after depreciation	364	454	354	456
Financial income	192	330	284	279
Financial expenses	−407	−489	−647	−627
Income after financial items	149	295	−9	108
Extraordinary items	−53	−228	−223	81
Income before appropriations	96	67	−232	189
Appropriations	−53	−42	−409	−382
Income before taxes	43	25	−641	−193
Taxes	−7	−7	−10	−10
Net income	36	18	−651	−203

Consolidated balance sheet for Zanussi Group (in million Skr.)

	1980	1981	1982	1983
Current assets excl. inventory	1559	1987	1811	2108
Inventory	965	1054	999	956
Fixed assets	1622	1539	2366	2902
Total assets	4146	4580	5176	5966
Current liabilities	1590	1832	1875	2072
Long-term liabilities	1273	1441	1864	2349
Reserves	259	301	472	627
Shareholders' equity	1024	1006	965	918
Total liabilities and shareholders' equity	4146	4580	5176	5966

privately-owned company in Italy with more than 30 000 employees, 50 factories and 13 foreign sales companies. Most of the growth came in the 1950s and 1960s under the leadership of Lino Zanussi, who understood the necessity of having not only a complete range of products but also a well-functioning distribution and sales network. Lino Zanussi established several new factories within Italy and added cookers, refrigerators, and washing machines to the product range. In 1958 he launched a major drive to improve exports out of Italy and he established the first foreign branch office in Paris in 1962. Similar branches were soon opened in other European countries and the first foreign manufacturing subsidiary, IBELSA, was set up in Madrid in 1965. Through a series of acquisitions of Italian producers of appliances and components, Zanussi became one of the most vertically integrated manufacturers in Europe, achieving full control over all activities ranging from component manufacturing to final sales and service. It is rumoured that, during this period of heady success, Zanussi had very seriously considered launching a takeover bid for Electrolux, then a struggling Swedish company less than half Zanussi's size.

The company's misfortunes started in 1968 when Lino Zanussi and several other company executives died in an aircrash. Over the next 15 years the new management carved out a costly programme of unrelated diversification into fields such as colour televisions, prefabricated housing, real estate, and community centres. The core business of domestic appliances languished for want of capital, while the new businesses incurred heavy losses. By 1982 the company had amassed debts of over L.1300 billion and was losing L.100 billion a year on operations (see Exhibit 2 for the consolidated financial statements during this period).

Between 1982 and 1984, Zanussi tried to rectify the situation by selling off many of the loss-making subsidiaries, reducing the rest of the work-force by over 4400 people, and focusing on its core activities. However, given the large debt burden and the need for heavy investment in order to rebuild the domestic appliance business, a fresh injection of capital was essential and the company began its search for a partner.

The acquisition process

The process of Electrolux's acquisition of Zanussi formally commenced when Enrico Cuccia, the informal head of Mediobanca and the most powerful financier in Italy, approached Hans Werthén on 30 November 1983, about the possibility of Electrolux rescuing Zanussi from impending financial collapse. It was not by chance that the grand old man of Mediobanca arrived in Sweden. Enrico Cuccia had close links to the Agnelli family – the owners of Fiat, the largest industrial group in Italy – and the proposal to approach Electrolux came from Mr Agnelli, who wanted to save the second largest private manufacturing company in his country. As a board member of SKF, the Swedish bearing manufacturer, Agnelli had developed a healthy respect for Swedish management and believed that Electrolux alone had the resources and management skills necessary to turn Zanussi around.

Meanwhile, Electrolux had been looking around for a good acquisition to expand its appliance business. Its efforts to take over AEG's appliance business in Germany had failed because the conditions stipulated for the takeover were found to be too tough. Later, Electrolux had to back away from acquiring the TI group in the UK because of too high a price-tag. Zanussi now represented the best chance for significant expansion in Europe. 'It was a very good fit,' recalled Anders Scharp. 'There were not many overlaps: we were strong where Zanussi was weak, and vice-versa.' There were significant complementarities in products, markets, and opportunities for vertical integration. For example, while Electrolux was well established in microwave ovens, cookers and fridge–freezers,

Zanussi was Europe's largest producer of 'wet products' such as washing machines, traditionally a weak area for Electrolux. Similarly, while Electrolux had large market shares in Scandinavia and Switzerland where Zanussi was almost completely absent, Zanussi was the market leader in Italy and Spain, two markets that Electrolux had failed to crack. Zanussi was also strong in France, the only market where Electrolux was losing money, and had a significant presence in Germany, where Electrolux had limited strength except in vacuum cleaners. Finally, while Electrolux had historically avoided vertical integration and sourced most of its components externally, Zanussi was a vertically integrated company with substantial spare capacity for component production that Electrolux could profitably use.

From 30 November 1983, until 14 December 1984, the date when the formal deal was finally signed, there ensued a 12-month period of intense negotiation in which, alongside the top management of the two companies, Gianmario Rossignolo, the Chairman of SKF's Italian subsidiary, took an increasingly active role. The most difficult parts of the negotiations focused on the following three issues:

Union and workforce reduction   At the outset, the powerful unions at Zanussi were against selling the company to the 'Vikings from the North'. They would have preferred to keep Zanussi independent, with a government subsidy, or to merge with Thomson from France. They also believed that under Electrolux management all important functions would be transferred to Sweden, thereby eroding the skills of the Italian company and also reducing local employment opportunities.

In response to these concerns, Electrolux guaranteed that all Zanussi's important functions would be retained within Italy. Twenty union leaders were sent from Sweden to Italy to reassure the Italians. The same number of Italian union leaders were invited to Sweden to observe Electrolux's production system and labour relations. Initially, Mr Rossignolo signed a letter of assurance to the unions on behalf of Electrolux confirming that the level of employment prevailing at that time would be maintained. Soon, however, it became obvious that Zanussi could not be made profitable without workforce reductions. This resulted in difficult renegotiations. It was finally agreed that within three months of the acquisition Electrolux would present the unions a three-year plan for investments and reduction in personnel. Actual retrenchments would have to follow the plan, subject to its approval by the unions.

Prior commitments of Zanussi   A number of problems were posed by certain commitments on the part of Zanussi. One major issue was SELECO, an Italian producer of television sets. A majority of shares in SELECO were held by REL, a government holding company, and the rest were owned by Zanussi and Indesit. Zanussi had made a commitment to buy REL's majority holdings of SELECO within a period of five years ending in 1989. Electrolux had no interest in entering the television business but finally accepted this commitment despite considerable apprehension.

Another major concern was the unprofitable Spanish appliance company IBELSA owned by Zanussi. Zanussi had received large subsidies from the Spanish government against a commitment to help restructure the industry in Spain, and heavy fines would have to be paid if the company decided to pull out. Once again, Electrolux had to accept these terms despite concern about IBELSA's long-term competitiveness.

Nevertheless, there was one potential liability that Electrolux refused to accept. In the later stages of the negotiations, an audit team from Electrolux discovered that a previous managing director of Zanussi had sold a large amount of equipment and machinery to a German company and had then leased them back. This could potentially lead to severe penalties and large fines, as the actions violated Italian foreign exchange and tax laws. Electrolux refused to proceed with the negotiations until the Italian government had promised not to take any punitive actions in this case.

Financial structure and ownership   Electrolux was not willing to take over majority ownership of Zanussi immediately since it would then be required to consolidate Zanussi into group accounts, and the large debts would have major adverse effects on the Electrolux balance sheet and share prices. Electrolux wanted to take minority holdings without relinquishing its claim to majority holdings in the future. To resolve this issue, a consortium was organized that included prominent Italian financial institutions and industrial companies such as Mediobanca, IMI, Crediop, and a subsidiary of Fiat. The consortium took on a large part of the shares (40.6%), with another 10.4% bought by the Friuli region. This allowed Electrolux to remain at 49%. While the exact financial transactions were kept confidential, since some of the parties opposed any payment to the Zanussi family, it is believed that Electrolux injected slightly under $100 million into Zanussi. One-third of that investment secured the 49% shareholding, and the remainder went towards debentures that could be converted into shares at any time to give Electrolux a comfortable 75% ownership. An agreement with over 100 banks which had some form of exposure to Zanussi assured a respite from creditors, freezing payments on the Italian debt until January 1987. At the same time the creditors made considerable concessions on interest payments.

One of the most important meetings in the long negotiation process took place in Rome on 15 November 1984, when, after stormy discussions between the top management of Electrolux and the leaders of the Zanussi union, a document confirming Electrolux's intention to acquire Zanussi was jointly signed by both parties. During the most crucial hour of the meeting, Hans Werthén stood up in front of the 50 union leaders and declared: 'We are not buying companies in order to close them down, but to turn them into profitable ventures . . . and, we are not the Vikings, who were Norwegians, anyway.'

The turnaround of Zanussi

It was standard Electrolux practice to have a broad but clear plan for immediate post-acquisition action well before the negotiation process for an acquisition was complete. Thus, by August 1984, well before the deal was signed in December, a specific plan for the turnaround and the eventual integration of Zanussi was drawn up in Stockholm. As stated by Leif Johansson, 'When we make an acquisition, we adopt a centralized approach from the outset. We have a definite plan worked out when we go in and there is virtually no need for extended discussions'. In the Zanussi case, the general approach had to be amended slightly since a feasible reduction in the employment levels was not automatic. However, clear decisions were taken to move the loss-making production of front-loaded washing machines from France to Zanussi's factory in Pordenone. On the other hand, the production of all top-loading washing machines was to be moved from Italy to France. In total, the internal plan anticipated shifting production of 600 000–800 000 product units from Electrolux and from subcontractors' plants to Zanussi, thereby increasing Zanussi's capacity utilization. Detailed financial calculations led to an expected cost savings of Skr.400–500 millions through rationalization. Specific plans were also drawn up to achieve a 2–3% reduction in Zanussi's marketing and administrative costs by integrating the organization of the two companies in different countries.

Immediate post-acquisition actions

On 14 December, a matter of hours after the signing of the final agreement, Electrolux announced a complete change in the top management of Zanussi. The old board, packed with nominees of the Zanussi family, was swept clean and Gianmario Rossignolo was appointed as Chairman of the company. An Italian, long-experienced in working with Swedish colleagues because of his position as chairman of SKF's Italian subsidiary, Rossignolo was seen as an ideal bridge between the two companies with their vastly different cultures and management styles. Carlo Verri, who was Managing Director of SKF's Italian subsidiary, was brought in as the new Managing Director of Zanussi. Rossignolo and Verri had turned around SKF's Italian operations and had a long history of working together as a team. Similarly, Hans Werthén, Anders Scharp, Gösta Bystedt and Lennart Ribohn joined the reconstituted Zanussi board. The industrial relations manager of Zanussi was the only senior manager below board level to be replaced. The purpose was to give a clear signal to the entire organization of the need to change work practices.

Consistent with the Electrolux style, a number of task forces were formed immediately to address the scope of integration and rationalization of activities in different functional areas. Each team was given a specific time period to come up with recommendations. Similarly, immediate actions were initiated in order to introduce Electrolux's financial reporting system within Zanussi, the clear target being to have the system fully in place and operative within six months from the date of the acquisition.

Direct steps were taken at the business level to enhance capacity utilization, reduce costs of raw materials and components purchased, and revitalize local sales.

Capacity utilization It was promised that Electrolux would source 500 000 units from Zanussi including 280 000 units of household appliances, 200 000 units of components, and 7500 units of commercial appliances. This sourcing decision was given wide publicity both inside and outside the company, and a drive was launched to achieve the chosen levels as soon as possible. By 1985, 70% of the target had been reached.

Cost cutting in purchases Given that 70% of production costs were represented by raw materials and purchased components, an immediate programme was launched to reduce vendor prices. The assumption was that vendors had adjusted their prices to compensate for the high risk of supplying to financially distressed Zanussi and should lower their prices now that that risk was eliminated. A net saving of 2% on purchases was achieved immediately. Over time approximately 17% gains in real terms would be achieved, not only for Zanussi, but also for Electrolux.

Revitalizing sales Local competitors in Italy reacted vigorously to the announcement of Electrolux's acquisition of Zanussi. Anticipating a period of inaction while the new management took charge, they launched an aggressive marketing programme and Zanussi's sales slumped almost immediately. After consulting with Electrolux, the new management of Zanussi responded with a dramatic move of initially extending trade credit from 60 to 360 days under specified conditions. Sales surged immediately and the market was assured once and for all that 'Zanussi was back'.

Agreement with the Unions

In the next phase, starting from February 1985, the new management turned its attention to medium- and long-term needs. The most pressing of these was to fulfil a promise made to the unions before the acquisition: the presentation of a complete restructuring programme. This programme was finalized and discussed with the union leaders on 28 March 1985, at the Ministry of Industry in Rome. It consisted of a broad analysis of the industry and market trends, evaluation of Zanussi's competitive position and future prospects, and a detailed plan for investments and workforce reduction. The meeting was characterized by a high level of openness on the part of management. Such openness, unusual in Italian industrial relations, took the unions by surprise. In the end, after difficult negotiations, the plan was signed by all the parties on 25 May.

The final plan provided for a total reduction of the workforce by 4848 employees (the emergency phone number in Italy!) to be implemented over a three-year period (2850 in 1985, 850 in 1986, and 1100 in 1987) through early retirement and other incentives for voluntary exit. In 1985, as planned, the workforce was reduced by 2800.

Paradoxically, from the beginning of 1986 a new problem arose. With business doing well and export demands for some of the products strong, a number of factories had to resort to overtime work and even hired new skilled workers, whilst at the same time the original reduction plans continued to be implemented. Management claimed that there was no inconsistency in these actions since the people being laid off lacked the skills that would be needed in the future. With the prospect of factory automation clearly on the horizon, a more educated and skilled workforce was necessary and the new hires conformed to these future needs. Some of the workers resisted, and a series of strikes followed at the Porcia plant.

Management decided to force the issue and brought out advertisements in the local press to highlight the situation publicly. In the new industrial climate in Italy, the strategy proved effective and the strikes ended. In 1987 the company made further progress in its relationship with the unions. In a new agreement, wage increases were linked to productivity and no limits were placed on workforce reductions. Further, it was agreed that the company could hire almost 1000 workers on a temporary basis, so as to take advantage of the subsidy provided by the government to stimulate worker training through temporary employment. It was clear that Zanussi management benefited significantly from the loss of union power that was a prominent feature of the recently changed industrial scene in Italy. However, its open and transparent approach also contributed to the success by gaining the respect of trade union leaders, both at company and national levels.

Strategic transformation: building competitiveness

The new management recognized that, in order to build durable competitive advantage, more basic changes were necessary. The poor financial performance of the company before the acquisition was only partly due to low productivity, and sustainable profits could not be assured through workforce reduction alone. After careful analysis, three areas were chosen as the focal points for a strategic transformation of Zanussi: improving production technology; spurring innovations and new product development; and enhancing product quality.

Improving production technology   Recalling his first visit to Zanussi, Halvar Johansson, then head of Electrolux's technical R&D, commented: 'What we found on entering Zanussi's factories was, in many respects, 1960s technology! The level of automation was far too low, especially in assembly operation. We did not find a single industrial robot or even a computer either in the product development unit or in the plant. However, we also discovered that Zanussi's engineers and production personnel were of notably high standards.' As part of a broad programme to improve production technology, Electrolux initiated an investment programme of L.340 billion to restructure Zanussi's two major plants at Susegana and Porcia.

The Susegana restructing proposal foresaw an investment of L.100 billion to build up the facility into a highly automated, high-capacity unit able to produce 1.2 million refrigerators and freezers a year. The project was expected to come on stream by the end of 1988. The Porcia project anticipated a total investment of about L.200 billion to build a highly automated, yet flexible plant capable of producing 1.5 million washing machines per year. This project, scheduled for completion in 1990, was the largest individual investment project in the history of the Electrolux group. When on stream it would be the largest washing-machine factory in the world. Both projects involved large investments to build flexibility through the use of CAD–CAM systems and just-in-time production methodology. As explained by Carlo Verri, 'The automation was primarily to achieve flexibility and to improve quality, and not to save on labour costs'.

Implementation of both projects was somewhat delayed. While the initial schedules may have been over-optimistic, some of the delays were caused by friction among Zanussi and Electrolux engineers. The Electrolux approach of building joint teams for implementation of projects was seen by some Zanussi managers as excessive involvement of the acquiring company in tasks for which the acquired company had ample and perhaps superior capabilities. Consequently, information flows were often blocked, resulting in, for example, a more than one-year delay in deciding the final layout of the Susegana factory. The delays were a matter of considerable concern to the top management of Electrolux. On the one hand, they felt extensive involvement of Electrolux's internal consultants to be necessary for effective implementation of the projects, since Zanussi lacked the requisite expertise. On the other hand, they acknowledged Zanussi's well-established engineering skills and the need to provide local engineers with the opportunity to learn and to prove themselves. They also worried about whether the skill-levels of the local workforce could be upgraded in time for operating the new units, and looked for ways to expedite the training process.

Innovation and new product development Zanussi had built its strong market presence on the reputation of being an innovator. This ability had, unfortunately, languished during the lean period. Both Rossignolo and Verri placed the greatest emphasis on reviving the innovative spirit of the company, and projects that had idled for years due to lack of funds were revitalized and assigned high priority.

The results were quite dramatic and a virtual torrent of new product ideas emerged very quickly. The most striking example was a new washing-machine design – the 'Jet System' – that cut detergent and water consumption by a third. The product was developed within only nine months and the new machine was presented at the Cologne fair in February 1986. Through a direct television link with Cologne, Carlo Verri himself presented the assembly line at Pordenone where the Jet-System was to be mass produced. By July 1986, demand for the new machine had reached the level of 250 000 per year and the company was facing delivery problems.

While the Jet System was the most visible outcome of the new emphasis on innovation, other equally important developments were in the pipeline. For example, the company developed a new rotary compressor to replace the reciprocating compressors that were being used in refrigerators. A major drive was also underway to improve product design and features through the introduction of integrated circuit (IC) chips. Interestingly, most of these proposals came not from the sophisticated and independent research centre of the company, but from development groups located within the line organizations which produced the products. How to maintain the momentum of innovation was a major concern for Verri, particularly as the company moved into the larger and more complex projects necessary for significant technological breakthroughs.

Enhancing product quality   Quality enhancement was viewed as the third leg of the strategy for long-term revitalization of Zanussi. At Electrolux, high quality was viewed as an essential means of achieving the primary objectives of the company: satisfied customers; committed employees; and sound profitability. Zanussi had a good reputation for quality, but the standards had slackened during the turmoil faced by the company for almost a decade prior to the acquisition. Committed to the policy that quality levels must be the same within the group no matter where a product was produced, Electrolux initiated a major drive to enhance product quality at Zanussi and set extremely ambitious targets to reduce failure rates and post-sales service requirements. The targets were such that incremental improvements did not suffice for their attainment and a new approach towards quality was necessary. The technical staff of Electrolux provided requisite guidance and assistance and helped set up the parameters for a series of quality improvement programmes launched by Zanussi.

Carlo Verri was involved in these programmes on an almost day-to-day basis. First, he headed the working group that set up the basic policy on quality for the entire Zanussi organization. In accordance with this policy, a total quality (TQ) project was started in May 1986 and a series of education and training programmes were introduced in order to diffuse the new philosophy and policy to all company employees. Supplier involvement was an integral part of the TQ project. As described by Verri:

Supplier involvement was crucial. Zanussi's suppliers had to demonstrate their commitment to effective quality control. This meant that all the procedures for quality assurance, for tracking down failures etc., had to be approved by us. In other words, suppliers had to have the capability to provide self-certification for the quality of their products. They had to provide service within days rather than weeks, given that our plants were becoming automated. Our gains in flexibility and quality through new production techniques could be lost if the suppliers did not become equally efficient.

Organizational revitalization: changing attitudes

One of the biggest challenges faced in the turnaround process lay in the area of revitalizing the Zanussi organization. During the troubled years the management process at Zanussi had suffered from many aberrations. Conflicts had become a way of life, and information flow within the organization had become severely constrained. Most issues were escalated to the top for arbitration, and the middle management had practically no role in decision making. Front-line managers had become alienated because of direct dealings between the workers and senior managers via the union leaders. Overall, people had lost faith in the integrity of the system, in which seniority and loyalty to individuals were seen as more important than competence or commitment to the company.

In addition, the acquisition had also created a strong barrier of defensiveness within the Zanussi organization. In its own acquisitions Zanussi typically eliminated most of the middle management in the acquired companies. As the acquired company it expected similar actions from Electrolux. Moreover, some Zanussi managers were not convinced of any need for change. They believed that Zanussi's financial problems were caused not by any strategic, operational or organizational shortcomings, but by the practices of the previous owners, including diversion of overseas profits through a foreign holding company in Luxembourg. Finally, most of the managers were also concerned that both Rossignolo and Verri, with their backgrounds in the Italian subsidiary of a Swedish company, 'were closer to Stockholm than to Pordenone'.

In an attempt to overcome these barriers, Verri and the entire executive management group at Zanussi participated in a number of team-building sessions that were facilitated by an external consultant. These meetings gave rise to a number of developments that constituted the core of the organizational revitalization of Zanussi.

Statement of mission, values, and guiding principles   One of the direct outcomes of the team-building meetings was a statement of mission, values, and guiding principles, developed to serve as the charter for change (see Exhibit 3). The statement identified the four main values of the company: to be close to the clients and satisfy them through innovation and service; to accept challenges and develop a leader

Exhibit 3   Mission values and guiding principles of Zanussi.

Mission

To become the market leader in Europe, with a significant position in other world areas, in supplying homes, institutions, and industry with systems, appliances, components and after-sales services.

To be successful in this mission, the company and management legitimization must be based on the capability to be near the customer and satisfy his needs; to demonstrate strength, entrepreneurship, and creativity in accepting and winning external challenges; to offer total quality on all dimensions, more than the competition; and to be oriented to an internal vision and engagement.

Values

Our basic values, ranked, are:

1. To be near the customer;
2. To accept challenges;
3. To deliver total quality;
4. With an international perspective.

Our central value, underlying all of the above, is transparence, which means that Zanussi will reward behaviour which is based on constantly transparent information and attitudes, safeguarding the interests of the company.

Guiding principles

1. A management group is legitimized by knowing what we want, pursuing it coherently, and communicating our intent in order to be believable.
2. Shared communication means shared responsibility, not power and status index.
3. The manager's task is managing through information and motivation, not by building 'power islands'.
4. Time is short: the world will not wait for our 'perfect solutions'.
5. Strategic management implies:

- professional skills;
- risk-taking attitudes and the skill to spot opportunity;
- integration with the environment and the organization, flexibility and attention to change;
- identification with the mission of the firm, and helping in the evolution of a culture that supports it;
- team work ability;
- skill in identifying strengths and weaknesses.

Policies to be developed

Specific policies were being developed in the following areas to support the implementation of the above mission, values and guiding principles: personnel, image and public relations, administration, purchasing, asset control, legal representation, R&D and innovation, and information systems. Members of senior management were assigned responsibility for developing policies in each of these areas, with completion expected by the end of 1986.

mentality; to pursue total quality not only in production but in all areas of activity; and to become a global competitor by developing an international outlook. Apart from these specific points, the statement also confirmed the new management's commitment to creating a context that would foster transparent and coherent behaviour at both the individual and company levels under all circumstances. As described by Rossignolo: 'We adopted the Swedish work ethic – everybody keeps his word and all information is correct. We committed ourselves to being honest with the local authorities, the trade unions and our customers. It took some time for the message to get across, but I think everybody has got it now.'

Management development workshops   In order to improve the flow of information among senior managers and to co-opt them into the new management approach, a set of management development workshops was organized. The 60 most senior managers of Zanussi, including Verri, participated in each of three two-day workshops that were held between November 1985 and July 1986. The next tier of 150 middle managers of the company were subsequently exposed to the same programme.

Middle management problems   An organizational climate survey in 1987 revealed an interesting problem. The top 60 managers of the company confirmed strong support for the mission statement and the new management style. Conversely, the 150 middle managers, who seemed to feel threatened by the changes, appeared considerably less enthused. Their subordinates – approximately 1000 front-line managers and professional employees – like the top management, fully approved the change and demanded greater involvement. In response to this problem, it was decided that the 60 top managers should establish direct communication with the 1000 front-line managers, bypassing the middle management when necessary. The decision was made known within the organization and a clear signal was sent to the middle managers that they should 'get on board' or else they would risk 'missing the boat'. At the same time, a special training programme was launched for the front-line managers and professional employees in order to broaden their management skills and outlook.

Structural reorganization   Before the acquisition, Zanussi was organized in five 'sectors', with the heads of each sector reporting to the managing director. The sectors, in turn, controlled the operating companies in their business areas. In practice, the sector managers were closely involved with the day-to-day operations of the companies under their charge. Both the managing director at the corporate level and the different sector managers had strong staff organizations to support their activities.

Verri abandoned the sector concept, even though the operating companies continued to report to the former sector managers who were now called managing directors. However, staff at the sector level were virtually eliminated and the operating companies were given full responsibility and authority for taking all operating-level decisions. Similarly, staff at the corporate level were also reduced very substantially, and the heads of planning, finance and control, organization and human resources, general administration, and legal and public affairs all reported directly to Verri. The four managing directors, the five heads of major corporate staff departments, and Verri constituted the executive management group of Zanussi. As Chairman, Rossignolo concentrated primarily on external relations.

Integration of the two companies

As described by Leif Johansson, 'With the acquisition of Zanussi, the Electrolux group entered a new era. In several respects we were able to adopt a completely new way of thinking'. Much of the new thinking emerged from the discussions and recommendations of the task forces that had been appointed, involving managers from both companies, to look at specific opportunities for integrating the activities of the two organizations. In total, eight such task forces were formed: two each for components, product development, and commercial appliances; and one each for the marketing function and management development. Each of these task forces had met three to four times, typically for half a day each time. Their recommendations formed the basis for the actions that were taken to integrate the production and sales operations of the two companies, rationalize component production, and develop specialization in product and brand development within the entire Electrolux group. At the level of individuals, a bridge had been built between the top management of Electrolux and the senior management team of Zanussi, and further actions were underway for creating similar understanding and mutual respect among managers lower down in the two organizations.

Electrolux Components Group (ECG)

Following Electrolux's acquisition of White Consolidated in the US in March 1986, an international task force consisting of managers from Electrolux, White, and Zanussi was created to explore the overall synergies that could be exploited within the activities of the three companies. The task force concluded that integration opportunities were relatively limited at the level of finished products because of factors such as differences in customer preferences and technical standards, and the high transportation costs. However, at the component level there were many similarities in the needs of the three companies, implying greater scope for standardization and production rationalization. As a result of this analysis, ECG was formed at the beginning of 1987 as part of the newly created industrial products division at Electrolux. The group was made responsible for the co-ordination and development of all strategic components used by Electrolux worldwide. Since over 50% of the

Exhibit 4 Electrolux Group: key data.

1. Group sales and employees worldwide

Nordic Countries

	Sales (Skr.m)	No of employees
Sweden	11 128	29 456
Denmark	1 735	3 078
Norway	1 505	1 299
Finland	1 445	1 563
	15 813	35 396

North America

	Sales (Skr.m)	No of employees
USA	19 488	29 750
Canada	1 580	2 150
	21 068	31 900

Rest of Europe

	Sales (Skr.m)	No of employees
Great Britain	6 377	10 589
France	5 098	8 753
West Germany	4 045	3 317
Italy	3 684	15 282
Switzerland	1 818	1 814
Spain	1 445	2 851
Netherlands	1 238	1 016
Belgium and Luxembourg	913	1 040
Austria	392	958
Portugal	96	193
Others	604	41
	25 710	45 854

Latin America

	Sales (Skr.m)	No of employees
Brazil	302	6 215
Venezuela	208	1 032
Peru	181	750
Colombia	104	1 865
Mexico	66	1 735
Ecuador	34	232
Guatemala	24	31
Others	443	198
	1 362	12 058

Asia

	Sales (Skr.m)	No of employees
Japan	707	1 175
Saudi Arabia	215	738
Hong Kong	152	1 340
Philippines	150	525
Kuwait	147	2 220
Taiwan	119	2 178
Malaysia	72	1 833
Thailand	56	15
Singapore	50	556
Jordan	28	137
Lebanon	22	35
Others	720	1 729
	2 438	12 481

Africa

	Sales (Skr.m)	No of employees
	414	

Oceania

	Sales (Skr.m)	No of employees
Australia	497	2 216
New Zealand	114	557
Others	14	—
	625	2 773
Total	67 016	140 462

group's component production came from Zanussi, Verri was appointed head of this group in addition to his responsibilities as Managing Director of Zanussi; the group headquarters were located in Turin, Italy. In order to preserve and enhance the competitiveness of the component sector, it was decided that 50% of the component group's sales must be made to outside parties and at least 20% of the internal requirement for components must be sourced from outside the newly formed group.

Exhibit 4 *continued*

2. Sales by business area

	1987 (Skr.m)	1986 (Skr.m)	1985 (Skr.m)	% of total (1987 sales)
Household appliances	39 487	31 378	19 200	58.6
Commercial appliances	5 619	4 250	3 348	8.3
Commercial services	2 893	2 504	2 266	4.3
Outdoor products	4 475	2 909	2 990	6.6
Industrial products	11 784	9 087	9 232	17.5
Building components	3 172	2 962	2 652	4.7
Total	67 430	53 090	39 688	100.0

3. Operating income after depreciation by business area

	1987 (Skr.m)	1986 (Skr.m)	1985 (Skr.m)	% of total (1987 sales)
Household appliances	2 077	1 947	1 589	49.2
Commercial appliances	484	349	260	11.4
Commercial services	169	172	132	4.0
Outdoor products	421	241	373	10.0
Industrial products	910	474	657	21.5
Building components	164	138	126	3.9
Total	4 225	3 321	3 137	100.0

Integration of production

At Electrolux, production, sales, and marketing had traditionally been integrated market by market. After the acquisition of Zanussi, all these activities were reorganized into international product divisions and national marketing/sales companies.

The larger volumes from the combined operations made it feasible to switch to a system in which large-scale specialized plants, equipped with flexible manufacturing technology, would each produce a single product for the entire European market. This new 'one product–one factory' strategy was exemplified by the new plants in Susegana and Porcia. Each of the product divisions carried full responsibility not only for manufacturing, but also for development and internal marketing of their products. In order to co-ordinate long-term development among these 43 divisions, three co-ordinators were appointed for 'wet', 'hot', and 'cold' products respectively. Based in Stockholm without staff, each of these co-ordinators would be on the road most of the time.

Integration of sales/marketing

Similarly, it was decided to create single umbrella companies over the separate sales/marketing organizations in all countries. Given the long-standing history of competition between the Electrolux and Zanussi organizations, this would turn out to be a difficult and complex process.

It was planned that in each country the stronger organization would absorb the weaker one. This did not mean, however, that the head of the larger organization in each country would automatically receive the top slot in the combined organization. A number of complaints arose on both sides over this issue, which became a source of much irritation. For example, it was because of this that Candotti, who had been the first to approach Electrolux for investment in Zanussi, resigned. In what remained a source of considerable frustration, Zanussi continued to operate through directly controlled sales companies in Germany, France, Denmark, and Norway.

Co-ordination among the marketing companies was achieved through an equally lean co-ordinating structure reporting to Leif Johansson, with an Italian manager co-ordinating all European countries and a Swedish manager looking after the rest of the world.

To facilitate operational co-ordination between sales and production, a number of new systems were developed. One, the Electrolux Forecasting and Supply System (EFS), involved the automatic co-ordination of sales forecasts and delivery orders. By 1988 computer links with EFS would be established in all European Sales subsidiaries and factories. The Zanussi evaluation system was changed to that of Electrolux, in which both sales and factories were assessed on the basis of return on net assets (RONA) rather than on a profit and cost basis. An overall RONA target of 20% was set for the group as a whole.

Brand positioning and product development

One of the consequences of Electrolux's history of international expansion through acquisitions was a proliferation of brands, not only in Europe but also in the US, where the acquisition of White had brought a number of brands. The task of co-ordinating these brands, some of which were local, others regional, and a few international, would fall to the two marketing co-ordinators, working closely with Leif Johansson and a task force involving product styling and marketing managers. The challenge was complicated by the fact that even the international brands did not always have the same position from market to market. Zanussi, for example, was not a brand name in Italy itself, where its products sold as 'Rex'. And its image in Sweden was not nearly as up-market and innovative as in other countries, for example the UK.

The approach chosen in Europe was to group the brands in four brand-name families, each targeted at a particular customer profile and destined to become a separate design family (see Exhibit 5). Two of these families would be international brands, based respectively on Electrolux and Zanussi and the other two would regroup a number of local brands (see Exhibit 6). The goal was to develop an integrated pan-European strategy for each brand-name family. For the international brands, the strategy would involve high-scale production of standardized products in focused factories and co-ordinated positioning and marketing across different

Exhibit 5   The four Electrolux brand-name family groups.

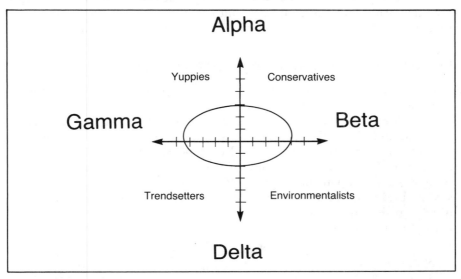

Exhibit 6   The Electrolux brand-name families.

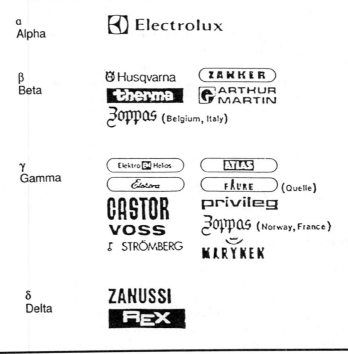

countries. For the families representing a collection of national brands, the products would again be standardized as far as possible so as to allow manufacturing on a regional scale; but each brand would be 'localized' in its country through positioning, distribution, promotion, and service.

Mutual respect and understanding among people

Since the acquisition Anders Scharp, Lennart Ribohn, and Leif Johansson had ensured that they jointly visited Pordenone at least once every two months for a two-day review of Zanussi's activities and progress. Hans Werthén and Gösta Bystedt also visited Zanussi, though much less frequently. The visitors would typically spend some time touring one or another of Zanussi's facilities and then move on to pre-planned meetings with Zanussi's top management. Over time these meetings had built a strong bridge of mutual respect between the two groups and helped diffuse some of the early apprehensions. As described by a senior manager of Zanussi:

> The top management of Electrolux really understands numbers. They look at a few key numbers and immediately grasp the essentials. That was very good training for us – we had the habit of analyzing and analyzing, without coming to any conclusions... Besides, the top two or three people in Electrolux have the ability of immersing themselves in a particular problem and coming up with a solution and an implementation plan. They are also so obviously excited by what they do, their enthusiasm is very contagious.

For most senior managers at Zanussi these meetings provided stronger evidence than could any words that the top management of Electrolux did not consider the acquisition as a conquest but rather as a partnership. 'We have had a lot of exchanges, and have learnt a lot from them, but we have not had a single Swedish manager imposed on top of us here.'

At the next level of management the joint task forces had helped build some relationships among individuals, but the links were still weak and apprehensions remained. 'We don't know them, but our concern is that the next level of Electrolux managers may be more bureaucratic and less open. To them we might be a conquest,' said a senior manager of Zanussi. 'In the next phase of integration, we must develop bridges at the middle and I frankly do not know how easy or difficult that might be.'

Future requirements

Whereas the acquisition of Zanussi and White Consolidated had catapulted Electrolux into a clear lead in the industry, the race was far from over. After initially failing to reach agreement with Philips in 1987, Whirlpool had come back in early 1988 agreeing to buy out 53% of Philips' appliance operations as a first step to taking full control. Upon full completion Whirlpool would have paid or assumed debt totalling

$1.2 billion for activities which in 1987 were generating $70 million pre-tax, pre-interest income on sales of $2 billion. The Japanese had started moving outside South East Asia. In the meantime, local European competitors such as GEC and Merloni were ensuring good returns and, more importantly, were gaining back market share.

All of this was taking place in a mature industry highly dependent on replacement demand. Industry analysts expected that, even in a moderately growing economy, appliance shipments would be 'on a downward trend for the next couple of years. Given the concentration of buyers and the shift toward specialized retailers, raw materials price increases were more and more difficult to pass on.

SUGGESTED QUESTIONS

1. How would you describe the key characteristics of Electrolux and Zanussi in 1983, in terms of their strategy, organization, capabilities, and performance?
2. As Leif Johansson, would you have recommended the Zanussi acquisition in 1983?
3. What lessons, if any, do you draw from Electrolux's approach to acquisition decision making?
4. What lessons, if any, do you draw from Electrolux's approach to acquisition integration? What would you have done differently?
5. What strategic and organizational challenges remain for Electrolux in 1988? What are the main options?
6. What should Leif Johansson do now?

GEC plc (A)

Case written by Tony Eccles

INTRODUCTION

GEC is a federation of over 160 operationally independent subsidiary companies, known as units, each unit engaging its own employees, investing in its own equipment, developing its own products, and selling its goods in the open market (see Exhibit 1). Less than 7% of GEC's turnover has been traded between GEC units.

In the year ending March 1987, GEC had a turnover of £5939 million (£5969m in 1986), including £384 million intra-group sales and a £308 million share of sales of associated companies. Turnover included £1291 million of exports from the United Kingdom. GEC's order book at March 1987 totalled £6050 million. (See Exhibit 2.)

The number of employees worldwide totalled 160 000, of whom 122 000 worked in the UK (see Exhibit 3). Pre-tax profits were £692 million compared to £701 million in 1986 and £725 million in 1985. In March 1987, GEC's cash and current asset investments amounted to £1697 million, an increase of £203 million during the year whilst net assets per share were 108p.

In 1986/87 GEC spent £620 million on research and development (R&D) including £330 million of its own resources. GEC has 18 000 people engaged in R&D (over 2000 at its central laboratories). It also invested £251 million on capital expenditure (with depreciation of £213m).

The GEC headquarters is a small, unobtrusive building in London's West End – not much bigger than the houses nearby. Less than one in a thousand of GEC's 160 000 people work there. The headquarter's personnel department employs eight people. There is no corporate planning department.

Exhibit 1   GEC: principal subsidiary companies.

The English Electric Company, Ltd*
Associated Electrical Industries*
The Marconi Company Ltd
GEC–Elliott Automation Ltd

Electronic Systems and Components

Systems
GEC Avionics Ltd – The Marconi
   Company Ltd
      Dr J G MacBean[‡]
      W H Alexander
   Navigation Group   P A Hearne
   Dynamics Group   P L W Howard
   Sensors Group   W R Paterson
   Airborne Radar Group   D J Fletcher
   GEC Avionics Inc, USA   W Broyles
   Marconi Command and Control
      Systems Ltd   K P Robinson
   Marconi Defence Systems Ltd
      D J Fletcher
   Marconi Space Systems Ltd
      W R Wignall
   Marconi Underwater Systems Ltd
      A A Bodnar
   Marconi Radar Systems Ltd
      D A H Chenery
   Marconi Communication Systems Ltd
      A J Glasgow
   Marconi Instruments Ltd
      Dr C S Gaskell[‡]
   Easams Ltd   A H Cairns
   The Marconi International Marine Co
      Ltd   G G Hill
   Canadian Marconi Company (51.6%
      Ordinary)   P E Wheatley
   Marconi Italiana SpA, Italy
      Dr R Piccini
   Cincinnati Electronics Corporation,
      USA   D G Dwyre
   Norsk Marconi A/S, Norway
      T W Bratlie
   Yarrow Shipbuilders Ltd*
      R W S Easton
   GEC Australia Ltd (Electronics Group)
      R G Elliot

Automation and Control
GEC Electrical Projects Ltd*   J A
Davies
GEC Industrial Controls Ltd*
      D W Prowse
   GEC Automation Projects Inc, USA
W & T Avery Ltd   K H Hodgkinson[‡]
   Avery–Denison Ltd   N Young
   Driver Southall Ltd   B Bullock
   Avery Australia Ltd   A C Matthews
   Avery New Zealand Ltd   C F Stewart
   South African Scale Co (Pty) Ltd
      P Van Heyningen
Avery–Hardoll Ltd   J M Duncan
PM Services Ltd   I J Macmichael
GEC Measurements Ltd*   M A Hughes
GEC Meters Ltd   R Harpum
Satchwell Control Systems Ltd   C
Smyth
GEC Mechanical Handling Ltd
GEC Traffic Automation Ltd   P Gogerly
GEC Marine & Industrial Gears Ltd
      Dr P N Jackson
GEC Australia Ltd   R G Elliott
   (Automation, Projects and
   Construction Divisions)
The English Electric Company
   of India Ltd (66.7% Ordinary)
      E S Chandrasekaran
   (Relays and Control Panels Division)
GEC Composants SA, France   J Lorvin

Medical Equipment
Picker International Inc, USA
      J N Williams
   Picker International Ltd
      A W L Mandy

Power Generation
GEC Turbine Generators Ltd
      R J Davidson[†‡]
   GEC Energy Systems Ltd
      J D Mowat
Ruston Gas Turbines Ltd   K A Bray[‡]
   GEC Diesels Ltd   Dr H J Perkins
      Ruston Diesels Ltd
      J M MacKinnon

Exhibit 1 *Continued*

Components
Marconi Electronic Devices Ltd
  A J Sadler
Circuit Technology Inc, USA
  B D Hunts
English Electric Valve Co Ltd
  M P Mandl
  The M-O Valve Co Ltd*   *P C Ruggles*
EEV Inc, USA   *P Plurien*
EEV Canada Ltd   *D Clissold*
Salford Electrical Instruments Ltd*
GEC Ceramics Ltd   *Dr R M Henson*

Telecommunications and Business Systems
GEC Telecommunications Ltd*
  R G Reynolds†‡
  Switching Division   *A J Snoad*
  Networks Systems Division
    G W Head
  Private Systems and Defence
    Systems Divisions   *B A Meade*
  Telephone Division   *T P Lowry*
  GEC Reliance Ltd*   *O Lamont*
GEC Computers Ltd   *P Rayner*
GEC Software Ltd   *D Alway*
Telephone Cables Ltd (74.5% Ordinary)
  M J Spoor
A B Dick Company, USA   *D Powell*†
  Videojet Systems International Inc,
    USA   *H Bode*
  Scriptomatic Inc, USA   *T O Moseley*
GEC New Zealand Ltd
(Telecommunications Division)
  J A Carter

Electrical Equipment
Power Distribution Group   *J D Gadd*‡
  GEC Switchgear Ltd
  GEC Distribution Switchgear Ltd
    A Baxter
  GEC Transmission and Distribution
    Projects Ltd   *K J Ralls*
  Vacuum Interrupters Ltd   *N Scoular*
  Vynckier NV, Belgium   *M Steyaert*
  GEC Transformers Ltd   *J V Grant*
  The Micanite & Insulators Company
    Ltd   *C J Salt*
The General Electric Company
  of India Ltyd (66.7% Ordinary)
    H. Singh

Power Generation *continued*
  Paxman Diesels Ltd   *J G Fryer*
  Kelvin Diesels Ltd   *A Whitehead*
  Société des Moteurs Baudouin SA
    France (99.6% Ordinary)
    A Lacroix
  Napier Turbochargers Ltd
    A J H Richardson
Ruston Gas Turbines Inc, USA
  J F Paull
GEC Diesels Inc, Canada   *J H Edlund*
GEC Australia Ltd (Diesels Division)
  R G Elliot

Distribution and Trading
Walsall Conduits Ltd   *D Wilson*
  GEC Distributors (Ireland) Ltd
    W P Browne
The English Electric Corporation, USA
  P Jancek
GEC Australia Ltd   *R G Elliot*
  (Lighting and Wholesale Divisions)
GEC (New Zealand) Ltd*   *J A Carter*
  (Wholesale and Consumer Products
  Division)
The General Electric Company
  of Bangladesh Ltd* (60% Ordinary)
    M S Haque
GEC Canada Ltd   *R D Merer*

Exhibit 1 *continued*

Electrical Equipment *continued*

The English Electric Company
  of India Ltd (66.7% Ordinary)
    E S Chandrasekaran
  (Fusegear and Switchgear Division)
GEC Australia Ltd *R G Elliot*
  (Heavy engineering and Industrial
  Products Divisions)
Wire & Cables Group *O S Johnson*[‡]
  AEI Cables Ltd
    Power Cables *L M Sloman*
    Rubber and Plastic Cables
    K Bennett
  F D Sims Ltd *H Stevenson*
  Kent Electric Wire Ltd *A J Taylor*
  Rodco Ltd (60% Ordinary) *I Stuttard*
  Vactite Ltd *A G Hickey*
GEC Traction Ltd *K Applebee*
  GEC Transportation Projects Ltd
    B McCann
GEC–General Signal Ltd (50%
Ordinary) *M L Boden*
GEC Large Machines Ltd *D R Edwards*
GEC Small Machines Ltd *R W Powell*
The Express Lift Co Ltd* *M L Dove*
Woods of Colchester Ltd* *D J Priest*
GEC Engineering (Accrington) Ltd
  M F Price
GEC Reinforced Plastics Ltd
  R Wolfendale
GEC Foundries Ltd *E Booth*
A G Hackney & Co Ltd *N L Wright*
L H Marthinusen (Pvt) Ltd, Zimbabwe
  C M Meek
GEC (New Zealand) Ltd* *J A Carter*
  (Industrial Machines and Power
  Engineering Divisions)

Consumer Products

Hotpoint Ltd *J E Samson*[‡]
  GEC (Radio & Television) Ltd
    D Swannack
  Redring Electric Ltd *M R Johnston*
  Cannon Industries Ltd *D Scahill*
GEC–Xpelair Ltd* *D J Blythe*
OSRAM–GEC Ltd* (51% Ordinary)
  R Sansom

Distribution and Trading *continued*

The General Electric Company
  of Hong Kong Ltd* *J Chiu*
The General Electric Company of
  Singapore Private Ltd* *S K Chan*
GEC Zambia Ltd*
GEC Zambibwe (Pvt) Ltd* *C M Meek*

Research

Research *Dr C Hilsum*
GEC Research Ltd *Dr J C Williams*

[†] Directors of The General Electric
Company, plc
[‡] Members of the UK Board of Management

1. The General Electric Company, plc
(GEC) (and/or a subsidiary or subsidiaries
in aggregate) owns 100% of each class of
the issued shares of the subsidiaries except
where a smaller proportion and the class is
indicated. Shares in companies marked with
an asterisk (*) are owned directly by GEC,
and in companies not so marked are owned
by a subsidiary or subsidiaries of GEC.

2. Companies are incorporated and
registered and operate in Great Britain, or,
in the case of overseas companies, in the
country indicated. The General Electric
Company of Hong Kong Ltd is registered in
England.

3. The list of subsidiaries includes
management companies and those which
had a material effect on the consolidated
results to 31 March 1987.

Exhibit 2   GEC: statistical information, 1978–87 (year end 31 March).

	1987 (£m)	1986 (£m)	1985 (£m)	1984 (£m)	1983 (£m)	1982 (£m)	1981 (£m)	1980 (£m)	1979 (£m)	1978 (£m)
Sales	5247	5253	5222	4800	4626	4189	3462	3006	2501	2343
Profit before taxation	668	701	725	671	670	584	476	416	378	325
Earnings per share*	15.8p	16.0p	14.9p	14.2p	14.2p	13.0p	10.9p	9.1p	7.8p	5.7p
Ordinary dividends	141	115	107	95	82	70	56	45	34	22
per share	5.30p	4.30p	4.00p	3.45p	3.00p	2.55p	2.05p	1.65p	1.25p	0.81p
Profit retained	294	338	308	316	312	292	272	209	219	133

* Excludes net credits for extraordinary items.

	1987	1986	1985	1984	1983	1982	1981	1980	1979	1978
Fixed assets	828	809	764	697	672	611	552	480	351	318
Investments	109	91	105	126	242	225	194	187	179	85
Inventories	1335	1275	1265	1129	1098	1055	944	795	621	589
Debtors	1434	1353	1258	1163	1047	913	873	748	569	526
Net cash and short-term investments	1730	1527	1414	1559	1319	1041	661	599	730	617
	5436	5055	4806	4674	4378	3845	3224	2809	2450	2135
Liabilities	2406	2292	2263	2215	1946	1705	1419	1225	1027	938
	3030	2763	2543	2459	2432	2140	1805	1584	1423	1197
Financed by:										
Shareholders' interest	2895	2614	2389	2239	2098	1793	1441	1188	1039	858
Loan capital	47	68	75	166	262	286	313	350	345	300
Loan capital	88	81	79	54	72	61	51	46	39	39
	3030	2763	2543	2459	2432	2140	1805	1584	1423	1197
Net assets per share	108.8p	98.0p	89.4p	81.5p	76.5p	65.4p	52.5p	43.3p	37.9p	31.3p

Note:
1 There was a capital repayment to shareholders in November 1982 amounting to £82 million.
2 £167 million of shareholders' funds unlisted in purchasing for cancellation 79 604 067 ordinary 5 p shares of the Company during the two years ended 31 March 1986.

The headquarters offers expert advice on a topics such as contract law, export finance, product licensing, trade marks, taxation, and industrial relations – units are free to seek this advice if they wish. Headquarters also controls the central R&D laboratories, though units also engage in their own research and development. Much of GEC's expenditure on R&D is externally funded research – notably on defence contracts for the British and other governments – though a proportion is for private venture.

The role of GEC's headquarters can be substantial where large overseas contracts are involved. It also liaises with the British government on such matters. Power stations, telecommunication systems, and overseas defence contracts often involve government to government negotiations as well as the packaging of the financial arrangements for the contract.

The GEC headquarters acts as a banker to the units and it controls cash, capital investment plans, and acquisitions. Each unit presents an annual budget plan for the operating year ahead. Starting in the autumn and continuing until near the year-end of 31 March, each unit's managers have to debate the merits of its forthcoming plan with some GEC directors. Whatever the outcome of that meeting, the unit remains solely responsible for the plan's fulfilment and is left to achieve – or beat – its budget in the way it thinks best.

Every month, each unit's managing director sends headquarters a management report on the key components of its operations – some 30

Exhibit 3   GEC: notes to the accounts.

1. Principal activities,
   profit contributions and
   markets

Analysis of results by classes of business

| Employees | | | Profit | | Turnover | |
1987 (thousands)	1986 (thousands)		1987 (£m)	1986 (£m)	1987 (£m)	1986 (£m)
59	58	Electronic systems and components	198.0	206.1	2016	1949
19	21	Telecommunications and business systems	93.8	84.2	749	773
16	17	Automation and control	45.4	47.2	457	444
6	6	Medical equipment	26.0	22.2	398	420
14	15	Power generation	49.9	58.3	594	638
28	29	Electrical equipment	51.3	43.0	723	770
10	10	Consumer products	34.6	33.4	387	331
4	4	Distribution and trading	12.4	13.1	202	209
4	5	Other activities	4.4	4.0	105	128
160	165		515.8	511.5	5631	5662
		Income receivable, less interest payment, from loans, deposits, and investments*	162.5	181.4		
		Associated companies	14.1	11.3	308	307
			692.4	704.2	5939	5969

Note:
* Includes profits on sale of equities of £4.4 million (1986 £34.4 million).

figures in all. These include sales, order intake, exports, remuneration and wage rates, numbers of direct and indirect employees, overhead spend, bank balance, debtors, creditors, inventory, capital employed, etc. – each compared with budget and with the previous years' achievements. It is accompanied by a monthly commentary, together with the figures for GEC's seven key ratios (see Exhibit 4).

GEC has no divisional organization and many units report directly to one director at headquarters. There are a few senior managers who each control a group of similar businesses and some of these group managing directors are on GEC's main board. From time to time, individual units were reallocated as the shape of GEC's operations developed, but this organizational system was used without major revision throughout the 1970s and early 1980s.

In 1984 GEC formed a 26-strong UK Board of Management (chaired

Exhibit 4   A GEC unit budget 1984/85.

		1982/83 Actual	1983/84 Forecast	1984/85 Budget
Net profit/sales	%			
Sales/capital employed				
Net profit/capital employed	%			
Sales/gross inventories				
Sales/net inventories				
Sales debtors				
Sales per employee	£K			
Added value per £1 of employee costs				

Index
Schedule

Schedule		Schedule	
1	Ratios	7	Cash flow trend
2	Salient figures	8	Provisions
3	Capital employed trend	9	Orders and commitments
4	Managing director's report	10	Research and development expenditure
5	Profit and loss account		
5A	Details of other income and expenditure	11	Capital expenditure
		12	Manpower
5B	Special items	13	Utilisation of resources – units
6	Summary of unit overhead account	14	Utilisation of resources – cost

Date of issue:

RATIOS

BUDGET 1984/85   SCHEDULE 1

UNIT

by Lord Weinstock) to create a forum for discussing group-wide operational decisions. Only four of its 25 members were neither main board nor associate directors of GEC plc.

BACKGROUND

In 1961 GEC took over Radio and Allied Industries (Sobell), then very successful and run by the 36-year-old Arnold Weinstock. As a result of the takeover, the Sobell/Weinstock families held £5 million of GEC shares. Weinstock and his Radio and Allied accountant colleague, Kenneth Bond, joined GEC's board, stopped GEC's overdraft rising and began to put in the better systems which had controlled cash in Radio and Allied. Bond was one of the earliest practitioners of cash flow management and soon became GEC's Financial Director. Weinstock was placed in charge of one of GEC's four divisions and in 1963 became GEC's Managing Director.

The GEC of today was formed in 1968 when, after its strongly resisted takeover of AEI in 1967, GEC merged peacefully with English Electric. The merger had the blessing of the British government, then encouraging the building of giant companies which could export worldwide in effective competition with leading American and European enterprises. The new combination of GEC, AEI, and EE employed assets of over £1000 million; had annual sales approaching that level – including £300 million in exports – and employed 240 000 people. It was the fourth largest industrial company in Britain and, excluding US corporations, was second only to Siemens among the world's electrical companies.

Speed of decision and insistence on action from the decision were the immediate hallmarks of Weinstock's management team (see Exhibit 5). The branches were dissolved; large groups were broken down into individual business units, each required to budget ahead and to produce monthly reports. Executives who failed to perform were replaced. GEC profits nearly trebled in two years. In one year Arnold Weinstock had moved from managing one of the British electrical giants to managing all three, increasing GEC's equity from £57 million to £136 million and spending only £15.6 million in cash. GEC's sales had expanded from £180 million to £890 million a year. Weinstock's family interests were the biggest individual shareholding in the group.

In the middle of 1967 the three companies had 268 000 staff, 240 000 in 1968, and by mid-1971 this had dropped to 225 000 (not strictly comparable because of the acquisition and disposal of units). In 1978 the number employed was 191 000. The cuts gave GEC a reputation for harshness, but GEC always defended the cuts on the grounds that they secured the remaining jobs which would otherwise have later gone due to uncompetitive manning levels.

A book about this period concluded that:

Weinstock's style of management is very different from that of other giant companies such as ICI, Shell and Unilever. Their leadership is collective; Weinstock's is much more personal. He is not a one-man band; there are many talented men around him at headquarters, such as Kenneth Bond. He devolves a great deal of responsibility to the operating companies and some of them have very able managers. But essentially the continued efficiency of the whole group depends on Weinstock's personal abilities, his energy, his attention to detail, his ability to analyse the weak spots in a company's performance,

Exhibit 5   The General Electric and English Electric Companies.

Every company has its own style of management. There is a distinction between 'style' and 'system' because systems can be changed at will, while style depends on the natural and developed characteristics of the managers. I am writing this memorandum sooner rather than later so that we may have the best chance of starting our relationships in what will be for us the right way, and to explain some basic attitudes to the job.

At HQ, the management directors and I are responsible to Lord Nelson as chairman for the performance of the business overall. Kenneth Bond (deputy managing director), Sandy Riddell (joint deputy managing director) and I are helped and prodded by T B O Kerr, R H Grierson, Lord Trevelyan on overseas matters, by David Lewis on commercial, legal and administrative matters, by Sir Jack Scamp on industrial relations, and by Bill Bird on sales and suchlike. You will hear from all of them in due course on one matter or another. These compartments of activity are not rigidly defined and in fact most of the directors are more or less involved in all company affairs, as too may be the non-executive directors. The deputy chairman, Lord Aldington, plays a particularly important role, as well as deputizing for the chairman in his absence.

But the real success of our new company depends on the individual managing directors of our many products units. Our help (or lack of it) from HQ does not relieve you in the least of the responsibility for that part of the business which is in your charge. You will, of course, see that your sub-managers are given well defined, specific tasks and objectives and then discharge their duties effectively.

Our philosophy of personal responsibility makes it completely unnecessary for you to spend time at meetings of subsidiary boards or of standing committees. Therefore, all standing committees are by this direction disbanded and subsidiary boards will not need to meet again (except, perhaps, for statutory purposes once a year). If you wish to confer with colleagues, by all means do so; even set up again any committee you and the other members feel you must have for the good of the business. But remember that you will be held personally accountable for any decision taken affecting your operating unit. And also remember that you are not obliged to join any such gathering. Incidentally, on this matter of personal responsibility, prior permission from HQ is required for any proposal to employ management consultants.

The managing director of every operating unit is responsible to me. My duties may be discharged (i) by me; (ii) through the management directors at Stanhope Gate; (iii) in specified cases, through others situated at operating sites to whom responsibility is given for groups of businesses. You will have very considerable autonomy in the running of your unit, subject to certain controls of which you will receive details soon; these are largely financial, but monthly reports should cover everything of consequence concerning the business, including important technical matters.

Up to March 31st, 1969, you will continue to send your monthly reports to Mr Riddell, with a copy to me, please. These will be based on your present budgets.

During February 1969 we shall arrange to see you here with your budget for the year April 1st, 1969 to March 31st, 1970. You will hear more about its form in due course.

Exhibit 5 continued

There is the point at which this memorandum should stop. But at the risk of being boring, I think it desirable that I should add a few general remarks.

The justification for our existence is to satisfy the needs of consumers. That satisfaction has a certain value to them which can be assessed by comparison with other offers from our competitors to meet similar needs. In order to perform this task, we have to make use of resources, and this process involves cost. The difference between the two, the created surplus, is profit. Clearly, in a competitive economy we operate most efficiently and creatively when profit is optimized. There are several indices we shall ask you to use to measure efficiency, but, at the risk of over-simplification, we may say that profitability in relation to capital employed is the main one by which your performance will be measured.

It is said to be possible to maximize short-term profitability by omitting to do those things which are required for the survival of a business in the long term. It would be extremely stupid to follow such a course, particularly in industries such as those in which we participate. But that is not to say that money may be wasted in injudicious investment or recklessly conceived programmes of research. We must always be concerned with getting value for the company's money.

There will be, in the coming months, a full dialogue between us on all these and related matters. But there are some things which can be done now with advantage. Administrative, commercial and similar overheads are uniformly too high throughout the group. See where you can reduce them – and save any other expenses, as well. So too, are stocks and debtors generally excessive. Try to cut these both by more rigorous production and stock control, and by more persistent debt collection. All that is required to achieve these simple things is more concentrated effort by your executives towards directly stated objectives.

We have begun the process of reorganization on which will be based the future form of our company. We will no doubt make mistakes, there may be disappointments; there will be frustrations. In these next ensuing months, patience and calm will be much needed. What is now thought best is not necessarily the shape of things for all time, and experience may require changes in some of our decisions.

We are embarking on a monumental task, nothing less than bringing up to the highest standard of efficiency a considerable part of the British electrical and electronics industries. Do not underestimate the difficulties. We simply cannot afford avoidable problems, such as personality clashes, personal prejudices, divisive, misplaced loyalties. We are now one company, one group, and, heaven only knows, we need each other's help in every way.

A Weinstock, 29 November, 1968

and above all, his decisiveness in ensuring that the weak spots are eradicated or strengthened. He does not fall into the pitfall that besets many men who control large enterprises – that of mistaking planning and exhortation for action.

There is no reason why the Weinstock style of management should not prove very effective for a huge corporation. The severe problems will arise when Weinstock retires.

The very qualities that have made him so successful make it difficult for him to provide for his own succession. The style of management that he has established requires an Arnold Weinstock at the top for it to work well. And yet it is unlikely that a man *like* Arnold Weinstock would work for the real Arnold Weinstock for very long. He would be too eager to go off and run his own show.

Jones, R. and Marriott, O. (1970),
Anatomy of a Merger, Jonathan Cape

Budget meeting 1: Dorman Diesels, February 1984

The group emerging from the budget meeting looked glum as they returned to the waiting room to collect their coats. 'How did you get on?' they were asked by the managers of the next GEC unit waiting their turn for the annual budget inspection. Both units were in the same general line of business, though operating separately in different segments of the market. 'It was going well until A W came in' was the reply, 'but you should be all right with your new range of equipment – they kept throwing that at us'.

Both units were operating in a difficult market. In the wake of the OPEC oil price rises, there had been a boom in the demand for fuel-efficient diesel engines and every major manufacturer in the world had expanded its capacity. Now demand was satisfied and as the recession had deepened, over-capacity was rife and the competitive struggle for orders had intensified.

Both GEC units had been suffering. The unit director waiting, with his team, for the budget meeting had been with GEC for three years. His unit had already been in difficulty when he had been brought in to avert the decline and to restore its commercial and market position. The work-force was contracting and eventually had been cut to less than half its previous 2000 and the new unit director had been given more associated units to control. Most were still struggling to perform to budget – though the trend showed signs of improvement.

In the main unit he had been notably active. He had led a major drive towards worker involvement, explaining, discussing, arguing, cajoling, and carrying the workforce along, despite the redundancies, to accept that openness, painful measures, commitment, energy, and investment were the only practicable conditions of survival.

The factory equipment was far from new ('my historic depreciation is less than £1 million a year; my replacement cost depreciation would be over £3 million – and we would not replace all the machines'). The products had not been substantially renovated for several years and there was a gap in the capacity range.

The new unit management team (for other fresh managers had joined the new director) had set a group to work to design a new range – to be lighter, smaller, and more powerful than existing designs. A multi-functional team of engineers, sales people, accountants, purchasing, and production personnel had been housed – along with some new computer-aided design equipment – in a highly visible office. Everyone knew why they were there and what it meant for the company's future.

A second decision had been to tell the team to 'believe the computers' and not to add the habitual engineering cautions to the designs. The resulting product was indeed lighter, more compact, more powerful, and cheaper to make – despite the fact that when the belief in computers was undercut by prototype parts breaking, the safest, if necessary the most expensive, cure was used to strengthen the design. Under these pressures, the development time had been surprisingly short and the new range looked impressive.

It had been launched earlier in the week of the February 1984 budget meeting in a professional presentation at a well-known conference centre. Before the overseas buyers had viewed the equipment, all employees who wanted to come, mainly in the evening, had been entertained to a rehearsal of the launch presentation – complete with video presentation, special effects, and electronic rock music. The atmosphere was jovial. As the dry ice drifted through the auditorium, good-natured laughter came as one employee said, 'It must be a new redundancy programme. They're gassing us now'. As the presentation reached its climax and the brightly enamelled engines appeared, the employees broke into spontaneous applause.

Before the budget meeting, the unit director had explained his concerns (one of which was the criticism he felt would be made about the cost and style of the launch presentation for his new range).

I've had to trim my capital investment because of the GEC commandment that thou shalt not make less profit or less ROC next year than this. (Note – these are not absolute GEC rules). It's too short term. I really wanted to invest £3 million not £2 million this year, particularly as my units have all under-invested in the past, but it would have pushed my return on capital down. Next year I want to invest over £5 million. GEC **is** releasing funds to me though. I haven't been tied down on my overdraft.

The trouble is that my profit this year is exceptional because I landed a big overseas contract with Iran. But it's not a reliable market and although my normal market is scheduled to go up substantially next year, I felt I had to put in another speculative overseas contract and I'll have to find half a million of profit from somewhere if the contract isn't repeated. These contracts shouldn't be in the budget; they should be seen as opportunistic and they've made next year more difficult because of this year's good profit. I wish I hadn't got that contract now.

They will be clever enough to see that I have been very conservative on provisions against that large contract profit in order to promote the whole business. I like my finance people to be conservative with provisions.

Although it was thought we might have to close down one of the units I've taken over, I found that their designs were better than ours and so I've improved their results by buying some of their output for our own market and incorporating their best features in the new design. There were over 20 variants and we have rationalized the range; that's cut the cost and so we are now more competitive on price and with better margins. But my other units are way below budget and GEC is used to getting high ROC out of electronics but, in a capital intensive capital goods company like mine it's difficult to make money now. I think I'll get a hard time at the budget meeting over last year's results in the units I've taken over – even though I have greatly improved the overseas unit's results. It's just taken a contract off a local firm backed by their own Government.

One GEC fault is that they only look at total overhead spend. Yes, you should save on overheads, but what matters is what you spend it on. Our sales overhead has doubled in the two years – that's good. If they criticize me, I'll argue that last year we spent half a million and lost money; this year we spent a lot more and made a profit. They're not good on marketing and they want everything to cover its cost. But we have to sell some small engines at a slight loss in order to keep our distributors going each week – otherwise they won't stay to sell one of our big engines every two months.

(In fact, when he revealed the slight loss on the small engines at the budget meeting, he was not criticized; it was seen as part of his overall, promising, strategy.)

To give them their due, they do extract development expenditure from overheads and don't press you to reduce that. In fact you get good support, there's positive encouragement.

A W will complain that inventory and debtors ought to come down but the inventory is rising to support higher sales and since GEC takes all the cash in the units, we get no credit for lower debtors. If a customer will pay cash for 2.5% discount, we simply lose 2.5% of margin. Some GEC units won't accept such an offer for that reason. On the other hand, we don't have to deal with banks and GEC doesn't charge interest either.

(GEC funds the balance sheet of each GEC unit with a Head Office loan. GEC levies half of the budgeted pre-tax profit spread evenly over twelve monthly payments. GEC pays tax and takes any interest on the monies it receives. The other half of the pre-tax profit remains in the unit and reduces the Head Office loan. Further cash needs for the units are obtained – whether for capital investment or working capital – through an overdraft/cash balance from GEC – for which the unit similarly is neither charged nor receives interest. The unit's Head Office loan also goes up and down by the amount that actual profit exceeds or falls short of budgeted profit. Thus a profitable unit

> which consistently beats its budgets could, depending on its
> capital employed needs, eventually eliminate the Head Office
> loan and have a notional cash balance.)

Our strengths are that orders are up; margins are up – even though
we're more competitive on price; we're hiring people as we increase
output and we're making good money on spares. That's slightly
misleading. You've got to look at equipment and spares as a total
product, because you can't charge development costs against spares.
If you were to charge development on current spares for old equipment, it wouldn't be relevant and if you charge it against future
spares, you're capitalizing development. That's dangerous.

The reason so few of our competitors close down is that they're
making money on spares for their old equipment which isn't being
replaced. Their installed base is going down. They're not investing
in the future. Nor were we tending to do so before.

Like his team, the unit director was obviously enthusiastic. 'I like
manufacturing. In British industry we've thrown away those skills. I'd
like to prove that it can be profitable if it's done properly. You've got to
market manufactures like any other product. We're picking up business
by aggressive marketing and we're now being taken seriously as suppliers.
The market is declining at several per cent a year, but we're going up
over 10%. It's got to come from others. We're just put our main UK
competitor down on a three-day week.'

Despite this ebullience, the unit director was not sanguine. 'The top
people don't like my style. They'll sack me if profits drop.' Despite his
concerns, the budget meeting gave no evidence of any distaste for his
performance from the headquarters group of Deputy Managing Director,
Sir Kenneth Bond, GEC Director, Malcolm Bates, and his assistant, Lord
Weinstock's son, Simon, together with Derek Roberts, GEC's Director
of Research. The group managing director of his unit was also present.

The unit director had held budget rehearsals with each of his four
companies and he and his team gave confident performances. His central
company was considered first and he went through the list of key points.

> Our new equipment was launched yesterday; it is the first variant
> of a more competitive range. Our sales are going up and we're
> selling aggressively. We've poached the best salesmen from our
> competitors.

'Good,' commented Bond as he turned to the group Managing
Director, 'Why don't we do that with xxxx (the unit whose budget
meeting had just ended) where we've got sales vacancies?' 'First we
change the head, then the rest will follow' was the reply. (The director of
that unit left the company and was replaced two months later.)

Competitors were considered (GEC has 7% of this world market). 'We
should have a schedule of our competitors in every budget.' One competitor had just been taken over by a rival and would now be run by an

ex-GEC man. The unit director had privately opined that the competitor would have been a good buy for GEC. But his group managing director had not agreed. It was thought that the unit director already had enough on his plate improving his existing four companies. (The competitor company had been offered to GEC for £25 million. It was barely profitable; had net assets of £15 million and had invested £70 million in two new ranges of its equipment. After GEC had turned it down, it was bought for less than £20 million – much of it on deferred terms – by a cash-poor multinational, itself then trying to recover.)

The headquarters group had spotted the provisions which had been tucked away, but the group managing director backed up his unit director: 'I like to feel that they are being cautious.'

'The ROCE is coming down with a bang' said Bond, 'though you say it's a growth business.' 'Yes,' responded the unit director, 'but that previous figure was obtained by not investing for years. We're increasing our capital employed. This is the first new engine range for over 10 years and our manufacturing machines are even older than that. The business used to make money years ago and we let it all go away. We're now going in again.'

In response to Bond's queries, the unit director explained his investment in new flexible manufacturing systems and the importation of some part-finished small engines from China. Everyone was interrupting everyone else amiably and without any sign of rank or inhibition. The unit's value-added, flat-rate bonus scheme was discussed, though the headquarters group weren't too pleased that, in telling employees quarterly about the accounts, the unit director had told them it had been a very satisfactory year. They worried for a while about the implications for the wage settlement – and moved on to inspect the budget figures.

'The margins on the new equipment are low.' 'That's because we're giving each unit an extended test and it's the extra cost of pre-production work. The worst thing we can do is to have failures in the early days.'

'We agree.'

'There's a big jump in selling costs but your turnover isn't going up a lot.'

'But our basic equipment sales are going up 50%. The rest was that exceptional overseas contract.'

'Travel expenses are high.'

'95% of our equipment ends up overseas because even our home sales go into people's packages – in and out of GEC – which go abroad. We're trying to do more of that. We still don't do enough travelling.'

After one hour Lord Weinstock came in from his adjacent office and sat at the side amongst the visiting team.

'Why were sales margins 10% last year, which was bad, and now when it's been a good year, they're down to 9%?'

'The overseas contract for kits was in there and it's brought down the spares margin though we're making X% on the spares.'

'That's half the normal margin,' reacted Lord Weinstock, 'It's the route to bankruptcy.'

'But our profit is going up and we're getting 25% more for our kit equipment than the previous supplier.'

'They're after a further large order there this year', commented Bates.

'I don't like large orders,' said Weinstock, 'I like small orders with big margins.'

'But we sold as many kits there this year as our total build in Britain,' protested the unit director.

'Then they must have been too cheap!'

Lord Weinstock began to go into the budget of one of the overseas units. Margins were too low, capital turnover too low, there were twice as many indirect employees as direct (this was because many components were brought in from suppliers rather than manufactured) and the productivity was suspect. The unit director pointed out that output was scheduled to nearly double with only 15% more employees and the unit's designs were now incorporated in his new British range. There was a discussion about the falling margin also being caused by increases in capital employed in the form of labour-saving machinery.

'But it's no good putting in labour-saving machinery if you don't save labour.'

The discussion switched to China and the imports which came from it. The headquarters team was enthusiastic that the unit director should set up a joint venture involving its government, for China had a huge potential as its market developed.

'I didn't think that was what GEC wanted,' reacted the unit director, 'you criticised me very strongly when I signed that existing deal with them.'

'That was yesterday,' responded Lord Weinstock, 'before it worked out.'

He returned to arguing about the general budget projections. The meeting had been going for three hours. In the end, Bond and Bates got up and said they'd leave Lord Weinstock on his own – still arguing. The meeting petered out.

In fact, the headquarters group had considerable confidence in the unit director's activities and plans and could see that major improvements were in train to weld together the several companies into a robust unit, though profits would not be large for several years and significant capital investment would be needed. The unit director and his team were, for their part, satisfied with the outcome of the meeting. In the two complete months of the 1984/85 year, the companies had been performing to budget.

Despite improvements in two of his four units, the profits of his main unit fell in the year 1984/85 and it did not obtain a repeat of the large overseas contract. He has since left GEC and is now managing director of another company in the same industry.

GEC's diesel businesses have suffered with both lower sales and profits arising from world over-capacity. The investment in China did not occur. GEC finally sold the main unit (Dorman Diesels) of his business in 1987 and another, Moteurs Baudouin, in 1988.

Budget meeting 2: Hotpoint, March 1984

'You come in with your previous company's techniques like strategy and formats. It is all very theoretical. We only understand money in and money out. We're very simple.' Lord Weinstock smiled. So did the managing director of the GEC Unit – not really believing the projected innocence. The annual budget meeting had been going for an hour when GEC's Managing Director, Lord Weinstock, had walked in from his adjacent office and sat shirt-sleeved against the wall, alongside the senior unit managers accompanying their director to the annual grilling at GEC's headquarters. Ranged in front of them were GEC's Deputy Managing Director, Sir Kenneth Bond, GEC Director, Malcolm Bates and his assistant, Lord Weinstock's son, Simon, together with Derek Roberts, GEC's Head of Research.

Though the unit director had known Lord Weinstock for 15 years, he was new to GEC but clearly had all the relevant facts at his fingertips. His 1984 orders were up over 15% on the previous year and a new factory was coming on stream. In an existing factory a twilight shift was being added, slowly, because, despite high unemployment, few applicants seemed suitable. Nearly all were being drawn from jobs in other companies. The extra output was being sold without dropping prices and, with the additional production being at a low marginal cost, there was a consequent boost to return on capital employed.

Inventories were set to rise to support promotions and sales fluctuations. The seasonality of sales made stocks high at budget time anyway and the unit director had taken personal charge of scheduling to promote long production runs. Some products were not manufactured at all by GEC, but obtained and badged from continental manufacturers. These continental products were either of advanced design or made in large European factories at low cost.

In its main product lines the GEC unit had become the British market leader. Its exports remained negligible.

The budget meeting had started by consideration of the market trends and product innovations. The GEC unit was planning to improve its existing technology and to introduce a new product variant which gave better value to customers.

Another new product market was expanding but the unit director was unenthusiastic about the high cost and long pay back of building a GEC plant to make it. The senior group persisted. 'If the tooling costs a lot, couldn't you buy old tools from the European market leader?' 'They're supplying us as well as selling themselves; they wouldn't want us to make against them.'

The main competitors were sketched out by the unit director. 'X is recovering but has an old image. Y has a thrusting image but a low market share. Z has dropped its price since introducing the new product – they're so scared of raising their price against their market share. Mind you, real prices have come down in the market over the last five years.

Inflation's been about 70%. Our price rises, about half that. Our reputation is rising in the trade. Our service organisation is good and we make money out of it.'

His explanations were lucid and confident, though this didn't save him from criticism. 'If you are selling all you can make, you could have raised prices and sold harder.' 'We're already at the top end of the price – we want to be a Hewlett Packard, not a Casio – but we're above most of the competition.'

Approval was difficult to find. 'This year's outcome is better than the budget – that makes next year's budget less attractive,' smiled Bond. 'We were having a quality problem at the new factory when we wrote the new budget. If we were writing it now we might be more opportunistic.'
(The unit director liked to have his budget meeting as late as practicable in the GEC season, so as to get close to the year in prospect. Unlike the capital goods and defence contract end of GEC's business portfolio, his business had a short and fluctuating order book.)

'If we had a quality problem, who did we sack?'

'Nobody. It was due to the organization structure.'

'Organization structures don't make wrong drawings.'

There was a lively discussion about the unit's profit-sharing scheme and about forthcoming pay rises. Vigorous questions were answered just as vigorously and the inspection moved on.

'Your distribution costs are going up.'

'Yes, but less than sales are going up. It's an improvement.'

Bond and Weinstock gave their well-honed response as a near duet:

'If there's room for improvement, there should be more of it.'

The cost of the incentive-driven sales force was queried by Lord Weinstock:

If customers aren't buying, then extra sales people won't sell. If your sales fall, it's the most stupid thing to do to increase advertising. If people aren't buying the product then advertising won't sell more. Cut back the extra advertising, you are still wasting money on advertising. It's too much because it's more than it was before. There's a lot of your advertising about. Unless you've got something different – and you haven't – all advertising can do is show people that you're there. If you're selling consumer goods, your sales don't go up and down with advertising – unlike soap powder.

The interrogating group became more benign.

'We worry about the year on year comparisons, actual against actual. If we did the budget it would be more difficult for you.' 'Then,' responded the unit director, 'we'd say it wasn't our budget.'

'When you are reporting, variances don't mean much to us. We want to see what's happening year by year.'

'I use variances in two ways – a variance from budget and a variance from standard cost. We might show a loss of margin, not because our trend is going off line, but because we're giving a lot of promotional support in the field. If I tell you my sales in money, it would give you no idea of my volume.'

'You're not tied to the past. Feel free to report in the way you think best. If we don't understand the terms, we'll need to be educated.'
Lord Weinstock had the last word as the two-hour meeting ended.

'Don't try to do good like your predecessor. Just try and make money.'

(This unit increased sales and profits to record levels in 1984/85 and again in 1985/86. It continued to improve. The unit director became responsible for three additional GEC units and was appointed to GEC's Board of Management, though not made an associate director. In 1988, having raised Hotpoint's UK laundry market share from 20% to 40% and made Hotpoint the most profitable white goods maker in Europe, this unit director – who had not been appointed to GEC's main board – left to become Chief Executive of the Yale & Valor group.)

Notes

1. Mulling over the style of these budget meetings with another senior GEC figure, the author opined that, contrary to the GEC myth, there was no sign of brutality or ruthlessness at the budget meetings. 'No, they are more polite the more junior you are and they rarely go for the jugular in those meetings – they mull it over afterwards and then act. The meetings you've seen were where the new unit directors are doing better than before – a honeymoon period. Yes, they say they really want to invest in new plants and more businesses, but its like soft pornography – it promises but doesn't deliver. You go and ask for £1 million to put in the UK and it's a different story.'

2. In the year ending March 1988, 154 GEC employees (apart from 12 of the 19 directors) earned over £40 000 pa.

3. Attempts by GEC to acquire sizeable companies have had varied results. In the mid-1970s GEC had been rebuffed when it tried to buy Cable & Wireless from the British government before privatization had been espoused as a government policy.

   A B Dick in the US was bought in the expectation that its product range could be transformed from electromechanical to electronic technology whilst taking advantage of its distribution and dealer network. This proved difficult and it took several years to become profitable.

   GEC had been over-bid by Racal for Decca in Britain and when GEC was buying Avery in 1979 its past reputation for labour shedding resulted in GEC having to concede a two-year post-acquisition redundancy moratorium. Redundancies later occurred at Avery, another company which had an obsolescent electromechanical product range until it introduced more advanced products. The question of post-acquisition employment policy was a difficulty for GEC in the 1970s, not only with organized labour but with British governments too – with the further possibility of union reaction having an effect on customers, not to mention problems of monopoly at a time when competition policy issues were growing at the expense of the previous drives towards rationalization and amalgamation.

In contrast, the acquisition of Picker in the US in 1981 took GEC deeply into the new area of medical electronics and has proved much more successful – particularly through GEC's body-scanning Magnetic Resonance Imaging system.

In 1982 GEC was courted by the top management of the struggling AEG–Telefunken group, but resistance by Siemens and the German trade unions led to the abandoning of any bid – even though, with GEC seeking only 40%, the majority of AEG–Telefunken shares could have remained in German hands. As it was, 80% of AEG was eventually bought by Daimler–Benz.

In 1984 GEC also attempted to buy British Aerospace, but BAe was not keen to become part of GEC – a combination which would have given GEC/BAe a near UK monopoly in some advanced space technologies, as well as putting GEC's electronics competitors at a prospective disadvantage as suppliers to BAe. The British government also let it be known that the GEC bid was unwelcome. In other cases, GEC has never got to the stage of making a bid because of the anti-trust considerations about a large company gaining yet more dominance via added market share – or upstream/downstream control of competitor's supplies or markets. GEC considers 100 acquisitions/partnerships/liaisons each year.

In December 1985 GEC announced its intention to seek agreement to purchase Plessey for £1.16 billion (160p per share). The scope for rationalization of telecommunications was seen as the central advantage of the link. However both companies' telecommunications sales were predominantly to British Telecom, although BT was in favour of the merger, believing that it would both cheapen and speed up its supplies.

The bid was rebuffed vigorously by Plessey and was rejected by the Monopolies and Mergers Commission on grounds of diminished competition within the UK which could lead to added costs of defence purchases and an erosion of R&D capability. Counter arguments by GEC that the markets were global and that economies of (non-duplicated) R&D would ensue were not accepted by the MMC, but it did endorse the merits of merging the GEC and Plessey public switching (System X) telecommunications interests.

SUGGESTED QUESTIONS

1. What are the best features of the GEC management style and what is its downside?
2. How effective are the financial control systems in GEC and what kind of managerial behaviour do they promote?
3. How and why might you seek to change GEC's management structure?

11

GEC plc (B): European links for the 1990s

Case written by Tony Eccles

INTRODUCTION

Between 1983 and 1988, GEC's sales grew by under 5% per year and there was a lower rise than this in pre-tax profits. In 1988 55% of turnover was in the UK (with a further 21% of exports from Britain), whilst 76% of profit also came from these British activities. Trading profits in 1988 rose 14% (from £492m to £561m) with £490 million having been spent on acquisitions in the year.

Despite paying higher dividends, GEC continued to throw up retained profits of approximately £300 million a year. This meant that, although shares were bought in and cancelled, and debt was repaid to the point where borrowings became negligible, GEC's cash assets remained within the range £1.3–1.7 billion, despite the sums invested in acquisitions. Cash and investments had yielded 9.7% return in 1987 compared to 42% return on operating assets.

GEC's ability to acquire further UK activities in its main business areas was curtailed by public policy considerations about competition. Whilst GEC had a few minor partnerships with competitors (and owned about 5% of Matra), its normal habit was to seek ownership or, at least, management control. Given GEC's unwillingness to step outside its existing areas of product expertise, together with monopoly concerns in Britain and the American government's reluctance to allow a key defence supplier to be foreign-owned, it was difficult to see what major initiatives GEC could take with which it could feel at ease.

Some new liaisons were formed, such as GEC's 1986 sale of 49% of its UK lighting company to Osram (Siemens). But such moves were described by the *Financial Times* as 'marginal tinkerings' and both press and analysts became markedly critical of GEC, as the Nimrod airborne radar project was cancelled in favour of the Royal Air Force buying Boeing's 'AWACS' alternative. The success of other Marconi activities was overlooked as were the 3000 changes made by the Ministry of Defence (MoD) to the original 'Nimrod' specification. Given the difficulties of making major bids, GEC then started to pursue the acquisition of more small and medium-sized businesses.

TOWARDS A NEW STRATEGY

Indications of a new approach had come in GEC's 1987 report when the Chairman wrote: 'We continue to seek opportunities to strengthen our position in international markets by acquisition, joint ventures and other forms of collaboration as well as through organic growth and the combination of our marketing and research and development expertise.'

RECENT ACQUISITIONS

In 1987 30% of the loss-making Dutch weighing equipment company, Berkel, was bought at the instigation of GEC's Avery subsidiary (as well as an option on a further 27%, later exercised) giving the UK/Commonwealth-oriented Avery group better access to European markets.

GEC also bought the Creda washing machine and cooker company for £126 million to add scale and scope to its Cannon cooker and Hotpoint white goods businesses. Creda had a turnover of £145 million (£110m in goods that GEC did not sell) – predominantly in Britain. This acquisition, together with the continued growth of Hotpoint, was to help GEC's consumer products group to raise profits from £35 million in 1987 to £60 million in 1988, just as the European industry was re-structuring. (The American firm, Whirlpool, took a controlling stake in Philip's $3 billion appliance business following the Electrolux takeover of Zanussi, which had given Electrolux–Zanussi a quarter of the European market.)

A further flurry of acquisition activity occurred with the purchase of Lear Siegler Astronics for $205 million and then Gilbarco for $250 million, a move which increased GEC's market share of petrol pumps/service station equipment to 50% in the UK and 40% in the US. These moves got a better reception. As the *Financial Times* put it: 'These... smaller acquisitions... play to one of the strengths of GEC... namely its decentralised management structure which can throw up information about acquisition opportunities which is not immediately available to head office.' Commentators felt that it could make sense for GEC to develop by strengthening its presence in specialist global markets.

MERGERS

Two major mergers were also attempted. In 1987 GEC agreed to merge Picker (sales $612m) with the medical electronics interests of Philips (sales

$1400m) to form the largest medical technology company in the world. The fit was good since most of Picker's sales were in the US, whilst Philips' sales were mainly in Europe. Being smaller, it was expected that GEC would inject $150–200 million into the joint company which was to be owned 50:50 with Philips. This joint venture failed to proceed after a disagreement over terms, when GEC learned that the Philip's interests were markedly less profitable than had been believed and that Philips was unprepared to compensate by adjusting GEC's financial contribution. This left GE as world leader, following its acquisition of the CGR division of Thomson–CSF, with $2 billion sales, just ahead of Siemens with $1.9 billion.

The other merger followed the recommendations of the 1986 Monopolies and Mergers Commission (MMC) report which had rejected the full merger of GEC and Plessey whilst backing the amalgamation of their telecommunications interests. These had been duly brought together early in 1988, thus creating a company (GPT) with 23 000 people, £600 million of assets, a £1.4 billion turnover and £160 million in operating profit. GEC's Richard Reynolds had become Managing Director of GPT. Both GEC and Plessey agreed a pre-emption right to purchase the other's stake in the event of the other being taken over or selling its interest in GPT.

Prior to the formation of GPT, Plessey had been trying to build a sustainable position of its own in five strategic areas (aerospace, computer services, defence, semiconductors, and telecommunications) and, during 1987–8, made several purchases of complementary businesses to strengthen itself.

GEC had been investing in specialist microchip design and the manufacture of Application Specific Integrated Components (ASICs) – previously known as semi-custom chips. But, even back in 1985, Siemens had entered a defensive alliance with Toshiba to develop standard 1-megabit memory chips, and analysts had then queried whether GEC could afford to sit out semiconductor technologies – so vital to its defence business – whatever its disinterest in selling standard components. Siemens had also entered a collaborative venture in semiconductors with Philips.

JOINT VENTURES

Joint ventures were also constructed. GEC's Ruston Gas Turbines took a stake in the development of a new small aircraft engine with GE of America (which already had a 50:50 partnership with SNECMA in the CFM consortium; the consortium which had won orders for 2000 engines for Boeing 737 and Airbus A320 planes, representing 46% of all commercial engines on order in the western world). The hope was that the work could lead to joint development between GE and Ruston in Aero engines.

GEC Transportation Projects entered a research and manufacturing agreement with Ansaldo Transporti for railway systems (GEC had recently completed the London Docklands light railway). GEC had a world lead in power semiconductors; GEC Transportation Projects exported about 80% of output and had similar sales (£120m) to Ansaldo.

These arrangements were, however, modest compared to the larger joint ventures which were initiated.

GEC and Siemens

There had long been informal links and contacts between the major western electrical companies and, with the growth of multicontractor projects, discussions about collaboration through joint interests had been growing. The link between ASEA and Brown–Boveri early in 1988 created a company with $18 billion sales and became the catalyst for intensified discussions, particularly as ABB then developed links with Westinghouse in the US and Finmeccanica in Italy.

By the middle of 1988 GEC had shifted further from its historical insistence on control of activities to a more flexible view of partnerships. It had started to talk with GE of America about amalgamating some of their similar businesses. GEC had also revived its discussions with Siemens about mutual interests in the broadening European markets, as EC governments and public utilities sought to enhance competition in these nationalistic markets. Siemens dominated its domestic German market where half its DM51 billion sales were made. Siemens had, in 1987, tried to buy control of the French telecommunications company CGCT (as had AT&T, keen to get into Europe and already developing partnerships with Philips and Italtel), but had seen CGCT acquired by a combination of Ericsson and Matra. Alcatel (56% controlled by CGE) had already merged with the European telecommunications interests of ITT.

In the middle of 1988 GEC had talked, perhaps as a smokescreen to disguise the plans then being developed, of a major repurchase of 15% of its own shares which could cost £620 million. This plan got a mixed reception with critics claiming it to be an admission that GEC could not think of anything to do with the money. GEC's perspective was different. Malcolm Bates, GEC's Deputy Managing Director, said: 'We are still looking for a deal, but if our share price remains low, we think it will be better for our shareholders to have a programme of share purchase to increase our earnings per share. It does not mean that we won't do anything else.'

Lord Weinstock claimed that the problem facing the group was that any acquisition would yield a less favourable return to shareholders in the long term than buying GEC shares.

We have been pressed like mad for years, ever since anybody found out that we had any money in the bank. People keep saying, spend it, spend it, spend it – but we haven't. Not because we don't want

Exhibit 1   EC production of telecommunications equipment (1987 total = 15.6 bn ECU).

	Share (%)
Alcatel (CGE = 50.3%; ITT = 37%)	28
Siemens	18
GPT (GEC = 50%; Plessey = 50%)	7
Ericsson	6
Bosch	6
Philips	6
Italtel	4
Matra	3
Sagem	3
STC (Northern Telecom = 27.5%)	2
Telettra (Fiat = 90%; Tefonica = 10%)	1
Racal	1
APT (AT&T = 60%; Philips = 40%)	1
Others	15
	100

Source: BIPE.

to, but because we didn't find enough things we wanted to buy. When we found things we wanted to buy we bought them.

Whether a company is in high or low technology, the duty of management is to husband its resources so as to preserve and enhance their value, which means earning a high rate of return through efficient operation of the business involved. This produces a paradox. If businesses are managed efficiently, the result will be the generation of large and probably increasing amounts of cash. Yet the reaction of the armchair strategists, especially in the media and politics, is to throw up their hands in horror at this manifestation of efficient management.

In November 1988 GEC and Siemens launched a joint bid of £1.7 billion for Plessey. It was evident that the bid had been constructed to allay monopoly fears in the UK. Plessey's defence interests would not be merged with Marconi; GEC would control GPT whilst Siemens would probably absorb both the GEC and Plessey semiconductor activities to create a firm with sales of $810 million, second only to Philips in Europe.

GEC would take a 50% stake in Siemens' small defence subsidiary. The logic of the bid rested on the growing need to build cross-border alliances to compete with major Japanese and American firms, and on the spreading of high costs of, for instance, developing the next generation of digital switches in telecommunications – exactly the argument about scale which had led to the formation of GPT (see Exhibit 1).

Exhibit 2 GEC–Siemens revised proposals for ownership of Plessey's main businesses.

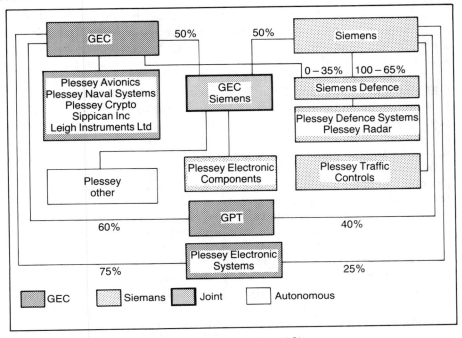

Source: MMC based on information supplied by GEC and Siemens.

Plessey reacted by rejecting the bid and seeking to find a 'white knight' as a more acceptable partner. It also tried to assemble a 'Pacman' defence via a consortium which would counterbid for GEC, but this proved impossible, particularly since a key consortium participant (GE) promptly announced a major link-up with GEC in which their European businesses in consumer products, medical equipment, and electrical distribution would be merged.

Plessey's takeover defence rested on the implausibility of GEC–Siemens being able to run the Plessey and GEC defence interests as separate businesses; the scope for conflict in joint ownership ventures; its own claims to having a more enterprising management; and the 'evidence' that strong domestic competition was a spur to competitiveness – citing as examples, BASF–Hoechst–Bayer, Nissan–Toyota–Honda, Boeing–Lockheed–McDonnell Douglas, and NEC–Toshiba–Hitachi in chip production.

The GEC–Siemens response focused on the ever-increasing cost of R&D in the rapidly evolving electronics world and pointed out that, in integrated circuits, as in telecommunications, only scale and access to multiple markets would enable companies to stay in the race – let alone have a chance of winning it. 'The recent co-operation between Hitachi and Texas Instruments shows that even large producers are looking for ways to share the ever-rising costs,' stated Karlheinz Haske, the Chief Executive of Siemens.

In April 1989 the MMC unanimously cleared the GEC–Siemens bid for Plessey, subject to some conditions. Evidently the MMC had felt that both British Telecom and the MoD were, as monopoly customers, able to withstand the market power of the merged companies. The MMC's worries centred around some parts of defence electronics, where GEC and Plessey accounted for 75% of the MoD's £1.8 billion purchases. Plessey's radar and defence systems would have to go to Siemens only, provided that Siemens could satisfy national security interests (e.g. that all directors of Plessey companies owned by Siemens or GEC–Siemens should be British citizens) (see Exhibit 2).

In avionics and naval systems on the other hand, there were no objections to GEC's takeover. GEC–Siemens would be required to allow MoD-authorized competitors access to the technology of the Joint Tactical Information Distribution System project – a NATO system which would enable ground forces, ships, and aircraft to communicate.

The MMC's report was widely seen as a victory for pan-European industrial logic over domestic considerations of competition policy. Despite strenuous efforts by Plessey, no partner or alternative bidder appeared, which was not surprising given GEC's blocking pre-emption right to purchase the other half of GPT. It dawned on an impressed financial community that GEC, by setting up GPT in this way, had got Plessey to agree to a partnership with GEC which meant that only GEC itself (with its chosen partner Siemens) could sensibly bid for Plessey, since any other bidder would lose GPT – one of Plessey's star attractions. The bid succeeded.

The agreement between Siemens and GEC for controlling different sections of Plessey had been affected by the MMC's conditions on the merger, with GEC later claiming that these undermined the original plan for a full joint venture. By early 1990 it was evident that a near-complete separation would occur between the Siemens and GEC-owned parts of Plessey – apart from the telecommunications operation of GPT, with which Siemens was to pool its computerized switchboards business. The 60% GEC: 40% Siemens ownership of GPT might yet be adjusted.

The British government decided to allow GEC to take over virtually all Plessey's US defence and aerospace interests to add to Plessey's avionics, anti-submarine, and semiconductor activities. Siemens would own Plessey's radar and communication businesses and the Hoskyns computing services business was to be sold off.

GEC and Alsthom

GEC had also announced a major joint venture with CGE of France's subsidiary, Alsthom, which would co-own their power engineering interests. It would be the largest power engineering enterprise in the EC

Exhibit 3 GEC Alsthom: sales breakdown by activity, 1989–90.

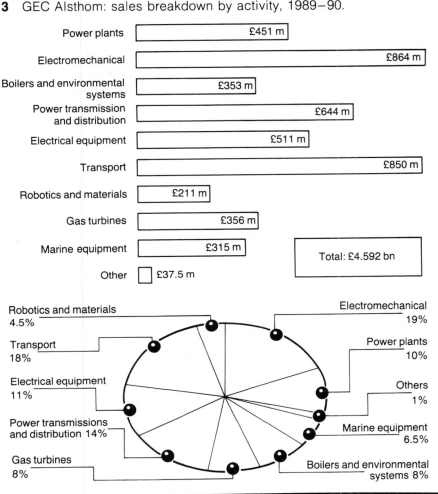

with sales of £4.6 billion and 85 000 employees, and would be world leader in power generation – some 35% larger than ABB, which in turn would be bigger than Siemens or Ansaldo. (ABB is biggest overall and had just bought the Italian power group Franco Tosi, to the annoyance of state-owned IRI–Finmeccanica which had wanted to merge Tosi with its Ansaldo subsidiary.) ABB's German subsidiary had pooled its nuclear technology with Kraftwerk Union (Siemens) and with Siemens' power station equipment division. In North America, ABB had put its power equipment businesses into two joint ventures with Westinghouse.

Alsthom already claimed a world lead in railway equipment and had a shipbuilding division (Chantiers de L'Atlantique). GEC would also put in its electrical distribution and transmission operations, its robotics

Exhibit 4   GEC Alsthom: organization chart.

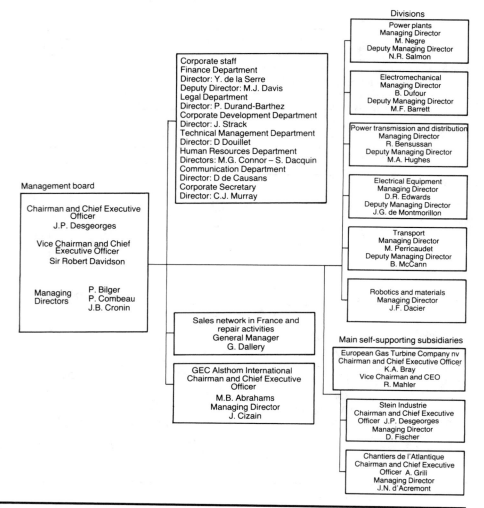

company, and its rail transport business. Alsthom came to the joint venture with GEC with its majority stake in ACEC, the Belgian energy and rail equipment group, and a 45% holding in the energy business of MAN of Germany. The deal excluded the joint venture in nuclear technology between GEC and Westinghouse and CGE's 40% stake in Framatome, the French nuclear power station builder, but nevertheless involved GEC putting almost a quarter of its assets into the partnership with Alsthom. GEC later extended the link by injecting its Electrical Projects and Industrial Controls activities into CGE through its subsidiary, CGEE–Alsthom (a dedicated projects and controls business).

The new alliance had been under discussion for some time. As Jean-

Pierre Desgeorges told the *Financial Times*, 'I first contacted Arnold (Weinstock) in 1984 but he was not interested in a merger then'. (Alsthom had also talked to Ansaldo (60% owned by ABB) and Siemens but there was no sensible hope of a deal.) 'The Germans say "I'm smaller than you, but I want to be the boss,"... Arnold was much more flexible.... This is going to be a big, new, dynamic company. We will no longer be Frenchmen and Englishmen or German or whatever in the company because of this common corporate culture which is developing. All senior managers have this feeling.'

This 50:50 amalgamation of GEC's power engineering and rail equipment activities with CGE's Alsthom subsidiary became the most fully delineated of GEC's joint ventures (see Exhibit 3). Half of GEC–Alsthom's sales were outside France and Britain and nearly half outside the EC. Following its formation, it had been structured into a series of transnational product and market divisions much as Alsthom was originally organized (see Exhibit 4). Heavily decentralized, according to its management, its £4.6 billion sales came one-third from GEC and two-thirds from Alsthom, but the GEC proportion had been more profitable due to 'historically low margins in Alsthom'. (In the last year before the merger, GEC's part made £90 million profit on £1.2 billion sales, whilst Alsthom's operations made £57 million on sales of about £2.9 billion).

However, the product and market complementarity was marked. In power stations GEC had a strong position in the UK, British Commonwealth, China, Far East, and South Africa; Alsthom's main markets were France, the Middle East, and North Africa, with interests in Latin America and Canada. In transformers and gas turbines the two ranges fitted rather than overlapped. Overlap was concentrated in steam turbines and electricity generators. Unfortunately, in the power generation industry there was a lack of orders worldwide and a 70% manufacturing overcapacity.

The new venture's initial business experiences were not wholly favourable. The privatization of electricity in Britain had reinforced concerns about the costs of combatting coal-fired pollution and the real costs of nuclear power generation. A further pressure grew from the attractive economics of high-efficiency, gas-turbine combined heat and power stations, particularly for industrial users with needs for both heat and power. Plans for three large coal-fired stations and two nuclear stations in Britain – in which GEC would have played a significant part – were abandoned in 1989–90 with only the Sizewell B nuclear plant continuing construction.

In January 1990 Siemens beat GEC–Alsthom for the contract to build a 900 MW, £350 million gas-fired power station for Power Gen at Killingholme, Humberside. ABB was planning to build a gas-fired plant in north-west England for its 80% subsidiary, Lakeland Power, which had proposals for three more such plants. In just over a year GEC had seen its UK power station orders curtailed and two major rivals enter the UK market.

With turbine generators forming 19% of GEC – Alsthom's £4.6 billion sales, rationalization of the group's Franco–British factories was inevitable since the French nuclear power station programme had also slowed down (more than 70% of French power is generated by nuclear stations). Labour costs in France had been 35% above British levels but, according to Alsthom, output per employee had also been higher due to lower staffing levels. Turbine generator activities employed 12 000 of GEC–Alsthom's 80 000 people.

Better circumstances prevailed in rail equipment where GEC–Alsthom had won contracts worth £580 million for Channel tunnel trains. French railways (SNCF) had also ordered 80 TGVs (Trains à Grande Vitesse) worth £630 million with options on buying 30 more.

GEC–Alsthom organization

GEC–Alsthom was headed by the previous Chairman of Alsthom, Jean-Pierre Desgeorges (sharing the joint Chief Executive role with Deputy Chairman, Sir Robert Davidson, the previous head of GEC's power engineering activities). Lord Weinstock chaired the GEC–Alsthom supervisory board (this chairman's role was planned to alternate annually between him and Pierre Suard, President of CGE, Alsthom's parent company), and so Desgeorges initially reported to Weinstock.

Whilst GEC–Alsthom had an organizational form closer to the Alsthom model than GEC's more individualistic unit-based management, the financial control system required the 130 GEC–Alsthom units to each report monthly in the GEC style. GEC–Alsthom had over 100 factories and was organized into six operating divisions (see Exhibit 4): **power plants** for power station project management; **electromechanical** for steam turbines and generators; **power transmission and distribution** such as switchgear; **electrical equipment**; **transport** (mainly rail equipment) (see Exhibit 5); and **robotics**. Subsidiaries included Stein (boilers), Chantiers de L'Atlantique (shipbuilding), and the European Gas Turbine company, EGT (where GE of America also held a 10% stake) included the West German gas turbine business of AEG, Kanis Energy.

In 1989 EGT won orders for nearly 3000 MW of equipment, much the same as ABB and Siemens but much lower than GE's 8000 MW. (The world market was 26 000 MW.) EGT hoped to supply gas turbine engines of up to 6000 horse power to military and civil aircraft. GEC's 50% of GEC–Alsthom displaced Marconi as GEC's biggest business.

GEC and GE

It took several months of detailed negotiations for the co-operation agreement to be finalized. The joint venture in household appliances would amalgamate their European interests and, in electrical distribution, GEC's Belgian-based Vynckier would combine with GE's Italian business, Cogemec. The plan to merge their European medical equipment

Exhibit 5   GEC Alsthom: transport division.

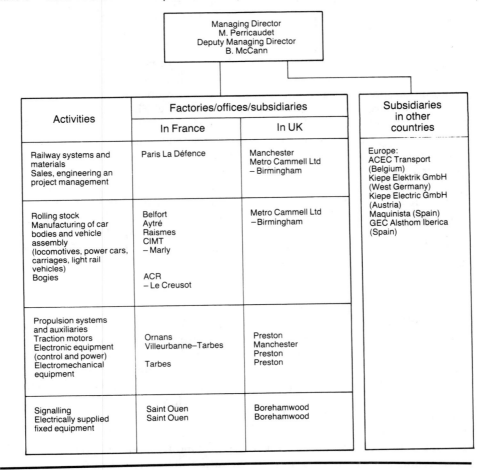

| Activities | Factories/offices/subsidiaries | | Subsidiaries in other countries |
	In France	In UK	
Railway systems and materials Sales, engineering an project management	Paris La Défence	Manchester Metro Cammell Ltd – Birmingham	Europe: ACEC Transport (Belgium) Kiepe Elektrik GmbH (West Germany) Kiepe Electric GmbH (Austria) Maquinista (Spain) GEC Alsthom Iberica (Spain)
Rolling stock Manufacturing of car bodies and vehicle assembly (locomotives, power cars, carriages, light rail vehicles) Bogies	Belfort Aytré Raismes CIMT – Marly ACR – Le Creusot	Metro Cammell Ltd – Birmingham	
Propulsion systems and auxiliaries Traction motors Electronic equipment (control and power) Electromechanical equipment	Ornans Villeurbanne–Tarbes Tarbes	Preston Manchester Preston Preston	
Signalling Electrically supplied fixed equipment	Saint Ouen Saint Ouen	Borehamwood Borehamwood	

businesses had been scaled down and now only consisted of GE buying GEC's British sales and service operation, because the strong links between GEC's German and US medical interests made Europe-wide collaboration impracticable. In gas turbines, GEC, GE, and Alsthom would all link up in a licensing deal giving the Europeans access to GE's technology through a new company called the European Gas Turbine Co (EGT) in which GEC would take a 10% stake.

GEC and Matra

Both GEC and Daimler–Benz had each acquired 5% of Matra when the French defence and electronics group had been privatized. Daimler–Benz had formed Deutsche Aerospace to include Dornier, the MTU aero-engine company, the aerospace part of AEG (Daimler–Benz owned 80% of AEG, including its domestic appliances division) and, despite objections from the German Federal Cartel office, Messerschmitt-Bolkow-Blohm (MBB) as well.

GEC strengthened its links with Matra by collaborating with Electronique Serge Dassault (ESD) in supplying Matra with jointly developed radars. British Aerospace then decided to turn from Marconi, its long-standing supplier of semi-active homing systems such as Sky Flash, and use a Thomson–CSF seeker on its Active Sky Flash missile; whilst Marconi would, with ESD, supply the active seeker to Matra's MICA missile, designed for use on France's planned Rafale fighter. Both missiles would compete on world markets via the two Anglo–French partnerships.

GEC–Marconi also tried to buy Shorts of Belfast from the British government in partnership with Fokker of Holland. Fokker, with a bulging plane order book, was after Shorts' aircraft building capacity whilst Marconi was interested in Shorts' Blowpipe missile. Shorts was instead sold to the Canadian company Bombardier, partly because it was thought that Bombardier might protect jobs better in Northern Ireland.

GEC'S ORGANIZATION

GEC had long been a collection of some 170 separate businesses each reporting directly to the head office at Stanhope Gate (see Chapter 10). Some of these business units had been clustered together under one senior manager, even though each continued to have a unit director who still reported directly to GEC's Stanhope Gate headquarters. Over the years, the clusters had been re-formed as the driving forces of markets or technology suggested better liaisons. However, in the early 1980s this system began to look odd in view of the convergent technologies – notably those featuring electronic and semiconductor innovations.

Attempts to create cross-linkages varied in style. Research under Deputy Managing Director (Technical), Derek Roberts, was seen as a unifying influence. In 1984 Lord Weinstock had set up the GEC UK Board of Management to bring together senior managers to discuss matters of joint interest. It included most of GEC's associate directors and was chaired by himself. Although it had been credited by some with the decision to invest more in semiconductors, the Board had no explicit powers. 'They don't take decisions, they talk things over,' said Weinstock. It met infrequently. In 1988 Roberts was appointed Provost of University College, though he remained a non-executive director of GEC.

Nor had the investment in semiconductors seemed more than half-hearted and, in any case, it was mainly directed at radiation-hardened chips for defence applications in GEC's own products. As Lord Weinstock said: 'That area has always been a worry to us. We have tried to make semiconductors three times and we did all of them very badly, none of them viable. We have never taken the plunge of a really big investment in semiconductor manufacturing – we spent several tens of millions, but that is not big.' (*Management Today*, January 1989)

In 1987 Lord Weinstock had unveiled a management reorganization aimed at creating larger divisional groups to bring together similar activities (linked by technology or markets) and so push operating decisions further down the organization. Asked if this would mean a decline in the importance of the annual unit budget meetings, he replied, 'You must be joking'.

The continuance of GEC's traditional unit-based management controls was seen by some as evidence that little had changed. As one commentator put it, 'Even with a two-tier board . . . it is hard to imagine adventures into new technology having any easier a time against performance controls that have shaped an entire management generation. In that case GEC will continue to be rated as the best recession manager in the UK . . .'.

OTHER STRUCTURES

Other companies chose different structures to cope with global diversity. The 1988 merger of ASEA and Brown Boveri had founded the largest power equipment maker in the world due to an acquisition programme described by the *Financial Times* as an 'insatiable appetite for buying just about any power station equipment manufacturer that comes on the market'. This had led to an empire of over 1000 companies, 215 000 employees and sales of £13 billion, making it almost twice the size of the world number two, Hitachi, with GEC–Alsthom being in fourth place, just behind GE.

Ten acquisitions had made ABB the world's biggest railway equipment maker, manufacturing in 10 countries. In environmental controls it bought ITT's Flakt group and the Swiss waste incinerating equipment firm of Widmer und Ernst. It had bought AEG's steam turbine business and entered a joint venture on nuclear reactors with Siemens. With burgeoning links with Eastern European firms and a sales split of EC – 25%, North America – 24% (where ABB had acquired the power transmission and distribution businesses of Westinghouse), and other European – 29%, the geographical spread was well balanced.

ABB evolved a matrix structure of eight globally responsible business segments, each reporting to one of the 12 members of the executive management who could also have responsibility for a geographic region, 50 product-based business areas, some 1000 companies and 3500 decentralized profit centres. This system was said to be 'in place and working'. The decentralization released managers to strengthen the executive management, and the executive management board of 11 members, under President and Chief Executive, Percy Barnevik, divided responsibilities so that some had product businesses, some regions or countries, and some a mix of the two. Barnevik saw the matrix, the

Exhibit 6   Reorganization at Siemens.

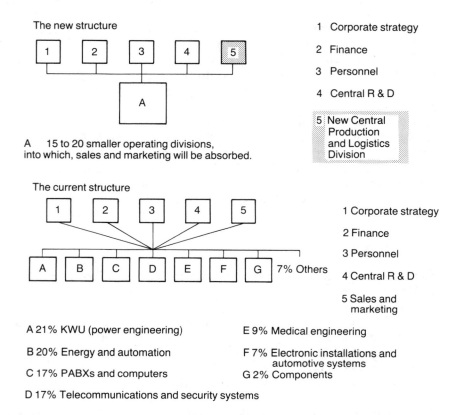

The new structure

1 Corporate strategy

2 Finance

3 Personnel

4 Central R & D

5 New Central Production and Logistics Division

A   15 to 20 smaller operating divisions, into which, sales and marketing will be absorbed.

The current structure

1 Corporate strategy

2 Finance

3 Personnel

4 Central R & D

5 Sales and marketing

7% Others

A 21% KWU (power engineering)

B 20% Energy and automation

C 17% PABXs and computers

D 17% Telecommunications and security systems

E 9% Medical engineering

F 7% Electronic installations and automotive systems

G 2% Components

decentralization, the opportunity-based acquisition programme, and the consequential efficiency potential as continuingly viable. 'I wish,' he was to say in early 1990, 'we had not been so cautious.' ABB's acquisition strategy later slowed as it sought to improve the effectiveness of its sprawling empire, but it was still extending into Eastern Europe. Joint ventures in power engineering were under way in Poland, with East Germany's steam turbine maker, Bergmann-Borsig, and with Skoda in Czechoslovakia.

Siemens reorganized from seven operating divisions to 18 smaller and more focused enterprises, with many of the head office functions – notably sales and marketing – moved out into the field and with the Executive Board slimmed down from 33 to 10 people (see Exhibit 6).

Whatever the respective merits of different forms of structure, critics of GEC often overlooked its persistence. GEC's power generating company had won, after seven years of negotiation, the £250 million turbine contract for the Chinese nuclear power station at Daya Bay near Hong Kong. GEC's Managing Director of Power Engineering, Sir Robert

Davidson, had made over 50 visits to China during those seven years, with up to 30 GEC personnel working there to secure the contract. In January 1988 GEC beat the Balfour Beatty–NEI consortium for the contract to build the Yue Yang coal-fired power station in south-east China.

In the year to March 1989, GEC reported trading profits up 16% (£653m compared to £561m) and with associated companies' earnings and net income on liquid funds remaining static, the pre-tax profit climbed from £708 million to £797 million on turnover up 16% at £6447 million (£5816m in 1988). Exports from the UK remained similar at £1256 million and the order book stood at £6403 million. Net cash and short-term investments amounted to £1086 million (£1383m in 1988).

The key questions were: Where next for GEC? And, could these joint ventures work (an important issue when GEC seemed to have put into joint ownership nearly half its operating assets)? As the *Financial Times* observed at the time: 'After standing aloof from big joint ventures for so long, Lord Weinstock has plunged right in with powerful companies that do not like to take a back seat in partnerships.'

By early 1992 the GEC–Alsthom venture was looking much better. EPON, the Dutch utility, had ordered the world's largest combined cycle power station outside Japan; Électricité de France would be supplied with a 1500 MW turbine generator for the Civaux nuclear station near Poitiers after the two ordered for Chooz in the Ardennes; and turbines were ordered for the Arak power station in Iran. Two combined cycle orders for East London and North Wales were also obtained. Along with the EFA contract (see page 232) and an order for three frigates (to add to the six already won under open, fixed-price contracts) GEC–Alsthom and GEC–Marconi had won over £2 billion in orders in the first few weeks of 1992.

OTHER REALIGNMENTS

Amalgamations, partnerships, and realignments had continued apace in the European engineering industries throughout 1989 and 1990.

Matra (where GEC and Daimler–Benz each had about 5%) took over the defence electronics and space activities of Fairchild for about $200 million and then Matra sought to link its space activities with GEC's Marconi. The two companies operated in complementary fields – Matra being strong in space avionics, space vehicles, navigation systems, and data management, whilst Marconi's space systems focused on satellite communications and payloads (such as those for the Skynet satellites) and power sources. With combined sales of £300 million, the new company would be owned 51% by Matra and 49% by Marconi, with GEC retaining a 5% stake in the Matra quoted parent company. An early aim of the new firm would be to bring in the space activities of Daimler–Benz from D–B's Deutsche Aerospace and MBB activities.

The military and civil flight electronics businesses of Thomson–CSF and Aerospatiale were also merged into a joint £500 million turnover company (Thomson–CSF having earlier acquired the bulk of Philips' defence electronics business). Given Thomson's missile links with British Aerospace, this liaison posed a threat to Marconi's own trade with BAe. Thomson–CSF formed a 50:50 missile company with BAe, called EuroDynamics, and gave themselves a year to work out how to implement the merger. BAe had already cut its workforce by several thousand and closed five of its nine manufacturing plants.

Underlying this kind of jockeying were major transnational defence contracts, such as the £22 billion European Fighter Aircraft (EFA) project. Only £6 billion had been raised for the contract but over £1.5 billion of this was for the development contract for the EFA's radar. The Germans, with about one-third of the overall EFA contract, wanted the radar work to come to a consortium which included AEG–Telefunken (Daimler–Benz) and GEC and which would offer a derivative of a GM–Hughes radar. The British were insistent that the radar contract should go to a new radar developed by Ferranti – as were the EFA's minority partners, Italy and Spain.

The deadlock was broken by Ferranti, whose plight after the discovery of major losses in its US operation was raising qualms about its ability to survive at all, let alone with sufficient strength to develop the EFA radar. Hence, in September 1989, GEC was allowed to buy Ferranti's defence business for £310 million, thus giving GEC a near UK monopoly in airborne radar systems at an exit multiple of 23 for the Ferranti radar business. As the *Economist* put it, 'Lord Weinstock has discovered an ingenious – if extreme – way to win contracts'.

Given the flux in Eastern Europe, it was not certain that the EFA would ever go into full production and, whilst it would probably not be displaced by the Dassault–Breguet 'Rafale', there remained the possibility that buyers might prefer the McDonnell Douglas F-18 'Hornet'. The EFA development contract was undertaken, however, and £300 million of it was awarded to the Ferranti-led group in May 1990.

Aerospatiale and Daimler–Benz had been talking since 1987 about merging their helicopter interests in order to win the European contract for the projected NH90 tactical transport helicopter. With combined sales of £800 million, this would make them the world number two after Sikorsky (United Technologies), leaving Augusta of Italy and Britain's Westland on their own in Europe.

In 1990 Daimler–Benz had initiated talks with Mitsubishi on technical/commercial collaboration and possible joint ventures in automotive, service, electronics, and aerospace. With both Thorn–EMI's defence interests and Ford's aerospace operations (with a turnover of £1.6 billion) for sale, the consolidation seemed likely to continue. Aerospatiale was reported as wanting to buy some of the Ford satellites business, in competition with Matra/GEC, while CGE–Alcatel (GEC's partner in GEC–Alsthom, later to rename itself Alcatel Alsthom) might want the Ford missiles business. The problem for French buyers was that much of Ford's work was on top-secret 'black programmes' for which no French company had Pentagon security clearance. Only 15 of these clearances were held outside the US, with 13 held by British and Canadian companies – including GEC.

These initiatives underlined the message that domestic and international defence procurement were not mutually exclusive. As BAe's then Chairman, Professor Roland Smith, put it 'You must get into a bigger group. There are fundamental changes in the nature of the industry. We have tried to structure our business with international alliances – the Rover/Honda tie-up and Airbus Industrie with Aerospatiale and Daimler–Benz. By the year 2000 there will be 3 or 4 players at most in Western European defence and aerospace'.

SUGGESTED QUESTIONS

1. What are the advantages/disadvantages to GEC's long term prosperity of engaging in joint ventures on this scale?
2. What issues would you expect to arise in GEC's joint ventures and how would you resolve them?
3. On what principles would you organize large, diverse, multi-linked organizations such as GEC, ABB, Siemens, British Aerospace or Alcatel?

12

Grand metropolitan plc (A)

Case written by Peter Williamson with Bernard Rix

It had been likened to a massive clearance sale. In just four years prior to 1988, Grand Metropolitan had disposed of over 25 businesses. A chunk of operations worth a total of £1.3 billion had gone. Some CEOs might have regarded this as a sign of defeat. To Allen Sheppard, who had taken over as group Chief Executive in November 1986 (adding the chairmanship in July 1987), it was the beginning of a new era: one of internally driven growth and focus on four core activities.

In fact, while it was selling with one hand, Grand Met was buying with the other. True to its roots as a deal-driven buyer of undervalued property assets, Grand Met continued to make acquisitions. In 1987, for example, it purchased Heublein Incorporated and its Almaden wine interests for £855 million. In a stroke, this netted it Smirnoff, the world's second largest spirit brand; a bigger leap forward than other companies might hope to make in decades. Nonetheless, there was a perceptible change in the mix of investment. In the same year, £340 million (equivalent to almost 6% of sales and 75% of pre-tax profits) went into the group's marketing budget for developing its existing consumer franchise.

IN AND OUT OF CITY FAVOUR

Watching these major portfolio shifts, the City financiers' assessments of Grand Met had been mixed. In the early 1980s it had enjoyed an undisputed premium rating. Then had followed a period of widespread disenchantment among the institutional investors. Despite good profitability in its core businesses, the group's growth in 'earnings per share' steadily declined between 1982 and 1986 (see Figure 1). Weakness in

© 1988, 1992 by Peter Williamson and London Business School
This case was prepared by Peter Williamson and Bernard Rix as the basis for class discussion rather than to illustrate either effective or ineffective handling of an administrative situation.

The casewriters gratefully acknowledge the assistance of Grand Metropolitan and the time and effort of Allen Sheppard and Peter Cawdron.

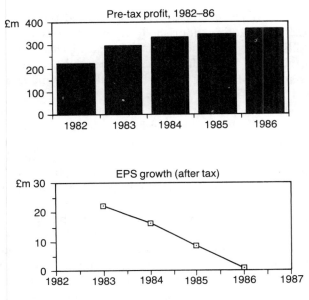

Fig. 1   Performance 1982–86

UK foods and contract services was followed by the disappearance of earnings growth in the novel combination of generic cigarettes and fitness products. The profitability of the moves into US health care looked doubtful and questions were being raised about Inter-Continental Hotels acquired from Pan Am in 1981. Sheppard had taken over as CEO at a time when some in the City were speculating that Grand Met, built on acquisitions, would itself soon be taken over and broken up.

The challenge then was to throw off the image of a loose conglomerate lacking strategic direction, and replace it with a conviction that the group represented a powerful combination of skills, more valuable than its independent parts, which could be relied upon for consistent profitability and above average earnings growth.

THE ASSET ESCALATOR

Despite market capitalization which ranked it number 14 in the UK by 1987, Grand Met was only 25 years young. Its founder, the late Sir Max Joseph, had registered the name 'Grand Metropolitan Hotels' in 1962 as the holding company for a chain of hotels he had been building up since the Second World War.

Bricks and mortar with an entrepreneurial spirit

Born in the East End of London in 1910, Joseph began his working life with a local firm of estate agents. Backed by borrowed capital he had started his own agency by the age of 20. Viewed by many as 'a natural entrepreneur', his venture flourished. Before he reached 30 he already owned a Rolls Royce and a house on Hampstead Heath. War service as a lance corporal in the Royal Engineers interrupted his business. His only regret, he remarked later, was that he would have made a much better field marshal.

In 1947 Max Joseph purchased his first hotel; the Mandeville in London's Mandeville Place. Despite high gearing, strong cash flows and rising property values made a second purchase possible in 1950: The Washington in Mayfair. Following a number of other hotel acquisitions, Joseph made an ambitious purchase of the Mount Royal at Marble Arch. With 712 bedrooms it was 600 rooms larger than anything the company had owned before.

With net worth now over £1 million, Max Joseph decided his business needed its own accountant. Stanley Grinstead was hired to fill the role. Ernest Sharp, also to become a leading figure in the group, joined in 1960. In 1961 the company went public, taking the Grand Metropolitan Hotels name in 1962. Hotel acquisitions continued, accompanied by a policy of actively marketing the company's hotel rooms, then a maverick concept, and centralized buying to cut costs.

Acquisitions continued rapidly: Gordon Hotels in 1964; the May Fair; the Metropole in Monte Carlo; the Carlton in Cannes; the Paris Lotti and Scribe hotels in 1966; the Manhattan in New York; the Castellana in Madrid; and three properties in Amsterdam in 1970.

During the 1960s Grand Met had very little corporate structure and the notable absence of a finance department, despite increasingly complex financial operations. The business was run by a triumvirate of Joseph, Grinstead, and Sharp, the latter men having been appointed as joint managing directors in 1967. At its most basic the strategy was to acquire 'trading property assets' in exchange for debt. The 'trading' element provided profits to cover the interest outgoings. Inflation led to rising values of the property assets while depreciating the real debt burden. Borrowing capacity was therefore automatically renewed, permitting the next acquisition.

From hotels to food and drinks

Hotels were not the only businesses to which this formula, parodied in the cartoon in Figure 2, might be successfully applied. Through experience in hotels, Grinstead and Sharp felt that Grand Met had acquired considerable skills in the management of catering and food. The company was also a very large buyer of drinks and knew what made them sell.

The catering business of Levy & Franks was purchased in 1966, bringing the property backed chain of Chef & Brewer pub–restaurants, grocery, and off-licence stores into the group. Bateman Catering, Midland Catering, and Empire Catering followed, some with substantial property interests.

Fig. 2 'I'm glad to see they're introducing tougher measures to keep up catering standards!'

In July 1969 Max Joseph made a £32 million bid for Express Dairy only 48 hours after learning that there was an opportunity to acquire. This family controlled company served almost one-quarter of all households in Britain through its door-to-door distribution of milk and dairy products under the Eden Vale, Express, and Ski trademarks. In addition to bottling plants, it also owned a portfolio of restaurants, hotels, grocery stores, and supermarkets. The price looked attractive to Joseph. The management problems which had led the former owners to sell a company with £18 million turnover and 16000 employees would be left to his deputies to sort out (see Figure 3).

1970 saw two other major acquisitions in the food and drinks sector. Berni Inns, which had grown from a single Exeter restaurant to a chain of 130 restaurant and hotel properties throughout the UK, was acquired for £14 million early in the year. With the Chef & Brewer chain this re-established Grand Met as the UK's largest hotel and catering group ahead of arch rival Charles Forte, who had pulled off a merger with Trust Houses.

In for a penny; in for a pound

The gaming company Mecca was the next major move. At a price of £33 million, Joseph felt the bingo halls, dance halls, and casinos, all of which brought new food, drink, and leisure operations, were a sure bet. With a

Fig. 3   Joseph lashes chief milkman.

Fig. 4   'The answer to our request for an increased offer was a lemon – and two raspberries, sir!'

network of high street betting shops they also netted a new catch of real estate assets (see Figure 4).

With the exception of Express, all of the acquisitions to date had been on 'friendly' terms. Max Joseph generally invited the former owners or top management to join the Grand Met board; examples included Frank Berni from Berni Inns and Eric Morley from Mecca. The result was a growth of the main board to 18. Many of the businesses continued to run much as they had prior to acquisition with little interference from the centre, short of sorting out major problems as and when they arose. It is probably fair to say that neither Joseph nor Grinstead showed much inclination to become deeply involved in day-to-day operations.

BUYING INTO THE 'BEERAGE'

Ask a brewer the classic strategy question, 'What business are you in?', and he will tell you 'brewing beer'. To Max Joseph, however, the breweries with their massive pub estates were a large and neglected set of 'earning' property assets. He first set his sights on Truman Hanbury Buxton, a medium sized brewery with an extensive property portfolio in London and the south-east, including 986 public houses, 138 off-licences, and 21 small hotels and motels. Again the successful Grand Met formula looked applicable. This time, however, Max Joseph was seeking to buy into a conservative and tight-knit industry run by a small group of families (known as 'the beerage'). Others had tried in the 1960s and failed. It was clear, nonetheless, that many of the breweries were poorly managed businesses, making inefficient use of their extensive assets. At the same time the brewing unions, who favoured Joseph, were becoming stronger.

Grand Met's initial bid for Truman had been blocked by one of its much larger 'beerage' brethren, Watney Mann, acting as a 'white knight'. After 14 bids the Truman board recommended Grand Met's offer of £48 million.

It was an irony that within nine months of the Truman acquisition a banker was to offer Joseph a stake in that former 'white knight' Watney Mann. As Britain's fourth largest brewer it enjoyed a 12% market share and, of course, a massive property portfolio of 4400 tenanted pubs. Being determined to fight the bid to the last and having learnt from the Truman battle, the Watney Mann directors decided to increase the stakes. Prior to the bid they had held a one-third interest in International Distillers and Vintners (IDV), an amalgamation of some of the oldest and most respected names in the wines and spirits business including Croft, W&A Gilbey, and Justerini & Brooks (J&B Scotch). Following Joseph's attack, Watney Mann purchased the other 67% of IDV with specially created, non-registered new shares. To take Watney Mann, Joseph would now have to pull off what in 1972 would be the largest ever industrial acquisition in the UK, doubling the size of the existing Grand Met (see Figure 5).

Fig. 5 'Never mind how many shares – I make it over 5 000 000 pints!'

Some 115 days and three offers later, and after five letters and a telegram to all 30 000 of Watney's shareholders, Grand Met's holding passed the critical 50.1% mark. The total cost was estimated at £435 million (or 2000 million pints at the prices of the day!).

As part of the Watney takeover, Joseph had been negotiating with Sir John Davis of the Rank Group to dispose of IDV. In the event the deal fell through. This added to the huge quantity of paper Grand Met was forced to issue to finance the move. In addition to £220 million of convertibles, its debt equity ratio was pushed to the limit.

CRISIS AND RECOVERY, 1973–79

Following the oil shock, the British economy entered deepening recession. Between 1973 and 1975 it faced plummeting production, the three-day week, and the secondary banking crisis. The property market burst.

The Watney Mann acquisition had left Grand Met facing this period with a heavy debt burden and associated interest payments. Worse still, Watney's excessive dependence on a single national brand, its low market share in the growing lager segment, and poor sales outside its tied houses, began to show through. This was followed by a disastrous advertising association with the 'red revolution' which irreparably damaged Watney's key 'red barrel' trade mark and heavily eroded its consumer franchise. As had long been his practice, Max Joseph had made only minor changes to the management of what had become WMT (Watney, Mann and Truman) after the acquisition. It was, it seemed, proving to be a mistake.

On what became known inside the company as 'black Monday', the shares (selling at £9.20 in 1992) reached a low, equivalent to nine pence. At these levels conversion of the debt would be unattractive to shareholders, and would leave Grand Met with the huge interest bill indefinitely. The banks, as one executive put it, 'were tapping Max on the shoulder'.

Joseph was convinced, however, that his property assets would ultimately prove a source of real strength as the only effective hedge against rapid inflation. Finding the profits to meet the interest drain and to ride out the storm now became the only priority. The urgency increased following the announcement in 1974 of the only fall in trading profits in the firm's history.

The first finance director of Grand Met, appointed in 1975, was charged with tightening up controls on the rather independent management of individual businesses, and at the same time working with the City to ensure conversion of the debt. Allen Sheppard, with experience of cost reduction and rationalization in the motor industry, was recruited as the Managing Director of WMT. His appointment saw the rapid resuscitation of WMT's regional brand names (such as Websters, Wilsons, Manns, and Ushers), along with concerted expansion of the Carlsberg and Holsten brands. Sheppard also quickly tackled the neglected production side of the brewing business, acting to increase productivity and reduce costs.

IDV was separated from WMT shortly after the acquisition, with Anthony Tennant, a former director of Truman, in charge. Tennant was from a strong marketing and advertising background and began to drive through new product introductions aimed at better use of the conservative IDV's worldwide distribution channels. Perhaps the most notable success was to be the launch of Bailey's Irish Cream, a joint venture with Express Foods. The product has since become the world's best selling liqueur.

By the end of the 1970s, cash flow and profit had sharply improved. The debt conversion was achieved. Joseph's property instinct had again proven correct: appreciation in the value of the property assets had added an extra £420 million to the balance sheet by 1979 leaving gearing back at very respectable levels.

INTERNATIONALIZATION

Turnover had reached £2583 million with a trading profit of £213 million when Max Joseph handed over to Stanley Grinstead as Chief Executive in 1980. The problems of the mid-1970s, however, had left an indelible imprint on the management. It was decided that priority should be given to reducing dependence on the UK economy and establishing a solid income stream out of the US.

Tobacco, alcohol, and fitness

The US company, Liggett Group Inc, was targeted. Their wines and spirits interests included IDV's distributor of J&B Scotch, the Paddington Corporation. Liggett's core business was cigarette manufacturing which had diversified into soft drinks bottling, fitness products, and Alpo pet foods, as well as wines and spirits. Joseph had doubts about Liggett, but left the final decision to Grinstead.

Prior to the hard fought acquisition for $450 million, Grand Met had intended to sell the tobacco businesses which, despite high cash flow, it regarded as a long-term liability. Despite a long decline in market position, under-investment in their brands, and some questionable diversification in the past, the incumbent Liggett management persuaded Grand Met that its move into generic cigarettes offered considerable growth and market share potential. Their plans for expansion of fitness products were also accepted by the new owners.

A jewel for the hotel crown

Finding itself in desperate financial straits, Pan Am was considering disposal of its premier Inter-Continental Hotels subsidiary (IHC) in August 1981. This time Max Joseph had no doubts. After only one week Stanley Grinstead had completed the deal for $500 million.

Concurrent with the IHC acquisition, Grand Met rationalized its existing hotel holdings. Around 10 were converted to the IHC standard, a number of others formed the basis of the group's second rank chain, Forum. The remaining 60 or so were sold, including 40 UK country hotels to Queens Moat. This brought a quiet, but important change in strategy: the vast bulk of IHC's hotels were managed on service contracts rather than owned.

Again the IHC management was retained; indeed, all of Grand Met's hotel interests now became their responsibility.

IN SEARCH OF A STRATEGY

Seeking its next source of growth, Grand Met began to acquire firms in US 'branded services' as from 1983. Its choice of Children's World (a chain of kindergarten/child care centres), Quality Care (home health care), and Pearle Optical (the largest US chain of retail opticians) reflected a desire to be on the right side of demographic and social trends.

Despite favourable growth prospects, these moves were controversial. Would profitability fall victim to a rush of new entry? Could these kinds of services be successfully branded? Without a consumer franchise and the associated opportunities for scale advantages in advertising and marketing, the historic fragmentation of these markets was likely to reassert itself: small, local entrepreneurs in child care and optical, and the hospitals themselves in home health care.

Grand Met was clearly taking a gamble on growth. The exit price–earnings ratio for the Pearle acquisition, for example, was 19. Physical assets were modest; $253 million of the $386 million purchase price represented goodwill.

The City again began to ask questions. The shine had been taken off Grand Met's premium rating; the conglomerate had become an unpopular animal and Grand Met's claim to a different classification seemed difficult to justify.

A NEW CORPORATE MISSION: ADDING VALUE

> The twenty-fifth anniversary of the founding of Grand Metropolitan would seem an auspicious time to add a new element to the communication of the group to its many and varied audiences. The message we have chosen to communicate is the value that the scope and scale of the group adds to its constituent companies.

Thus wrote Sir Stanley Grinstead, Chairman of Grand Metropolitan, in a supplement to the 1986 Annual Report (see Exhibits 1 and 2). The sceptics saw in it more than a passing irony. Even for a company with turnover exceeding £5 billion, employing 130 000 people worldwide, its activities were diverse. In 1986 its businesses embraced brewing (Ruddles, Manns, Webster's, Watney's, and UK licences for Carlsberg, Budweiser, and Fosters); restaurants (Berni Inns, Chef and Brewer); catering (Compass Services); betting and gaming (Mecca); branded foods (Express, Eden Vale); US consumer products and services (ALPO pet foods, Pepsi bottling interests, DP Corp fitness products, Pearle opticians, Quality Care home health care, Children's World kindergartens); hotels (IHC); branded wines and spirits through IDV (Bailey's, Malibu, Le Piat d'Or, J&B); oil exploration (with interst in four North Sea blocks); off-licences and licensed premises (Peter Dominic, Watney Mann and Truman); to name only its better known businesses. Moreover, after making an acquisition it had often made few changes to the incumbent management or its policies and, historically, deal making had seemed to take precedence over close involvement in individual activities as the concern of the corporate centre.

BEHIND THE SCENES

While Grand Met's acquisition deals continued to capture the headlines, a new group of 'operational managers', led by Allen Sheppard, were bringing about what were to become even more significant changes in the company. Many of these went largely unnoticed by outsiders at the time, yet the individual actions were forming a pattern which was to dominate the strategy of the company in the period which followed. The emergence of this strategy can be traced through UK brewing and retailing, the turnaround of Express Foods, replacement of management and disposal

Exhibit 1 A new corporate mission – 'adding value'.

A hallmark on a piece of gold or silver communicates the intrinsic value of an object over and above the design and character of the piece itself. Thus, analagously, the use of a corporate symbol based on the traditional English system of hallmarking allows Grand Metropolitan to communicate the added value that membership of the group confers on its component companies and brands.

Grand Metropolitan's record of success over the last twenty-five years is evidence of the many ways in which the group does, indeed, add value to its individual operations.

The group has used its assets with shrewdness and imagination to achieve rapid growth by acquisition, using the property base to achieve high gearing at those times when borrowings have been needed to fund an acquisition.

It has invested its funds strategically to develop companies at times when, for reasons of competition, modernisation or growth prospects, one part of the group was judged to have a higher priority than others.

The group has a varied portfolio of companies but at the same time ensures that each company is a substantial competitor in its own market place.

It has developed, through operational experience and consumer research, a remarkable knowledge of the hotel, leisure, food, property, retailing and alcoholic beverage markets in the United Kingdom and United States in particular, and in African, Australasian, American, European and Asian countries. Such knowledge of distribution channels, consumer behaviour and motivation has given valuable insight into local and world trends and developments.

The group has built brands in many markets which are of immense value and which are continuously maintained and strengthened by skilful marketing. In addition it has an enviable record of success in new brand introduction.

The breadth of the group's activities provides an exceptional opportunity for the training of management. The range and variety of its international markets allows the development of a cadre of senior management which compares very favourably with those of other United Kingdom or United States corporations. Our managers are capable both of setting strategic objectives and executing programmes to achieve them. They are quick to identify change and adapt to it. They are not narrow-minded in their approach to problems.

These are some of the most important ways in which Grand Metropolitan 'adds value' to the planning and activity of its component companies. To communicate this special characteristic of Grand Metropolitan, we have introduced our new symbol - a 'hallmark' of the intrinsic value of the group itself. The English system of hallmarking consists of at least three elements which serve as a kind of symbolic language. The three marks denote, by registered symbols, the place of origin, the date and the material out of which the piece is made.

In adapting this symbolic system to the corporate identity of Grand Metropolitan there was a happy coincidence that the group itself has three main operating areas - the United Kingdom, the United States and International.

The three elements of the symbol have been chosen with care. The 'lion passant' is a historic Standard hallmark for silver and is used to symbolise the United Kingdom base of operations. The sun - which aptly symbolises the international sphere of operations - has been used as the London Assay mark for imported gold and silver. The eagle provides a convenient symbol for Grand Metropolitan's North American operations.

Just as a hallmark on silver or gold attests to its guaranteed value, so we trust that the Grand Metropolitan 'hallmark' will serve as a reminder of our past record and as a pledge of our future success.

GRAND METROPOLITAN

....adding value

Exhibit 2   Financial performance to 1987.

Five-year record based on the consolidated financial statements for years ended 30th September

	1983 (£m)	1984 (£m)	1985 (£m)	1986 (£m)	1987 (£m)
Balance sheet					
Fixed assets	2242.1	2430.2	2787.6	2755.5	2902.4
Other assets	307.7	308.8	230.3	249.4	221.2
	2549.8	2739.0	3017.9	3004.9	3123.6
Less: net borrowings	943.9	961.0	1019.4	932.8	1358.2
	1605.9	1778.0	1998.5	2072.1	1765.4
Capital and reserves	1566.4	1744.1	1965.0	2045.5	1737.1
Minority shareholder's interests	39.5	33.9	33.5	26.6	28.3
	1605.9	1778.0	1998.5	2072.1	1765.4
Profit and loss account					
Turnover	4468.8	5075.0	5589.5	5291.3	5705.5
Trading profit	407.0	443.9	453.2	487.4	571.6
Reorganization costs	(19.2)	(36.1)	(40.7)	(27.1)	(9.3)
Profit on sale of property	10.2	22.6	4.7	8.7	14.0
Interest	(111.8)	(109.6)	(105.9)	(101.3)	(120.2)
Profit after taxation	286.2	320.8	311.3	367.7	456.1
Taxation	83.3	85.6	64.4	91.8	120.1
Profit after taxation	202.9	235.2	246.9	275.9	336.0
Minorities and preference dividends	5.0	4.0	4.7	2.8	2.8
Profit attributable to ordinary shareholders	197.9	231.2	242.2	273.1	333.2
Extraordinary items	1.6	(20.2)	29.9	(11.7)	127.8
Profit for the financial year	199.5	211.0	272.1	261.4	461.0
Ordinary dividends	58.0	67.1	79.2	87.5	103.1
Transferred to reserves	141.5	143.9	192.9	173.9	357.9
Earnings per share (see note 1 below)	25.0p	28.9p	29.0p	32.1p	38.9p
Ordinary dividends per share	9.625p	9.2p	10.0p	10.25p	12.0p
Dividends as adjusted (see note 1 below)	7.29p	8.36p	9.09p	10.25p	12.0p
Dividend cover	3.4	3.5	3.1	3.1	3.2

Notes:
1 Adjustments have been made to take account of the 1984 and 1986 capitalisation issues.
2 The figures for 1983 to 1986 have been restated to reflect the change in accounting policy for routine sales of property and those reorganization costs which were formerly included in extraordinary items.

of much of the Liggett businesses, and the development of IDV's portfolio.

UK brewing and retailing

After steady growth in volume during the 1970s, the UK beer market declined sharply in the face of the 1980 recession, contraction of the heavy 'thirst creating' industries such as steel and coal, and heavy increases in duty between 1980 and 1982. A radical reassessment of cost structures, capacity, and the returns on the brand and retail property assets became necessary. This was impeded, however, by the vertical integration, from production through distribution and marketing, in the brewing business and the cross-subsidization which resulted.

Since his appointment as the head of Watney's in 1975, Sheppard had been strengthening the management team. Key figures included Clive Strowger, a former colleague from the motor industry recruited in 1977, Ian Martin, recruited from ITT in 1979, and David Tagg in 1980, who would become responsible for the organization's management development. Together this team set about tackling the problems, now intensified by declining demand.

The brewing and wholesaling functions (WMTB) were separated from the pub retailing business. The result was a sharp decrease in the transfer price of beer from the brewery, reflecting commercial reality.

In the face of their now meagre profits, the production and wholesaling divisions began to implement an aggressive rationalization programme to put costs in line with revenue. The now more powerful pub retailing division, with the freedom to buy outside, demanded WMTB supply brands with a strong customer franchise; products which would aid the flow of custom in to the pub. A more realistic view of pub profitability, meanwhile, underpinned the allocation of investment to pub refurbishment, enhancing an asset which had formerly been run down as a 'poor cousin' of production.

WMTB cut its workforce by 5000 (50% of the former total), eliminated surplus capacity and inefficient sites, pared the administration, and disposed of peripheral soft drinks, machinery production, and continental brewing interests, releasing £82 million of capital by June 1986.

With four brewery sites instead of nine, and dramatically improved productivity, WMTB arguably became the UK cost leader at the production end of the business.

The early 1980s also saw major innovation and expansion of WMTB's brand portfolio, shifting it from heavy reliance on the protection of tied sales to a set of strong, sales-generating customer franchises. In the lager segment, WMTB negotiated rights for Fosters (launched 1981) and Budweiser (launched 1984) to complement the development of its existing Carlsberg and Holsten brands. It also obtained an exclusive 'on-trade' franchise for the Guinness non-alcoholic Kaliber. In the ale segment, it began by strong re-establishment of its regional brands. This was followed by the gradual transformation of Websters Yorkshire Bitter into a national brand and the acquisition of Ruddles to meet the growing 'real ale' demand. Testimony to the success of this brand development strategy is the 59% of WMTB products currently sold to the take-home market and non-tied houses (compared with an industry average of 51%), while maintaining the second lowest discounts among the national producers. A programme of aggressive advertising spend accompanied the changes with media spend settling at around 15% of the industry total.

Finally, returns on the pub real estate portfolio were carefully analysed and improved. The tenanted estate was culled and rents reviewed. The managed houses have seen the introduction of high-margin food, and the gradual conversion of sites into segment specific 'styles' under three brand names: Chef & Brewer (450 outlets) covering three traditional pub formats, namely food based 'taverns', 'ale houses', and 'locals'; Open House (250 locations) covering contemporary pubs, namely 'Open House Bar', music and light 'Style Bar', and the snooker table equipped 'Sports'; and Clifton Inns covering the portfolio of 130 independent character, high-quality pubs.

These moves culminated in 1987 with the complete managerial separation of three distinct activities: Grand Met Brewing and Branding (responsible for production and marketing); Grand Met Estates (which owns the entire estate portfolio); and Grand Met Retailing (which is responsible for running the non-tenanted pubs). Specialist management is employed in each company: a 'property man' runs Grand Met Estates; a 'retailer' manages Grand Met Retailing. Market rents and selling prices are charged in intra-company transactions with each business reporting separately up to the main board. This permits a clarity of separate objectives: selling beer, maximizing property returns, and maximizing total sales of all products from each pub, respectively. It differs from the 'integrated' structure, prominent among competitors, in which maintaining beer volumes may artificially dominate the other imperatives of the business.

The Berni restaurant chain was subject to a similar transformation from the early 1980s. A substantial proportion of the 300-site portfolio had occupied poor locations in town centres with restricted parking. The chain was described by one commentator as having a 'tired formula with indifferent quality of premises and service to match'. After management control passed to the Sheppard team, some 100 sites were sold, releasing capital to be reinvested in upgrading the remaining more promising sites. Decor was upgraded, menus improved to meet growing demand for variety, and staff retrained. Purchasing and distribution were centralized to improve the chains cost position and ensure quality and consistency.

Express Foods

The £36.4 million trading profits earned by Express Foods in 1980/81 had dropped to £16.4 million by 1983/84. Recently appointed as director of

Grand Met's UK operations, Sheppard transferred Clive Strowger in to head Express in 1984. Mike Hodgkinson, another member of his former brewing team, followed as deputy in 1985.

Morale was low, the management structure highly centralized, and distribution systems failing. Peripheral businesses, such as tomato processing and paté manufacture, had added complexity to the task of management and diverted the focus from key issues of cost structure in the core business. Retailers' own label in products such as yoghurt were threatening the weakened brands and EEC quota restrictions were creating an imbalance between capacity and supply.

A four-part plan was put into action by the new team. Firstly, improved product quality and cost reductions of £6 million per annum were achieved in parallel through tighter process control, reduced raw material wastage, upgrading of quality assurance personnel, capacity rationalization, reduced manning, and plant modernization. Secondly, new computer systems with a customer service orientation were introduced. Thirdly, the peripheral businesses were disposed of.

The final part comprised a far-reaching product development and marketing programme. Express became a leader in additive-free products following the trend to more healthy, natural products. The Ski brand was relaunched, backed by new packaging and a wider product range, supported with a targeted 'lifestyle' advertising campaign.

By 1985/86 profits had recovered to £39 million with a further £100 million cash contribution to the group flowing from disposals and reduced working capital. A dramatic turnaround was also achieved in the contract services (catering) business; a loss of £11 million in 1983/84 had become a profit of £10 million by 1985/86.

THE LIGGETT AND MECCA DISPOSALS

The UK brewing and food operations – Sheppard's area of responsibility – had been the first to undertake a systematic disposal of businesses aimed at focusing the portfolio and concentrating development effort. The belief in the disposal of businesses lacking either growth potential or 'fit' – thinking quite absent from Grand Met's earlier history – began to spread.

A management buyout of the Liggett generic cigarette interests, which had grown its US market share in this segment from 1.5% to 5% on the initiative of the incumbent management, was proposed for $325 million. Before the deal was completed, however, a severe price war broke out in the generic market, undermining profitability. The buyout plans collapsed. In the event the major divisions were subsequently disposed of separately: Pinkerton Chewing Tobacco in August 1985 for $137 million; L&M do Brazil (leaf tobacco) in November 1985 for $19 million; and the remaining Liggett Group interests in October 1986 for $137 million.

Mecca Leisure, which operated bingo halls, catering, entertainment, and UK holidays, was also sold off. This represented another turning point: sale of a significant business (worth £95 million) which had con-

Exhibit 3   Trends in the world spirits market.

World spirits depletion by category
(excluding local traditional spirits and communist countries)

Category	1975	1986	%
	Millions of cases		
Whisk(e)y			
Scotch	68	64	−6
Japanese	25	27	+8
Canadian	29	27	−7
Bourbon/Tennessee	33	20	−39
American blended	24	12	−50
Irish/other	7	6	−14
Total whisk(e)y	186	155	−7
White spirits			
Vodka	53	61	+15
Rum	56	62	+11
Gin	42	41	+2
Tequila	8	7	−12
Other	17	13	−4
Total white spirits	176	184	+5
Specialities			
Liqueurs	41	62	+51
Brandy	75	77	+3
Bitters/aperitifs	29	24	−17
Anise/pastis	24	25	+4
Cocktails and mixed drinks	3	7	+133
Other	10	10	u/c
Total specialities	182	205	+12
Total distilled spirits	544	544	u/c

Source: *Impact*; Industry Forecasts Ltd, The Brewer's Society and Media Expenditure Analysis Ltd.

tinued to perform satisfactorily. The rationale here was twofold. First, given the nature of its markets and expertise, Mecca leisure had little chance of growing into a material part of the total Grand Met group. Second, its success depended largely on hands-on, entrepreneurial style. In this case it would almost certainly perform best under fully independent management. It was perceived as having little to gain and much to lose by being under a large, corporate umbrella.

DEVELOPMENTS WITHIN IDV

Since the time of its acquisition as part of Watney Mann in 1972, IDV's trading profits had risen from £12 million to £147 million in 1985/86 on turnover of more than £1 billion. Against a background of stagnation or decline in the volume consumed in the world's major spirits markets (see Exhibit 3), this was an exceptional performance.

IDV's success derived from the confluence of several key policies. First among these was an emphasis on direct sales to retailers in contrast to the standard industry reliance on a network of single nation distributors. This improved access to market intelligence as well as aiding the launch of new brands by removing the marketing slippage which commonly arose between manufacturer and retailer.

The second key element was a stronger commitment to new product development than its competitors. With 55 launches between 1980 and 1986, IDV accounted for 32% of all new product introductions made by the world's seven leading spirits companies. These included Bailey's Irish Cream (2.5 million cases pa), Piat d'Or (2 million cases pa) and Malibu (1.4 million cases pa). In 1986 there were a further 25 new products being test marketed.

A third factor was above average spend on brand marketing, some 33% above the industry norm per pound (£) of sales. Fourthly, IDV concentrated its efforts on the growth segments: vodka, tequila, liqueurs, and cocktails, with less emphasis on new sales in the declining 'brown spirits' sector.

Finally, IDV had been active in forming alliances as a means of accessing powerful brands. These included the purchase of agency marketing rights, taking 'friendly' equity stakes, and forming joint marketing companies as an alternative to full acquisition. This policy provided IDV with key brands like Amaretto di Saronno, Cinzano, and Cointreau which were becoming recognized across the increasingly global upmarket consumer segment. For their owners, often European family companies, they preserved independence while offering greatly enhanced global distribution.

Under Anthony Tennant, who had been Marketing Director of Truman at the time of the 1971 acquisition, moving across to IDV in 1975, the company had developed a strong culture based on branded price premia for its products. Discounting was an anathema. This was combined with belief in rigorous market analysis, proximity to the customer, and heavy promotional support. This team, led by Tennant and his deputy George Bull, had largely operated in parallel with Sheppard's initiatives in the Brewing, Retailing, and Foods groups. While the two 'streams' had many management approaches in common, IDV had not been involved in the same heavy cost rationalization or disposal of peripheral activities.

THE SHEPPARD ERA

In a matter of weeks after Sheppard's appointment as CEO in 1986, two Board resignations were to follow. Clive Strowger became Finance Director of the group, as well as retaining operating responsibility for Express. Ian Martin was moved into another key slot, becoming chairman of Grand Met USA. George Bull continued as Chief Executive of IDV, a position he had held since 1985. Tennant became Deputy Chief Executive, but was soon to resign, subsequently joining Guinness.

The result was a four-man team of executive directors at the top, all with extensive operating experience and a shared managerial ethos. They were supported by a small, high-level staff comprising ex-merchant banker, Peter Cawdron (strategic planning), David Tagg (personnel and group services) who had headed this function in the UK divisions, and Tim Halford (public affairs). This was rounded out by a strong group of non-executive directors: R V Giordano (Chairman and Chief Executive of The BOC Group); Sir John Harvey-Jones (Chairman of ICI); and F J Pizzitola (a Lazard Frères & Co. partner). In 1988 Sir Colin Marshall of British Airways and David Tagg joined this existing Board (see Exhibit 4).

Operation 'declutter'

Following reform of the management structure, 1987 saw portfolio rationalization continue rapidly. Disposals included: the Scottish brewery Drybrough; an interest in the Queens Moat Houses hotel group; the dairy interests of Express Foods USA; the North Sea oil interests; the Contract Services division; the US home nursing operation Quality Care; DP fitness products; and the child care and kindergarten subsidiary Children's World.

The two US branded services businesses were perhaps the most radical disposals for different reasons. Quality Care, which had been purchased in 1985 for a net price of $115 million, was sold for $102 million. Children's World sold for $117 million, the multiple of 58 times earnings implying enormous growth potential. Sheppard argued they were 'clutter'. Their ability to develop a strong brand franchise and sustained profitability was doubtful at best; their fit with the strategic vision now binding the Group together was poor, and lacking the critical size to be a significant contributor to Grand Met's portfolio; they diverted management attention from the core businesses disproportionately to their potential. He might add that both were sold to buyers with other operations in the same sectors.

The largest of the 1987 disposals was Contract Services for £160 million; this was a business which was making money. However, again the Sheppard team doubted the scope for true consumer branding as a route to higher margins. Increases in market share, without further acquisitions, looked unlikely, especially against the dominance of Trusthouse Forte. In the event, the business was sold as a management buyout.

In early 1988 the decision to dispose of the US Pepsi bottling interests was taken. The successful sale of this business for $705 million in July signalled the completion of the 'declutter' operation.

Exhibit 4   The organizational structure in early 1988.

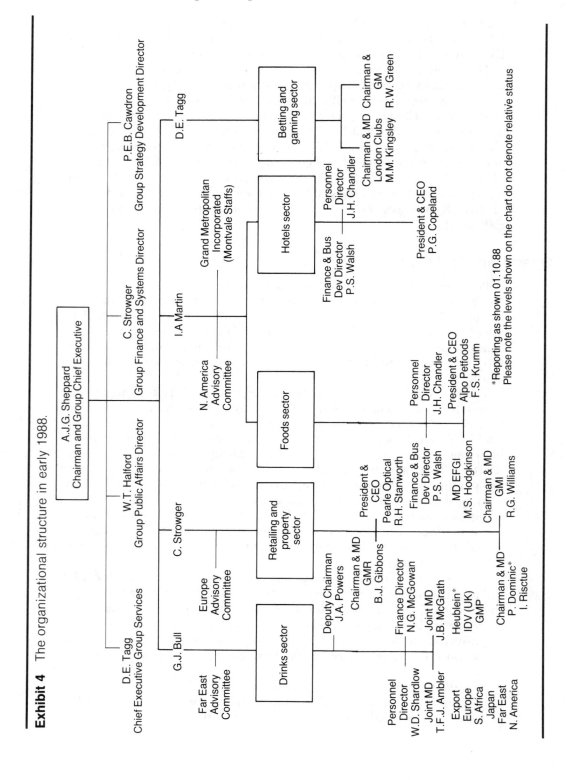

Exhibit 5   The IDV–Heublein product portfolio.

IDV–Heublein brand portfolio (excluding wines)

Brands	Category	US	Canada	UK	Europe Inc. Eire	Japan	Australasia & Rest of Asia	Latin America	Africa	Duty free and other	Total
							Thousand cases				
Smirnoff	Vodka	7020	900	1850	950	20	150	1700	850	660	14100
J&B	Scotch	1900	90	70	1800	170	65	100	320	385	4900
Popov	Vodka	3800	85	155	10			150			4200
Bailey's	Liqueur	1100	180	375	480	10	155			200	2500
Black Velvet	Canadian	1750	300		50						2100
Malibu	Liqueur	120	35	425	500	5	75	10	20	110	1300
Arrow	Liqueur	1200									1200
Gilbey's†	Gin		150	170	230	40	140	50	120	200	1100
Jose Cuervo*	Tequila	1100									1100
Club Cocktails	Cocktails	1100									1100
Croft	Sherry			690	115					295	1100
Dreher	Brandy							1100			1100
Absolut*	Vodka	1000									1000
Relska	Vodka	725									725
Amaretto di Soronno*	Liqueur	700									700
Croft	Port			80	240					230	550
Wild Turkey*	Bourbon	535									535
Grand Marnier*	Liqueur	455									455
Silk Tassel & Gold	Canadian		390								390
Sambuca Romana	Liqueur	280			20						300
Bombay Gin	Gin	205									205
Yuhon Jack	Liqueur	215									215
Finlandia*	Vodka	190									190
Delaforce	Port		15	140						15	170
Sub total		23395	2130	3830	4535	245	580	3110	1310	2095	41230
Other brands and agencies		2005	3900	800	300			1300	600	400	6270
Total case vols.		25400	3030	4630	4835	245	580	4410	1910	2495	47500
% of Total		53.4%	6.4%	9.7%	10.2%	0.5%	1.2%	9.3%	4.0%	5.3%	100%

Notes:
1 Fortified wines, i.e. sherry and port, have been counted in the spirits definition.
2 *Denotes US agency distribution rights.
3 †This excludes the licence to James B Beam in the US; similarly the licence for Gilbey's vodka to James B Beam in the US is excluded.

The Heublein acquisition

A number of City analysts commented that at $1.3 billion, the Heublein–Almaden acquisition was another example of Grand Met's ability to execute a large acquisition quickly. Despite this commonality with the past, however, Heublein was a very different kind of acquisition in many respects.

IDV had held the licence for Smirnoff (Heublein's major brand) for over 30 years in the UK, Canada, South Africa, Australia, and Eire, accounting for around 30% of the brand's worldwide volume. The managements knew each other well and enjoyed strong rapport. They rapidly integrated under IDV's CEO, George Bull.

The businesses also had very similar strategies at the operating level. A major tenet of Heublein's strategy was to convince consumers not to purchase a 'commodity brand' for home use, as reflected in its 'Friends are worth Smirnoff' advertising campaign. It had strongly avoided discounting, introducing two second-line products, Popov and Relska as 'flanking brands' to fight lower priced competition. It has invested heavily in new products in the growth segments of the market including prepared cocktails (Tropical Freezer) and fruit-flavoured liqueurs (Peaches and Cream). Heublein has also made use of marketing alliances to obtain access to strong existing brands, the best example being Jose Cuervo in the growing tequila market.

The 'fit' of the two businesses had been highly complementary. Sales of 'super-premium' imported vodkas in the US market were growing, especially in the bar trade. IDV was already the importer of the largest of these (Absolut from Sweden) through its US company Carillon. As well as doubling IDV's sales of spirits, the merger rounded out its product line (see Exhibit 5). Together the companies now control some 15% of a concentrating US spirits market.

At the same time, the acquisition of Heublein's Almaden wine subsidiary led to a five-fold increase in IDV's wine volumes, giving it 11.5% of the US market, a business which IDV had consciously avoided. Trading conditions here had become difficult following a slowing of the rapid growth of the 1970s combined with large increments in market capacity. The problems, however, had close parallels with the earlier state of UK brewing. Grand Met moved to rationalize plants and increase capacity utilization and productivity. IDV began to look like a cost leader in the business, while a number of other major players including National Distillers and Chemicals and Seagrams announced withdrawal from this market.

Inter-Continental Hotels

In line with the policies of its former parent, Pan Am, the roots of IHC had been firmly planted in the hotel management, rather than property ownership, business. Plans to depart from this policy at the time of the takeover in 1981 seemed to strike a responsive chord with Grand Met's tradition as both hotel owner and manager combined. Construction of three wholly-owned IHC hotels in the US went forward.

Their completion in 1984 coincided with a sharp drop in US occupancy rates, not the least in oil-impacted Houston where a new 'flagship' property was located. The result was a trading loss estimated at $8 million, plus interest on the $130 million development costs of the three properties in 1985/86. This profit hit was subsequently aggravated by a decline in US travel to Europe in the wake of a declining dollar, Chernobyl, and increased terrorism.

Running a luxury, premium price hotel chain had hardly acted to nurture cost cutting skills in IHC. In June 1987 Sheppard appointed Ian Martin as Chairman of IHC in addition to his existing responsibilities as Chief Executive of Grand Met USA. The former international marketing director of IDV was installed as the CEO of IHC, and the key finance, personnel, and marketing functions were filled by proven executives from WMTB and Express.

Determined focus on cash flow and overhead reduction followed, lines of management communication were shortened, and unnecessary layers removed. The business definition was clearly shifted back to hotel management and away from property ownership: the plans for 12 new hotels were split between nine management contracts and three franchises, none of which would be wholly owned; the property function was separated in respect of the existing portfolio. Resources were channelled into a renewed brand positioning centring on an international image, rather than the 'refuge for American travellers' flavour which had tended to result from Pan Am's emphasis on cross-selling other goods and services to its airline passengers.

MANAGEMENT STYLE AND THE ROLE OF THE CENTRE

Sheppard has been credited with describing his management style as 'a light grip on the throat'. Whether true or not, it is not a label he has tried to throw off; he has simply emphasised the 'light'. Other quotations include:

'We as a Group thrive on controlled conflict'

'The problem was a high degree of indiscipline and no constant image and uniformity throughout the chain (Berni)'

'I actually remember writing a memo saying that if anyone isn't clear what authority they have – do it and ask afterwards'

His colleagues agree that he promotes a culture where managers should not avoid taking appropriately considered risks, and that, 'He is not afraid of rolling up his shirtsleeves and mucking in'.

Against the background of this style, Grand Met faced the issue of balancing devolved responsibility and autonomy at the operations level with the need to maintain a consistent strategic focus across the group and meet its corporate financial goals. Its solution has been what the company calls a managerial 'challenge culture' driven from the centre in parallel by the strategy finance and personnel functions. Through these networks, the corporate centre monitors, encourages, and questions the operations. The strategy of each business is constantly probed and challenged by the centre. As the environment changes and competitors play their moves, the assumptions on which the strategy was built are revisited and questioned. Progress in building the strategy is reviewed. The strong personnel function is designed to spot potential problems before they ultimately show up in the numbers, to attract good management, train them, and understand their skills so as to accumulate a critical

Exhibit 6   Grand Met's organizational philosophy

Organizational Philosophy
- Decentralized authority
- Open communications
- Challenge culture
- Small corporate centre adding value
- Avoidance of bureaucracy
- Strong performance orientation
- No compromise on high management standards
- Development of people
- Tolerance of different personalties and styles
- Action orientation
- Major role in trade and industry affairs

mass of knowledge within the group and a pool of proven managers who can be transferred into a subsidiary when problems arise or market developments necessitate unfamiliar shifts in strategy and organization.

Grand Met also emphasises motivation of its line managers. Based on the conduct of a regular survey of rewards offered by comparable large companies, it aims to maintain its senior managers' compensation in the upper quartile of industry. Performance-related bonuses and stock option incentives also play an important role.

The centre's role is a great deal more proactive than the 'holding company' model. The executive directors are each wearing two hats: that of a corporate officer with a responsibility toward the group, and that of an operating officer responsible for their division's performance. This includes Sheppard, to whom Brewing, UK Retailing, and Betting and Gaming directly report. Grand Met's organizational philosophy is summarised in Exhibit 6.

MANAGERIAL PROCESS

Central to the process are the following elements:

- agreed strategy;
- business plan;
- budget;
- monthly reviews.

Strategy is reviewed on an ongoing basis as part of the 'constant probing' process. Progress on strategic goals is monitored and the course of development re-examined. Once a year this is written into an agreed 'vision statement' for each business and details of four types of development thrust: growth of the core business, development of new brands, acquisition of new brands, and expansion of distribution. Budget type numbers are strictly prohibited at these meetings which involve the central executive and the key operating managers.

Agreed strategy is converted to a business plan which is separately reviewed. Numbers are taken five years out, being increasingly specific over the first two years. This involves the board and the operating management, and commonly takes several days.

The annual budget follows. Its first section must be a *bridge* to the business plan; the 'free hanging' budget is not a recognized species.

Sheppard closely monitors performance against budget with a half day 'call over' meeting with each of the four operational executives every month, sometimes fortnightly. Additional strategy meetings are held with individual businesses in response to unexpected market developments, such as a major competitor move. These reformulate the market scenario and decide what response, if any, is appropriate.

Each year a report on around 550 of the senior operating managers is carried out, with the top 150 being the subject of detailed board review of their developing capabilities and the future positions they may fill. Succession plans and the transfer of skills throughout the organization are therefore assured.

OPERATION BUILD?

Eighteen months after Sheppard became CEO, the shape of Grand Metropolitan had undergone another series of major changes. In many ways the long term repositioning of the organization which originated in UK brewing and retailing and IDV in the latter 1970s, had been completed. It permeated not only the strategic focus, but also the organizational structure, management style, and decision-making processes.

The strategy, centred on the power of global brands underpinning both above average margins and increases in market share in industries undergoing concentration and structural change, is very different from that which drove the company forward through its early history. In supporting a high quality of earnings it has undoubted attractions. A premium stock market rating, however, also requires sustained high growth. Both the opportunity and the problem were perhaps best captured by the increasingly common adage in the international drinks industry: 'Drinking less but drinking better'. Sheppard's next challenge lay in achieving widespread organic growth across the now focused portfolio. 'Operation Build' would have to be the next chapter in Grand Met's history.

SUGGESTED QUESTIONS

1. Assess the major strategic moves which have made up Grand Metropoliatan's history. How would you divide them between (1) ad hoc opportunism; and (2) integrated parts of a deliberate long-term strategy?
2. What problems and what strengths within Grand Met. did Grinstead inherit from Max Joseph?
3. How would you describe the Grand Met. culture? How has this

changed over time? To what extent is it reflected in the organizational structure, management style and decision making processes in Grand Met. in 1988?

4. Set out the major strategic issues facing Grand Met. at the close of the case. Why was Allen Sheppard chosen to steer the company into the 1990s?

13

Infoservice: Strategic decision-making simulation game

Written by Michelle Bergadaà and Raymond–Alain Thiétart with
C Chapot

INFOSERVICE: A HISTORY

Infoservice is a software development company. It was created in 1978 by
two engineers: Alain Barbet and Christian Dubarry, who had graduated a
few years before from the same school. During a training period with
another firm, they both realized the potential growth of computer
services.

They started their business by developing a new software package for
data management and analysis. At the same time they developed new
contacts with prospective customers. The first software was sold as early
as 1979; very rapidly, customer demands became more precise. To satisfy
this demand, additional engineers where hired.

In 1981 Infoservice employed 10 engineers in addition to its two
founders. These two founders functioned more as managers than technicians. Alain Barbet took responsibility for the newly-formed technical
department and Christian Dubarry took charge of marketing. Dubarry
was responsible for developing new client contacts, for researching
market trends, and for guiding software development at Infoservice.

The first version of the data management and analysis software was
progressively abandoned. The demand for an integrated system (software
plus hardware) with new applications appeared. A five-engineer team was
given the task of developing such a system.

At the same time, engineers were sent on tempory assignments to a
number of clients' offices. In this way, corporations could acquire top-

level specialists for limited periods of time in order to solve specific problems. The lengths of these assignments were variable and could last up to two years. The need for qualified personnel increased further and several new engineers had to be hired.

In 1985 Infoservice, with a staff of 30 people, had to change its structure. Alain Barbet was named Chairman of the Board and CEO, and Christian Dubarry became President. The departments were reorganized. Eric Letellier (an engineer who had been hired three years before) was given the position of Director of the Technical Department.

A marketing department was formally organized with Jean-Pierre Valois, a former engineer, managing two subordinates. In addition, a new accounting and finance department was created. A new manager was hired to deal with personnel matters. He was in charge of allocating the human resources between the 'customer in-house' services and the software department activity. 'Renting' engineers was a profitable business and was providing one-third of the revenue. To suppress this activity would have impeded the development of new software products.

The new version of the data management and analysis software package was reaching maturity (numerous versions existed). The software engineers were highly specialized, but thanks to the commercial network and 'mission' engineers who were working at important customer sites, a new need was identified. Firms were looking for means to improve their external as well as internal communication. The President, Christian Dubarry, had the idea of developing a new system – the Videotex system (see Exhibit 2). This system, entirely modular, would address the majority of the various client demands. A team of engineers and marketing department representatives was put in charge of this new product development.

In 1988 Infoservice experienced a smooth growth curve. It employed 45 people of whom 30 were engineers. The data management and analysis software was progressively abandoned in favour of the Videotex system. The Videotex system has several applications; its functions are very diverse. Many small and medium size firms are interested in this very adaptable product, which is aimed at customer services and information.

Beyond this new development, a recent technological trend has drawn the attention of Infoservice: 'the Memory Card' (see Exhibit 2). The Memory Card can be used as a credit card, as a cinema voucher, and so on. Five engineers are working on the software used with the card.

Alain Barbet and Christian Dubarry, who are convinced that their company's future is tightly linked to market growth in computer and information systems, have created a new 'innovation unit'. This unit is charged with forecasting market trends and analysing the technical feasibility of new products. An engineer and a marketing person work in this unit.

At the beginning of 1990 Infoservice had 55 employees. The 'mission' (i.e. assignment) activity has developed rapidly: clients frequently require tailor-made, ready-to-use equipment.

Videotex has now reached a peak in its life-cycle. The system has a vast and diversifed library and controls a significant share (estimated between 5% and 10%) of a very fragmented market.

The innovation unit is starting to make its first recommendations. Among these recommendations is the improvement of the Videotex system through the introduction of digitalized images. With this new capability, any document (charts, graphics, pictures, etc.) can be used as simple written material. Numerous applications are expected to be derived from this new development.

Today, Infoservice markets its first 'Memory Cards' to the following types of customer: department stores, chains of sporting goods stores, cinemas, and corporations (restaurants, identity checks). New applications such as subscription-TV and medical files should follow.

Infoservice has developed close relationships with the national telecommunications company, France–Telecom. It can use the card readers of France–Telecom which are installed in many firms. This card-reader (LECAM) allows a standardization of the Memory Card technology and thus facilitates its growth.

At the beginning of 1990 Infoservice had a sales breakdown as follows:

- Videotex system   50%
- Memory Cards   10%
- Missions   40%

THE PROBLEMS

At the beginning of 1990, Infoservice was faced with several problems:

Personnel management

November 1989: Christian Dubarry's secretary, by chance, found the résumé of a young employee – an engineer – on the Xerox machine. Two engineers had resigned only a month before. For the President, it was more than a coincidence.

The personnel management problems were acute. Christian Dubarry and the personnel manager made the following diagnosis:

- Staff turnover is very high during the first three years of an appointment. It often happens that an employee becomes fully operational, starts being profitable for the firm – and then leaves. Since salaries at Infoservice are above the industry average, the technical manager suggests the following explanation: 'I have the feeling that we are just a training centre. We don't know how to keep our young employees. If we had real opportunities to offer, then they would stay.'
- Specialized training of engineers usually takes place at Infoservice when they are put in charge of product development. After this training period, some of the engineers are sent on a 'mission' at the request of a customer. However, some engineers are sent to work at the clients'

sites without having had any real training. One of the engineers, Philippe Lucas, declares: 'When we arrive at the client firm we are mixed with engineers from other software development firms. Sometimes, I wonder if I work for Infoservice.'

Several 'mission' engineers wish to be reintegrated at Infoservice, but the personnel manager can rarely grant their request: 'We are forced to find new incentives for these positions which are unfairly perceived as being unrewarding. It is a fact that the average mission length is one year. However, we continue to monitor our engineers' performance. They are not left alone.'

- Because of the specificity of each task, the new engineers rapidly become very specialized. This leads to a fairly rigid career path. The technical manager says, 'We don't want to be separated from a well trained and efficient employee. We are completely dependent on our personnel. If a product manager leaves us, the product development might require six extra months.'

The marketing–technology relationship

The technical department manager admits that there is a lack of co-ordination between the technical and the marketing departments.

The computer services market, after the fast growth of the 1980s, is approaching maturity. Competition between software development companies is very intense. Customers may play one supplier against the other. According to the marketing manager, 'Price cutting is mandatory if we want to win a market'. The marketing department is sometimes forced to negotiate and to commit Infoservice beyond its available resources if it wants to make a deal. 'I perfectly understand the constraints of our salesmen, but our engineers can't be submitted to the most idiosyncratic demand from the clients,' is the view of the technical manager. 'These unanticipated and so-called urgent missions break the pace of our work. This reveals the lack of organization of the marketing department'.

For the CEO, Alain Barbet, the problems have a deeper root. Engineers prefer to explore and develop products in-house before marketing and supplying them to clients. They also think that the best response to competition is through innovation in order to differentiate Infoservice products. The marketing people, however, have a different point of view. They stress the importance of having a presence in the market. They also emphasize the critical aspect of the missions which can be used as an introduction to future business. Furthermore, the missions provide a large share of the revenue. 'How could we finance product development without our lucrative direct service to the customers?' is their view.

Opinions also diverge concerning the allocation of profit. Which is the most profitable business? Is there a link between product development and the engineers' assignments at customers sites? As the marketing manager says, 'if the clients would not use us as a service supplier, would they think of us for our Videotex and Memory Card products?'

The two founders of Infoservice think that many customers complain because of the lack of co-ordination between marketers and technicians. In fact, the lack of co-ordination does lead to extra delays. Would organization by product solve the problem? A Product Manager could then reconcile the diverse technical and commercial demands subject to the human resource constraints.

The environmental change

An industrial shakeout   The end of the 1980s witnessed several significant changes in a very fragmented industry:

- Mergers and strategic alliances between software development companies seeking to open new markets and develop synergies;
- Takeovers of software companies by large industrial groups in the computer and telecommunication industries.

These changes gained momentum as the single European Market of 1992 approached. The local French markets were to become global. It would be essential for software development companies to be present in other countries, either by means of an alliance with a foreign competitor or through a subsidiary.

A market in constant innovation   The market for computer services is evolving very rapidly. The ever-growing processing speed of micro-chips and memory capacities shorten the product life cycle of equipment and software.

Companies often find they have compatibility problems with their equipment. For example, Videotex use is limited to a specific piece of equipment. To cope with this problem, the innovation unit proposes two solutions:

- Infoservice develops its software for each type of equipment, which will require a significant investment of resources;
- Infoservice uses a market standard, in which case co-operation with a leading computer firm would be necessary.

The innovation unit has another problem: how to forecast the market for the next five years when the market growth rate is still very fast.

SUGGESTED QUESTIONS

1. Must Infoservice be organized along product lines (structured by product) to improve management of personnel and the co-ordination between marketers and technicians? Can the present structure be maintained with minor adjustments? If so, what should these adjustments be?
2. Where should the Infoservice market be: France or Europe? If its market should be in Europe, what would be the best strategy to attack

it? To create one or several subsidiaries in some European countries? To build a strategic alliance (or several) with foreign software development companies? To have a joint-venture with a competitor or a large industrial group? Or to choose another route?

3. To reduce conflict at Infoservice, should the firm attempt to define its vocation more clearly? Should Infoservice invest in developing additional innovative products which could differentiate it from competitors? Or should it choose a middle-of-the-road policy (differentiated products and engineers 'rental' to clients) for financial reasons? In summary, should Infoservice orient its strategy differently?

Exhibit   265

Exhibit 1 Managers' profiles, objectives, and positions with respect to Infoservice problems.

Technical manager

Eric Letellier is 42 years old; he is married, with two children. He is an experienced engineer, having been hired in 1982 after working as a computer scientist in a consulting firm specializing in information systems management.

Since his arrival at Infoservice he has worked on several applications, based on the first software the firm designed. Working with Alain Barbet, he acquired a very good knowledge of the software, and was appointed to the post of technical manager in 1985.

He is very attached to the quality and the innovative potential of Infoservice, and is in favour of intensifying the development of new products. He is convinced that the success of the company is based upon the know-how of its engineers. He sees software performance as a way to seize new market opportunities, especially in the Memory Card business sector.

Letellier wants the innovation unit to grow. New products for new markets need to be found. As he says: 'Innovation is a base for Infoservice's growth.'

For him, opening up new markets in Europe is an excellent idea. As he frequently says, 'France is well-known for its technological advance in the field of telecommunications networking'.

Videotex product manager

The Videotex product manager is 30 years old; he is married with no children. A member of the technical department, he has been in charge of the Videotex system for the past four years.

The product manager is in favour of developing new applications for the Videotex system. As he says, 'We have a very high-performing product that we can easily sell. We should now increase the range of its applications'.

He thinks that Infoservice should be organized along product lines – Videotex, Memory Card, etc. – instead of the current functional structure.

He is also very concerned with the technical level of the firm, which needs to be reinforced. He hopes that, very soon, new engineers will be hired to compensate for the departure of young employees. This will reinforce the growth of new products.

For the moment, he is not very satisfied with the way the firm is run. On several occasions, engineers of his department have been sent on a long-term mission. Sometimes he wonders, 'how is it possible to develop new products in such unstable conditions?' He also has the impression that his colleagues in the marketing department treat him as a subordinate. A reorganization along product lines would probably relieve some of his frustrations – and it would present a wonderful career opportunity!

Memory Card product manager

The Memory Card product manager is 34 years old; he is married with one child. He is a real computer fanatic, and one of the key members of the technical department.

Exhibit 1   *continued*

He was hired by Infoservice in 1981 as a young, inexperienced engineer. He was promoted to the post of product manager for the Memory Card in 1988. He perceived this promotion as a recognition of his skill.

He is entirely dedicated to his work, and wants to develop the potential of the Memory Card: memory capacity, access speed, new applications, etc. According to him, finding new applications and developing synergies with the Videotex system are part of the Infoservice dedication to innovation.

He sees the European market as an opportunity to achieve his product development objectives. For example, the Memory Card is not yet fully accepted outside the French market. This is a growth opportunity, but he does not fully favour an agreement or a merger with another software development company as a means of grasping this opportunity, since this could be detrimental to his own position at Infoservice.

He is frequently upset because of the short notice given by the marketing department. He would prefer a larger autonomy for his engineers and himself. He is aware that the engineers do not like being sent on a 'mission' at short notice.

Mission manager

The mission manager is an electrical and telecommunications engineer. He is 33 years old and a dedicated sportsman, spending his leisure time in very active pursuits such as skiing and mountain climbing.

He was appointed mission manager in 1987. He has well-developed interpersonal skills, and is perceived by other people as being trustworthy. This was probably a major deciding factor in him being offered the position of mission manager.

His job is very challenging, being in charge of young engineers who work at clients' locations and are 'rented' for long periods of time (1–2 years). He is in regular contact with the marketing department, and it is via the marketing department that information about client needs is forwarded. He also has direct contact with firms which are looking for an engineer with specific skills; it is essential to provide the right profile of skills to meet the client's needs.

The diversity of his responsibilities has led him to challenge Infoservice's position as merely a software development firm. His ongoing contact with the competitive market has made him a pragmatic person: 'When we don't satisfy a customer need, we lose it! And sometimes for good,' he says.

He is very favourable to the idea of changing the Infoservice structure. For him, the differentiation between the marketing and technology departments is very stimulating. What will he do if he has to work with a marketing expert in the same organizational unit?

Marketing manager

Jean-Pierre Valois, 38, is an engineer who rapidly turned to marketing. Even though he has not forgotten his technical background, he is very marketing oriented.

He has a staff of four: all graduates from business schools. He tries to 'teach' them as much technical know-how as possible, so that they can understand clients' needs and can talk to them.

Exhibit   267

Exhibit 1   *continued*

Sometimes he has to challenge commitments (for example in terms of delays) made by his staff without the agreement of the technical department. But whatever he does, this does not seem to be appreciated by the technical manager. In fact, the technical manager thinks that he is more interested in his career than in the welfare of his colleagues.

His relations with the executive president are good. His arguments are perceived as being realistic and are in agreement with the Infoservice corporate policy. 'It's a long-term investment to have engineers sent to a mission!'

Valois is in favour of attacking the European market. 'It is a formidable growth opportunity. Maybe, some day, Infoservice will need a manager for one of its foreign subsidiaries!'

Videotex marketing chief

The Videotex marketing chief is 29 years old, and not married. He was hired four years ago by Jean-Pierre Valois. A graduate from a prestigious business school, his task is to look for new customers for the Videotex system.

His job consists of listening to and analysing clients' needs. He believes he has a good knowledge of the market; six months after he was hired, he won the largest contract ever for Infoservice.

His skills are recognized at Infoservice, and when he speaks people usually listen. From his point of view, Infoservice needs to have a strong presence in the market if it wants to fight the ever-growing competition.

'Customers need to be pampered,' he says. To do so he proposed improving the after-sales service by offering new applications, through updating the software or data bank.

He is a very independent person and refuses any restructuring which could put him under the authority of an engineer. Of course, the expansion into new markets will probably offer many career opportunities. He likes to tell people around him that he is trilingual and a lover of Latin countries.

Memory Card marketing chief

The Memory Card marketing chief is 44 years old and among the oldest employees at Infoservice. He was hired three years ago after a 15-year career with a major French company. Infoservice wanted someone with a sound knowledge of the computer industry. He is aware of the value of his personal contacts and this helped him negotiate his contract with Infoservice.

He is a quiet and rather conservative person who does not like having other people interfering with his business: 'The Memory Card — it's me!' he says. This statement does not please the development engineer in charge of the Memory Card.

He is not averse to restructuring. After all, it may help him move up the career ladder. It could, perhaps, present him with an opportunity to manage both the marketing and the technical sides of his business.

Exhibit 1   *continued*

Technical innovation specialist

The technical innovation specialist has just turned 28. He has a doctorate in engineering with a specilization in telecommunications. He is very familiar with numerical networks, digital images, and telecommunications. He frequently writes in professional journals and has good relations with the research centre where he wrote his dissertation.

His task is to monitor technical evolution. Based on his observations, he then makes propositions which can lead to the development of new product. However, he is sometimes disappointed by the lack of positive reaction to his suggestions. The Videotex–Memory Card link was his idea. Other ideas include linking digital images or fax machines with the Videotex system.

From this point of view, Infoservice should have one objective: innovation. He does not ignore market constraints, but he thinks that the only way to reduce market pressures is to foster technological innovation. His major goal is to preserve his autonomy at Infoservice and he is in full agreement with the other engineers who want a product-based organization. In this way, project co-ordination will be reinforced.

Innovation manager

The innovation manager is married, with two children. At 35 years old, he has had training in both engineering and business, so what he has 'lost' in terms of specialization, he has gained in breadth of experience.

He devotes his time to analysing the competition and the market, looking at the five- to ten-year implications. His analysis of the market and the industry as a whole makes him think that:

- strategic alliance with another software development company, not directly in competition with Infoservice, could be a good thing. Synergies could be found and they could prove profitable (e.g. new projects, new clients, etc.);
- expansion on a foreign market could be an important growth opportunity. To do this, a joint venture would probably be the best option.

As far as his career is concerned, he would like to have line management responsibility. He likes new challenges.

Software development engineer

After graduating at the age of 22 from a computer science department of a major university, the software development engineer has already worked for three years at Infoservice. He has worked on the data bank application of the Videotex system, and he has created a library of financial information to be used by the banking industry.

He is looking for career opportunities at Infoservice. For example, he is interested in the Memory Card–Videotex system project. He sees it as a means of attracting the attention of the management in his direction. As with many other young employees, he thinks that the best positions are in the hands of the 'old guard'. He sometimes wonders if, finally, he will not have to change his job if he

Exhibit   269

Exhibit 1   *continued*

wants a faster career track. Recently, one of his friends made the move and left the company.

Furthermore, he has the feeling that he is not employed to his full potential. Projects are badly co-ordinated; customer contacts are always mediated by the marketing department, and they do not know much about computer techniques. A restructuring, without any doubt, will bring him a higher degree of job satisfaction. If will also probably be an opportunity for him to receive a salary increase.

Mission engineer

At 24 years of age, the mission engineer is a specialist in mainframe networks. He was hired two years ago and was immediately sent on a mission. He started a second mission six months ago at a large public transportation firm. His task consists of developing new software for Metro lines automation.

Even though he is very interested in his current duties, he would like to work on an Infoservice project. He has never been at Infoservice since he was hired; his only contact is with his boss, and this is usually by phone.

Being dissatisfied with this situation, he has recently asked to be put in charge of a project; he does not want to be sent on a mission again for the time being.

However, while working as a mission engineer, he has observed clients' needs for such a service. He has also observed the fierce rivalry between software development companies. Clients continually monitor and compare the performance of engineers from different companies.

He believes that being 'close to the client' is a prerequisite to success. However, he regrets that there is not enough movement of personnel at Infoservice. There is the possibility that he may one day be tempted by offers from client companies.

Controller

In his forties, and married with three children, the controller has been with Infoservice for six years. He was trained in a business school and started his career at an audit firm before turning to cost accounting and control.

From this early experience he has maintained an interest in figures. The financial statements he prepares are first-rate. His last report, for example, emphasized the increasing cost of labour that he attributed to the high turnover among young employees. He has suggested the need to achieve greater stability among the personnel, and to do this he advises offering higher salaries, which could be performance-related.

He also stresses the large borrowing capacity of Infoservice. He would be pleased to see this capacity put to use, for example in new projects such as the digital images project which he firmly believes in.

Finance manager

At 45 years of age, the finance manager has an MBA in finance from a top American university. He has been the finance manager for seven years. From his experience in the US, he has maintained a strong pragmatism and a solid sense of

Exhibit 1 *continued*

reality. For him, financial results and forecasts are the only meaningful starting points for any important decision: investment, new markets, advertising, co-operative agreements, etc.

He likes to reiterate a number of facts, for example 'Infoservice is 40% dependent on its mission activity'. He would refuse, at least in the short term, to concentrate Infoservice's activities on product development. In the very long term, however, this alternative should not be ruled out.

As regards a merger with another firm in the same industry, he likes to stress the risk of capital dilution that this would present.

Personnel manager

The personnel manager has a masters degree in psychology. He is 48 years old, and married with two children. He has two passions: corporate organization and personnel management. He was hired in 1985, when Infoservice decided to establish a new structure. He was immediately 'seduced' by this high-tech firm where he was allowed to work without the direct supervision of a boss. To be part of the executive team of a young and dynamic company was sufficient motivation for him.

He wants to play the role of 'expert in human resources'. He stresses the need to train young employees. According to him, it is the only way to integrate them rapidly into the firm. He also advises on a need to move personnel from product development to mission work, and vice versa. This is the main thrust of his personnel policy. His aim is to 'hang on' to the best people. 'It's so hard to find highly qualified computer experts on the market.' Some competitors have had to hire inexperienced personnel with no computer background. This creates a number of training problems and puts the firm in a difficult position, *vis-à-vis* its customers.

The European expansion can be implemented if Infoservice recruits men and women with European stature. However, this will be difficult to achieve. A co-operative agreement with a foreign software development company appears to present a solution.

Executive president

Alain Barbet, the 37-year-old executive president, is the founder of Infoservice. He remembers when he had to write the software himself; the long nights spent working at the computer have taught him patience and disclipline.

Since the outset, the Infoservice policy has always stressed two activities: pro-duct development and service (missions). However, the mission activity has continuously expanded to acount for 40% of sales in 1990. This illustrates the dependence of the company on a few large clients. Other problems upset him: the resignation of young engineers after just a couple of years with the company; the strained relations between the technical and marketing departments; the takeover by large firms of some of his competitors; the merger wave between software companies and the future European competition.

Is the time right to revise Infoservice's strategy? After all, in 1985 everything was put into question when they had to find a new structure. Is Infoservice entering the third phase of its growth?

Exhibit   271

Exhibit 2   Videotex.

The Videotex is a software equipment system. It can perform several functions: external communication; data bank; and internal or external electronic mailboxes.

The Videotex system can be entirely adapted to the needs of the client. The software is the keystone of the system. It is composed of two main elements:

- the monitor is the basic software; its function is to regulate the flow of instructions from the upper level software. It is the 'common denominator' of the different Videotex systems;
- the applications which are adapted to the needs of clients. For example, a data base is one application. A second application, such as an electronic mailbox, can complement the configuration.

The software development company can market the complementary applications that it has developed. It can also sell a complete configuration: equipment, monitor, and application. The Videotex system is connected to a network which can be used to transfer data.

Exhibit 3   Memory Card.

This card resembles a banking card: it has a plastic frame and an electronic chip is inserted in the card. The chip is programmed and has numerous applications.

If the client has neither the software nor the equipment, he can ask the software company to program the card. If the client has the resources he can program the cards himself. In any case, the client will have to have a card reader. The software company sells the system (software plus equipment) which is fitted to the needs of the client: from a simple Memory Card to the entire integrated system.

Exhibit 4   Markets and competition.

	Memory Card	Videotex system
Competition		
Position	Ranked third, behind two large competitors (35% and 30% market share respectively) which are specialists in the Memory Card	Many competitors. Industry is extremely fragmented
Market share	20%	5% (estimated)
Trend	Infoservice has lost some market share due to its lack of specialization in this product	Competitors tend to specialize in this product
Market		
Size	FF 30 million	FF 250 million
Growth rate per year	100%	30%
Products	Cards for professional use (personnel management, restaurants, hospital management, etc.)	Data bank on firms (external promotion) and on products (internal use)
	Cards for personal use (cinema, paid TV, medical file, department store, etc.)	Electronic mail box (internal communication)
Customers	Large companies, banks, public institutions	Other software development companies which want to market their own applications. Independent firms which want to exploit a service based on the applications
Potential	Advertising media	Integration of digitalized images
	Management of the Memory Card with Videotex	

Exhibit   273

Exhibit 5   Infoservice: organizational structure in 1990.

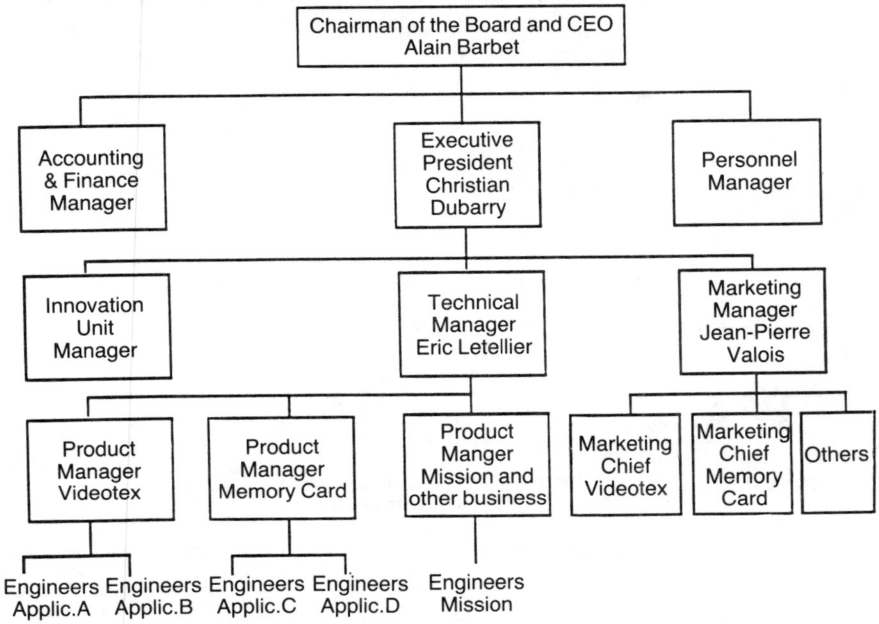

```
                    ┌─────────────────────────┐
                    │ Chairman of the Board   │
                    │ and CEO                 │
                    │ Alain Barbet            │
                    └─────────────────────────┘
          ┌──────────────────┼──────────────────────┐
┌──────────────┐    ┌──────────────┐       ┌──────────────┐
│ Accounting   │    │ Executive    │       │ Personnel    │
│ & Finance    │    │ President    │       │ Manager      │
│ Manager      │    │ Christian    │       │              │
│              │    │ Dubarry      │       │              │
└──────────────┘    └──────────────┘       └──────────────┘
          ┌──────────────────┼──────────────────────┐
┌──────────────┐    ┌──────────────┐       ┌──────────────┐
│ Innovation   │    │ Technical    │       │ Marketing    │
│ Unit         │    │ Manager      │       │ Manager      │
│ Manager      │    │ Eric         │       │ Jean-Pierre  │
│              │    │ Letellier    │       │ Valois       │
└──────────────┘    └──────────────┘       └──────────────┘
```

Product Manager Videotex — Product Manager Memory Card — Product Manger Mission and other business — Marketing Chief Videotex — Marketing Chief Memory Card — Others

Engineers Applic.A   Engineers Applic.B   Engineers Applic.C   Engineers Applic.D   Engineers Mission

Exhibit 6 Infoservice financial statements, 1985–89.

Balance sheet (millions FF)											
Assets							Liabilities				
	1985	1986	1987	1988	1989		1985	1986	1987	1988	1989
Fixed assets (gross)	28	32	38	44	52	Common stock plus surplus	20	21	22	23	25
Depreciation	(7)	(10)	(14)	(19)	(25)						
Fixed assets (net)	21	22	24	25	27	Long-term debts	7	7	9	10	12
Inventory	0.5	1	1	1	1.5	Accounts payable	1	1.5	2	2	2
Accounts receivable	6.5	7	8.5	9.5	11.5	Other current liabilities	0.5	1	1	1	1
Cash	0.5	0.5	0.5	0.5	0.5						
	28.5	30.5	34	36	40		28.5	30.5	34	36	40

Income statement (millions of FF)											
Income statements											
	1985	1986	1987	1988	1989		1985	1986	1987	1988	1989
Cost of goods sold	16.5	20	24.5	28.5	32	Sales	24	30	37	44	50
Selling, general and admin. expenses	3	4	5	6	6						
Depreciation	2	3	4	5	6						
Interest	0.5	0.5	0.6	0.7	0.8						
Earnings before tax	2	2.5	2.9	3.8	5.2						
	24	30	37	44	50		24	30	37	44	50

14

International Distillers and Vintners (A)

Case written by Tony Eccles with Martin Stoll

Since its acquisition in 1972 by Grand Metropolitan, International Distillers and Vintners (IDV) had grown from a collection of long-established British family firms to become the world's largest drinks company, measured by case sales of wines and spirits. IDV's annual profit for 1987 was £268 million compared to £338 million for Guinness/ United Distillers Group (UDG) (see Table 1A and Table 1B).

The IDV trading record for 1980–89 (£m) was as follows:

Year to September	1980	1981	1982	1983	1984	1985	1986	1987	1988	1989
Turnover	475	525	769	860	942	1055	1076	1796	1936	2148
Trading Profit	36	49	98	105	129	150	147	223	274	335
Margin (%)	7.6	11.4	12.8	12.1	13.7	14.2	13.7	12.4	14.2	15.6
ROCE (%)				25.3	30.0	31.8	28.8	16.0	21.2	23.3

(1987 includes seven months of Heublein)

During the 1980s IDV achieved a compound annual profit growth of 25%, fuelled by acquisition, expansion of existing brands, development of new brands, and vertical integration into the distribution network. By 1987, however, the world market for wines and spirits was in gentle decline, consolidation in the industry had begun to accelerate, and acquisitions were becoming increasingly expensive; the era of easy growth had ended and competition had intensified. Should IDV change its hitherto successful strategies to meet a changing environment, and if so what should these new strategies be?

Table 1A The 9 largest spirits companies, 1986

	(million nine-litre cases)
IDV	46.7
Seagram	43.7
Guinness	44.7
Allied–Lyons	31.5
Suntory	24.2
Jim Beam	19.3
Bacardi	23.1
Pernod–Ricard	16.5
Brown–Forman	14.0

Note: These figures do not completely agree with earlier data in this case study since double counting can occur when brands are owned by one company and marketed by another.
Source: Impact.

Table 1B The leading wines and spirits companies, 1985–86 and 1988–89 (million nine-litre cases)

	1985–86	1988–89
IDV	82.5	91.2
Seagram	65.0	79.6
Pernod–Ricard	56.6	57.0
Guinness/UDG	44.0	45.0
Allied–Lyons	41.0	51.6 (includes Hiram Walker)
Suntory		28.7
Bacardi		28.3
Jim Beam		19.2
Brown–Forman		16.8

Source: International Drinks Bulletin.

THE WORLD WINE AND SPIRITS INDUSTRY

The world wine and spirit industry included 3000 spirit brands and over 9000 wine brands, the vast majority of these being locally produced and consumed. The market operated at three levels: global brands; international brands sold country by country; and local products. Growing globalization of tastes had tended to drive international brands towards the global category and some of the stronger local products had extended into the international category. Yet, at the same time, the leading global brands enhanced their position at the expense of weaker products.

Worldwide consumption of alcoholic spirit beverages in 1987 was

Table 1C   The top 100 spirit brands; numbers owned

	1981	1987
IDV	7	10
Guinness	9	10
Seagram	8	11
Allied–Lyons	6	7
Suntory	4	6
Pernod–Ricard	4	4
Brown–Forman	4	4
Moet–Hennessy	1	1
	43	53

Source: Impact International.

1.7 billion cases, including local products and communist block consumption. Excluding the communist spirit sector, the top 100 brands sold 260 million cases. Globally, these top 100 brands accounted for less than 50% of the world branded spirit market (see Table 1C and Table 1D). However, there were large profit margins to be made in these brands.

The growth in consumption seen in the late 1970s had not continued. US, Canadian, and West German volumes declined while Europe saw a modest increase. The most vivid expansion occurred in Japan where consumption more than doubled in the decade to 1987.

Anti-alcohol lobbies, tax policies, drink–drive legislation, and increased concern about health were significant factors as people swung away from high-volume consumption in the more developed countries.

INDUSTRY STRUCTURE

The drinks industry was only moderately concentrated, but concentration was growing in premium products. The top 10 companies held 50% of the world branded spirit market. The world market brand share of the top five wine and spirit companies had risen from 28% in 1981 to 36% in 1986.

Production

The location of production facilities for some liquor categories was dicated by the nature of the product and enforceable limits on its description. Whisky was made in Scotland to use the Scottish spring waters; wine was made in the region whose name it carried; and similar restraints applied to Cognac, Armagnac, Champagne, Port, and Sherry. For other categories, the physical production location was not a legal requirement. The costs of setting up a new production facility did not present a barrier to entry into this industry.

Table 1D   Leading companies; main brands

IDV	Guinness
Smirnoff Vodka	Gordons Gin
J&B Scotch Whisky	Johnnie Walker Red Label
Popov Vodka	Bells Scotch Whisky
Bailey's Irish Cream Liqueur	Dewars Scotch Whisky
Gilbeys Gin	Johnnie Walker Black Label
Black Velvet Canadian Whiskey	White Horse Scotch
Malibu Liqueur	Gordons Vodka
Arrow Liqueurs	Haig Scotch Whisky
Dreher Brandy	Black & White Scotch
Seagram	Allied–Lyons
Seagrams 7 Crown American	Ballantine's Scotch
Blended Whiskey	Canadian Club Whiskey
Seagram Gin	Kahlua Liqueur
Seagram Co Canadian Whiskey	Teachers Scotch
Chivas Regal Scotch Whiskey	Hiram Walker Liqueur
Martell Cognac	Courvoisier Cognac
Crown Royal Canadian Whiskey	Ten High Bourbon
Captain Morgan Rum	
Kessler American Blended Whiskey	Suntory
Canadian Lord Calvert Whiskey	Suntory Old Japanese Whiskey
Passport Scotch Whisky	Suntory Red Japanese Whiskey
100 Pipers Scotch Whiskey	Suntory Reserve Japanese Whiskey
	Suntory White Japanese Whiskey
Pernod–Ricard	Suntory VSOP Brandy
Ricard Pastis	Suntory Mild Vodka
Pastis 51	
Suze Aperitif	
Pernod Pastis	

Advertising and promotion

In 1987 the world's top five wine and spirit companies spent over £1 billion of advertising and promotional money, and this largely excluded trade discounts. IDV's proportion of that was just over one-fifth (see Table 2). As the consumer became more health conscious the industry moved increasingly into an era of 'drinking less but drinking better' with a beneficial effect on brands and margins. The cost of adding value through advertising did not diminish and, even though some types of advertising might be further restricted, total advertising expenditure looked unlikely to drop in the early 1990s.

Suppliers and customers

No supplier dominated the drinks industry although Guinness was a powerful player in the supply of malts for blended whiskies, owning 34

Table 2   Competitor (net) AMP spend (year ending 1987)

	(£m)	cases	AMP/case
IDV	193	85	2.3
Guinness	220	47	4.7
Allied–Lyons	230	51	4.5
Seagram	223	76	2.9
Pernod–Ricard	137	58	2.4
Brown–Forman	65	30	2.2

malt distilleries (of which 24 were working). However, it was not clear how Guinness could restrict the supply of malts sufficiently to disrupt the flavour of other blends.

As the purchasing powers of the supermarkets developed, they put more pressure on the margins of the drinks manufacturers. The trend to supermarkets was expected to spread across the world into markets presently supplied by small (usually family) retail outlets. In the long term, global margins for the drinks companies might be eroded. Undistinguished commodity brands were expected to have difficulty in gaining retail distribution.

National distribution

The lack of growth in the spirits market put pressure on companies to change their national distribution systems. The traditional system was very different from that of most other consumer goods. It had been relatively common for some major brands to be distributed by other companies, sometimes competitors, in key markets throughout the world.

The industry faced two growing problems with this traditional system:

1. As the industry consolidated into fewer and fewer players, so the problem of conflicting brands in portfolios became more intense.
2. Increasingly, companies wanted to control the marketing and sales of their own brands and, in the process, hope to maximize profit by taking the margin on the distribution.

Controlling national distribution had, in most cases, meant controlling the distributor, and acquisitions and mergers grew apace. Guinness/UDG, on a global scale, claimed in 1990 that 75% of its products went through distributors which it owned or controlled, compared to 25% about two years earlier. IDV controlled 86% of its distribution and Seagram more than that.

THE COMPETITION

Guinness

UDG – the spirit arm of Guinness – comprised the Bells whisky company and the old Distillers Company Ltd (DCL), which historically consisted of a number of largely autonomous brand companies, such as Johnnie Walker, John Dewar, and Tanqueray Gordon. These had formed a loose federation of spirits businesses under the Distillers corporate umbrella. DCL was above all a production driven company. It saw itself as a producer and exporter of Scotch whisky and gin. Although pricing had been centrally controlled, there was competition between Distillers' brands for volume, and lack of control of the brands in the marketplace during a period when sophisticated brand management was becoming critical to success. In 1970 DCL had 75% of the UK Scotch whisky market; by 1985 this had fallen to 15%.

The Guinness Board under Ernest Saunders had bought Bells (1985) and Distillers (1986), and had determined that the strategic direction of the group should be the international marketing of high-volume, high-quality consumer products with world famous brand names and a principal focus on spirits and brewing. Other current group businesses with good brand development potential were to be retained and non-strategic businesses, including wines, divested. In 1987 Anthony Tennant, IDV's Chairman, left to become Managing Director of Guinness and developed this policy further. To reflect this new policy, the company was reorganized into three major divisions: UDG, Guinness Brewing Worldwide, and Commercial and Development Group. UDG contributed over 80% of Guinness's profits.

The restructuring included the establishment of new UDG international sales and marketing headquarters in London; the concentration of UK sales and marketing for all UK brands at Arthur Bell Distillers at Perth; and the centralization of all Scotch whisky distilling, blending, and bottling activities under a single management structure in Scotland. The new managing director of UDG was from the Dunhill Group.

UDG's new management organization was geared to management on regional rather than brand company lines. The world had been divided into: Europe, the Far East, USA, International, and Duty Free. Each region was headed by a managing director with full profit responsibility for that region covering both profits made locally and on sales from the UK.

Guinness then acquired Schenley, its major US distributor, for over $400 million. The first step in the implementation of the recent Guinness alliance with Moet–Hennessy took place when they merged both their US distribution companies.

UDG subsequently acquired Caldbeck (the marketing and distribution companies which handle UDG's products in the Far East) and, together with Moet–Hennessy, took a controlling stake in Jardine Matheson's wine and spirit distribution business. Through these two transactions UDG gained control of businesses that accounted for the great bulk of their products sold in the Far East.

In Japan – a very large and high-margin market for Scotch and bourbon – the Jardine operation handled White Horse and I W Harper (both category leaders). The bourbon category in Japan more than doubled between 1986 and 1988. In North America UDG sold almost 16 million cases in 1987 of which 90% went through their own distributors. This established them as the fourth largest distributor of spirits in the US and the third largest producer of bourbon. UDG formed joint ventures with Bacardi in Spain and Germany, another joint venture in Germany with Underberg (a powerful local distributor), and two joint ventures with Moet–Hennessy (later LVMH) in France.

Guinness dramatically reduced costs in Distillers after the acquisition. Bulk sales of excess whisky stocks were stopped except where UDG was contractually obliged to continue. UDG's pricing policy was to raise the price of whisky brands ahead of inflation.

Allied–Lyons

Like Grand Metropolitan, Allied–Lyons had extensive food interests. The size and nature of its drinks interests had markedly changed through its acquisition of the Canadian company Hiram Walker. Allied–Lyons bought Hiram Walker in two stages, starting with the acquisition of 51% of the company in 1986 for £400 million and £466 million of debt, followed by the 1987 purchase of the remaining 49% from Olympia and York for £572 million. The purchase aproximately doubled Allied–Lyons drinks interests, and wines and spirits contributed £250 million of the company's £436 million pre-tax profit in 1988. It was estimated by analysts that 64% of the drinks profit came from Hiram Walker's operations.

While it may have been a good financial deal, a number of industry analysts were not convinced that the deal made business sense. Critics did not see the logic of the fit, pointing out that Allied–Vintners, Allied's drinks subsidiary, was essentially a UK drinks producer with a mixed portfolio of UK brands, including VP British wines, Harveys and Cockburns sherries and ports, Gaymers ciders, and Babycham. Even its major whisky, Teachers Highland Cream, was primarily a UK brand. In Hiram Walker, Allied had acquired a North American company which was also very dependent on its domestic market. Despite its ownership of some international brands, including Canadian Club, Ballantines, Kahlua, Courvoisier, and Tia Maria, 73% of Hiram Walker's group volume had come from North American sales.

Writing in May 1987, stockbrokers Wood Mackenzie expressed their 'crucial reservation' about the acquisition:

Allied is essentially a domestic (UK) liquor business taking over a domestic (North American) liquor business. The scope for a global marketing approach therefore seems limited since the combined grouping does not yet posses the requisite international distributor network.

Allied set about remedying that weakness. By May 1988 all Allied's brands, with the exception of Ballantine's whisky, were distributed in North America by Hiram Walker. But in mainland Europe, Allied had only a limited control of some of its major brands, though at least in France and Spain the brands were mostly sold through a single distributor – Seagram.

In the important Japanese market, Allied–Lyons took a distinctly different route from its competitors with its October 1988 deal with Suntory, Japan's largest liquor company, which had been handling some of Allied's brands since 1970 – notably Canadian Club. Under the deal, by which Suntory acquired 2.5% of Allied's shares and Allied acquired a 1% stake in Suntory (netting Allied £106m), a jointly owned Japanese distribution company would import Allied's brands and distribute them through Suntory's sales force. With Japanese duty on imported Scotch having been reduced in April 1989 to almost the same level as duty on quality Japanese whisky, Allied hoped to capture a substantial share of the Japanese market. The deal also involved Allied in selling Suntory products outside Japan, especially in North America.

Aside from distribution, Allied also used the acquisition of Hiram Walker to introduce a new management structure in the form of seven autonomous divisions. Some of these were brand based, such as Allied Distillers, which handled the top whisky brands Teachers and Ballantines; others were regionally based, such as Allied–Lyons International Brands, which was set up to develop the important duty-free market. It also used the merger to rationalize some aspects of purchasing and production.

The Seagram company

Seagram was the second largest world wines and spirits company with annual sales of wines and spirits totalling $3.8 billion in the year to 31 January 1988. Still effectively controlled by the Bronfman family, its move into the international market had been relatively recent.

Until the late 1970s, about three-quarters of Seagram's sales of wines and spirits were made in North America, though the company owned Scottish distillers Robert Brown, Chivas Brothers and Glenlivet, the Champagne house Perrier–Jouet, the port and sherry house Sandeman, and the French wine shippers Barton & Guestier.

The 1980s saw a rapid expansion of Seagram's overseas operations, mostly by acquisition. It acquired full ownership of Mumm champagne and bought Cinzano's operations in Portugal. Seagram's strategy of building Seagram into a 'truly international company', highlighted by its 1988 acquisition of Martell, was easier for Seagram than for other would-be world players for two reasons. The first was the Bronfman family's controlling interest in the company. This meant that it could be relatively indifferent to short-term losses. It had also used its 'family business' image to good effect in its approaches to other family businesses, most notably Martell. The second was Seagram's 23% equity stake in Du Pont whose dividends provided what the company described as 'a steady unencumbered cash flow'. In 1987 Du Pont accounted for more than 70% of Seagram's earnings and the $165 million Du Pont dividends alone provided $20 million more than its after-tax income from wines and spirits. In addition, Seagram's interest in unremitted Du Pont earnings was worth $211 million in the same year.

On the international front, Seagram's worldwide strategy had been to develop links with Allied–Hiram Walker, in part fuelled by a mutual worry about IDV, though the Martell acquisition forced Seagram into a closer relationship with IDV in the Far East. Seagram International considered itself as being 'multi-local' and it built success through 'local' brands and through its persistent strategy (since emulated by its competitors) of distributing its products through wholly-owned distributors wherever it could.

Bacardi International

Based in Cuba, all Bacardi's Cuban production facilities were confiscated after the Cuban revolution in 1959. The Bacardi trade marks were registered outside Cuba which prevented Castro from marketing the output of the Bacardi distilleries as Bacardi rum. Bacardi concentrated on its rum, realizing that, without a home market, it had to operate internationally. Worldwide supply continued from Bacardi's production facilities in Mexico and Puerto Rico. Eight bottling plants were set up spanning the world from Australia to the US.

The company concentrated on building its brand through high product quality and consistent market positioning as a mixer, particularly through joint promotions with Coca-Cola. Bacardi rum flourished, overtaking Smirnoff to become the best-selling brand in the world. Bacardi's brand developments have been line extensions of rum together with Bezique, a lime-flavoured spirit launched in 1984.

In 1986 Bacardi signed an agreement for Cusenier, the Pernod–Ricard subsidiary, to distribute Bacardi in France. In 1987 the company established a joint venture with Guinness in Spain to market selected UDG brands. A similar arrangement was made with Guinness in 1988 in the German market, despite Bacardi's concerns about loss of control, especially of its principal trade mark. As a private family company it was not preoccupied with short-term profit.

Suntory

Suntory introduced Japan's first whisky in 1930 and started exporting in 1931, though it had problems building an export market for something that was not a traditional Japanese product. Initially a foreign taste to the Japanese, whisky sales were boosted by the Americans after the Second World War and Japan became the second largest whisky drinking nation after America. By the early 1970s, Suntory's share of the domestic whisky market had risen to between 60% and 70% and it owned the largest distillery in the world.

During the 1970s and 1980s product diversification and international penetration was pursued. Suntory opened Japanese restaurants in Mexico, Milan, Paris, and London; set up local production in Thailand, Mexico, and Brazil; and arranged two barter deals – obtaining bulk wine from Bulgaria and vodka from the USSR in return for Japanese whisky.

Suntory protected its domestic market from imported Scotch by intensive lobbying of government for a favourable tax consideration for Japanese whisky. (The Japanese drinks industry, to this day, remains one of the larger contributors to the ruling Liberal Democratic Party's funds.) The company continued to build its domestic market share in beer (5% in 1977). It also set up a soft drinks and fruit juice division, a fast food chain in Tokyo and, by 1979, it had 25 000 tied or controlled bars to sell its products.

In response to increased interest in the buoyant Japanese market by the world's major wine and spirit companies, Suntory started to secure further sources of product supply. It already represented Haig, Jack Daniels, Martell, Beefeater, and Bacardi, and it had an 11% stake in the Glenlivet Distillery. Suntory later agreed to distribute Perrier and Chateau Lafite Rothschild; started to brew Budwieser beer under licence; bought a prestigious Bordeaux Chateau, the largest US bottled water company, a California Winery; entered a marketing alliance with Allied–Lyons; and set up a joint venture with the Chinese.

Despite Suntory's attempts at international penetration, less than 5% of its revenue came from foreign sales in 1985. In 1986 the company's dependence on its home market was dramatically demonstrated. An increase in taxes caused a swing in fashion away from whisky and towards Shochu. Suntory dropped seven million cases of whisky sales and despite its marketing abilities did not recover the lost sales.

In 1988 Seagram bought Martell. Martell had been supplying Suntory with bulk Cognac, but Seagram did not renew the Martell distribution contract with Suntory. In the same year Suntory acquired another US bottled water company, giving it a substantial presence in this market. Suntory has remained a private company although funding for recent acquisitions may have caused the sale of some family shares. There was no clear succession candidate for the president (second son of the founder) whose preferred strategy is believed to be the development of the alliance with Allied–Lyons.

Pernod–Ricard

Pernod–Ricard was the largest spirits producer in France and the eighth largest spirits producer in the world, having the world's third largest selling brand – Ricard. Though a public company, Pernod–Ricard remained under family control.

The company had the largest single share of the EC spirits market with an estimated 8.3% (Guinness, 6.1%; IDV, 3.8%; Allied-Lyons, 4.8%; Seagram, 3.4%; Bols, 3.3%).

The 1974 merger between Pernod and Ricard, had given the company dominance in the large French anise market – which accounted for 40% of the total French spirits market. Conscious of its dependence on this, Pernod–Ricard set out to diversify both its product range and its territorial sales. By 1986 it had set itself the objective of making half its sales in France and half through exports, with sales in each half split equally between alcoholic and non-alcoholic drinks.

Its major diversification had been to buy Orangina – France's leading non-alcoholic drink – in 1984. This was soon being produced and distributed under licence through eight plants in seven countries, including the US, UK, Canada, and West Germany, and was being launched into more overseas markets. Pernod–Ricard also became a world leader in fruit preparations for use in milk products, especially yoghurts. However, in 1989, it lost its French distribution rights for Coca-Cola. These had contributed over 40% of Pernod's non-alcoholic drinks volume and, with earnings of around FF140 million, had contributed 10% of group pre-tax profits. (Coca-Cola paid £90 million compensation to Pernod–Ricard).

Pernod–Ricard remained predominantly a French wines and spirits company. About three-quarters of its 1987 wine and spirits profits still came from the sale of anise drinks in France. Anise drinks sell in France at prices approaching those of Scotch whiskies – without their maturation costs – and so anise has remained a profitable sector. In 1988 the French wines and spirits operation produced 62% of group net profits on 43% of the total sales of FF13 500 million.

Pernod–Ricard's spirit range included Calvados (apple brandy) as well as its own Armagnac (Montesquiou) and Cognac (Bisquit). It also had its own Scotch whiskies (Clan Campbell; White Heather) as well as a single malt whisky (Aberlour) and Bourbon (Wild Turkey). Since France was the world's third largest market for Scotch (after the US and the UK), Pernod–Ricard was well placed to capture part of this growing market, having two of the top 15 Scotch brands in France.

With a 90% share in Société des Vins de France, Pernod–Ricard supplied approximately 10% of the French wine market and was the market leader in branded table wines. It also produced a number of branded wine-based aperitifs including Cinzano, Dubonnet, and Byrrh, and distributed brands such as Cutty Sark, Bacardi, Stolichnaya vodka, and Gilbey's gin from IDV.

Pernod–Ricard had been more cautious than some of its competitors in extending its alcoholic interests outside France and concentrated on European markets. Its export wing (SEGM) had a network of subsidiaries such as IGM Deutschland in Germany, Parkington in Britain, Ramazotti In Italy, Perisem in Switzerland, and Prac SA and Ambrosio Velasco in Spain. Acquisitions of producers had mainly been of one-country companies such as the Dutch spirits manufacturer Cooymans, Italy's leading food aromatics company San Giorgio and, after an extraordinary competition with IDV in 1988, the Irish Distillers Group – the only producer of Irish whiskeys – including Old Bushmills. Elsewhere, Pernod–Ricard had a number of joint distribution agreements for its spirits, including ownership of 30% of Heublein in Brazil and Japan. Heublein has 30% of Pernod–Ricard's Austin Nichols distribution company in the US.

Brown–Forman

Founded in 1870, three family members still own 100% of the voting stock of this Kentucky company. Wines and Spirits accounted for 80% of its operating income, of which 80% came from spirits and, of that 80%, half came from Jack Daniels, a 'Tennessee Whiskey' (US sales, 3.3 m cases; international, 0.5 m cases), despite it only accounting for 26% of the spirits volume. Its other major brands were the liqueur Southern Comfort (US, 1.3 m; international 0.8 m), Early Times bourbon (US, 1.5 m; international 0.2 m), Canadian Mist which was claimed to be 'America's best selling Canadian (whiskey)' (4.0 m cases, all in US).

The profitability of Jack Daniels, Southern Comfort, and Canadian Mist had all been enhanced in the late 1980s through proof reduction or reformulation.

Brown–Forman also acquired 'prestige' businesses outside the drinks industry. Lenox was the major North American manufacturer of fine china and crystalware and Hartmann was a manufacturer of up-market luggage. These companies were profitable but other ventures into candles and jewellery were less successful and had been sold.

Brown–Forman's only manufacturing plant outside North America was at Irish Distillers Group in Ireland where it produced Southern Comfort for the European market. Southern Comfort and Jack Daniels were the only company products which sold in any volume outside North America.

Performance ($ million)	Years to 30 April			
	1986	1987	1988	1989
Net sales, less excise tax	995	1098	1067	1287
Net income	86	90	103	144

Jim Beam

American Brands, the owner of the Jim Beam company, bought the spirits business of National Distillers and Chemicals in 1987 for $545 million.

Whilst operating economies of the order of $20–30 million resulted from bringing the two organizations together, most of the expanded range were mid-priced rather than premium (Brown–Forman produced nearly three times as much operating profit from 12.5 million cases as Jim Beam did from 17 million.)

In addition, Jim Beam bought De Kuyper Cordials at the peak of its growth curve (driven by the Peach Schnapps fashion in the US) and, with the rapid decline of De Kuyper, offset by the savings from rationalizing the two overheads and sales force costs, the interest costs of the acquisitions may have exceeded their operating income. In 1987 operating income from spirits was $68 million before interest, other expenses and tax. There were significant cut-backs in advertising in 1988.

Jim Beam	3.4 + 1.2 overseas
De Kuyper	3.3
Windsor	2.2
Kamchatka	1.4
Gilbeys Gin	1.3
Gilbeys Vodka	1.3
Old Crow	0.6
Old Grand Dad	0.4
Beam 8 Star	0.4

International Distillers and Vintners

IDV was formed in 1962 from the businesses of Justerini & Brooks and Gilbey. Owning Chateau Loudenne, Scottish whisky distilleries, and Croft in Portugal, Gilbey also distilled in Canada. In 1953 the US company Heublein had granted Gilbey the licence to produce and market Smirnoff Vodka internationally.

During the 1960s IDV's technical proficiency grew but little attention was placed on the marketing of the brand portfolio, the company relying instead on existing brand strengths and consumer tastes. There was little central management control, central marketing structure or strategic marketing direction. The brand companies continued to operate much as they had always done. From a marketing perspective IDV looked like an uneasy confederation of fiefdoms (not unlike Distillers), each one at odds with the centre, rather than a rationally organized business enterprise.

In 1967 Showerings, the UK manufacturer of Babycham (now part of Allied–Lyons), made a takeover bid for IDV. The bid was countered by the UK brewer Watney taking a defensive shareholding in IDV. In 1972 Watney itself was the target of a takeover bid by Grand Metropolitan. As part of its defensive strategy, Watney acquired majority control of IDV. However, Grand Met acquired Watney and so IDV became the wine and spirits arm of Grand Met. At the time, property-based Grand Met was not very interested in wines and spirits and chose to leave IDV as a free-standing profit centre, in case Grand Met wanted to sell it at a later stage. (Some 10 years later, a similar lack of attention from Seagram was to allow Seagram International to flourish.)

Nevertheless Grand Met pressed IDV to increase its profitability and return on investment. During the mid-1970s the production orientation of IDV gave way to a new marketing influence and its value to Grand Met grew.

In 1975 Bailey's Irish Cream liqueur was launched and became the world's largest premium liqueur.

In 1976 Anthony Tennant had been appointed IDV Group Managing Director. With a background in marketing, he saw the need for the centre to play a more important role. He created a group marketing department whose role would be to guide the international development of the group's brands and to develop more new brands. Shortly afterwards the first IDV corporate strategy was developed with an emphasis on long-term profit through marketing of international brands.

In 1979 Grand Met acquired the Liggett group which included two important US drinks importers, Paddington and Carillon, thus helping IDV to gain a direct marketing presence in the US in order to build its brands. Paddington had built up the J&B brand in the US. Carillon had the US rights to Grand Marnier, Absolut Vodka, and Bombay Gin.

In 1984 Grand Met purchased a 25% shareholding in Cinzano International plus management control, thus strengthening IDV's brand portfolio and distribution network. In 1986 IDV acquired Sambuca Romana and the US agency for Amaretto di Saronno. A joint venture marketing and sales agreement with Cinzano, Cointreau, and IDV was initiated, covering a number of key European markets. In 1987 IDV acquired Saccone & Speed, the wine and spirit arm of Courage, the UK brewer. The acquisition added two important dimensions to IDV. First, it greatly expanded the wholesale division and secondly, the UK agencies for Southern Comfort and Jack Daniels were obtained. Capping all these moves was Grand Met's $1.3 billion acquisition of the US drinks group Heublein in 1987.

Heublein

One of Heublein's earlier products was prepared cocktails – 'The Clubs', as they were known – but prohibition brought hardship to the company as it struggled to survive. Having revived after the end of prohibition, Heublein purchased the rights to Smirnoff Vodka in the late 1930s and, with Smirnoff sales soaring in the 1950s, Heublein launched the brand internationally. Heublein chose Gilbeys as its international agents.

In 1984 General Cinema began to build an apparently hostile stake in Heublein. About a month later a friendly acquisition between Heublein and R J Reynolds was announced.

In 1987 R J Reynolds sold Heublein to IDV. In acquiring its long-time trading partner Heublein, IDV almost doubled in size and acquired the ownership of Smirnoff Vodka, the world's second largest selling spirit brand (after Bacardi). IDV acquired Heublein to protect its Smirnoff licences around the world, to increase its power with the US distributors, and to acquire critical mass in a declining world market.

The acquisition also brought IDV a substantial presence in the US domestic wine market with Inglenook, Almaden, and Beaulieu wines, pushing up IDV's share of the US domestic wine and spirits market from 2% to 13%. Heublein included market leaders such as Popov Vodka, Lancers wines, and brands imported under licence such as Jose Cuervo Tequila and Finlandia Vodka.

In strategic terms, the acquisition had two major effects on IDV. First, it made it more reliant on vodka and other 'white' spirits. In 1986 vodka and white spirits accounted for 54% of IDV's spirit sales by volume, compared to white spirits' 33% share of the total world spirits market.

Secondly, the acquisition increased IDV's dependence on the US market. In 1987 about half of its spirit sales and over 60% of its wine sales were in the US.

Due to post-prohibition legislation, the US still had an unusual market structure. Liquor producers were not only forbidden to fully vertically integrate, but they were also obliged by law to virtually sell at the same price to all distributors. US liquor distributors prior to 1986 had mostly operated on profit margins of up to 20%. An increase in Federal Excise Tax then caused margins to fall to nearer 10% due to customer price resistance. As stockbrokers Panmure Gordon put it in 1987:

> As the number of distributors declines in any one state, their primary concern is to attach themselves to the brand owners with the largest, most profitable and most resilient brand portfolios. Of the major US companies, IDV/Heublein to a considerable extent best fits that description. In these circumstances IDV has a powerful bargaining position in cushioning its margins from the pricing pressures evident at the retail end of the distribution chain.

IDV and Martell

In 1987 IDV signed a trading agreement with the family controlled Martell company by which IDV and Martell would distribute and market each other's brands in various territories. To cement the agreement IDV acquired a 10% equity interest in Martell.

The agreement was designed to add a cognac to IDV's portfolio, and also to gain access to Martell's extensive distribution network in the Far East which accounted for 22% of world cognac sales by volume and 33% by value. Cognac, a premium spirit in Far Eastern markets, could produce a profit at least three times that of exported Scotch whisky. Additionally, by forming a close tie with Martell, IDV had hoped to make Martell unappetizing to any other suitor.

However, the majority of the Martell family were not involved with the business and, frightened by the potential loss in value of their shares if

IDV's presence locked out other suitors as Grand Met tried to increase its stake to 20%, they wanted to sell the company. A bid battle developed between Grand Met and Seagram for control of Martell, culminating in Seagram outbidding Grand Met and buying Martell for $920 million.

Grand Met had gained a £37 million net profit on its shares, and Seagram and IDV soon reached a new agreement by which Seagram marketed and distributed all IDV brands (as well as its own) in Hong Kong, Malaysia, China, Singapore, and Thailand. IDV was to market and distribute all Seagram brands in those territories where Seagram's extensive distribution did not operate. Wood Mackensie commented: 'The deal gives IDV the distribution and Seagram the brands to put through its distribution system in the Far East.' IDV still did not have a cognac of its own. It had, however, bought Metaxa brandy (its Greek J&B distributor) and a 30% stake in the leading ouzo (an anise-flavoured aperitif) producer, thus gaining world distribution rights to Ouzo 12 (then selling 900 000 cases a year) for a price believed to be something over £100 million. Metaxa sold 1.5 million cases a year in 130 countries – 1 million through duty-free outlets – and was ranked number 82 in the world league of spirit brands.

In May 1989 IDV bought (for a sum believed to be $100m) the wine and spirits operation of a Californian order of monks – The Christian Brothers – whose brandy was the second largest brandy in the US (1.1 m cases; 27% market share; and no 94 world spirit brand) behind Gallo's E & J brand. With it came the largest vineyard in Napa Valley (1200 acres; 800 000 cases). IDV had grown to become the single largest part of Grand Met in terms of both turnover and profit.

Premium branding and profitability

While parts of the European market were more buoyant than the North American market, IDV's aim in both markets had been similar. The basis of IDV's core business strategy was that profits were intended to come from increased market share and/or pricing up through adding perceived value to the consumer. This policy, backed up by an annual advertising, merchandising, and promotion spend of over £200 million, had enabled IDV to maintain better margins on many brands than its competitors.

In financial terms, IDV's return on capital grew from 25% in 1983 to over 30% in 1987, and its 307% growth in profits since 1980 was only equalled among the 10 largest wine and spirits companies by Moet–Hennessy. (Note: Because of the habit of capitalizing brands – and because of acquisition accounting – return on capital numbers for all companies must be treated with caution.)

Organization structure

IDV believed that there were a number of elements behind this success. One was IDV's approach to brand management. Instead of having conventional brand managers answering to a single marketing director, each of IDV's major brands was controlled by a separate IDV international brand company (IBC). Each IBC had its own international sales force and production and it concentrated on the marketing of its own brand. The international brand manager dealt with individual market distributors, whether or not they were IDV-owned companies, and agreed with them on the individual brand strategy. It was a system that IDV felt provided major advantages over conventional structures, mainly in focus, continuity, dedication, and commitment.

The other component of this structure was the national marketing company (NMC). IDV controlled, with its partners, 32 NMCs in countries around the world. Each NMC was charged with the responsibility for building the finest possible portfolio of brands. It was the responsibility of the NMC to maximise profit with IDV and competitors' brands. For example, in the US, Carillon's portfolio included Absolut Vodka. Carillon built this brand successfully, but in so doing helped dislodge Smirnoff from its reputation as a premium/super-premium vodka. In a world of consolidating brand ownership, having multiple NMCs in a country was a way of marketing competing brands.

New brand development

IDV's approach to new brand development (NBD) is different from that used by most fast-moving consumer goods companies. Instead of making a single department responsible for NBD, all senior executives were encouraged to 'champion' ideas for new brands from their inception to their market launch. With pilot plants in Harlow (England) and Hartford (Conn), its chain of off-licences, and other Grand Metropolitan owned pubs and restaurants, IDV could test market its brands inexpensively before launching.

IDV had outstanding new brand successes, notably with Bailey's Irish Cream. Launched in 1975, Baileys accounted for about 25% of the UK liqueur market and 75% of the cream sector 10 years later. Baileys success was followed by that of Malibu liqueur, launched in 1980 (and originally from South Africa) and Le Piat d'Or wine. Baileys, with annual world sales of 3.3 million cases (making it the world number 23 spirit brand), Piat d'Or with sales of 2 million cases and Malibu with 1.5 million cases (number 76 in the world), together contributed 16% to IDV's total profits.

Unfortunately for IDV, repeating these successes proved difficult as the market became much more competitive. As *Marketing Week* reported in 1986:

Times have changed since the days of IDV's early successes. With between 300 to 400 new drinks launches over the past three years the market clutter is enormous. 'Seven or eight years ago we were virtually the only people in there. Now any company of any standing is there.'   IDV UK Marketing Director, Tony Scouller.

For this reason, if no other, it was often easier to buy a stake in an established successful brand than to develop one; a strategy that IDV also followed, as in its purchase of Sambuca Romana.

Some shifts were two-sided, for example the increasing willingness of consumers to experiment in their drinking habits was a factor behind the fragmentation of brand preferences, but provided the opportunity for the development of profitable new brands.

Panmure Gordon suggested that IDV's 'propects for maintaining its record of substantial real profits growth' would depend on some key influences.

1. The prospects for the US wines and spirits markets and the ability of IDV/Heublein to cope with, and competitively exploit, the pressures of declining consumption and an adverse fiscal climate.
2. The question of whether the past record of successful new product development could be maintained.
3. The ability to ensure that the alliances formed with Cinzano, Cointreau, and Seagram were successfully managed to exploit the potential in the trends of rising European and Far Eastern spirits consumption.
4. The effect of the emulation factor: Would IDV's success, which was inspiring initiatives by competitors, undermine IDV's competitive advantages?
5. Given the consolidation in the world's wine and spirit industry, should Grand Metropolitan adjust its return on investment criteria (to match those used by family companies) to allow IDV to acquire the brands and companies which would be important for its long-term profitability? (See Table 3.)

For example, after fighting off Remy Martin, Benedictine was purchased in 1988 by Martini & Rossi for a price–earnings ratio of 135 times its 1987 earnings. Benedictine's chairman said, 'Our products are difficult to reproduce and it would cost a fortune if you had to create them from scratch'.

In October 1988, Piper–Heidsieck, one of the last family-owned champagne houses, was taken over by Remy Martin for FF1.25 billion. In 1987 Piper–Heidsieck made attributable net profits of FF19.1 million on sales of FF382.6 million. Remy already controlled Krug and the separate Charles Heidsieck champagnes and became the fourth largest champagne producer, behind LVMH, Seagram (with Mumm), and BSN.

Having linked with LVMH in an international distribution and marketing arrangement in 1987, Guinness sold Hine cognac to LVMH, thus raising LVMH's share of the world cognac market (130 m bottles in 1987) from 18% to 20%. (Martell had an estimated 19%.) Apart from Hennessy and Hine cognacs, LVMH owned Moet et Chandon, Veuve Clicquot, Canard Duchene, Mercier, and Dom Perignon champagnes. Louis Vuitton luggage, Givenchy, and Christian Dior perfumes were in the group too. Of LVMH's sales of FF13 billion in 1987, FF4.5 billion

Table 3   Exit multiples of industry acquisitions

		Target	Buyer	Exit p.e.
1	1981	Makers Mark	Hiram Walker	16
2	1982	Barton Brands	Argyll	13
3	1982	All Brands	Whitbread	18
4	1984	URM	Allied–Lyons	22
5	1984	Tia Maria	Hiram Walker	17
6	1984	Somerset	DCL	15
7	1985	California Cooler	Brown Forma	17
8	1985	Bells	Guinness	15
9	1985	Buckingham	Whitbread	15
10	1986	DCL	Guinness	14
11	1986	Hiram Walker	Allied–Lyons	15
12	1987	Heublein	Grand Met	15
13	1987	Morton	Seagram	17
14	1987	National Distillers	James Beam	24
15	1987	Caldbeck	Guinness	15
16	1987	Schenley	Guinness	13
17	1987	Burroughs	Whitbread	27
18	1988	Martell	Seagram	34
19	1988	Benedictine	Martini & Rossi	135

Table 4   The leading liquor companies average operating profit per case*

	Company	(US$)
1.	Moet–Hennessy	32.72
2.	United Distillers Group	13.29
3.	Allied–Lyons	7.41
4.	Whitbread	6.06
5.	Brown–Forman	5.83
6.	Bols	5.50
7.	IDV	4.87
8.	Suntory	3.82
9.	Seagram	3.81
10.	Pernod–Ricard	3.07

* Estimated for 1987
Source: *International Drinks Bulletin*.

were in wines, FF3.0 billion in spirits, FF2.3 billion in luggage and FF3.2 billion in perfumes/beauty care.

Following the managerial convulsions within LVMH during the summer of 1988 and the entry of a major new shareholder (Jacques Rober), Guinness became a significant shareholder in LVMH. Jacques

Table 5 IDV/Heublein brand portfolio, 1987 (excluding wines)

Brands	Category	US	Canada	UK	Europe, incl. Eire	Japan	Australia and Rest of Asia	Latin America	Africa	Duty free and other	Total
						(thousand cases)					
Smirnoff	Vodka	7020	900	1850	950	20	150	1700	850	600	14 000
J&B	Scotch	1900	90	70	1800	170	65	100	320	385	4900
Popov	Vodka	3800	85	155	10			150			4200
Bailey's	Liqueur	1100	180	375	480	10	155			200	2500
Black Velvet	Canadian	1750	300		50						2100
Malibu	Liqueur	120	35	425	500	5	75	10	20	110	1300
Arrow	Liqueur	1200									1200
Gilbey's **	Gin		150	170	230	40	140	50	120	200	1100
Jose Cuervo *	Tequila	1100									1100
Club Cocktails	Cocktails	1100									1100
Croft	Sherry			690	115					295	1100
Dreher	Brandy							1100			1100
Absolut *	Vodka	1000									1000
Relska	Vodka	725									725
Amaretto di Soronno *	Liqueur	700									700
Croft	Port			80	240					230	550
Wild Turkey *	Bourbon	535									535
Grand Marnier *	Liqueur	455									455
Silk Tassel and Gold	Canadian		390								390
Sambuca Romana	Liqueur	280			20						300
Bombay Gin	Gin	205									205
Yukon Jack	Liqueur	215									215
Finlandia *	Vodka	190									190
Delaforce	Port		15	140						15	170
Sub Total		23 395	2130	3830	4535	245	580	3110	1310	2095	41 230
Other Brands and Agencies		2005	3900	800	300			1300	600	400	6270
Total Case Vols.		25 400	3030	4630	4835	245	580	4410	1910	2495	47 500
% of Total		53.4%	6.4%	9.7%	10.2%	0.5%	1.2%	9.3%	4.0%	5.3%	100%

Notes: 1 Fortified wines, i.e. sherry and port, have been counted in the spirits definition.

2 * Denotes US agency distribution rights.

3 ** This excludes the licence to James B Beam in the US; similarly the licence for Gilbey's vodka to James B Beam in the US is excluded.

Rober was owned 55% by Bernard Arnault's group, Financiere Agache, and 45% by Guinness and it held 43.5% of LVMH (fully diluted) of which nearly half (19.6%) belonged to Guinness. In turn, LVMH was the largest shareholder in Guinness with 12%.

In April 1989 Guinness disclosed that it planned to buy 16.8% of the Christian Dior fashion house from Financiere Agache, which would effectively raise the Guinness stake in LVMH to 24%. The gross investment by Guinness was nearly £1 billion, offset by LVMH investing in Guinness. LVMH might raise its 12% stake in Guinness.

SUGGESTED QUESTIONS

1. What should IDV do, given the market trends for wine and spirits?
2. What are the opportunities for branding wines?
3. Great emphasis has been placed on controlling distribution of products. Why?
4. How would you set about developing new products in wines and spirits?

15

Iskra Power Tools

Case written by Per Jenster with William Fischer and Robert Howard

As he walked through his factory in January 1991, Miro Krek, General Manager of Iskra in Kranj, Yugoslavia, commented to his visitors: 'There are certain things we need to do in aligning our marketing and manufacturing. Our efficiency could easily be improved by 10–15%. For example, we could put in longer lines and plan larger volume runs to get better efficiency. At the same time, we are considering concentrating our manufacturing on certain parts such as motors.' Placing his hand on his chest, he said with considerable emotion, 'Motors are at the heart of any power tool – we need to manufacture them!'

Krek explained: 'Over the last three months, Yugoslavia has undergone incredible political change towards adopting a Western style market economy. This change has forced us to rethink our entire power tool business. Should we try to become a major player in the West and East European power tool markets or should we only focus on a few select markets or customers? What would be the consequences for the Iskra organization?'

Prior to these events, Iskra had concentrated its sales primarily on western power tool markets, where the management believed their competitive advantages were low labour costs and, to a lesser extent, a few niche products. In fact, these two dimensions had formed the basis of Krek's plans for leading the Iskra Power Tool Division into the 1990s. Now, new markets were emerging, and old advantages were threatened. It was necessary to review the interrelated issues of manufacturing and marketing power tools.

As Krek saw it, there were three options available for Iskra Power Tools. First, to continue to capitalize on Yugoslavia's low labour costs and compete on price in Western markets. Second, Iskra could build on

This case was prepared by Research Associate Robert C Howard under the direction of Professors William A Fischer and Per V Jenster as the basis for class discussion rather than to illustrate either effective or ineffective handling of an administrative situation. Reprinted by permission of IMD, Lausanne, Switzerland.

the two major successes that it had enjoyed, and manufacture and market a select few power tools in western niche markets. Third, Iskra Power Tools could try to build on Yugoslavia's tradition as a commercial link between east and west, and develop the power tool markets of Eastern Europe.

Krek also had the worry of how to preserve Iskra's domestic position at a time when the firm was under attack from a Black & Decker assembly operation in Yugoslavia. With less than two weeks to prepare for his final presentation to senior management of the Iskra Group, he knew a full review of the options for the 1990s was necessary.

The Iskra Group of Companies had been founded in Ljubljana in 1961 through the merger of four major electrical companies in Slovenia, Yugoslavia's northernmost republic. By 1991 Iskra had become the leading electronic and electrical manufacturer in Yugoslavia, manufacturing and marketing a broad range of products through 14 domestic subsidiaries and 18 foreign offices. Iskra had 25 000 employees, making it the largest Slovenian employer.

Until the early 1950s, Iskra's employees had channelled their expertise into industrial and consumer products for rebuilding the Yugoslavian infrastructure and meeting the needs of the domestic market. Included among the group's industrial products were electric power meters, transformers, capacitors, and electric motors. In the consumer area, products included automotive products such as starters, alternators and voltage regulators, and household appliances such as vacuum cleaners, toasters, and power tools. In time, the Kranj production facility became too constrained to continue manufacturing the entire Iskra product offering, and several products were transferred to other sites in the area. Power tool production, however, along with kilowatt meters and telecommunications switching equipment remained in Kranj. (See Exhibit 1 for the Iskra Power Tools organization chart.)

ISKRA COMMERCE

As was typical in centrally-planned economies, the production and distribution of Iskra Group's products were separate responsibilities. While the factories concentrated on production, a separate sales organization, Iskra Commerce, handled the marketing and distribution responsibilities. Originally, Iskra Commerce had conducted all purchasing and selling for the Iskra Group, both inside and outside Yugoslavia. In the early 1970s, Iskra's domestic companies began to purchase and sell directly in Yugoslavia. However, Iskra Commerce retained responsibility for foreign commercial intercourse.

In foreign markets, Iskra Commerce continued purchasing and selling for all companies within the Iskra Group until the late 1980s. Thereafter, Iskra's foreign companies also began to establish direct commercial links with suppliers and buyers. Mitja Taucher, former Senior Advisor of Iskra Commerce, recalled: 'When Yugoslavia had strong regulations regarding

Exhibit 1 Iskra Power Tools organization chart.

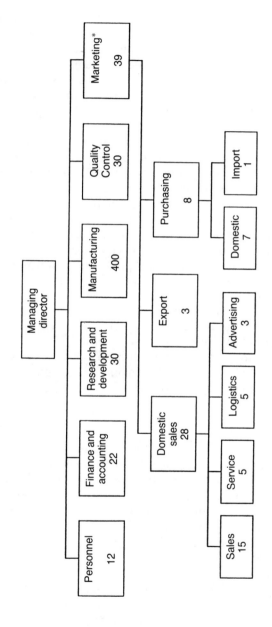

*Includes 10 people who also work in Iskra Commerce

imports, it made a lot of sense to channel all the group's purchases and sales through one organization; the group was stronger as a whole than as individual companies. Now, however, with the changes in Yugoslavia concerning imports and the strength of our individual companies, it makes sense for Iskra Commerce to serve in a different capacity.'

THE POWER TOOL INDUSTRY

Power tools usually included a motor capable of being guided and supported manually by an operator, and had a role between traditional hand tools and sophisticated machine tools. Typical products included the household drill, circular saw, jigsaw, router, angle grinder, hedge trimmer, chain saw, and more specialized products such as nut runners and impact wrenches used in assembly-line manufacture. The relatively low cost of electric tools facilitated their use in small workshops, the building and construction industries, and in households.

The industry was classified into two broad segments according to end usage: professional and hobby. Professional users worked in industries such as assembly-line manufacture, foundries, shipbuilding, and woodworking. The building and construction trade covered both segments, using tools for the professional builder as well as tools designed for the home enthusiast or do-it-yourself (DIY) market. Worldwide, power tool purchase behaviour varied as a function of labour costs and disposable income. Generally, the professional power tool sector was most developed in high labour cost countries; the DIY market tended to be more pronounced in countries with higher personal disposable incomes.

In 1989 the worldwide electric power tool industry was valued at just over DM10 billion, with sales concentrated in North America (28%); Europe (47%); and the Far East (18%). Although the industry had grown at 3% per annum since 1980, market growth rates varied considerably (see Table 1). In Europe, where the industrial segment had traditionally dominated, Germany, France, Great Britain, and Italy represented 75% of the region's sales (see Table 2).

SEGMENTS AND CHANNELS

Professional tools were traditionally bought from hardware stores, wholesalers, large tool specialists, or from a manufacturer's or distributor's direct sales force. Important buying criteria were quality for specific tasks, durability, and after-sales service. In addition, some manufacturers of professional tools viewed education and problem solving as part of the sales effort, with trained sales people needed to meet the technical requirements of the user.

In the hobby segment, customers bought from wholesalers, hardware stores, department stores, home improvement centres, mail order houses, and hypermarkets. Manufacturers considered image, product quality, and price as important purchase factors. In this segment, as with other con-

Table 1   Percentage growth of European power tool markets in 1989 and 1990

Country	Growth in 1989 (%)	Country	Growth in 1990 (%)
Portugal	20	Greece	35
Spain	18	Germany	18
Italy	15	Portugal	18
Greece	15	Italy	12
Finland	12	Netherlands	10
Austria	12	Sweden	10
Sweden	10	Ireland	8
Great Britain	8	Belgium	6
Germany	8	Spain	6
France	8	Austria	4
Belgium	8	Denmark	3
Switzerland	8	Switzerland	3
Netherlands	5	France	0
Ireland	5	Great Britain	0
Denmark	−5	Norway	0
Norway	−5	Finland	−3

Source: Databank (1989); Bosch (1990).

Table 2   1989 unit sales in Europe's four largest markets

Country	(thousand pieces)	European Sales (%)
Germany	7 000	28
France	5 000	20
Great Britain	4 300	17
Italy	2 500	10
Other countries	6 200	25
Total	25 000	100

Source: Bosch.

sumer products, brand name and packaging were gaining in importance relative to other product features. At the low end of the market, products were designed to meet an expected lifetime of 25 hours in use. At the high end, which tended to enlarge as the market matured, there was more emphasis on durability and ergonomic characteristics, similar to professional products.

In Europe, a shift in purchasing patterns had changed the distribution of power tools. In the professional sector, direct sales had begun to play a more significant role in the distribution process, particularly in the more mature and structured markets. And, in the consumer segment, the volume of tools sold through mass merchandisers was growing at the expense of conventional tool sellers. In short, increased specialization in

Table 3 Percentage of country sales by distribution channel, 1990

Channel/country	DIY segment Germany	Italy		Professional segment Germany	Italy
Wholesalers	5	25	Direct	10	
Hardware stores	55	45	Hardware	50	55
Department stores	15	11	Wholesalers	40	25
Home centres	21		Large tool		
Others (cash and			specialists		20
carry, mail order)	4	19			

Source: Black & Decker; Iskra company records.

power tool usage, combined with a proliferation of applications, was leading manufacturers to establish more direct links to professional users and more visible links to the DIY segment. The volume of power tools sold through any one of these channels varied as a function of country. Generally speaking, the markets in northern Europe were more mature and more structured than those in the Mediterranean countries. Likewise, mass merchandisers and direct sales played a more significant role in the north than in the south (see Table 3).

MANUFACTURING

Power tool manufacturers relied heavily on subcontractors to produce many components. The major firms only made components that were central to the performance of the final product, such as the motor.

Portable electric power tool components:

Outer shell	Electric Motor	Screw Machine Parts	Switches and attachments	Packaging

Power tools were mass produced, although the extent of mechanization varied with the volume of production, nature of the product, and the efficiency of the individual manufacturer. According to one analyst, purchased materials accounted for 50% of manufacturing costs, machining 15%, diecasting/moulding 9%, motor winding and assembly 12%, and final assembly 14%.

TRENDS

By the late 1980s, a number of trends had begun to influence competition in the industry. Among these were a growing preference for battery-powered tools, globalization of the industry, and the opening up of Eastern Europe.

Battery-powered tools

Because of their low energy storage, cordless products had been limited to the DIY market. However, the combination of superior power storage and lighter materials permitted battery-operated tools to be used in more demanding applications, thus facilitating their penetration of the professional market. At the end of the 1980s, cordless tools represented 20% of all power tool production worldwide. Further advances in materials and batteries were expected to increase the life between recharges and the number of applications which cordless tools could handle.

Globalization

Throughout the 1980s, the electric power tool industry became more globalized, enabling larger players to have an operational flexibility unavailable to smaller companies. By decreasing a firm's reliance on a single market, multinational power tool companies were able to leverage their positions worldwide. Firms with manufacturing as well as sales in many markets were able to exploit uncertainties in exchange rates, competitive moves, or government policies better than their smaller rivals.

Eastern Europe and the USSR

During 1989, communist regimes were replaced by a variety of governments which expressed their commitment to develop market economies. Analysts believed that these developments would influence the power tool business in two ways. Firstly, these newly-opened markets and their power tool manufacturers were expected to be the targets of firms already established in the west. Secondly, once the legal issues surrounding privatization became clear, the surviving power tool manufacturers in Eastern Europe could begin to restructure their own operations, and market their products at home and abroad.

COMPETITION

In 1989 there were some 75 power tool manufacturers worldwide. These competitors could be grouped into two categories: large multinationals and domestic manufacturers. The large players offered a full range of power tools to both the professional and the DIY segments, as well as a complete line of accessories such as drill bits, saw blades, battery packs, and after-sales service. Smaller power tool makers tended to concentrate production on a limited line of tools, augmented by OEM (original equipment manufacturer) products to one or a few segments of the market. These small firms were well known and usually respected for their expertise in their chosen fields.

Black & Decker

Black & Decker was the largest power tool maker in the world. With manufacturing plants in 10 countries and sales in nearly 100, the company reported 1989 power tool sales of $1077 million and held about 25% of the total market, more than twice that of its next biggest rival. Like most of its competitors, the company segmented the industry into professional and DIY sectors, deriving two-thirds of its revenue from consumers and one-third from professional users. In addition to its size, Black & Decker enjoyed a number of competitive advantages. New product introduction was a high priority: the company launched 77 products in 1989 while new and redesigned products accounted for 25% of revenues. By 1991 the company expected new entries to represent more than half its sales.

In Europe, where Black & Decker pioneered the introduction of products to the DIY segment, its name was virtually synonymous with power tools. One company spokesman attributed his company's success to proper market segmentation and a restructuring that had begun in the mid-1980s. Thus, when the market for power tools as a whole was growing at a rate of only 5–6%, Black & Decker achieved 11% growth in 1989 due in part to its concentrated focus on accessories and cordless products. Although the latter grew 30% in 1989, Black & Decker's successful identification of the trend toward cordless products allowed its sales in this segment to grow by 70%, reaching $100 million in 1989.

From the mid-1980s onward, the management of Black & Decker devoted significant attention to 'globalizing' its worldwide operations and, by the beginning of the 1990s, design centres, manufacturing plants, and marketing programmes were adept at making and selling products to a worldwide market. As early as 1978 Black & Decker had standardized its motors and armature shafts, and it had consistently pursued manufacturing approaches that combined product variety with volume output such as: dedicated lines and facilities for specific items (focused factories and group technology); flexible manufacturing systems, just-in-time manufacturing, and significant vertical integration of the fabrication and assembly process. In addition, Black & Decker achieved substantial cost savings through global purchasing programmes and by restructuring its manufacturing facilities. In one facility, for example, the company standardized production around a limited number of motors. In another case, the company consolidated production of drills from five different plants to two.

To strengthen its presence in Eastern Europe, Black & Decker had recently established an assembly operation via a joint venture in Kranj. Although the company owned only 49%, its proximity was seen as a serious challenge to Iskra's position in Yugoslavia. And, in May 1989 in Czechoslovakia, Black & Decker entered into a joint venture to produce DIY tools and lawnmowers for the Czechoslovakian and West European markets. Once the joint venture reached full capacity in 1990, Black &

Decker intended to cease production at its French and Italian facilities, and rely on its new Eastern European manufacturing platform.

Makita

Based in Japan, Makita had entered the power tool market in the 1950s. By the 1980s, Makita had established itself in a number of foreign markets by emphasizing its price competitiveness. At one point Makita products were selling at price levels that were 20–30% lower than the industry average. By 1990 Makita had established a solid reputation for quality and after-sales service, supported by a three-day repair policy. Through engaging a large number of distribution outlets in target markets to promote and service its products, Makita had climbed to number two in the industry by 1991.

In contrast to Black & Decker, Makita concentrated only on supplying a broad range of tools for professionals, attributing its success in overseas markets to superior after-sales service and a close working relationship with well-informed retailers who kept in touch with consumers regarding the latest in product development. Beginning with two factories in Japan in the mid-1970s, Makita had globalized its operations during the 1980s, establishing factories in the US, Canada, and Brazil.

In Europe, Makita's 1989 sales increased by 15% and it stated that it intended to become the largest power tool supplier in the region. In a step towards fulfilling that vision and meeting the company's expressed goal of supplying 25% of European sales with locally manufactured products, Makita constructed a power tool plant in the UK. Scheduled to open in early 1991, the plant would initially make cordless and percussion drills, angle grinders, and circular saws for the professional sector. Ultimately, the plant was to produce only electric motors. As of January 1991, Makita had not begun to compete in any of Iskra's markets.

Robert Bosch

Robert Bosch was the third largest power tool producer in the world with manufacturing plants in Germany, the US, Brazil, and Switzerland. Bosch produced a variety of power tools for both the professional and the DIY markets, buying the portable tool division of Stanley Tools in the US in 1979. The company was particularly strong in Europe where it distributed through all channels. In 1990, despite an unfavourable trend in the dollar/Deutshmark exchange rate, Bosch's sales increased 14% to over DM2.2 billion.

Following the unification of Germany, Bosch announced plans for a joint venture with VEB Elektrowerkzeuge Sebnitz to assemble power tools in Dresden (formerly East Germany) to be distributed through the latter's network of 1400 hardware outlets. By the end of 1990, the Sebnitz facility was a fully-owned subsidiary and earmarked for DM50 million in investment, initially for producing one-handed angle grinders and small drills. In the longer term, Bosch planned to concentrate all export production in Sebnitz.

Skil

Skil was a major US manufacturer of power tools, where the company was originally known as a professional tool supplier. More recently, Skil had concentrated on developing tools that fulfilled needs somewhere between the professional and consumer levels. In Europe, Skil had positioned itself in the Nordic markets as a professional tool company. It approached the rest of Europe through the DIY market with a strong price emphasis, and was particularly strong in Germany and France.

Niche players

There were quite a number of successful smaller players in Europe which pursued niche strategies. In Germany, for example, Festo and ELU were well known for their fine-crafted woodworking tools, especially circular saws. Likewise, Kango, a British company, was renowned for its percussion drills. Generally speaking, niche players in the European power tool business charged premium prices and earned the majority of their sales in their home markets (see Exhibit 2 and Exhibit 3).

ISKRA POWER TOOLS' COMPETITIVE POSITION

Initially, Iskra Power Tools concentrated its sales in the Yugoslavian market, venturing into Western Europe in the 1960s, based on the company's expertise in small electric motors, mainly for electric drills. The cornerstone of this expansion strategy was exchange programmes with other power tool makers.

In 1966 Iskra entered into a co-operation agreement with Perles, a small Swiss power tool manufacturer, with Perles' angle grinders being sold under the Iskra name in Yugoslavia and Perles distributing Iskra's drills under the Perles label. In 1971 Iskra sought to build on the Perles name and distribution network by acquiring the Swiss-based manufacturer. Mitja Taucher commented that Iskra management realized they would have difficulties with an unknown name in Europe and, thus, acquired Perles in 1978. 'Perles is still in existence mostly for its name and distribution network, not its manufacturing capacity, which is small,' recalled Mitja. 'It was a good name across Europe for large angle grinders and some drills.'

In 1972 Iskra entered into an agreement with Skil Europe. In exchange for Iskra's small drills, sold under Skil's name through its European distribution network, Skil supplied Iskra with percussion drills, belt sanders and circular saws, sold in Yugoslavia under the Iskra name.

Iskra Power Tools began to strengthen business ties in Eastern Europe, beginning in 1978 with Naradi, a power tool manufacturer, and with

Exhibit 2   Iskra's main competitors in Europe.

Competitor	Location of corporate headquarters	Specialist (S) or Generalist (G)	Perceived successful by Iskra
AEG	D	G	
Black & Decker	US	G	Yes
Bosch	D	G	Yes
Casals	E	G	
ELU	D	S, woodworking tools, especially circular saws	
Fein	D	S, metal working tools, especially drills, and angle grinders	
Festo	D	S, same as ELU	Yes
Hilti	D	S, drills	Yes
Hitachi	J	G	
Impex	D	S, drills	
Kango	UK	S, percussion drills	
Kress	D	G	
Makita	J	G	
Metabo	D	G	
Peugeot	F	G	
Rockwell	US	G	
Rupes	I	S, table saws	
Ryobi	J	G	Yes
Skil	US, NL	G	
Stayer	I	G	Yes
Wegoma	D	S, same as ELU	

Key: D = Germany; USA = United States; E = Spain; J = Japan; UK = United Kingdom; F = France; I = Italy; NL = Netherlands.
Source: Company records.

Merkuria, a trading company, both based in Czechoslovakia. Due to a lack of convertible currency in Czechoslovakia, Iskra devised a three-way trading agreement: Perles shipped drills from Switzerland to Naradi, which marketed the products under the Naradi name, and to Merkuria, which sold products under the Iskra name. In turn, both Czech firms delivered products to Iskra and Iskra sent its power tools to Perles. Although Iskra achieved nearly a 10% market share through these two agreements in Czechoslovakia, its success was not without problems.

The power tools made by Naradi did not measure up to the quality standards demanded by Yugoslavian consumers and, after a few years, Naradi's products were out-of-date in comparison to competitors' offerings. Because of these difficulties and the lack of real distribution channels or a service network in Czechoslovakia, Iskra management terminated the agreement in 1988.

Exhibit 3   Iskra Power Tools: competitor positioning diagram.

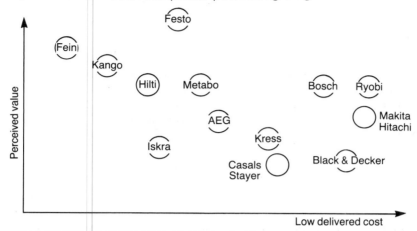

Iskra had also participated in a co-operative arrangement to exchange power tools with Celma, a Polish power tool maker. Iskra marketed Celma's products under the Iskra name in Yugoslavia. However, Celma's products were of such low quality that Iskra soon found itself inundated with repair requests. Consequently, the management of Iskra devised a new agreement for co-operation on specialty tools such as shears, steel cutters, and die grinders.

Iskra Power Tools had tried sourcing from the USSR. Unfortunately, due to the length of the negotiating period, the products were out-of-date on arrival and Iskra brought its Russian efforts to a halt in 1984.

Limited domestic competition had almost always provided Iskra with a source of funding to manufacture tools sold outside Yugoslavia. By the beginning of the 1980s, however, the management of Iskra grew concerned about becoming too dependent on the domestic market. Moreover, when it combined the uncertainties of the domestic market with its unsuccessful ventures in Eastern Europe, the management concluded it was time to strengthen its ties with Western power tool producers.

Iskra as OEM supplier

In 1980 Iskra signed a co-operation agreement with ELU, a German manufacturer of woodworking tools. Despite Iskra's successful development and initial manufacture of a small circular saw for sale under the ELU label, the management of ELU cancelled the agreement after two years. According to Branko Suhadolnik, Export Manager for Iskra Power Tools, Iskra was simply unable to supply the quantity of saws specified in the contract because of delays in starting production.

Iskra also began manufacturing for Kango, a UK company specializing in drills. In exchange for Kango's rotary hammer, sold under the Iskra name in Yugoslavia, Iskra provided Kango with circular saws sold under the Kango name in the UK.

Iskra as volume OEM

In the mid–1980s, Iskra management expanded its co-operation with Skil. In addition to supplying Skil with a small drill, Iskra provided a small angle grinder, a circular saw, and an orbital sander. These items were sold under the Skil name in support of Skil's low price strategy. In November 1990 the management of Iskra approached Skil to discuss strengthening their partnership still further. However, as of January 1991, no additional co-operation had been agreed.

In 1990 Iskra began negotiating a joint venture agreement with Ryobi. Ryobi was considering Yugoslavia as an entry point into the European Community and wanted to capitalize on Yugoslavia's comparative advantage in labour costs. In return for supplying angle grinders to Ryobi, Iskra was to market Ryobi's battery-operated power tools in Yugoslavia. Although the management of Ryobi was impressed with Iskra's products, they said that the manufacturing costs were too high; in order to meet Ryobi's terms, Iskra had to invest in more equipment. Shortly thereafter, the management of Ryobi postponed further dealings in Eastern Europe until the political environment stabilized.

In its most recent effort to supply a foreign manufacturer, Iskra approached Bosch concerning a router that complemented Bosch's offering. This deal was contingent on Iskra's dissolving its independent sales network in Germany and elsewhere. Because Bosch was not willing to purchase what Iskra management believed was the required volume necessary to compensate for the loss of its sales network, Iskra declined the offer.

In summary, the management of Iskra had made several attempts over the years to increase its attractiveness to foreign firms. With Skil, Iskra's competitive advantage was being a low-cost supplier; with ELU, Kango and Bosch, Iskra's success was based on the high perceived value of a niche product. With Ryobi, price competitiveness and market presence in Eastern Europe were important.

ISKRA'S PRODUCTS AND CHANNELS

At the beginning of 1991, Iskra marketed a range of 200 products; 10 of these were obtained from other manufacturers via exchange agreements, while the balance were designed and produced by Iskra itself. Accessories accounted for 20% of Iskra Power Tools' turnover, while drills and angle grinders accounted for approximately 50% and 30% of tool sales. Outside Yugoslavia, Iskra distributed its own products under the Perles name, almost exclusively through specialist hardware outlets in both the DIY and professional segments. In addition, Iskra Commerce marketed Iskra's power tools through its own offices.

In Yugoslavia, where Iskra had a market share of 50% in 1989, the company sold its power tools through Iskra Commerce with its own network of shops in each republic. It had a significantly larger market share in Serbia than in Slovenia or Croatia where, according to Branko, because of their proximity to Italy and Austria, customers were better informed as to western power tool alternatives, and could more easily get them. Power tools were also sold through the Iskra Power Tools sales organization, and directly from the factory in Kranj.

Design

There were two ways of developing new products at Iskra. One was via direct co-operation with manufacturing on existing product lines – a process which tended to focus on minor changes and had been practised for at least 15 years. The second pertained to new products and was primarily concerned with shortening product development time, through interdisciplinary teams, to a level comparable to Iskra's competition. The interaction between design and marketing was based on a philosophy of 'we design, you sell'. This relationship began to change as collaboration on new designs began to increase with Iskra's partners – Skil and Perles – and greater and earlier co-operation between the two functions began to evolve.

Iskra was receptive to ideas from the marketplace, communicated to the design team via Iskra's customers and foreign distributors. In 1988, for example, Iskra formed a multidisciplinary team to determine which products had to be produced in the subsequent five years, at what price and what quantity. In the export market, ideas were solicited from Iskra's agents and distributors via an annual conference. Iskra conducted market research for both its professional and its DIY users, albeit only in Yugoslavia.

Manufacturing

Despite Iskra's large product range, most were variations of a common mix of 10–15 models, all made in one factory using traditional batch production. Depending on the model, the array of products was manufactured on a monthly, quarterly, or annual basis. For example, Iskra had 70 variations of its drill, which was produced throughout the year in the same way as its angle grinders and circular saws. On the other hand, smaller volume products such as sanders and routers were made only on a quarterly basis.

Planning

Batch sizes and sequencing were developed by a central planning department located in the Kranj factory. Typically, the planning department estimated the year's production and adjusted their forecast quarterly.

Differences between the batches produced and the amounts needed for assembly at any point in time (due to lead time varations) were stored in inventories until needed. In other words, purchasing of components and product fabrication at Iskra were always begun before the ultimate destination of a power tool was known, thereby limiting the ability to use dedicated machining in the first and last stages of the production process. From 1987–89, Iskra Power Tools' inventory turnover averaged 4.4, with the biggest inventories occurring at the beginning of the assembly process. By comparison, one manager estimated that Bosch's inventory turnover was in the range of 5–10 per year.

Whether Iskra produced or purchased its parts, all were stored until the full range was available to make a particular product. Igor Poljsak, the Financial and Accounting Department Manager, mentioned that the constant shifting of parts between Iskra's many buildings added 10–15% to production costs and interest on working capital was 10–12%.

Productivity

Productivity at Iskra Power Tools was somewhere between that of eastern and western power tool makers, with direct labour estimated at 10–12% of the cost of goods sold (see Table 4 and Table 5, Exhibit 4 and Exhibit 5).

The management of Iskra acknowledged that the company probably had three times as many people as necessary. As one executive commented: 'indirect costs are always too high, and we think that we have

Table 4   Productivity figures for selected power tool firms

Company or location	No of workers	Output (units/year)
Iskra	550	600 000
Bulgarian	5000	40 000
Czechoslovakian	2000	150 000
Western Firm	250	600 000

Source: Company records.

Table 5   Breakdown of manufacturing costs for angle grinders (%)

Purchased materials	65.1
Machining, diecasting and moulding	15.9
Motor assembly	9.1
Final assembly	9.9
Total	100.0

Source: Company records.

Exhibit 4   Income statement for Iskra Power Tools.

Year to December 31	1987	1988	1989	1990
($US thousands)				
Sales revenue				
Domestic	24 842.5	18 196.4	20 658.6	24 886.9
Exports	12 311.6	11 882.3	10 204.6	12 815.1
Others	1 852.7	486.0	406.2	548.5
Total sales	39 006.8	30 564.7	31 269.4	38 250.5
Cost of sales	27 596.4	22 948.2	23 676.4	27 425.9
Gross income	11 410.4	7 616.5	7 593.0	10 824.6
Selling and Admin expenses	8 226.5	5 032.3	5 191.8	6 020.4
Operating income	3 183.9	2 584.2	2 401.2	4 804.2
Other income:				
Interest	3.3	36.6	14 928.1	797.5
Sundry income	269.3	152.8	406.2	2 320.8
Total other income	272.6	189.4	15 334.3	3 118.3
Other expenses:				
Interest	907.9	1 753.9	12 201.8	4 558.6
Sundry expenses	583.0	482.5	13 664.8	4 781.7
Total other expenses	1 490.9	2 236.4	25 866.6	9 340.3
Obligatory contributions to community funds	1 521.9	507.6		
Net income (loss)	443.7	29.6	(8 131.1)	(1 417.8)
Allocation of net income (loss):				
Business fund				
Reserve fund	292.8	26.6		
Collective consumption Fund	128.6			
Joint venture partners	22.3	3.0		
Depreciation	1 402.7	1 269.9	1 470.2	2 591.5
Net income	443.7	29.6	(8 131.1)	(1 417.8)
Cash generation	1 846.4	1 299.5	(6 660.9)	(1 173.7)

Source: Company records.

extremely high indirect costs for our production volume. For example, we have data indicating that Skil, with approximately the same number of people as Iskra, produces nearly one million pieces. Kress employs 400–500 people and produces around one million pieces. We have around 550 people, recently reduced from 760 without any strikes; however, I don't believe that will hold if we try to reduce further.'

Iskra's productivity was also influenced by significant differences in production. Work was performed both in batch and in sequence, and, because all parts (except motors) were continually moved in and out of physical inventory, the flow of goods through the factory was complicated. (See Exhibit 6 for the flowpath of a typical item.) On the dedicated motor assembly line there was little apparent continuity among workstations and, although the production machinery was only about 10 years old, the manufacturing process appeared much older. Lastly, the final assembly of tools had lots of discontinuities as newly-finished goods often sat for several days waiting for complementary parts, such as chuck-keys, which were out of stock.

Quality

The Iskra management was well aware that it needed to establish, improve and maintain quality in products and processes. The quality

Exhibit 5 Iskra balance sheets.

Year to December 31	1987	1988	1989	1990
($US thousands)				
Current assets:				
Bank balances and cash	71.9	13.7	29.0	24.3
Bills and trade receivables	6 815.3	4 954.3	5 791.2	10 257.3
Prepayments and other receivables	1 497.4	4.931.1	520.8	137.3
Current portion of long-term receivables	1.8	0.5	408.6	184.1
Inventories:				
Raw materials	3 506.8	2 289.7	856.8	3 367.0
Work-in-process	1 367.4	957.8	245.9	1 148.0
Finished products	1 211.4	640.9	802.2	1 750.0
Subtotal	6 085.6	3 888.4	1 904.9	6 265.0
Total current assets	14 472.0	13 788.0	8 654.5	16 868.0
Long-term receivables	67.8	56.6	2 503.3	3 500.0
Investments	1 324.7	1 289.1	34.1	—
Deposits for capital expenditure	16.9	201.8	28.9	998.4
Fixed assets:				
Land and building	1 343.1	1 199.8	1 453.9	2 611.6
Equipment	12 804.9	11 697.2	17 554.8	32 520.9
Deferred expenditure	15.8	14.0	188.0	—
Construction in progress	24.9	70.5	107.5	191.9
Total gross fixed assets	14 188.7	12 981.5	19 304.2	35 324.5
Less: accumulated depreciation	7 495.2	7 542.2	12 363.5	25 093.6
Net fixed assets	6 693.5	5 439.3	6 940.7	10 230.9
Net assets allocated to funds				
Reserve fund	338.6	94.1	69.6	137.4
Collective consumption fund	847.3	466.1	169.6	380.6
Other funds	21.4	9.6	21.3	168.5
Subtotal	1 207.3	569.8	260.5	686.5
Total assets	23 782.2	21 470.5	21 089.8	35 987.9

Exhibit 5   *continued*

Liabilities and funds	1987	1988	1989	1990
Current liabilities:				
Bills and trade payables	2945.6	2581.5	7656.1	4282.7
Payables for fixed assets	6.5	1.3		
Customers deposits and other current liabilities	2648.2	2689.5	0.9	3836.9
Short-term loans	5381.4	5981.1	4325.3	7188.4
Current portion of long-term loans	889.5	511.1	502.7	263.2
Amounts due to reserve and collective consumption funds	309.3	17.3		
Deferred sales	1355.9	1111.5	172.1	4207.3
Total current liabilities	13536.4	12893.3	12657.1	19778.5
Long-term loans	3362.5	3345.4	2788.3	5001.0
Joint venture partner investments:				
Domestic partners	17.8	22.1	0.7	
Foreign JV partners				
Business funds	5668.0	4659.5	5368.9	10541.4
Other funds:				
Reserve fund	338.6	94.1	160.2	137.4
Collective consumption fund	847.2	448.8	69.6	380.6
Other funds	11.7	7.3	35.2	149.0
Subtotal	1197.5	550.2	265.0	667.0
Total liabilities and funds	23782.2	21470.5	21080.0	35987.9

Source: Company records.

Exhibit 6   Flowpath for power tool gear manufacturing.

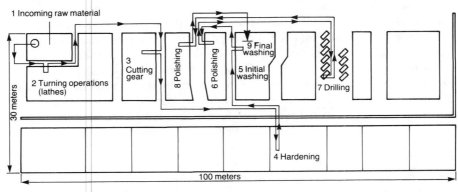

Source: company records.

manager had organized statistical process control (SPC) procedures within the factory but the level of quality was nowhere near that required to move to a production process, such as just-in-time (JIT), which could significantly reduce work-in-process inventories. Incoming goods were checked on arrival, according to prearranged contractual standards, using a standard acceptance sampling (Acceptable Quality Level) system. Acceptance sampling was done at final production and final assembly, as well as with incoming items. In all cases, quality control was based on the first five pieces in a batch, followed by statistical sampling.

In future, the quality manager hoped to embed a quality attitude throughout the company. As part of the process, management had prepared a book containing quality standards, based on the International Standards Organization (ISO) 9000 series standards. As of January 1991, management had not had much success implementing quality improvement. To do so, management believed, would require reshaping the attitudes of Iskra's workers.

The production workers

Iskra Power Tools' production process was characterized by low employee involvement, poor changeover performance between different models, and relatively poor maintenance performance. The assembly line workers were analysed using modern time and methods analysis, and the analysis used to allocate labour staffing. However, since assembly was performed on a paced line, it was not possible for the employees to work faster. Thus, no pay incentives existed for higher output and workers were paid as a group. On occasion, quality bonuses were paid within the factory, despite the fact that some of the production being 'rewarded' was not perfect.

Jakob Sink, Quality Assurance Manager, commented on the difficulties met in transforming the mindset of Iskra employees. 'It is a new idea to send back a QC approval form within a few weeks. "Why not do it in a couple of months?" is still very much the attitude of those working in production.' Sink added that workers were concerned in case identifying poor quality could cause either themselves or any of their co-workers to be fired and that some employees might resist new manufacturing processes designed by management to deal with high-variety manufacturing more efficiently. In defense of the workforce, Sink said that incoming materials played a key role in the quality problem and that, although Iskra controlled what it bought, it sometimes cost as much to control incoming materials as to produce a finished product.

The supply situation

There was widespread agreement among the Iskra management team that the supply relationships were a competitive disadvantage. In fact, some thought that Iskra's manufacturing costs were 20–25% more expensive than for Bosch, for example, because of the supply situation. The company faced the added complication that one of its major suppliers was based in Serbia, with which political tensions had been growing.

Within Yugoslavia, the manufacturing director distinguished suppliers according to raw materials or finished components such as gears and cables. He commented that, aside from having a lower quality, raw materials were also more expensive in Yugoslavia than in Western Europe. Furthermore, there were few finished component suppliers to choose from in Yugoslavia, and those that did exist did not possess a high quality standard. To use domestic components, Iskra would have to take what was available from several firms and re-machine them before assembling its power tools.

As one remedy, Iskra forged close working relationships with those local suppliers who were able to respond to major design changes without any real problem, but efforts to upgrade the quality of the finished components had been unsuccessful. Despite the close relationships, it was highly unlikely that Iskra could put SPC into a supplier facility. According to Milan Bavec, 'SPC is still too new, and even though we've held seminars, run films and the like, our results are still poor. At present, the real problem is getting the suppliers to comply with Iskra's own quality checklists. And that will take at least another two to three years'.

Foreign suppliers

Another manager pointed out that an obvious remedy to the problems encountered with domestic suppliers was to source from foreign firms. In general, sourcing at Iskra began after Iskra Power Tools had identified a potential supplier and negotiated the contract. Iskra Commerce then handled the commercial issues, such as invoicing and foreign exchange, for which it charged a fee of 4–6%. In addition, Iskra Power Tools paid an import duty of 4–5% on all items which it re-exported. For items sold on the domestic market, however, the import tax was 45%.

Another sourcing disadvantage for Iskra was customs delays. Typically, it took the company up to one month to obtain import clearance. To counter such delays, Iskra was obliged to order large stocks in advance. Additional factors that complicated Iskra's sourcing arrangements were premium prices because of small order volumes, payment problems due to foreign exchange availability, and the problem of Yugoslavia's external political image.

To summarize the above, one Iskra executive prepared a business system depicting the company's contribution to added value. For a customer paying a price of 100, distribution accounted for 50%, while parts, fabrication, and assembly represented the balance (as summarized below).

The Iskra business system

Parts	Fabrication	Assembly	Distribution	Customer
32.5	8.0	9.5	50.0	100.0

$\rightarrow$ VALUE ADDED $\rightarrow$

Source: Company records.

FORMULATING A STRATEGY

In formulating Iskra's future strategy, Branko Suhadolnik believed the company would only succeed by concentrating on less mature and less structured markets such as France and Italy, and by establishing the Perles brand name and structuring the distribution. Revamped manufacturing facilities would play a primary role in associating the company's image with quality products. Although he also supported the idea of serving as an OEM, he favoured serving the niche players, provided Iskra could overcome what he believed was the company's inability to supply a requested volume of product at a competitive price.

On the other hand, Miro Krek believed the company's future lay in concentrating on becoming an OEM supplier to high volume producers, not trading under the Perles brand or worrying about distribution. As an OEM supplier, Krek felt that Iskra's inability to attract outside co-operation was due to a lack of price competitiveness, quality, and supply reliability. Consequently, special attention should be devoted to developing its price competitiveness and strengthening its ties with volume players such as Skil. A third group of Iskra executives believed that now was the time to attack Eastern Europe and the USSR. Specifically, these executives believed that western suitors saw Iskra as a possible route into the Soviet Union.

Western markets with Perles branding

Branko Suhadolnik felt that any activity in western Europe required a concentrated focus on France, the second biggest market in Europe. Branko emphasized that with more than 8% growth in 1989 and five million power tools sold, France represented 20% of the total European market and warranted further attention.

There was no strong French producer of power tools. The market was not nearly as developed as in Germany or the Netherlands and, therefore, customers bought more on price, less on quality and tradition, and the distribution channels in France were not well defined. 'Then too,' Branko added, 'we believe the Latin way of life in France is closer to our way of life than the Germans, who are more formal and direct.'

Suhadolnik also stressed the need for Iskra to target the Italian market. 'Italy has a small power tool producer, but most of its production is exported; almost 60%. In value, almost 70% of the Italian market is imported. Bosch is number one, and Black and Decker number two with its own production through Star, a local company. Moreover, all the Japanese and other companies are minor, the market is close to Yugoslavia and, therefore, transport costs are low. Finally, Yugoslavia and Italy have a clearing agreement that allows unlimited import and export.' One of Suhadolnik's colleagues added that the clearing agreement was one reason why Iskra entered the Italian market in the first place; Italy was the cheapest source of raw materials for cables, switches, plastic, and blades – almost half of Iskra Power Tools' raw materials.

In developing a strategy for the Italian market, Suhadolnik proposed to concentrate on that half of the professional segment which catered to specialty repair shops. 'In Italy,' one manager commented, 'where the first thing for an Italian man is his car, there are an abundance of repair shops to service those cars.' The manager then referred to a market research survey stating that Italy had about 100 000 known repair shops of all kinds; the unknown number was anyone's guess. The study also mentioned a trend in these shops toward building maintenance. 'That's why,' the manager concluded, 'we believe Iskra can reach a 3% market share in Italy within two years, up from our present 1.3–1.5% share of market.'

Western markets as volume OEM

One of Iskra's competitive advantages in foreign markets was low price. In Germany Metabo sold one of its drills for DM299, AEG sold a comparable drill for DM199, and Iskra, under the Perles name, sold its drill for DM139. A number of Iskra managers believed that a low price should be vigorously pursued. In their opinion, bolstered by favourable comments from foreign power tool manufacturers, Iskra's products possessed good value for money. Therefore, one executive added, he saw no reason why Iskra could not continue to use its low labour cost advantage and underprice the competition.

Western markets as Niche OEM

Suhadolnik emphasized that Iskra was simply too small and had too few resources to offer a full range of products the way Bosch did and so Iskra should concentrate on angle grinders and drills, beginning with a new focus on R&D and production. Iskra should focus on those products that represent its distinctive competence, beginning with design, followed by component sourcing and new manufacturing technology. Taucher added, 'Our output is 600 000 pieces per year. All our large European competitors are in the order of 1.5 to 2 million pieces per year. That is probably the threshold; we are much too small to compete on their terms and we don't have a name like Bosch or AEG. To be a niche manufacturer, you still need the name. We are not a Formula 1 car, but a Yugo on which we have put a Maserati label.'

Eastern Europe

In Eastern Europe, Iskra management knew about power tool manufacturers in the DDR and Bulgaria as well as Poland, Czechoslovakia, and the Soviet Union where Iskra had had some experience. Suhabolnik explained that all these markets were virtually untapped and thus presented a tremendous opportunity for Iskra. Nonetheless, with the exception of the DDR, which was now part of Germany and where the one power tool manufacturer had been purchased by Bosch, none of the remaining countries could pay hard currency for Iskra's products. Therefore, Iskra was required to sell its products via counterpurchase agreements as it had done with Naradi in Czechoslovakia. Despite these countries' hard currency shortages, an executive pointed out that some of Iskra's competitors had not been discouraged from taking a further look at these markets. In particular, both Bosch and Black & Decker had planned to start manufacturing in the Soviet Union and were actively looking for personnel to run these facilities and market their products.

SUGGESTED QUESTIONS

1. Describe the power tool industry in Europe and the dynamics that are shaping it.
2. Identify Iskra's position in this market as well as in Eastern Europe and Yugoslavia.
3. Think about specific recommendations which would help Iskra's management clarify its marketing strategy.
4. Assess Iskra's manufacturing capabilities; what are its relative advantages or disadvantages?
5. Given Iskra's competitive position, what are the manufacturing options and what are the tactical implications of moving in different competitive directions?
6. What would you propose in terms of a manufacturing strategy for Iskra, and how should it be implemented?

16

J & M Airframes Ltd

Case written by Cliff Bowman

HISTORY

J & M Airframes Ltd is the result of a merger in 1958 between two aircraft manufacturers, Javelin and Morton–Harman, both based in Yorkshire. Prior to the merger Javelin tended to concentrate on military transport aircraft, whereas Morton–Harman were essentially light aircraft specialists who had particular success with crop-spraying planes.

The merger was seen at the time as a defensive measure. These two were almost the last remaining independent aircraft manufacturers in the UK. Due to the increasing complexity of aircraft design and the rapidly escalating costs of developing new aircraft, fewer and fewer firms had the resources to 'go it alone'. The industry had seen specialization in the 1920s and 1930s, with the emergence of airframe manufacturers and aero-engine firms. And in the 1950s a spate of merger activity had reduced the number of firms in the industry dramatically.

The merger was a 'gentlemanly' affair; a process that was considerably assisted by the retirement of the founder of Javelin. Following the merger there was some rationalization of production facilities. This process has continued over the years and now all manufacturing is concentrated on one site on the outskirts of York.

The most urgent task facing the combined companies in the late 1950s was to design and develop a new aircraft to replace their ageing range of models. J & M responded by successfully launching a low-level heavy bomber (the 'Tempest') which proved to be the mainstay of the company throughout the 1960s and 1970s. The Tempest took the industry by surprise, out-performing competing models from more established suppliers of military aircraft, and securing as a result a large long-term contract with the RAF.

This major contract tended to eclipse J & M's previous areas of specialism, so that by the end of the 1970s they could be regarded as a 'one product' firm. However, although there are disadvantages in being dependent on a single product, there have been major compensations. The original contract for 80 aircraft has expanded to the point where there are now over 400 Tempests in service with air forces around the world. Specialization has enabled them to keep production costs down through the development of better methods, and through design improvements. Although production of new aircraft has been winding down since 1975, there is still a large volume of work to be done refitting older models with, for example, more modern avionics and weapon systems.

J & M IN 1980

There are 4500 people working on the York site; 2800 are in production, the remainder being split between technical, commercial, and support activities. Since the decline in demand for new Tempests, the company has tried to utilize its capacity in other ways (Tempest-related work now only accounts for about 30% of the firm's activity). Since 1975 the firm has begun to take on subcontracted work from other major aerospace manufacturers based in the UK, Europe and the US.

This work is extremely variable in the size of the unit to be manufactured (from a complete wing to a minor sub-assembly), and the number of units in any one order (from one-offs, to large batches).

NEW CHALLENGES FACING J & M

This shift, from a one-product firm selling to only a handful of customers, to a multiple-product operation dealing with many diverse customers, has created many strains on the management, the workforce, and the organizational structure, as indicated in the words of a number of the firm's managers:

> From our point of view in production planning, the problems have escalated with every new job we take on. When we were churning out Tempests we could see bottlenecks, shortages, and delays quite easily. Now, we have eight major programmes on the factory floor requiring upwards of 30 000 separate components. To be frank, we often have little idea what is actually going on on the shop floor. Part of the problem is that with Tempest we never really had to develop sophisticated production planning and control systems. I wouldn't say it was anarchy out there, but it seemed to work OK. Consequently, even when we have tried to put in systems, there isn't the discipline on the shop floor to maintain them; often they can't see the point of logging 'waiting time', for instance, but this is vital information for us.
>
> Tony Fuller, Production Planning Manager

It's difficult to motivate the shop floor now. In the old days they saw a Tempest fly out of here nearly every week. I know that gave everyone a tremendous thrill; knowing that they had contributed to that aircraft. Now all the guy sees is a truck loaded with sub-assemblies leaving the site.

Brian Simons, Foreman, Conventional Machining

We suspect that efficiency has declined dramatically over the last two years. You can put this down to the running down of the Tempest programme, but we also made some decisions which, although they seemed right at the time, they have since exacerbated our problems. To try to cut costs we offered an attractive early retirement deal to 150 of our supervisors and foremen. Unfortunately, the supervisors we wanted to leave stayed, and our best people took the money; I know that a lot of them had already lined up good jobs in other firms. I think we lost an awful lot of experience as a result. The other decision was the scrapping of the Payment by Results system. This had to go; it was so corrupt it was a joke. Rate fixers were intimidated, absurd times were not amended, and in many respects the system was running the factory, rather than the management.

Sarah George, Personnel Manager

For most of my department the shift of work away from the Tempest has meant a more varied job. We need to be much more flexible now, because we don't know what the next job will involve. Some of the younger graduates like the challenge of new jobs, but I know that a lot of the older hands preferred the way it use to be. In the old days you could be working on a problem for months, especially when we were trying to lower the production costs of Tempest in the late sixties and early seventies. In those days we used to work very closely with the production people, working as a team to solve the problems. But now I would say most of the department don't like going down to the shop floor. The atmosphere has changed; there's a lot of cynicism down there.

Rowly France, Head of Production Engineering

ORGANIZATION STRUCTURE

The firm is organized functionally (see Figure 1). This structure has remained essentially the same since the merger. Although over time departments have grown and new ones have been set up, the basic functional arrangement has been maintained. Management generally accept that this organization served them well over the life of the Tempest. When everyone was working on the same programme there was not much need for communication across the organization. Over the

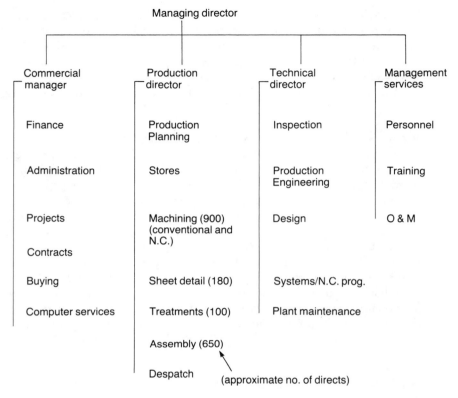

Fig. 1   J & M Airframes Ltd, 1980.

years each function got on with its own job, and the long-term nature of the project provided the stability needed to refine the procedures and systems in the factory.

But the sheer size of the firm has caused some problems. Communication from the top downwards is reasonably effective (although the shop floor do not think they get anywhere near enough information), but upward communication is almost nonexistent. The few individuals that have moved functions (e.g. from the technical department to production) reflect on the differences between departments. These differences cause particular problems in the areas of discipline, standards of behaviour, and management style.

Longer serving production foremen complain that their powers have been eroded over the years:

> I used to be able to hire and fire, set quality standards, load the jobs into the shop, discipline a lad that had got out of line. Now my hands are tied. If I so much as raise my voice to an apprentice I have to give him a written apology copied to half the factory.

Although this is a somewhat jaundiced view, there has been a large increase in the number of staff positions over the years. Now there are separate departments dealing with work study, production control, quality assurance, value engineering, training, costing, production scheduling, procurement, etc.

Along with the growth of the firm there has been an increase in the number of management levels. There are chargehands, supervisors, senior supervisors, foremen, superintendents, production managers, and manufacturing managers, who report to the production director.

CURRENT WORKLOAD

Apart from the refits on existing Tempests, there are the following major programmes on the site:

Programme	Workload (%)
Firefly tailplane	15
Panther flaptracks	12
Scanscope (for aerial photography)	10
Otter fuselage	9
Galaxy winglets	8
ARV cockpit mods	6
A350 ribs	6
Miscellaneous	4

The Tempest refits account for the remainder (30%) but this programme is forecast to represent less than 10% of the workload within two years.

THE EXECUTIVE COMMITTEE

J & M's executive committee is the most powerful senior management group. It is made up of the managing director, the production director, the commercial manager, the technical director, and the head of management services. At a recent meeting the commercial manager had some disturbing news to impart:

'I heard a whisper at the Paris show that Lockheed were getting much tougher with their suppliers. Apparently, they pulled out of a long-term deal with Hughes following an unannounced QA audit. I dread to think how we would shape up to a really thorough examination of our quality systems. As I see it, we might not only lose the Galaxy work; bad news travels fast. Our other customers might start wondering whether they should keep dealing with us.'

The technical director responded:

'Come on, Frank, we've heard all this before. This is just another scare story put around to keep us on our toes. Our quality is OK. I know we've had some problems with the ARV cockpit mods, but that was down to a lack of communication between the design office and the machine shop. Anyway, we are still approved by the MoD, so what's the problem?'

At this point the production director intervened:

'I can't believe I'm hearing this! How can you say we don't have a problem with quality when our scrap and rework costs are going through the roof! I'm convinced that most of your inspectors enjoy rejecting jobs. I sometimes think they are secretly paid by our competitors.'

The technical director reacts forcefully:

'It's a good job somebody takes quality seriously here. If it was left to your supervisors we'd be letting all sorts of crap leave the factory.'

Then the managing director took control:

'Look, there's little point in having a slanging match. We know we've got problems, so let's look for some solutions rather than blaming each other. We have got a problem with quality. We've also got problems with delivery, and costs. It seems that nobody can tell me precisely where we are on any of our contracts. Far too often we only know we have a problem when it's too late to do anything about it. To be honest, sometimes I feel this place is running out of control.'

Frank agrees, adding:

'Yesterday I had a most embarrassing phone call from Panavia. They wanted to know why they had not received the last batch of sub-assemblies yet. Well, I said I'd get right back to them with an explanation. I spent the next two hours trying to track down somebody who could give me a straight answer. It seems to me that nobody is taking responsibility for the customer anymore. Everyone passes the buck. Assembly blamed treatments, treatments criticized the NC machining. NC machining said the delays were caused by poor NC programming. And when I eventually spoke to Alan Gough in NC programming he said that design kept changing the drawings.

'If we're looking for solutions, I think we need to organize the factory differently. There needs to be a focus on the customer's requirements. I can't see, in principle, why we shouldn't split up the site into lots of mini-factories, each one concentrating on one project.'

The production director responds:

'Good grief, Frank, have you any idea what's involved in this kind of change? I admit you've got a good point, but it would mean a lot of changes for everybody, and some activities, like treatments, couldn't be split up between different projects.'

Then the technical director intervened:

'Well, what you do in production is your business, but I would be very unhappy about splitting up my designers, production engineers and, particularly, the inspectors. To be honest, I think this would be a big mistake, and I'm sure quality would suffer if we moved inspection staff to be under the control of production. Anyway this sounds like a matrix organization, and I've never seen one that worked!'

Then the managing director commented:

'OK, well we haven't time at this meeting to go into something as big as this. I suggest we get somebody to look into what options are available to us. Maybe he could take a look at what other firms have done; or should we bring in consultants? Anyway, Frank, could you get something moving on this?'

SUGGESTED QUESTIONS

1. What was the situation of J & M Airframes in 1965–70? What was the strategy? Did the organization structure 'fit' the strategy?
2. What has changed in the period 1970–80?
3. What problems do J & M face in 1980?
4. Recommend an appropriate organization structure which addresses the problems you have identified.

17

Nouvelles frontières

Case written by Pierre Dussauge with C Labarde and B Quelin

Created in the mid-1960s as a student association that organized low-price holidays, mainly in Third World Countries, Nouvelles Frontières has since grown very rapidly. By 1990 Nouvelles Frontières was the second largest tour operator in France, behind Club Méditerranée, with about 1 200 000 customers, and sales totalling 4 billion francs★ (see the ranking of France's largest tour operating companies in Exhibit 1).

THE DEVELOPMENT OF AIR TRAVEL

The organization of air transport

The post-war years saw the first efforts to rationalize the use of air space. Right after the Second World War it became necessary to define the conditions under which an aircraft could fly over a given territory, make technical stopovers, pick up or drop off passengers, etc. More generally, all the rules regulating air traffic between two or more countries had to be established. After general concerting on a worldwide level, international air transport was organized on the basis of:

A legal framework The Chicago accords (1944) laid down the foundation for bilateral agreements according to the terms of which airlines, supervised by government aviation administrations, share inter-city traffic, decide flight frequencies, and ratify fares and all other conditions for ensuring the profitability of routes.

★ US$ averaged about 5.5 French francs in 1990.

Exhibit 1 The largest tour operators in France.

Rank	Company	Sales		Profit/Losses	
		1989 (FF millions)	1988 (FF millions)	1989 (FF millions)	1988 (FF millions)
1	Club Méditerranée	7597	6386	409	306
2	Nouvelles Frontières	3608	3280	23.9	0
3	Sotair	2030	2200	8.3	12.1
4	Voyages Fram	2000	1600	47	39
5	Chorus	1140		−22	
6	Voyage Conseil	807	902	−16.6	−90.8
7	Kuoni France	663	571	3.7	6
8	Voyageurs du Monde	599	542	4.8	6
9	Mondial Tours	520	357	−2.4	1
10	Frantour Voyages	490	454	n/d	n/d

An international association IATA (International Air Transport Association, based in Geneva) comprises most of the world's airlines, with the exception of Aeroflot, a number of US domestic airlines, and some airlines of Third World countries. Its influence has been decreasing steadily since the late 1960s, owing to a growing number of non-member airlines, and to the fact that its regulations are being stretched more and more frequently, even by member airlines. Nevertheless, IATA continues to establish the 'official' guidelines with respect to international air fares.

A classification of flights Air traffic can be divided into two major categories of flight:

- scheduled flights (which are operated on a regular basis according to predetermined timetables);
- non-regular flights, chartered on the demand of a customer who assumes the commercial risk associated with operating such charter flights.

It should be noted in passing that air travel growth forecasts conducted in the post-war years did not envisage the considerable development of charter flights that was to take place. Legislation concentrates on scheduled flights and, even today, is not explicit with respect to charter flights.

A well-defined legal framework founded on inter-government agreements thus allowed, at least at the beginning, for the growth of the air travel industry. On this basis, air fares are decided through bilateral agreements between countries★ for international traffic, and according to the specific legislation of each country for domestic traffic. In France, all air fares proposed by airlines must be ratified by the Direction Générale de l'Aviation Civile (DGAC), the civil aviation department of the transport ministry.

A number of structural as well as more circumstantial factors have strongly influenced the development of air transport since the early 1960s:

- After having obtained independence, most Third World countries created their own national airline in order to support their economic development and for reasons of prestige. These airlines could hardly make profits by operating under normal circumstances. However, protected by their respective governments, which were usually the major shareholders, they tended to sell off a number of seats at very attractive – though 'unauthorized' – prices to obtain a satisfactory passenger load, whether or not they were members of IATA.
- At the end of the Vietnam war, a large number of planes, operated for military purposes during the war, were allowed to sell their services to civilian charterers in peace time. These operators (Trans America, Arrow Air, Capitole among others) were responsible for the sharp increase in transport capacity after the Vietnam war, selling their services at very low prices.
- The international agreements, having originally largely underestimated the development of charter flights, do not offer any satisfactory protection to the governments and regular airlines concerned, and instead present a legal vacuum. In this context, chartered flights increasingly tend to compete with airline operated flights on popular tourist destinations.
- The regular airlines, finding it almost impossible to legally oppose those who do not follow the rules, and bound by bilateral agreements and IATA regulations, are often compelled to sell off their unsold seats in a quasi clandestine manner at discounted prices.
- Technological development has led to larger aircraft which are more reliable and less expensive to operate (in passenger per mile cost), provided that their passenger load is sufficient.

All these factors combined have created a situation of permanent overcapacity in the air transport market. According to some specialists, however, the general overcapacity which characterized air travel in the 1970s and 1980s should gradually evolve towards a better adaptation of the airlines' supply to market demand. The airlines are making efforts to better adjust their supply, to ensure greater passenger loads and thus improve their profitability. This general tendency, however, should not obscure differences between specific situations.

★ This can sometimes lead to surprising results: the most distant destinations are not necessarily the most expensives ones. It may cost less to fly to the final destination rather than to one of the stopovers on the route (e.g. Paris – Kuwait – Bombay – Bangkok).

In fact, competition on the tourism and air travel markets can be very diverse and fluctuating. It depends notably on the destination and the time of the year. For example, on the Europe–Bangkok route, which was long one of the cheapest because of supply exceeding demand and because of keen competition, fares have risen steadily in recent years as a result of increasing demand. Conversely, in the summer of 1986, air fares between Europe and the US fell steeply owing to the decrease in the number of American visitors to Europe (because of terrorism and a falling dollar).

Finally, air transport, which was deregulated in the US in the late 1970s, is gradually being deregulated in Europe since the late 1980s.

The evolution of tourism in Europe and in France

It was not until the 1950s that European tourists began to be attracted by holidays in the sun. This led to a desire to travel to the south, to countries on the coast of the Mediterranean sea (e.g. Spain, Italy, Greece, Turkey, Tunisia, Morocco, etc.) or even farther afield.

Long considered a luxury, air travel thus became a necessity. However, the structure of air transport as described above was ill suited for this mass movement. Concerned solely with a clientele of well-to-do people or businessmen, the airlines happily shared a market in which the price of the ticket was of little importance even though the passenger load rarely exceeded 50% of aircraft capacity. The evolution of tourism, by creating a new demand emanating from price conscious travellers, incited airlines to lower their fares and offer discounted prices on certain routes. Indeed, since 1960, prices have shown a marked downward trend while the volume of air traffic has been increasing steadily (between 1975 and 1985, air traffic grew by an average of 6% per year).

The growth of tourism and associated air travel has greatly benefited in Europe from the general increase in standards of living as well as from the increased length of legal holidays (a minimum of four to five weeks in most countries). It can be noted, in this context, that the number of people who travel by air during their holidays is much lower in France than in other countries of northern Europe (half the number of West Germany or the UK though total population is about the same size); this is due to the fact that France has a coast on the Mediterranean which is easy to drive to or travel to by train from most regions of the country.

THE DIFFERENT PARTIES INVOLVED IN AIR TRAVEL

Air travel involves various parties that can be classified in four major categories: air carriers; providers of holiday services; tour operators; and travel agencies.

Air carriers Air carriers are either private or, in many countries (including France), state-owned or semi-state-owned. We can distinguish between 'regular' airlines which fly according to predetermined time-tables and 'charter' airlines flying on demand. In recent years, many airlines have set up specialized charter subsidiaries. There is not always a clear dividing line between scheduled flights and charter flights, since airlines often sell block bookings on scheduled flights to tour operators. The latter, instead of chartering a complete plane, buy a given number of seats on a scheduled flight and are responsible for marketing them, thus taking the commercial risk on the seats that they book.

Providers of holiday services   Their activities, which are extremely diverse, are not necessarily associated with air travel. They include resorts, hotels, coach and car hire firms, excursion guides, and all organizations offering tourist facilities at the place of destination.

Tour operators   Tour operators offer a finished product that can comprise various components: the flight and different services (accomodation, local transport, excursions, entertainment, etc.) which make up a packaged holiday.

Travel agencies   Travel agencies, which are in contact with the final customer, are responsible for marketing the finished products offered by different tour operators. In France, there are some 2200 travel agencies, either independent or part of chains (the largest of which controls up to 300 outlets) and which are almost all members of the Syndicat National des Agents de Voyage (National Association of Travel Agents). Travel agents are paid on the basis of a commission granted by airlines, providers of services or tour operators. The commission, which varies according to the nature of the finished product distributed (from a rate of about 6% for plain ticketing, to 10–12%, sometimes 15% or even 18% for marketing more elaborate tours and holidays,★ is the subject of long negotiations between travel agents and tour operators. In the event of a conflict, the concerted action of the travel agents can easily block the access of a tour operator or of a specific product to the market. Even Club Méditerranée had a serious conflict with the travel agents' association on commission issues and was boycotted for several months.

NOUVELLES FRONTIERES IN 1990

The growth of Nouvelles Frontières was extremely rapid (1000 customers in 1967; 4000 in 1968; 500 000 in 1985; 1 000 000 in 1989; and 1 200 000 in 1990).

This phenomenal growth was always marked by considerable risk taking. In order to develop their company as fast as possible, the managers of Nouvelles Frontières chartered large transport capacities, increasing

---

★ For tours and holidays offered by tour operators, the travel agents' commission is 12% on average.

Exhibit 2   The financial structure of the Nouvelles Frontières Group in 1990.

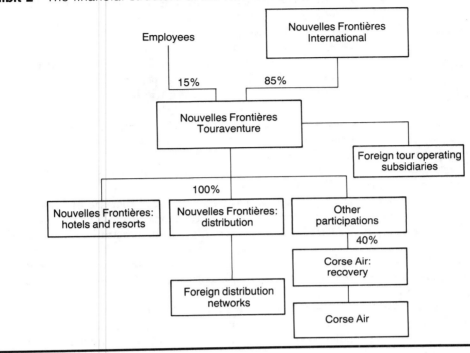

spectacularly from one year to the next, and offering a wide range of destinations. An insufficient number of bookings one year could have led to serious problems for the company.

From the very beginning, Nouvelles Frontières has simultaneously carried out the two activities of **tour operator** and **travel agent**. Nouvelles Frontières has its own network of agencies (throughout France and a few agencies abroad) selling exclusively Nouvelles Frontières products which, in turn, cannot be found in any other sales outlet (in contrast, most other tour operator products can be bought from any travel agency). This exclusive distribution organization is supported by a computerized reservation system to which each Nouvelles Frontières agency is connected.

Nouvelles Frontières sets its prices by adding to the purchase price of flights, accommodation, tours, and other services an average coefficient of 11.5%. These normative prices are then compared to the market situation and lowered if other competitors offer more attractive prices, or inversely increased if the competitive context makes it possible to do so. The aim of this price setting system is to make Nouvelles Frontières the lowest-cost competitor in the marketplace.

Nouvelles Frontières' total gross margin, which varies from year to year, according to a number of parameters (exchange rates, number of bookings, etc.) ranges between 9% and 11% of sales★. This gross margin must cover the costs of both the tour operating activity, and the distribution network. The tour operating activity accounts for about 60% of internal operating costs, and the distribution activity for 40%.

The company's net operating margin is – voluntarily – very low (generally less than 1%) and sometimes negative when losses are incurred on particular operations or when the growth of operating costs[†] (hiring of new personnel, opening of new agencies, etc.) is higher than that of sales.

Nouvelles Frontières' management is convinced that the exclusive and specialized distribution system they have created is a significant source of competitive advantage for the company. They point to the fact that average sales per salesperson – or per square foot of outlet – is about three times that of non-specialized agencies.

Nouvelles Frontières' management is also convinced that the firm has a cost advantage over its competitors on the tour operating (i.e. tour and trip producing) part of its business. Internally conducted studies seem to show that the cost of the tour operating activity is 10–15% lower than that of relatively small competitors (100 000 to 120 000 customers per year) and 2–5% lower than that of major competitors (400 000 customers per year and above).

The company's own exclusive distribution network is also an asset in its dealings with airlines. When the latter end up with unsold capacity they can entrust available seats to Nouvelles Frontières which can put them on the market in less than 48 hours through its computerized sales network. In such a context, Nouvelles Frontières benefits from extremely favourable buying conditions for these products which it can promote in the form of special offers. In addition, Nouvelles Frontières' size and the high percentage of total sales that certain airlines make with Nouvelles Frontières (for example, Nouvelles Frontières is Royal Air Maroc's largest customer and is a very large customer of Tunis Air, Bangladesh Biman, Syrian Air, etc.) create very favourable bargaining conditions. Nouvelles Frontières can often negotiate fares 50–80% lower than the normal coach fare and, on average, purchases air transport capacity from regular airlines or charter companies 10–15% cheaper than its main competitors in France.

Finally, having its own exclusive distribution network makes it possible for the company to have a direct contact with the market and customers and is one of the necessary conditions for being constantly aware of changing customer demands and for being able to develop new products to meet needs that have not yet been satisfied.

In 1990 the Nouvelles Frontières network comprised 72 travel agencies in France and about 40 offices abroad. Of the 72 outlets in France, 30

★ Gross margin rate $= \dfrac{\text{sales} - \text{purchases}}{\text{sales}}$.

[†] Which takes place, at least partially, in stages.

were franchised. The franchise-holding agencies, which exclusively sell Nouvelles Frontières products, get a 5% commission on their total sales and turn in the cash they generate through their operation to Nouvelles Frontières on a daily basis.

Unlike certain other tour operators (in the UK and Germany in particular), Nouvelles Frontières was able to grow very rapidly in the tour operating business without owning any airplanes. Until 1989 it carried out its business by:

- negotiating with airlines to obtain preferential fares on scheduled flights;
- buying charter blocks on scheduled flights, or chartering entire planes.

Contrary to the general belief, more than 50% of Nouvelles Frontières' air travel was undertaken through scheduled flights until 1989, when the firm acquired a controlling stake in the equity of Corse Air, a small charter airline.

700 000 copies of Nouvelles Frontières' catalogue are distributed twice a year (total cost: 5 million French francs in 1990). Thanks to the catalogue, most customers have already selected the tour, trip or holiday they want by the time they step into a Nouvelles Frontières agency to make a reservation and make a down payment. The Nouvelles Frontières catalogue offers 10 different types of tours and holidays:

1. *Individual discovery*: the customer only buys an air ticket;
2. *Package discovery*: the customer buys an air ticket and some services at the place of destination (e.g. accommodation for a few days);
3. *Travel as you choose*: this formula includes the air ticket and all the necessary services at destination. With this product, customers travel on their own and are not assisted by a Nouvelles Frontières guide;
4. *Initiation to travel*: this includes the air ticket and a tour in a small group without advance reservation of services, but under the supervision of a Nouvelles Frontières guide;
5. *Semi-conducted tour*: it comprises the air ticket and the same type of tour as in 4, but with some advance arrangements;
6. *Adventure holiday*: this formula includes the air ticket and a tour in a small group for those prepared to renounce a certain degree of material comfort (canoes, Land Rovers, frugal food, spartan accommodation, etc.);
7. *Minibus tour*: the same type of formula as in 4, but with the group travelling by minibus;
8. *Packaged holiday*: as the name implies, includes all services and is totally organized;
9. *Relaxation holiday*: comprises the air ticket and accommodation in one place including all or some meals;
10. *Language and sports holidays, skiing holidays*.

The company does not limit its efforts to the transport and trips themselves, but takes a great interest in preparing holidays. It offers its customers technical information concerning each country, organizes preparatory meetings and forums, and has an information service for those interested. Nouvelles Frontières also publishes (in collaboration with another publisher) travel guides for certain countries.

In the early years of Nouvelles Frontières, the trips and holidays had a clearly marked orientation. The company offered study tours with a Third World bent (work in villages in India, visit to self-managed estates in Algeria, etc.); a tourism 'on the cheap' where comfort was of secondary importance. Even today, the different types of holiday as well as the means offered to the customer to prepare for the trips indicate the firm's desire to promote as far as possible 'intelligent holidays', and to make every effort so that those who choose to travel with Nouvelles Frontières become 'more than mere customers'. The managers of Nouvelles Frontières define the objective of the company as 'being the cheapest tour operator in all categories: from budget travel to luxury tours and trips'.

In 1990 Nouvelles Frontières' sales (measured by the number of customers) were more or less evenly divided between the sale of air tickets alone and the sale of a package tours and holidays (air tickets and accommodation and other services). In comparison, in the early 1970s, air tickets contributed 80–90% of sales, with package holidays accounting for only 10–20%. Since air transport represents more than 40% of the cost of a package tour or holiday, a significant proportion of total sales is derived from air transport alone.

As Jacques Maillot often declares, 'transport is a very essential component of our business'. Availability of air transport capacity conditions the entire business of Nouvelles Frontières, even though a clearly stated objective is to sell, together with air tickets, the greatest possible amount of services because the margin derived from services is higher than that from air tickets.

Suppliers are usually paid (as is the habit in France for inter-firm contracts and transactions) 45–60 days after they deliver their services. Customers pay 30% of the price of the trip as a down payment at the time of reservation, the balance being paid a month before the departure date at the latest. This system allows Nouvelles Frontières to dispose of surplus cash amounting to sales made over a 70-day period (i.e. 20% of annual sales) – a classic distribution situation in France. This excess cash is invested in bonds and earns interest on the basis of a 8–10% annual rate.

THE AIR TRAVEL MARKET IN FRANCE AND THE NOUVELLES FRONTIERES CUSTOMER BASE

A 1988 study highlighted the following points concerning the current major trends in tourism, the image of Nouvelles Frontières as perceived by the travelling public, and the nature and evolution of the firm's customer base.

Growth of Nouvelles Frontières' activity

		1973	1980	1985	1990
Number of customers	France	40 000	130 000	410 000	950 000
	Abroad	–	10 000	90 000	250 000
Sales		fr. 50m	fr. 350m	fr. 1.6bn	fr. 4bn
Breakdown of sales	Air tickets	90–100%	80%	60%	50%
	Packaged tours and holidays	0–10%	20%	40%	50%
Breakdown of destinations	Long-haul flights	80%	70%	50%	45%
	Medium-haul flights	20%	30%	50%	55%

Current trends

- The attitude towards the Third World has changed considerably in the last few years (the feeling of guilt at the sight of poverty, prevalent in the 1960s and 1970s, has been replaced by a self-justifying attitude: 'We are lucky enough to live better than they do').
- Society continues to be strongly marked by **individualism**.
- Even when they are interested in discovery and adventure, tour operator customers are increasingly attracted by **leisure** holidays, thus creating more market opportunities for holiday formulas.

In this context, Nouvelles Frontières took steps to modify its traditional image and turn to a different, more mature and more socially integrated type of customer (white collar workers, professionals, etc.). A new logo was adopted; advertising campaigns, more oriented towards this new type of clientele and highlighting such products as hotel accommodation, family holidays, resorts, etc., were launched.

The public's image of Nouvelles Frontières

- Nouvelles Frontières is no longer perceived as a student association or a small vulnerable organization, but rather as a large and powerful company.
- Nouvelles Frontières' corporate goal (making travel accessible to all by striving for low prices) is perceived as strong and extremely positive.
- Nouvelles Frontières, however, continues to be associated with the

notion of 'youth' (and thus with a lack of rigour, reliability, and professionalism).

The Nouvelles Frontières customer base

The 1990 customers of Nouvelles Frontières are older than they were in previous years.

Less than 25 years	25–45 years	35–44 years	45–64 years	More than 65 years
16%	45%	30%	6%	3%

(in 1973, 80% of Nouvelles Frontières' customers were between 18 and 35)

They are also:

- socially integrated (54% are single and 31% are executives or professionals);
- urban, with a level of education far above average (51% live in the Paris region; 57% have a university education).

The evolution of sales parallels that of the market and the clientele. In the early 1970s, most of the sales were made with long-haul flights. However, since then, the proportion of medium-haul flights has risen steeply; medium-haul flights are often associated with holiday formulas in the countries of the Mediterranean basin.

In all cases, the most attractive feature of Nouvelles Frontières is its prices, even though customers also attach great importance to the human and cultural aspects in their choices of holiday formulas.

THE COMPETITIVE ENVIRONMENT

Air travel in general and the use of charter flights in particular developed earlier in other European countries. In West Germany and Britain, for example, there are very large tour operators that control their own airlines and infrastructures for tourist accommodation (hotels, resorts, etc.). The largest German and British tour operators have a domestic market which is far bigger than the corresponding French market, and count several million customers each year.

In France, apart from the Club Méditerranée (whose main activity is the management of resorts all around the world, air transport being only a side activity) and Nouvelles Frontières, there are only a few tour operating companies of significant size:

- Fram, which sold tours and holidays to 400 000 customers in 1990;
- Sotair, which is the tour operating subsidiary of Air France and had 300 000 customers in 1990. Sotair sells its products under the Jet Tour, Jet Am, Jumbo, and Jet Air brands;

- the Chorus Group (Air Tour Euro 7, Cruise Air, Touropa, etc.), which had 250 000 customers in 1990. One of the Chorus Group's main shareholders is TUI, the number 1 tour operator in Germany.

Nouvelles Frontières can be considered as a 'non-specialized tour operator'. As a result, it has specific competitors for each product line (Kuoni for up-market holidays, Terre d'Aventures for trekking holidays, etc.). Other smaller tour operators however, resemble Nouvelles Frontières as it was in its early years, while some small agencies offer very specialized products (Explorator, Terre d'Aventures, etc.).

DEVELOPMENT PERSPECTIVES

Until 1989 the development of Nouvelles Frontières took place essentially in the context of its main tour operating business, complemented by its direct distribution activity. This development was made possible by the growth of the market and the consolidation of Nouvelles Frontières' position in the industry to the detriment of its competitors. During the 1980s, sales increased by an average of 20–25% per year in volume, and 15–20% per year in value.

In the late 1980s, the growth of the industry seemed to be slowing down in France. In this context, Nouvelles Frontières could continue to expand by trying to take market share away from its competitors, and could also look for new development alternatives.

The company can adopt several possible measures in order to strengthen its position on the French tourism market and attract new customers to air travel:

- It can continue to open new travel agencies and reinforce its presence throughout France. The opening of a new agency requires an investment of fr. 100 000 to fr. 300 000 per year, over two to three years. Franchising limits the investment to fr. 80 000 per outlet. The creation of 50 new agencies were planned for the 1990–92 period.
- It can develop new information and marketing channels (data communications services, etc.). In 1990, 16 500 customers (plus 15% compared to 1989) bought a trip or tour from Nouvelles Frontières through the 'Minitel' (the French public electronic mail system).
- As part of its basic activities, it can offer new services to its customers (multi-year subscriptions, 'free mileage' or 'free vacation' systems, credit facilities and staggered payments, etc.).

Several new development orientations, more or less linked to the basic activity of Nouvelles Frontières, have been the subject of in-depth analysis by the top management. Some options have already been chosen and are being implemented, while others are still being studied.

Nouvelles Frontières has begun to develop a new 'group' service offering trips and custom-built services for corporate groups, associations, etc. This sector is growing rapidly and may, in the coming years, represent a significant share of sales. Nouvelles Frontières has also developed a 'business' department, using its competence in the field of air transport. Thus, businessmen can benefit from preferential fares for business-class tickets, which the company is in a position to obtain from airlines. The activities of the 'group' and 'business' departments form the subject of two separate brochures which are published in addition to the general catalogue. The two departments are managed as profit centres.

Nouvelles Frontières also organizes language courses as part of its holiday preparation programmes. The success of the formula has led the company to set up a subsidiary for this activity. The Nouvelles Frontières Language School is no longer limited to Nouvelles Frontières travellers, being open to all who are interested, and offering very attractive prices (far lower than those of the Berlitz language school, for example). Data processing and software services, developed internally as part of the computerization of the group, are today marketed to 'non-competitor' tour operators and travel agents, by means of a computer subsidiary. The possibility of creating an air freight service has been contemplated, but still remains at the project stage.

The internationalization of Nouvelles Frontières began at the end of the 1970s with the setting up of subsidiaries in a number of other countries. The subsidiaries were originally meant to provide services and support to travellers from France, but they soon began to market trips in the country where they were set up. In 1990, 20% of sales (close to fr. 1 billion, i.e. 250 000 customers) came from its foreign subsidiaries.

Setting up a subsidiary abroad requires considerable investments. In order to consolidate its position on a foreign market and grow to a significant size, Nouvelles Frontières must provide financial support for the subsidiary for several years (amounting to investments of several million francs over three to five years). The opening of agencies abroad also requires subsequent investments equivalent to those for setting up an agency in France. International development prospects seem extremely encouraging owing to the growth potential of various foreign markets and synergies with the French market. However, in the last few years, Nouvelles Frontières has encountered difficulties with respect to the management and supervision of its foreign subsidiaries.

As far as air transport is concerned, Nouvelles Frontières – which, prior to this, was totally dependent on outside suppliers – acquired a 40% stake in a charter company called Corse Air in 1989. Nouvelles Frontières replaced Corse Air's management and appointed the new management of the airline. At the beginning of 1990, Corse Air's fleet consisted of two Boeing 747s (long-haul jets with a 350-passenger capacity which, on average, can fly one to two trips a day) and two Boeing 737s (medium-haul jets with a 120-passenger capacity that can make two to three flights a day). Corse Air lost fr. 50 million in 1988 and fr. 105 million in 1989; 1989 sales totalled fr. 180 million. When Nouvelles Frontières took over Corse Air in 1989, a seven-year recovery plan was developed and approved by the other shareholders, banks, and other creditors.

In the area of tourist services, Nouvelles Frontières operates a dozen hotels and resorts that are located in France, Greece, Tunisia, Senegal, the West Indies, and so on. Most of these hotels and resorts are now part of a chain created by Nouvelles Frontières in 1988, called 'Palladien'. The 'Palladien' concept remains relatively vague and the various hotels and resorts form a fairly heterogeneous chain. Accommodation in its own resorts represents between 5% and 10% of all tourist services (excluding air transport) sold by Nouvelles Frontières. New projects in the area of hotels and resorts are being studied by Nouvelles Frontières' management.

The opening of a new resort requires an investment of about fr. 5–10 million to be financed directly by Nouvelles Frontières. By managing tourist facilities directly, the company can better monitor the quality of services provided to its customers. In the field of services Nouvelles Frontières is also examining the possibility of creating its own networks for car rental, a coach fleet, and so on.

In 1988 Nouvelles Frontières signed a memorandum of understanding with the Club Méditerranée for the two groups to merge. The merger, which would have resulted in one of the largest tour operating companies in Europe and even the world, was never carried out because of differences of opinion between the top managers of the two firms on a number of strategic issues.

Exhibit 3 Who owns Nouvelles Frontières?

Nouvelles Frontières International SA

Jacques Maillot, Chairman	25%
Christian Pinot	15%
Mikel Landaburu	15%
Patrick Billebault	15%
Patrick Nottin	15%
Noël Picato	10%
'NF Feu Vert pour l'Aventure' (Chairman: J Maillot)	5%

Nouvelles Frontières Touraventure (France)

Nouvelles Frontières International SA	85%
NF employees	15%

SUGGESTED QUESTIONS

1. Analyse the structure of the tour operating industry in France.
2. What are the sources of Nouvelles Frontières' competitive advantage?
3. Evaluate the various strategy alternatives now being examined by top management.

18

Rockware plc (A)

Case written by John Hendry

In September 1983 Sir Peter Parker returned from a seven-year spell running the state-owned British Rail to resume his former role as Chairman of Rockware, a manufacturer of glass bottles and jars. With him he brought a newcomer to the glass container industry, Frank Davies, who had been head of the aluminium extrusion division at Alcan, and had now been appointed Managing Director of Rockware.

When Sir Peter had left Rockware, as plain Peter Parker, in 1976, things had looked pretty good. Demand for glass containers was booming. Rockware's sales were growing by around 15% a year in real terms, while operating profit had doubled in the past two years. By September 1983, however, the picture was very different. Having peaked in 1979, demand for glass containers had declined each year since then. Despite high levels of inflation, prices had remained static in money terms and had even started to fall slightly. Rockware, in common with other manufacturers, had been forced to close furnaces and make workers redundant, and by 1983 the workforce had dropped to just 4500 from a 1979 peak of 7600. The redundancy and rationalization costs of £19 million had virtually wiped out the modest operating profits of the years 1980–82, and for the first six months of 1983 the firm had declared a loss of about £8.5 million. The full year figures would show an operating loss of over £6 million with further interest costs and exceptional losses of over £6.5 million. A successful placing of £10 million worth of convertible preference shares by the firm's merchant bankers in the summer of 1983 had given some breathing space. But although these shares had been placed without difficulty (Pilkingtons, the large British float and safety glass manufacturer who owned 20% of Rockware's ordinary shares, took up a large tranche of the preference shares, and this helped City confidence), the ordinary share price had collapsed to around 20–30p from 80p in the spring of 1982: before the year ended it would drop further to just 16p. Looking to the future, the prospects for glass containers were not encouraging. Capacity cuts across the industry were beginning to restore the balance between supply and demand with the prospect of a stabilization of real prices. But there seemed little prospect of any growth in the market, and every prospect of a continuing shrinkage as glass containers lost market share to plastics, and in particular to polyethylene terephthalate (PET). Launched commercially in 1979, PET was still not an adequate substitute for glass in many applications, but technological development, funded by the large multinational petrochemical companies, was proceeding rapidly. PET bottles were already beginning to eat away at the glass bottle market, and this process looked likely to continue and accelerate. Rockware itself had had an interest in plastics containers for many years, and in 1980, after a series of acquisitions, these accounted for about 30% of its turnover. But a combination of management problems with overseas plants, continuous price squeezing in an intensely competitive market, and the need to raise extra cash to support the glass manufacturing rationalization had since led to a series of disposals, so that by the end of 1983 plastics accounted for just 12% of turnover.

GLASS CONTAINER TECHNOLOGY AND MATERIALS

Modern glass container manufacture differs little in essence from traditional glass-blowing. The main raw materials are silica sand (about 70%), soda ash (12%), and lime (12%); these are heated with other additives in furnaces to about 720–750 °C to make molten glass. After refining to remove impurities the molten glass is machine blown in blobs into hollow moulds and then cooled under controlled conditions. Each furnace feeds several bottle-making machines, each of which produces 10 or 12 bottles at a time. The furnaces are fuelled by natural gas. In Britain this is supplied by a monopoly supplier, British Gas, and accounts for about 60% of total production costs. Silica sand is supplied by BIS with about 70% of the market and soda ash by ICI with about 80% of the market. Both these companies have strong control over the available sources of supply.

The main feature of the manufacturing technology is its lack of flexibility. A glass container plant cannot be used for the manufacture of any other form of glass product (such as flat glass, or optical glasses). Nor does the technology allow transfer of operations between different types or colours of bottle glass. Thus a brown glass bottle plant is effectively dedicated to brown glass bottle manufacture, and similarly for green, clear or opal glasses. Because of the energy costs of keeping a furnace going, the costs of running a plant at under full capacity (i.e. with one or more of the bottle-making machines idle) are severe, as are the costs of switching from one product to another: to change the moulds is a significant and time-consuming operation, during which the furnace has to be kept going.

THE GLASS CONTAINER INDUSTRY

The British glass container industry has traditionally been very fragmented, but by the mid-1970s it had become concentrated into six major companies of which Rockware, with a market share of about 25%, was the largest. The others were Redfearn (about 14%), Beatson Clark (9%), and three subsidiaries of major bottle users who had integrated backwards: United Glass (owned jointly by Distillers and Owens–Illinois, 25%), Canning Town (Arthur Bell, 9%) and the glass division of the Co-operative (9%). Of these Beatson Clark specialized in brown glass pharmaceutical containers, and Rockware in opal glass. But both Rockware and Redfearn supplied a wide range of bottles and jars in clear, brown, and green glass, and with United Glass they dominated the open market for glass food and drink containers.

Elsewhere in Europe, and in the US, the industry structure tended to be rather different, with each national market being dominated by one or two glass manufacturers, each diversified across a range of different glass process technologies and products. Although diversified, most of these companies were much larger glass container producers than Rockware. Thus the glass container business of Saint Gobain in France, for example, was one-and-a-half times the size of the entire British glass container industry. The bottling business of BSN, a French brewing, mineral water, and soft drinks company which, like Distillers and Guinness, had integrated backwards, was even bigger. Part of this difference of scale was due to a much larger demand for glass bottles in Europe, primarily for the packaging of wine, mineral water, and bottled beers, than existed in Britain.

In the late 1970s there had still been very little overlap between national glass container markets, and given the high transport costs of empty glass containers this situation had been expected to continue. From a base of about 4%, however, imports to Britain had grown to 11% in 1982, and were still rising as customers, uncertain of the future of the precariously placed British industry, placed orders with the diversified European manufacturers as a precaution against the possible bankruptcy and close-down of the British firms. Meanwhile, imports of ready-bottled products were also increasing, at the expense of bulk shipments for local UK bottling, and though difficult to measure this was clearly having a significant impact on the British bottle market.

THE CONTAINER MARKET: GLASS, CARDBOARD, PVC, AND PET

As a container material, glass has many distinctive advantages. Rigid as a material it is flexible as a design medium. It is strong, attractive, chemically inert, and almost totally impervious. It is also recyclable. Against this, it is breakable and, above all, heavy, and in the early 1980s it was losing ground to three substitutes: cardboard, PVC, and PET.

The use of cardboard was restricted largely to the packaging of milk and fruit juices, but nevertheless posed a serious threat to the bottle manufacturing industry, especially in the case of milk. In Britain milk has traditionally been delivered by the dairies in glass bottles, which are then returned and recycled. Although a glass bottle costs about twice as much as a cardboard container to manufacture, the fact that it can be used 20 or more times makes the delivery system extremely cost effective. Glass is much less suitable, however, for packaging milk for sale in supermarkets and other retail outlets. Although the weight of a pint milk bottle has been halved in the last 50 years, it still adds almost half as much again to the overall weight of the milk, and this is a nuisance to both shoppers and stock-handlers. Glass bottles are less easily packed in bulk than square cardboard containers, and the supermarkets do not find it cost effective to accept empty returns, which both destroys the cost advantage of glass and creates an extra nuisance for the customer who has to dispose of the bottle. During Sir Peter's absence from Rockware, the supermarkets' share of milk sales doubled to about 15%, and a move towards the European and American situation, where all milk is sold in retail stores with no deliveries, was a distinct possibility. On the other hand, some of the supermarket chains had no wish to carry large stocks of milk. The dairies had an interest in maintaining the delivery system, as foreign experience showed that its demise was accompanied by a drop in milk consumption, and consumer research indicated that customers believed milk tasted better from bottles and kept fresher in them.

Of wider significance was the increasing use of plastics, in particular PVC and PET, both of which were cheaper, lighter, and less breakable than glass. As yet this use had been limited by the technical properties of these materials, which did not share glass's imperviousness. In the early stages of their development, they could not be used for fizzy drinks, wines, beers, or sauces subject to oxidization because of the migration of gases through the containers. The technology was improving all the time, however, especially in respect of multi-layer PET bottles. By 1983 these had been developed sufficiently to allow for their use as large soft drinks bottles, where the high volume-to-surface ratio minimized the problem of gas containment, and there was every reason to expect that they would in due course provide potential substitutes for the great majority of glass container applications. Work was even progressing on a recyclable PET. When PET products did become available they would certainly be cheaper than glass (because of much lower energy costs – about half those of glass), lighter, and easier to handle: significant advantages to retailers and consumers alike.

THE SITUATION AT ROCKWARE: GLASS

The Rockware group had been built up in the 1960s and early 1970s through the acquisition of three long-established independent glass manufacturers, Garston, Forster, and Jackson, and glass manufacturing had remained a decentralized activity. The four sites (five plants), scattered right across Britain, retained their individual characters and loyalties, and although group marketing was centralized in the wake of the acquisitions they had continued to operate in most respects as independent companies. During the boom years of the mid-1970s this had resulted in a healthy spirit of competition, but with the industry recession the limited degree of centralization had been abandoned and, with closures threatening, competition between the sites had become more pointed and less friendly, with accusations being made of factories stealing each other's customers. As with other long-established craft-based industries, there was still a strong craft tradition, with long periods of training and with firm and industry loyalties built up over lifetimes and generations. This personal, emotional investment made the recession both harder to accept and harder to bear.

Throughout the industry there remained a deep-seated conviction that things must get better and that the current downturn could only be a temporary phenomenon. As the recession bit, workers had to be made redundant and furnaces closed, but this process lagged well behind the fall in demand and overcapacity continued. The situation was not helped by the economics of bottle manufacture, discussed above, which encouraged firms to run their furnaces at full capacity even if the demand was not there to meet it. Price-cutting had inevitably followed, and although Rockware had tried to hold out against this they had lost market share as a result and had ended up having to follow the market. They had, however, led the move to rationalization. By September 1983 Rockware had spent £19 million on rationalization, closing furnaces, making workers redundant, and eventually closing down the original Rockware factory at St Helens. United Glass and Redfearn were also on the point of closing down factories, and the overcapacity problem looked to be coming to an end. But Rockware were still manufacturing on negative margins, the glass container market was still declining, and imports were still rising.

THE SITUATION AT ROCKWARE: PLASTICS AND ENGINEERING

Besides its dominant glass container business, Rockware also manufactured in two other areas. The engineering businesses, Burwell Reed and Kinghorn, and the Birstall Foundry, served primarily to provide moulds and other equipment for use in Rockware's own container manufacture, though they also traded outside the group. Plastic container manufacturing had begun under Sir Peter's earlier tenure as Chairman and had grown to form a major part of the group's overall business before being cut back again during the downturn in the glass business.

The main growth in Rockware's plastics business had come in the late 1970s. In late 1978 they had taken over Alida, a producer of flexible plastic film packaging, for £4.7 million. The following year they had bought the overseas plastic bottle-making concerns of Dart Industries Inc of America, with a book value of £6.4 million, for £2.94 million, and paid £0.75 million for two small plastics companies. This gave them a total of 12 plastics factories in Britain, Spain, Holland, Belgium, and Australia. The move into plastics had appeared to make sound strategic sense, but in a highly competitive industry all the Rockware plastics operations experienced a chronic squeeze on prices and margins. Some of the businesses also experienced technical and managerial problems, and far from boosting group profits, plastics proved a severe drain on resources at just the time the core glass manufacturing business was running into serious problems. In 1981 the overseas Dart operations were all disposed of, and in late 1982 negotiations began with the Alida management on a management buy-out of that company. This was agreed upon in 1983 and the sale finally took place at the end of that year. The agreed price of £2.9 million was in real terms under half what Rockware had paid for the company, but with glass manufacturing losses the money was badly needed.

With the sale of Alida, Rockware was left with three plastics divisions specializing in clean air injection blow moulding and extrusion blow moulding, and supplying PVC bottles primarily for the pharmaceuticals and cosmetic markets. Two of these, at Norwich and Kingston, were expanding, profitable businesses, but the other two, at Golborne and Reading, were encountering serious problems at both the technical and the managerial levels, and their losses more or less cancelled out the others' profits.

BACK FROM THE BRINK

Despite the capacity cuts being made by all the leading British glass container manufacturers in 1983, the industry had not yet come fully to terms with a declining market. Many people still treated the recent problems as a temporary aberration, and thought in terms of 'reserves of capacity to meet an upturn of business', rather than of overcapacity in a declining business. Right across Europe, the overwhelming response was still to cut prices rather than capacity, while at the same time planning on the basis that they would soon rise again.

To Frank Davies, this was ludicrous. Coming into the industry as an outsider, he saw a 27% decline in the UK glass container market in the previous four years and a level of prices at which no one in the industry could make a profit. As PET development continued, the best that could be hoped for was a stabilization of the glass container market, while a continued decline looked more realistic. In any price-cutting war, the continental manufacturers, with their diversified product ranges and much greater corporate resources, would inevitably be the victors. Rockware could only be a heavy loser.

Faced with this view of the situation, Frank Davies and Sir Peter Parker determined on a package of short-term measures to save the company. The £10 million issue of convertible preference shares, arranged by Sir Peter in anticipation of his return to the company, provided them with

Exhibit 1   Rockware 10-year summary.

				(£ thousand)						
	1975	1976	1977	1978	1979	1980	1981	1982	1983	1984
Sales										
Glass	52 630	67 697	80 794	96 684	106 178	116 178	112 971	103 980	101 310	107 410
Plastics	3 165	4 146	7 134	9 825	33 812	48 919	46 221	33 163	26 914	15 240
Engineering	668	711	1 295	1 910	3 261	4 668	2 388	4 610	3 246	1 521
Total	56 463	72 554	89 223	108 419	143 251	169 765	161 580	141 853	131 470	124 721
Operating profit (loss)										
Glass								4 504	(8 344)	5 700
Plastics								935	537	0
Engineering								(384)	(84)	300
Total	5 748	7 155	8 014	7 970	7 893	5 773	5 558	5 215	(6 216)	5 909
Interest and exceptional losses	(442)	(1 230)	(603)	(951)	(2 709)	(5 301)	(4 659)	(4 610)	(6 611)	(2 741)
Profit before taxation	4 306	5 925	7 411	7 019	5 184	472	899	605	(12 827)	3 168
Capital expenditure	6 863	5 234	9 549	10 778	13 901	10 829	5 369	9 593	6 569	7 053
Average number of employees	6 321	6 238	6 955	7 048	7 643	7 595	6 593	5 174	4 541	3 669
Share capital and reserves	17 839	32 317	40 517	43 905	58 698	56 559	49 420	49 412	30 437	33 050
Preference shares										10 700
Loans etc.	22 060	6 353	10 505	16 001	31 650	39 256	42 447	41 524	29 107	20 786
Fixed assets plus net current assets	39 899	38 670	51 022	59 906	90 348	95 815	91 867	90 936	70 244	64 536
Inflation rate (RPI: 1.1.1974 = 100)	134.8	157.1	182.0	197.1	223.5	263.7	295.0	320.4	335.1	351.8

necessary resources and breathing space, but with losses running at £1 million a month they had to move very fast.

The first step, taken by Davies on his first day, was to raise prices by 7.5%. Nobody followed, and the company lost volume in the short term. But the move was necessary if losses were to be stemmed, and it was well-timed to coincide with plant closures at both Redfearn and United Glass. A strike at United Glass also helped. Within a month or two it was becoming clear that Rockware's customers would stick with the company and shortly afterwards their competitors also began raising prices. Six months later, in May 1984, Davies raised prices again, this time by 8%, and this time the industry followed.

The second measure taken was to make a further 1000 Rockware staff redundant and, at the same time, negotiate a six-month wage freeze (in the face of wage increases elsewhere in the industry of about 6%) with the remaining employees. This step was made possible by very generous redundancy packages (helped by the £10 million of new finance), and by the personal skills of Parker and Davies. Sir Peter Parker is a warm, approachable, and extremely articulate man, with a strong sense of public justice. When, on leaving British Rail, he chose to return 'fully committed' to the relatively small Rockware company rather than take up one of the more lucrative and prestigious appointments that would have been

Exhibit 2 Proportion of glass bottles recycled (selected European countries, mid-1980s).

Holland	53%	Italy	24%
Belgium	36%	Denmark	20%
West Germany	31%	Great Britain	9%
France	25%		

Exhibit 3 Estimated non-glass packaging turnovers of selected UK companies (1984 £ million).

Metal Box	850	DRG	200
Reed	300	Rockware	15
Lin Pac	280		

his for the taking, the Rockware workforce responded by returning his loyalty. He believes in being open and straightforward with his firm's employees, treating them as 'citizens', and his powers of communication were such that no-one in the company could be in any doubt as to the seriousness of the position they were in. Frank Davies is also a friendly and approachable figure, who shares Parker's commitment to honesty and plain speaking, and though an outsider to both firm and industry he was quickly accepted on the basis of these qualities, reinforced by Parker's own recommendation.

Alongside these two very drastic measures, Davies also set about pulling the company together, improving its cohesion and tightening controls. The separate companies in the group (including the three glass bottle companies) continued to be run at local level, with a large degree of operating autonomy. But a new Marketing Director, Don Fairley, was recruited from Britain's largest packaging company, Metal Box, to build up a central marketing organization and co-ordinate between the different factories, and between the glass and plastics groups, which were previously quite isolated: 'don't think glass, think customer' was the new message. Group financial controls were also strengthened, and the practice of running over orders so as to improve capacity utilization was stopped: a directive was made to the glass factories to manufacture to orders only, and stocks were cut dramatically as a result, freeing up further capital. To increase productivity and cut down on energy costs, the existing programme of furnace modernization was accelerated. An improved ordering and order call-off system was introduced. A strategic group, comprising heads of business units and of staff functions, was set up.

Exhibit 4   UK glass container market.

	1980	1981	1982	1983	1984
Million units	6800	6500	6100	5925	5976
£ million	384	381	386	366	376
Imports (%)	6%	7%	11%	12%	14%
By end use (million units)					
Drink					3180
Food					1920
Chemicals and pharmaceuticals					515
Toiletry and perfumery					361

Note: these figures do not allow for indirect imports, e.g. wines, waters, and beers bottled in country of origin.

Exhibit 5   Forecast UK PET container market.

	1985/86		1986/87	
Million units				
Carbonated soft drinks				
1 litre bottles	139		166	
1.5 litre bottles	147		164	
>1.5 litre bottles	314		395	
Other	93		117	
Total	693		842	
Turnover (approximate)	£85 million		£105 million	
Market shares				
In-plant operations*	46%	Metal Box	10%	
Fibrenyl	23%	Lin Pac	10%	
Redfearn	11%			

*Aggregate of ten firms manufacturing and bottling products who have backwards integrated to make their own bottles.

These measures between them enabled Rockware to turn in a profit of £3.2 million in 1984, as against a loss of £12.8 million the previous year (see Exhibit 1), but with the basic problem of industry-wide overcapacity unresolved, they could afford only a temporary respite. Rockware needed a strategy.

SUGGESTED QUESTIONS

1. What were the problems facing Rockware when Peter Parker returned? How appropriate were the measures taken so far and what were the alternatives?

2. How were the senior management able to implement the tough measures they did as smoothly as they did?
3. Analyse the structures of the principal industries in which Rockware is competing. How attractive are these industries? How can Rockware position itself to compete in them in the future?
4. Should Rockware consider diversification, and if so what type of diversification would be appropriate?

19

Note on the European airline industry

Note written by Sumantra Ghoshal with Ronald Berger Lefèbure, Johnny Jorgensen and David Staniforth

THE MARKET ENVIRONMENT

Most industry forecasts projected the European air-transport market to grow steadily between 5% and 6% per year to 1990, and about 4% annually to 2000, somewhat better than the 2–4% recorded during the early 1980s. Although some 60–70% of scheduled air traffic in Europe was for business travel, this market segment was expected to remain stagnant over the next 10 years with the majority of the growth coming from the leisure travel market. Part of this future growth was expected to come from greater freedom to compete as the market was progressively deregulated. This anticipated effect of deregulation was confirmed by the 13% increase in traffic between Great Britain and the Netherlands in the year following the signing of their liberalized bilateral agreement, compared with the 8% increase for all intra-European traffic. (See Exhibit 1 for data on size, growth, and share of some of the major international airlines.)

THE COMPETITION

Traditionally, competition in the highly regulated European market had focused on route negotiations and access to other nations' airports. The largest European carriers were British Airways, Air France, Lufthansa, Iberia, Swissair, Alitalia, and Scandinavian Airlines System (SAS), with the first three controlling 40% of the available passenger–kilometres on

Exhibit 1   Air traffic market data: transatlantic and Europe.

Transatlantic scheduled and charter passengers, selected airlines

	1975 (thousand)	(%)	1980 (thousand)	(%)	1985 (thousand)	(%)
TWA	1736	14	2352	13	3757	16
PanAm	1643	9	2230	12	2631	11
British Airways	1217	10	2201	12	2136	9
Lufthansa	673	5	1052	6	1182	5
KLM	593	5	818	4	1079	5
Air France	613	5	736	4	843	4
Swissair	346	3	536	3	649	3
SAS	401	3	525	3	537	2
British Caledonian			149	1	430	2
Sabena	243	2	291	2	356	2
Delta			252	1	374	2
American					367	2
Others	4953		7633		8894	
Total	12418	100	18775	100	23235	100

Source: Travel and Tourism Analyst, May 1986.

Intra-European scheduled passenger kilometres for selected European carriers

	1980 (million)	(%)	1984 (million)	(%)
British Airways	8066	16	7698	14
Lufthansa	5732	11	6302	12
KLM	2236	4	2541	5
Air France	7397	15	7794	14
Swissair	3736	7	4092	6
SAS	3250	7	3623	7
Sabena	1209	>2	1202	2
British Caledonian	321	<1	396	<1
Others	18053		20860*	
Total	50000	100	54504*	100

*Estimate.
Source: Travel and Tourism Analyst, May 1986.

scheduled intra-European flights. (See Exhibit 2 for a comparison of the international route network of SAS with those of some of its competitors.) A large country with a strong national carrier had a lot of leverage in route negotiations, and could often choose the most profitable time slots for arrivals and departures. The product offered did not vary much among competing airlines, and fares were usually fixed in bilateral agreements that were strictly adhered to. These fixed fares allowed

Exhibit 2   Comparison of competing airlines' route structures.

1987−88 world airline route structures
(Approximate no. of major* international destinations served)

Airline	N. America	S. America	Europe	Africa	Austral-Asia
SAS	5	1	40[†]	0	6
Air France	12	16	75	25	33
British Airways	19	7	65	9	33
British Caledonian	5	0	13	13	7
KLM	11	16	55	18	26
Lufthansa	18	10	74	17	28
Pan American	35	13	40	1	5
Sabena	8	0	n/a	26	10
Singapore Airlines	3	0	12	1	32
Swissair	7	4	52	18	21
United Airlines	55+	0	n/a	0	13

Notes:
* The distinction is somewhat arbitrary, and the numbers are intended as an indicator only.
[†] This number does not include smaller Scandinavian destinations.
Source: Company annual reports and routemaps.

airlines with higher operating costs to remain competitive due to the presence of an artificial price umbrella.

For SAS there was not one major competitor, but rather one in each market it served, e.g. British Airways in the UK sector and Braathens SAFE on domestic routes in Norway. In the late 1970s, the impact of the second oil-shock led to poor financial results for most airlines and the competition for passengers increased (see Exhibit 3). The airlines tried to differentiate their products, and to improve in-flight service by offering free drinks, better meals, and introducing a separate class for business travellers. However, new service elements introduced by one airline were quickly copied by others, so it was difficult to sustain a competitive advantage.

In addition to the obvious threat from the major national carriers, increased competition came from the regional feeder and charter airlines (regional in this context includes international flights and is defined as flights with aircraft capacity of 70 passengers or less). The former category had a fairly small share of the market at less than 5%, but had exhibited high growth. From 1978−86, the number of regional airlines, aircraft, and seat capacity in Europe doubled. This trend was expected to continue, or accelerate, as regulations were relaxed, and as regional carriers were allowed into major traffic hubs. However, the major airlines had not passively watched their markets erode, but had countered by 'expropriating' developed regional routes, or by expanding their own regional traffic. This had been achieved either by operating a separate

Exhibit 3A   Air traffic vs. economic trends: economic activity and air traffic, 1971–85.

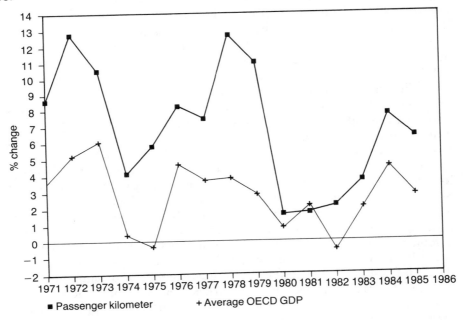

■ Passenger kilometer   + Average OECD GDP

Exhibit 3B   Change in real oil prices (%) 1971–86.

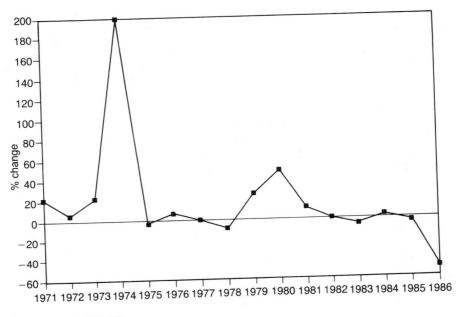

Source: AEA/OECD/TTA.

commuter division, or by partial acquisition of, or a joint venture with, a regional carrier. According to AEA (Association of European Airlines) data, in 1986 SAS offered the highest number of 'regional' seats on international departures in Europe, while in 1978 it was not even among the top 10. However, even if around 10% of total scheduled international departures within Europe were with regional aircrafts, this figure dropped to 3% in terms of passengers, and only 1.5% of passenger-kilometres.

In 1985 charter traffic in Europe accounted for 57% of the world's non-scheduled revenue–passenger–kilometres (RPK), versus only 38% in the mid-1970s. In 1986 around half of the intra-European air traffic was non-sheduled. European charter traffic had grown at an average annual rate of around 5–6% from 1975–85, compared to only 1.7% for the world charter market. Scheduled carriers usually operated charters, or a charter subsidiary, to improve aircraft utilization on weekends and during low demand periods. SAS was no exception, having a charter subsidiary Scanair, which operated eight McDonnell–Douglas DC-8s on long-term lease from the parent company. In addition, Scanair leased extra capacity from SAS during weekends and holiday periods. Although charter traffic accounts for only 1–3% of the major airlines' RPKs, this market segment could be quite important for the smaller and medium-sized carriers (for the Irish flag-carrier Aer Lingus, it represented 18% of revenues in 1986). The major players in the charter market were the independents. The UK's Britannia Airways, Europe's largest charter operator, carried as many passengers a year as KLM. The trend in the charter market was towards larger aircraft and increased capacity so as to reduce operating costs.

The 'seat-only' concept (when a charter airline offers only basic transport) was a growing threat to the scheduled airlines. On certain routes, seat-only accounted for up to 25% of passengers carried by ACE airlines (Association des Compagnies Aeriennes de la Communauté Européenne, representing charter airlines in Europe). The demand for seat-only services was expected to grow significantly. Diversification into scheduled services by charter airlines was another trend seen in the mid-1980s, although in 1987 it represented only about 3% of total RPKs for these airlines. In the future, this proportion was expected to increase, not only to meet the growing demand for seat-only, but also to counter the scheduled carriers' increased presence in the cut-price holiday segment.

The air charter industry had traditionally been much less regulated than the scheduled carriers. An early International Air Transport Association (IATA) provision stating that a package holiday should not be priced lower than the lowest sheduled fare kept prices high, but by the mid-1970s several governments had abolished most price and capacity controls. However, in many countries the charter industry remained under quite strict control.

EFFECTS OF REGULATION/DEREGULATION

The European airline industry was entering a period of liberalization as a result of increasing competitive pressures. European consumers were urging their national governments towards deregulation in an effort to bring travel costs down. Some individual countries, notably Great Britain and the Netherlands, had modified their bilateral agreements with other nations to allow more competition on capacity and fares. However, a number of factors made the situation in Europe quite different from that experienced in the US following deregulation of the airline industry in that country.

The cartel within the IATA had given member airlines a protected market. In addition, bilateral treaties between European nations allowed their airlines to share the market through pooling arrangements. According to a study by the European Civil Aviation Conference (ECAC), 75–85% of the tonne-km on European scheduled flights were subject to these pooling agreements. These could take several forms, such as agreements to share revenues and capacity (although not always equally), agreements to limit the number of flights between two cities, and agreements by one carrier to pay another not to fly certain routes. A final important feature of these agreements was a commitment to price-setting. The bilateral treaties usually declared that the airlines should, subject to government approval, reach agreement on their air fares and it was often stated that the price-setting machinery of IATA would be used whenever possible.

Through these pooling agreements, capacity had been divided up on a 50:50 basis between the respective countries. If, for example, KLM offered 150 seats from Stockholm to Amsterdam, SAS was entitled to offer 150 seats on the same route. A number of proposals had been put forward to modify this procedure. One proposal supported by the European Parliament was to increase the maximum capacity that could be offered by airlines of one country from the present 50% to 75% of the total capacity on the route without the consent of the other country. The AEA/IATA proposal limited this to 55%, and this latter modification had been adopted in some of the new agreements, such as the one between Britain and France. The agreement signed between the UK and the Netherlands in 1984 was the most competitive in Europe with no limits on route entry or capacity. As a result, a total of seven carriers were flying the London–Amsterdam route, but the average fare had not decreased significantly although the range of fares and services has expanded considerably. This is illustrated in Exhibit 4, which compares fares on this route in 1983 and 1985.

The European market was too fragmented to enable a surge of new competitors with significant fare reductions on major routes as happened in the US in the late 1970s. The size of the US market and the presence of only one regulatory authority allowed rapid deregulation to take place. This led to the entry of new competitors in virtually all markets, and

Exhibit 4   Example of fare structure: London–Amsterdam.

London–Amstersdam Air Fares, 1983 and 1985
(Nominal pounds sterling)

	1983	1985
British Airways and KLM		
Economy fare	148	162
Eurobudget (any flight)	126	138
Eurobudget (designated flights)	105	115
PEX (stay over one Saturday)	99	109
SuperPEX (more restrictive than PEX)	88	91
Late saver (very restrictive)		55
British Caledonian		
Peak fare	148	109
Shoulder fare		89
Off-peak fare	98	69
Average	116	104

Source: *Travel and Tourism Analyst*, March 1986.

low-cost carriers, such as People's Express, were formed. These carriers typically employed non-union personnel and operated used aircraft. Consequently, they had lower operating costs compared to the established major carriers and they used this advantage to undercut the majors on price. They were helped further by falling fuel prices since their older aircraft were not as fuel efficient as those of the established carriers. These lower prices could be profitable in the long term only if traffic bases were increased. The resulting scramble for volume led to a shake-out and seven major carriers came to dominate the US market after a series of takeovers and mergers: American Airlines; Texas Air Corporation (having acquired Continental, Eastern, and People's Express); United Airlines (having acquired Pan-Am's Pacific routes); Northwest (having acquired Republic); Delta (having acquired Western); TWA (having acquired Ozark); and USAir (having acquired Piedmont and Pacific Southwest). These airlines had also forged links with regional carriers to feed more traffic into their respective systems.

Although the EEC commission was urging its members towards greater liberalization, it only represented about half of the countries that made up the more conservative ECAC. There were also significant differences within the EEC countries themselves. Great Britain and the Netherlands were the most liberal, followed by Luxembourg, West Germany, and Belgium. They were still outnumbered by the seven other members who remained more conservative.

Deregulation was progressing on a piecemeal basis, with new bilateral agreements being negotiated with individual countries, instead of on a Europe-wide basis, which would be necessary to provide the level of free competition which existed in the US. The EEC was pressing for a more unified European stance to enable negotiations with the US on a multi-lateral, rather than bilateral basis. A problem with the piecemeal approach was that single routes themselves did not provide a viable network for new entrants. This factor limited the possibility of a new carrier gaining a major foothold in a more competitive European market in the manner that People's Express did in the US. Although it was widely believed that deregulation would result in lower overall fares for European travellers, studies of the US experience do not necessarily confirm this view. In a 1983 study, Britain's Civil Aviation Authority (CAA) concluded that normal fares on US routes with limited competition were only 10–15% below UK–Europe equivalents, although where additional competitors had entered, fares were as much as 33% lower. Much of these differences could be attributed to higher labour, fuel and associated costs of operating in Europe compared with the USA. Some UK–Europe routes were found to offer promotional fares which were actually lower than any fare on an equivalent US route. The Dutch aviation authorities undertook a similar study of deregulation's effect on fares. Applying the results of these studies to European scheduled routes in general suggested possible fare reductions of approximately 10% if service levels were maintained, and up to 20% if service levels were reduced. Actual realization of such reductions, however, depended on the pace of new entry, for which the opportunities, as noted earlier, were not as great in Europe as they had been in the US.

NEW DEVELOPMENTS

Confronted with these environmental changes, many of the major air-lines were expanding their range of services by integrating into related aspects of the travel sector, such as hotels, travel agencies, car rental, and financial services. Among the European carriers, seven companies had built substantial interests in hotels: Aer Lingus, Air France, British Caledonian, KLM, Lufthansa, SAS, and Swissair. Airlines were also considering expanding into the field of credit cards to increase the range of services offered to customers and provide management of corporate travel expenses for business related travel.

In February 1987, United Airlines was grouped together with Westin and Hilton International Hotels and Hertz car rental under the Allegis corporate name, becoming the world's most vertically integrated travel service company. However, only five months later, Allegis's board rejected the travel supermarket concept. Both the car rental and hotel chains were put up for sale. In spite of the Allegis experience, the trend towards travel service integration was expected to continue as the industry became more global and competitive.

New areas of co-operation for mutual cost savings and benefits were developing among European carriers. For example, most airlines were under pressure to provide automated ticket and boarding-pass facilities to improve customer service. Prototype machines were purchased jointly by AEA member airlines and testing began in 1987. Worldwide interest in the concept had increased and discussions had been held to develop a common design to supply most of the IATA carriers.

Computer Reservations Systems (CRS) and their implications for the airlines' sales distribution networks had become increasingly important, particularly in the light of worldwide developments. These networks were expected to become the primary link between the airlines and the marketplace. The major US airlines had launched a drive to place their CRS systems in travel agencies outside the US, and were focusing on Europe. The retailing of airline tickets in the US prior to deregulation was relatively straightforward, since distribution was via a cartel system. Deregulation meant that the airlines had to build marketing relationships with individual travel agencies, and the CRS system was a key element in that strategy. The massive investments required to develop these systems made this area a good candidate for co-operative ventures.

20

Scandinavian Airlines System in 1988

Case written by Sumantra Ghoshal with Ronald Berger Lefèbure, Johnny Jorgensen and David Staniforth

When the Scandinavian Airlines System (SAS) group financial results for the fiscal year 1986–87 were released, it marked the trinational transport group's sixth straight profitable year, and their best year ever with a net operating income of Skr.1.6 billion on revenues of Skr.23.9 billion. This was a huge improvement over the situation in 1981 when losses were mounting and the airline was rapidly losing market share. A summary of the company's recent financial results, along with relevant exchange rates, are shown in Exhibit 1.

Much of the credit for the company's dramatic turnaround was ascribed to Jan Carlzon who succeeded Carl-Olov Munkberg as President and CEO in 1981. Carlzon quickly initiated a number of major changes in the airline and its associated companies. He reoriented SAS towards the business travel market and gave top priority to customer service. This involved a complete reorganization of the company and a major decentralization of responsibility. As a result, SAS had become the leading carrier of full-fare traffic in Europe. Carlzon had joined SAS as Executive Vice-President in 1980, after serving as President of Linjeflyg, the Swedish domestic airline. Previously, he had been Managing Director of the SAS tour subsidiary Vingresor.

Despite these successes, dramatic as they were, the company still faced considerable threats and many analysts questioned if it could survive as a viable competitor in the increasingly global and competitive airline industry. Its population base of only 17 million spread out over a large

Exhibit 1   SAS group financial and operating results, 1977/78–1986/87.

Financial summary-group	1977/78	1978/79	1979/80	1980/81	1981/82	1982/83	1983/84	1984/85	1985/86	1986/87
(Skr. millions)										
Operating revenue	7 050	8 066	9 220	10 172	12 807	15 972	18 005	19 790	21 585	23 870
Operating expenses	(6 437)	(7 551)	(8 920)	(9 664)	(11 895)	(14 696)	(16 415)	(18 256)	(19 369)	(21 524)
Depreciation	(347)	(360)	(391)	(430)	(474)	(483)	(545)	(574)	(863)	(1 126)
Financial & extra items	(140)	(7)	28	(129)	10	(192)	(77)	57	162	443
Net operating income	126	148	(63)	(51)	448	601	968	1 017	1 515	1 663
Exchange Rate – Skr. $US	4.60	4.15	4.17	5.61	6.28	7.83	8.70	7.40	6.91	6.40

Revenue by business area	1982/83 (%)	1983/84 (%)	1984/85 (%)	1985/86 (%)	1986/87 (%)
(Skr. millions)					
SAS Airline Consortium	12 600 (79)	14 151 (79)	15 434 (78)	16 495 (76)	17 510 (73)
SAS International Hotels	732 (5)	843 (5)	948 (5)	1 083 (5)	1 230 (5)
SAS Service Partner	1 681 (11)	2 049 (11)	2 393 (12)	2 712 (13)	3 223 (14)
SAS Leisure (Vingresor)	1 311 (8)	1 474 (8)	1 537 (8)	1 897 (9)	2 379 (10)
Other	456 (3)	460 (3)	390 (2)	415 (2)	730 (3)
Group eliminations	(808) (−5)	(972) (−5)	(912) (−5)	(1 017) (−5)	(1 202) (−5)
Total	15 972 (100)	18 005 (100)	19 790 (100)	21 585 (100)	23 870 (100)

Income by business area	1982/83 (%)	1983/84 (%)	1984/85 (%)	1985/86 (%)	1986/87 (%)
(Skr. millions)					
SAS Airline Consortium	461 (77)	729 (75)	811 (80)	1 207 (80)	1 453 (87)
SAS International Hotels	14 (2)	21 (2)	67 (7)	72 (5)	73 (4)
SAS Service Partner	75 (12)	15 (2)	81 (8)	123 (8)	180 (11)
SAS Leisure (Vingresor)	41 (7)	43 (4)	81 (8)	133 (9)	141 (8)
Other	17 (3)	5 (1)	(15) (−1)	(31) (−2)	(99) (−6)
Group Eliminations	(25) (−4)	(21) (−2)	(7) (−1)	(22) (−1)	(85) (−5)
Extraordinary Items	18 (3)	176 (18)	−1 (0)	34 (2)	0 (0)
Total	601 (100)	968 (100)	1 017 (100)	1 516 (100)	1 663 (100)

Operating statistics SAS Airline	1977/78	1978/79	1979/80	1980/81	1981/82	1982/83	1983/84	1984/85	1985/86	1986/87
Cities served	98	102	103	105	99	93	91	88	89	85
Kilometers flown (millions)	123	124	20	113	113	120	124	125	136	n/a
Passengers (thousands)	7 886	8 669	8 393	8 413	8 861	9 222	10 066	10 735	11 708	n/a
Cabin load factor (%)	56.4%	59.9%	59.4%	60.9%	63.6%	65.5%	67.2%	67.2%	66.2%	68.9%
Employees	16 010	16 755	17 069	16 425	16 376	17 101	17 710	18 845	19 773	n/a

Source: annual reports.

area was too small by itself to support a comprehensive international traffic system. In addition, its geographic location at the periphery of Europe was a disadvantage when compared to Western Europe's densely populated areas.

The most pressing problem was the airline's operating costs, which were among the highest in the industry (see Exhibit 2). It was estimated that labour charges accounted for 35% of SAS's total costs, compared with only 25% for the major US carriers since deregulation, and 18% for the large Asian airlines. The evolution of the US 'mega-carriers' was a major concern as they eyed Europe as an area for continued expansion.

Senior managers of the company were fully aware of these challenges. In discussing future developments in the airline industry, and SAS's role in particular, Helge Lindberg, Group Executive Vice President, noted:

> I doubt very much that SAS can survive alone as a major inter-continental airline. We need to expand our traffic system in order to compete with major European carriers having much larger population bases, as well as with the major American and Asian carriers who maintain considerably lower operating costs. We need to develop with other partners a global traffic system with daily connections to the important overseas destinations. The nature of our industry is such that if you are not present in the market the day the customers wish to travel, the business is lost. Another priority is to reduce our costs. Our social structure in Scandinavia leaves us with one of the highest personnel costs in the industry, coupled with the fact that increased emphasis on service caused us to lose our traditional budget consciousness over the past few years. A third

Exhibit 2   Comparison of airline operating costs.

Estimated airline operating costs
(US cents per available tonne–kilometer)

Airline	1982	1983	1984	1985	1986
Singapore Airlines	36	36	33	32	30
British Caledonian	37	37	29	35	38
United Airlines	39	39	38	44	40
KLM	35	29	26	35	44
Pan American	34	36	38	36	n/a
British Airways	40	38	31	37	44
Delta	42	43	43	45	44
Lufthansa	51	44	40	53	57
Swissair	54	47	41	53	58
Sabena	53	43	44	56	63
SAS	53	53	50	65	76

Source: company annual reports.

major issue is to develop a competitive distribution system, a problem we are about to solve in partnership with Air France, Iberia and Lufthansa, with the so-called Amadeus system.

THE TURNAROUND

Sweden, Denmark, and Norway had always shared a common interest in creating an ambitious air service, both to link their scattered communities, and to ensure a role for Scandinavia among the world's international airlines. They first considered a joint airline in the 1930s when all three countries wanted to establish a route to America. No firm agreement was reached until 1940 however, when they decided to operate a joint service between New York and Bergen, on Norway's west coast. This plan was unfortunately scuttled by the German invasion three days later.

The Bermuda conference on international air travel in 1946 put an end to any hopes of true freedom of the air, and served to underline the importance of developing a common airline in order to establish a stronger world presence. The three countries agreed upon an ownership structure, and in the summer of 1946 a DC-4 lifted off from Stockholm bound for Oslo and New York bearing the Scandinavian Airlines System name. Sweden controlled three-sevenths of the new airline and Norway and Denmark two-sevenths each, with ownership split 50:50 between the respective governments and private interests.

SAS gained a strong foothold in the European market – at the expense of the Germans who were forbidden from establishing their own airline – and quickly developed a worldwide route network. The airline established numerous firsts in the early years of worldwide air travel, beginning with the Swedish parent company ABA in 1945, who were the first to re-establish transatlantic service after the war. SAS pioneered the Arctic route in 1954 with a flight from Copenhagen to Los Angeles via Greenland, and in 1957 inaugurated transpolar service to Tokyo, cutting travel time by half. The Scandinavians were the first to operate the French Caravelle, introducing twin-engine jet travel within Europe, and worked with Douglas Aircraft to develop the ultra-long range DC-8-62, capable of flying non-stop to the US west coast and Southeast Asia. A list of the airline's major milestones is shown in Exhibit 3. SAS had often looked for overseas partners, and purchased 30% of Thai Airways International in 1959. This stake was bought back by the Thai government in 1977, but the two airlines had since entered into a co-operative service agreement.

The 1960s and early 1970s were the golden years for the airline. Apart from 1972 when profits shrank to $8 million due to currency fluctuations, average annual net profits from 1969–75 were between $15 million and $20 million. In the late 1970s, the second oil shock had a severe effect on profits, and the airline sustained considerable losses in 1979–80 and 1980–81.

Exhibit 3   SAS milestones.

1946–July 31–August 1
DDL, DNL, and SILA found SAS for the operation of intercontinental services to North and South America.

1946–September 17
Route to New York opened.

1946–November 30
Route to South America opened.

1948–April 18
ABA, DDL, and DNL form ESAS to co-ordinate European operations.

1948–July 1
SILA and ABA amalgamated.

1949–October 26
Route to Bangkok opened.

1950–October 1
ABA, DDL, and DNL transfer all operations to SAS in accordance with a new Consortium Agreement dated February 8, 1951, with retroactive effect.

1951–April 18
The Bangkok route is extended to Tokyo.

1951–April 19
Route to Nairobi is inaugurated.

1952–November 19
First transarctic flight by commercial airliner.

1953–January 8
The Nairobi route extended to Johannesburg.

1954–November 15
Polar route to Los Angeles inaugurated.

1956–May 9
Pre-war route to Moscow reopened.

1957–February 24
Inauguration of North Pole short cut to Tokyo.

1957–April 2
SAS participates in formation of Linjeflyg.

1957–April 4
Route opened to Warsaw.

1957–April 16
First flight to Prague.

1958–October 6
Agreement of co-operation signed by SAS and Swissair.

1959–August 24
SAS and Thai Airways Co. establish THAI International.

1960–July 2
Monrovia added to South Atlantic network.

1961–October 1
SAS Catering established as subsidiary.

1962–May 15
Inauguration of all-cargo service to New York.

1963–May 4
Route opened across top of North Norway to Kirkenes.

1963–November 2
First service to Montreal.

1964–April 2
Route to Chicago inaugurated.

1965–April 5
Non-stop service New York–Bergen begun.

1966–September 2
Inauguration of service to Seattle via Polar route.

1967–November 4
Opening of Trans-Asian

Express via Tashkent to Bangkok and Singapore.

1968–March 31
Dar-Es-Salaam added to East African network.

1969–November 1
Route opened to Barbados and Port-of-Spain in West Indies.

1970–February 18
KSSU agreement ratified.

1971–April 3
Trans-Siberian Express to Tokyo inaugurated.

1971–November 1
SAS participates in formation of Danair.

1972–April 5
Route to East Berlin opened.

1972–May 24
New York–Stavanger route opened.

1973–November 4
All-cargo express route opened to Bangkok and Singapore.

1973–November 6
Dehli added to Trans-Orient route.

1975–September 2
Inauguration of Svalbard route, world's northernmost scheduled service.

1976–April 21
Route opened to Lagos.

1977–April 7
Kuwait added to Trans-Orient route.

1977–November 2
Opening of Gothenburg–New York route.

Source: 'The SAS Saga'; Anders Buraas, Oslo 1979.

SAS had developed close relationships with Swissair and KLM. An agreement between the three airlines (the KSSU agreement) was signed in 1969 with the objective of strengthening technical co-operation and of jointly assessing any new aircraft entering the market. For example, it was agreed that SAS would be responsible for overhauling the Boeing 747 engines of all three airlines, while the other partners performed other joint maintenance activities.

Although the trinational airline had generally functioned smoothly, there had been some problems among the constituent groups, particularly when Denmark joined the EEC in 1973. This underlying rivalry was reflected in Norway by the statement, 'SAS is an airline run by the Swedes for the benefit of the Danes', in reference to the airline's head office in Stockholm and its main traffic hub at Kastrup airport in Copenhagen. Nonetheless, the larger traffic base and increased bargaining power afforded by the union had helped to make SAS a major world airline.

Problems facing SAS in 1981

When Jan Carlzon assumed the presidency of SAS in August 1981, he realized that major changes would have to be made to restore the airline and associated companies to profitability, and to meet the growing challenges of an increasingly competitive industry. After 17 profitable years, the SAS group had posted operating losses of Skr.63.1 million and Skr.51.3 million in fiscal years 1979–80 and 1980–81 respectively. This dramatic decline had given rise to rumours that the three constituent countries were considering disbanding SAS and running their own separate airlines.

In addition to the problems that beset the industry – the international recession, higher interest rates and fuel costs, overcapacity and less-regulated competition – specific problems had plagued SAS in recent years. The airline had been losing market share, even in its home territory; its fleet mix and route network did not meet market needs; and its reputation for service and punctuality had deteriorated. For example, on-time performance (defined as percentage of arrivals within 15 minutes of schedule) had slipped from over 90% to 85% – a major drop by airline standards.

In addition, many regular travellers from Norway and Sweden were increasingly avoiding Copenhagen's troublesome Kastrup airport – SAS's major hub – in favour of more attractive and efficient terminals at Amsterdam, Frankfurt or Zurich. Under the umbrella of regulation, bad habits had developed within the company's management ranks. Carlzon felt that SAS, like most airlines, had allowed itself to become too enamoured with technology – new aircrafts, new engines – often at the cost of meeting the customer's needs. They had become a product-driven airline instead of being a service-driven one. A typical example was the acquisition of the state-of-the-art Airbus A300 aircraft in the late 1970s. These larger planes required high load factors to be profitable and this necessitated lower flight frequencies – not in the best interests of customers who needed frequent and flexible flight schedules. In the past, when air travel was still somewhat of a novelty, customers had been willing to plan their trips according to a particular airline's schedule, and had even been willing to sacrifice some time to do so. The market had since changed, and experienced travellers now chose flights to suit their travel plans, not vice-versa. 'In the past, we were operating as booking agents and aircraft brokers,' said Carlzon. 'Now we know, if we want the business we must fight for it like the "Street fighters" of the rough-and-tumble American domestic market.'

New strategy – 'the businessman's airline'

Faced with the situation of a stagnant market, general overcapacity in the industry, and continuing loss of market share to competitors, Carlzon recognized that a new strategy was necessary to turn SAS around. In a similar situation when he was the President of Linjeflyg, Carlzon had decided to increase flight frequency and cut fares dramatically in order to improve aircraft utilization and boost load factors. These actions had proven to be very successful and profitability had improved substantially. However, the market SAS operated in was quite different from that of Linjeflyg, and it was not clear that a similar strategy could be applied successfully. Another possible option was to initiate a major cost reduction programme aimed at obtaining a better margin from a declining revenue base. This strategy would have required significant staff cuts, fleet reduction, and an overall lower level of flight frequency and service.

In the airline industry, the most stable market segment was the full-fare paying business traveller who provided the vast majority of revenues. First class travel within Europe was declining, mainly because businesses could not justify the extra expense, especially during a recession. All the major, scheduled airlines were after the business traveller, and some had created a separate 'business' class priced at a 10–20% premium over economy, which offered many of the amenities of first class.

SAS chose the strategy of focusing on the business traveller. As described by Helge Lindberg, then Executive Vice President–Commercial, 'although other options were considered, we quickly decided there was no alternative but to go after the business traveller segment with a new product which offered significant advantages over the competition'. In the words of Jan Carlzon: 'We decided to go after a bigger share of the full-fare paying pie.'

There were a number of risks involved in this strategy. Increasing investment to provide an improved level of service at a time of mounting losses could bankrupt the airline if revenues did not improve sufficiently. On the other hand, if investment was the way to go, perhaps it could be better spent on more efficient aircraft so as to reduce costs. Another concern was that differentiating the product could alienate the tourist class passengers, especially among Scandinavian customers, who might resent any increase in passenger 'segregation'. In spite of these considerable risks, management increased expenditures and staked the future of the airline on their ability to woo the European business traveller away from the competition.

As a result, first class was dropped and 'EuroClass' was introduced, offering more amenities than competing airlines' business classes, but at the old economy fare. (A similar service, First Business Class, was introduced on intercontinental routes, where first class was retained.) Thus any passenger paying the full fare would be entitled to this new service, which included separate check-in, roomier seating, advance seat selection, free drinks, and a better in-flight meal. The other European airlines reacted strongly. Air France saw EuroClass as a serious threat to its own 'Classe Affaires', which cost 20% more than economy, and at one point refused to book any EuroClass fares on its reservation system. Other airlines protested to their local government authorities, but to no avail, and the new fare structures were allowed to remain. SAS backed up the new service with the largest media advertising campaign ever launched by the airline (see Exhibit 4).

In conjunction with the new EuroClass services, a drive was launched

---

Exhibit 4   Example of EuroClass advertisment, 1981.

SAS Advertisement:
'Of the eight major airlines competing in Sweden for European traffic, five do not give you separate check-in and seating, separate cabin or free drinks. Of the three remaining airlines, two do not give you extra room and larger seats. Only one airline in Europe has EuroClass which gives you more service and comfort for the economy fare.'

Lufthansa Advertisement:
'You can still fly first class in Europe!'

Source: 'Advertising Age' 1981

to improve flight schedules and punctuality. The aircraft fleet mix was modified in order to meet the demands of increased flight frequency. The recently acquired, high-capacity Airbus aircraft were withdrawn from service and leased to SAS's Scanair charter subsidiary since they were not suitable for the frequent, non-stop flights which the new schedule demanded. For the same reason some Boeing 747s were replaced by McDonnell–Douglas DC-10s, and the older DC-9s were refurbished instead of being replaced since they were of the right size for the new service levels.

On certain short-distance routes such as Copenhagen–Hamburg, a new 'EuroLink' concept was introduced. This involved substituting 40-passenger Fokker F-27s for 110-passenger DC-9s and doubling flight frequencies to provide a more attractive schedule. In short, the previous high fixed-cost, high capacity fleet was changing into a lower fixed-cost, high frequency one. This evolution of the SAS fleet is shown in Exhibit 5.

Every effort was made to differentiate the business traveller product as much as possible from the lower priced fares. In this respect, 'Scanorama' lounges were introduced at many of the airports served by SAS in an effort to further improve service. These lounges were for the exclusive use of the full-fare paying passenger and offered telephones and telex machines and a more relaxing environment to the business traveller. A joint agreement with the Danish Civil Aviation Authority was reached to invest in refurbishing Kastrup airport to bring it up to competitive standards. The objective was for Kastrup to be Europe's best airport by the end of the decade.

The introduction of these new products and related services represented a change in the overall philosophy of SAS. All tasks and functions within the organization were examined. If the business traveller benefited from a particular service or function, it was maintained or enhanced, otherwise it was cut back, or dropped altogether. Managers were urged to look upon

Exhibit 5   Evolution of SAS's fleet.

Aircraft type*		Seat Cap.	1977–78	1978–79	1979–80	1980–81	1981–82	1982–83	1983–84	1984–85	1985–86	1986–87
Boeing 747		405	3	4	4	5	5	3	5	5	2	0
Airbus Industries	A300	242	0	0	2	4	1	1	0	0	0	0
McDonnell–Douglas	DC-10-30	230	5	5	5	5	5	5	6	8	9	11
	DC-8-62	N/A	5	5	2	3	3	3	3	3	3	0
	DC-8-63	170	5	3	4	2	2	2	2	2	2	0
	DC-9-21	75	9	9	9	9	9	9	9	9	9	9
	DC-9-33	(freight)	2	2	2	2	2	2	2	2	2	2
	DC-9-41	100/122	45	49	49	49	49	49	49	49	49	49
	DC-9-81	133	0	0	0	0	0	0	0	0	6	8
	DC-9-82	156	0	0	0	0	0	0	0	0	6	8
	DC-9-83	133	0	0	0	0	0	0	0	0	0	4
Fokker F-27		40	0	0	0	0	0	0	4	6	9	9
Total			74	77	77	79	76	74	80	84	97	100

* Aircraft owned or leased by SAS that were leased to other operators are not included in this table.
Source: company annual reports.

expenses as resources; to cut those that did not contribute to revenue, but not to hesitate in raising those that did. Administrative costs were slashed 25%, but at the same time an extra Skr.120 million was invested on new services, facilities, aircraft interiors, and other projects that affected the passengers ·directly. As a result, annual operating costs were increased by Skr.55 million at a time of deep deficits and continuing losses. Furthermore, these additional investments for improved service delayed the acquisition of new, more efficient aircraft to replace the ageing DC-9 fleet.

The results of this new strategy were dramatic. Full-fare paying passenger traffic rose over 8% in the first year, and profits rose to Skr.448 million for the 1981–82 fiscal year. In punctuality, SAS improved on-time performance to 93%, a record in Europe. The share of full-fare paying passengers rose consistently, and by 1986 it had risen to 60%, giving SAS the highest proportion of any airline in Europe. Accompanying this change in passenger mix were impressive profit gains. In 1986 SAS turned in the third best profit performance among the world's major airlines with a net operating profit of Skr.1.5 billion (a comparison of financial and operating results of major world airlines is shown in Exhibit 6).

Corporate cultural revolution

Due in part to the protected, stable growth environment, the SAS organization was not ready to meet new competitive challenges without a major restructuring. Previously, the reference point had been fixed assets and technology, with emphasis on return on investment, centralized control, and orders from top management. Across the board cost-cutting was the usual approach to improve profits and to adapt to changing market conditions. The customer interface had been neglected. As described by a senior manager of the company:

> In those days, many employees felt that passengers were a disturbing element they had to contend with, rather than the ones who were in fact paying their salary. Taking control of a situation, and bypassing the regulations in order to please a customer were not the things to do in SAS.

Thus personal initiative was discouraged, and adherence to the company policy manuals was the norm. A large corporate staff was needed to run this bureaucracy, with layers of middle management to follow up directives from the top. Throughout the organization the morale of employees was low, and the level of co-operation among them, such as between ground staff and air crews, was not always the best. 'There was a feeling of helplessness, and a fear for the future of the company,' remarked an SAS pilot when asked to comment on the situation prevailing prior to 1981.

A transformation 'from bureaucrats to businessmen' was essential, and

Exhibit 6   Comparison of major world airlines' statistics.

1986 world airline operating and financial statistics

Passengers	(thousands)	RPKs	(millions)
1. Aeroflot	115 727	1. Aeroflot	188 056
2. United	50 690	2. United	95 569
3. American	45 983	3. American	78 499
4. Eastern	42 546	4. Eastern	56 164
5. Delta	41 062	5. Delta	50 480
6. TWA	24 636	6. TWA	48 100
7. All Nippon	24 503	7. Northwest	46 346
8. Piedmont	22 800	8. British Airways	41 405
9. USAir	21 725	9. Japan Air Lines	38 903
10. Continental	20 409	10. Pan American	34 844
22. SAS	11 700	30. (est) SAS	12 471

Fleet size	(No. aircraft)	Employees	
1. Aeroflot	2682	1. Aeroflot	500 000
2. United	368	2. American	51 661
3. American	338	3. United	49 800
4. Northwest	311	4. Eastern	43 685
5. Eastern	289	5. Federal Expressa	43 300
6. Delta	253	6. Delta	38 901
7. Continental	246	7. British Airways	37 810
8. CAAC (China)	241	8. Air France	35 269
9. TWA	167	9. Lufthansa	34 905
10. Republic	165	10. Northwest	33 250
18. SAS	106	22. SAS	19 773

Operating revenue	(US $ million)	Operating profit	(US $ million)
1. United	6688	1. American	392
2. American	5857	2. Federal Express*	365
3. Air France	4747	3. SAS	260
4. Japan Air Lines	4578	4. Delta	225
5. Eastern	4522	5. Cathay Pacific	206
6. Delta	4496	6. Swissair	200
7. Northwest	3598	7. Northwest	167
8. TWA	3181	8. USAir	164
9. Federal Express*	2940	9. Continental	143
10. Pan American	2580	10. KLM	131
11. SAS	2387		

* Freight only.
Source: *Air Transport World*, June 1987.

an emphasis on the customer was needed. A major reorientation had been contemplated by Carlzon's predecessor, Carl-Olov Munkberg, but it was felt that implementation of a new organization would be more effective under a new CEO. 'New brooms sweep clear,' remarked Carlzon in relating his decision to replace or relocate 13 of the 14 executives in the management team of SAS. Helge Lindberg, the sole survivor in the top management team, was put in charge of the day-to-day running of the airline. Lindberg's extensive knowledge and experience was valued by Carlzon, who saw him as a 'bridge between old and new', and a valuable asset now that the time for change had arrived.

In the past, SAS had focused on instructions, thereby limiting potential contributions from the employees. A key element of the cultural revolution under Carlzon was a new emphasis on information instead of instructions. The practical implications of this were that any employee in the 'front line' (i.e. in the SAS–customer interface) should have the decision-making power necessary to do, within reasonable limits, whatever that person felt appropriate to please the customer. Each 'moment of truth', when the customer encountered the service staff, would be used to its full potential so as to encourage repeat business. 'Throw out the manuals and use your heads instead!', was the message from Lindberg. The underlying assumptions, made explicit throughout the organization, were that an individual with information could not avoid assuming responsibility and that hidden resources were released when an individual was free to assume responsibility instead of being restricted by instructions.

Exhibit 7   Examples from 'Carlzon's Little Red Books'.

Hopeless odds.
When we looked around a year ago, our hopes of 'getting our nose up' were sinking. Demand had stopped increasing. We could no longer regard ourselves rich, i.e. there was less hope for continued growth and thus automatically increased revenues. The competition got harder. How could we survive?

Source: SAS.

Exhibit 7   *continued*

Certain competitors 'throw in the towel'
At the time when SAS achieves its best result ever, the majority in the airline industry are doing poorly. The IATA companies are this year losing around US$2 billion! But they should be making a profit of US$3 billion (7.5% of turnover) to have a chance of meeting their future aircraft investments. From this we can draw two conclusions:

- SAS is not like the other IATA companies. Our result is nothing less than a world sensation.
- The IATA companies will probably fight for their lives in the future – just as we started to do a year and a half ago. They will probably use all their force to beat us in the coming rounds.

Note: Translation from Swedish by casewriters.

Some of the tools used by Carlzon in the reorganization were personal letters and several red booklets ('Carlzon's little red books') distributed to all employees. In these booklets the company's situation and its goals were presented in very simple language, using cartoon-like drawings to emphasize their importance (see examples in Exhibit 7). Some employees found this form of communication too simple, but overall, the response was very positive. In his first year Carlzon spent approximately half of his time travelling, meeting with SAS employees all over the world. This made it very clear to everyone that management was deeply committed to turning things around, and helped to implement the changes quickly.

Education was considered necessary to reap the full benefits of the new organization, and both managers and front-line staff were sent to seminars. The courses for the front-line personnel were referred to by many as the 'learn-to-smile seminars', but the real benefits probably resulted more from the participants' perception that the company cared about its employees, than from the actual content of the courses.

Certain problems were encountered in the process of change. Confusion and frustration were typical reactions of many middle managers when they suddenly found themselves bypassed by the 'front line', on the one hand, and by the top management, on the other. 'You can't please everyone, and some people will have to be sacrificed,' said an SAS manager when asked to comment on this problem. Cross-training of employees to perform several tasks was attempted, but met with resistance from the unions. An example was the 'turnaround' check – a visual check of the aircraft performed between each flight. This could very well be done by the pilots, but the mechanics' union insisted upon this task being done by their people, resulting in higher operating costs.

Another problem was that the first reorientation had short-term goals, and when these were achieved, the early momentum diminished. By 1984 SAS had received the 'Airline of the Year' award from the Air Transport World magazine, and its financial situation had improved dramatically. These factors led to a feeling of contentment, and people started to fall back into old habits. Demands for salary increases were again raised. Some people thought that SAS was now out of danger, and wanted to harvest the fruits of hard work. Small 'pyramids' started to crop up in the organization, and it became evident that the problems in the middle management were not solved. 'The new culture was taking roots, but we had problems keeping up the motivation,' noted Lindberg.

Consequently, a 'second wave' of change was launched, and new goals with a much longer time horizon were outlined. Management wanted to prepare the company for the coming liberalization in the airline industry, and ensure a level of profitability sufficient to meet upcoming fleet replacement needs. The ultimate goal was for SAS to be the most efficient airline in Europe by 1990.

THE SECOND WAVE

SAS wanted to integrate the various elements of the travel package offered to the business traveller: to develop a full service product for the full-fare paying passenger. In the words of Lindberg: 'We wanted to be a full service, door-to-door travel service company. We aimed to offer a unique product which we could control from A to Z.' To meet this objective, the SAS service chain concept was established by creating a distribution system and network of services that met the needs of the business travellers, from the time they ordered their tickets to the time they got back home. This meant that the development of a hotel network, reservation system, and credit card operation were decisive for the company's future.

SAS International Hotels (SIH)

In 1983 SIH became a separate division within the SAS Group. A new concept, the SAS Destination Service – 'ticket, transport and hotel package' – was introduced in September 1985. SAS market research indicated that ground transportation and hotel reservations ranked high among the needs of business travellers. Indeed, surveys also indicated that more than 50% of Scandinavian business travellers had no prior knowledge of the hotels where they had been booked, and thus would appreciate the standards and facilities guaranteed by the SAS Destination Service. The hotels where guaranteed reservations could be made under this scheme totalled 80, and the chain, already one of the biggest in the world, was marketed as SAS Business Hotels. With this new service, passengers were able to order airline tickets, ground transportation, and confirmed hotel reservations with one telephone call.

At each SAS destination where public transport from the airport to the city centre was time consuming or complicated, a door-to-door limousine service was made available at reasonable prices to full-fare paying passengers. A helicopter shuttle service was introduced for travellers transferring between New York's Kennedy and LaGuardia airports. Many of the hotels featured SAS Airline Check-in. This meant that passengers could check their luggage and obtain boarding-passes before leaving the hotel in the morning, and then go directly to the gate at the airport for afternoon or evening departures. With the creation of the SAS Destination Service, a complete door-to-door transport service was offered, and it reflected SAS's conviction that, to a large extent, the battle for full-fare paying passengers would be won on the ground. The total product had to be seen as an integrated chain of services for the business travel market, including reservations, airport limousines, EuroClass, hotels, car rentals, airline check-in at the hotel, hotel check-in at the airport, airport lounges, and the SAS 24-hour telephone hotline.

SAS reservation system

SAS was facing a rising number of reservation transactions: one million in 1980, and two million in 1983. This demand created the need for an integrated information system, and a network able to accept higher access without increasing the response time. To respond to this need, the company introduced a new reservation system in 1984. Developed at a cost of over Skr.250 million, the new system had more than 13 000 terminals around the world which were connected with SAS's centralized computing centre. The company believed that innovative and aggressive applications of computerized information and communication technology would decide which airlines would survive. The strategy was to ensure that SAS products found the shortest and least expensive access to the market, either directly or via travel agencies. Management believed that the company had to retain independence from credit card companies and the huge distribution systems of the major US airlines. By creating its own information and communication system to assure continued direct access to markets, SAS would have control of the complete purchase process.

Exhibit 8   Selected operating data for US CRS systems.

	Sabre (American)	Apollo (United)	System One (Texas Air)	Pars (TWA/NWA)	Datas II (Delta)
Terminals: USA	54 800	40 688	21 450	17 907	9 600
abroad	316	330	100	352	300
Subscriber locations	13 018	8 944	6 350	4 816	3 100
% total agency sales processed Jan–June 1986*	43	30.1	8.5	8.5	4.1
% US RPMs of airlines Jan–May 1987	14.136	17.124	19.212	17.766	12.317
1986 revenues[†]	$336m	$318m	. . .	. . .	. . .
1986 profits	$412m	. . .	. . .	. . .	. . .
Airline booking fees					
–basic	$1.75	$1.85	$1.75	$1.75	$1.50
–direct access	$2.00	$.185	$1.75	$1.75	$1.50
Direct access airlines as of July 1987	13	30	20	13	5
Current strengths	Size: depth of data: most	Size: depth of data	Aggressiveness	International pricing; large number installed in corporations; flexibility	

Notes:
* USA only, Sabre estimate;
[†] American is the only airline reporting publicly; Apollo estimate as published previously by the author and not disputed by the company;
. . . not available
Source: CRS vendors; *Travel Weekly*; *Aviation Daily*; author's estimates; *Travel and Tourism Analyst*.

Controversy over ticket distribution had increased in Europe and European carriers manoeuvered to protect their national markets. The threat of competition from the US systems and the danger of losing control of the distribution process forced Europe's major airlines to improve and update their computer reservation systems. (A summary of the major American systems can be found in Exhibit 8.) In 1987 SAS joined a computer reservation system (CRS) study group formed by Air France, Lufthansa, and Iberia. Later that year, the group announced its intention to develop one of the world's largest and most complete reservation and distribution systems. Known as AMADEUS, the system was expected to provide travel agencies with product and service information, reservation facilities for a worldwide array of airlines, hotels, car rentals, trains, ferries, and ticketing and fare quoting systems. Representing a total investment of US$270 million, the system was scheduled to be operational in mid-1989, and was expected to handle 150 million annual booking transactions. Finnair (Finland), Braathens SAFE (Norway), Air Inter and UTA (France) had joined the AMADEUS group by the end of 1987. A competing system, known as GALILEO, was also announced in 1987 grouping, among others, British Airways, KLM, Swissair, Alitalia, and Austrian Airlines.

Credit cards

In 1986, through the acquisition of Diners Club Nordic, SAS took over franchise rights in the Nordic countries for the Diners Club card, which had 150 000 card holders in Scandinavia, Finland, and Iceland. The annual sale of hotels and transport services was a multibillion kronor business in Scandinavia. SAS alone sold Skr.11 billion worth of airline tickets in Scandinavia during its 1984/1985 fiscal year. Credit card purchases accounted for 13 per cent of these sales, and the share was steadily rising. The credit card acquisition was seen as an important element in SAS's distribution strategy, being a practical tool for the business traveller.

SAS service partner (SSP)

SSP, an SAS subsidiary in the catering business, was expanded from 12 international airline flight kitchens to an enterprise with more than 7000 employees in over 100 locations. The subsidiary operated in 13 countries from the US to Japan, delivering 18 million airline meals a year. SSP was made up of a group of independent companies in airline catering and the international restaurant business. In 1984 SSP catered for more than 100 airlines, operated flight kitchens for several others, and ran airport restaurants in all three Scandinavian countries as well as in England and Ireland. It had a separate unit for its Saudi Arabian business, which was expected to have possibilities for growth in the Middle and Far East. In the early 1980s, Chicago had been chosen as the entry point in a planned expansion among US airports. Despite the cyclical nature of the airline business, the subsidiary had remained consistently profitable. SAS believed that more and more airlines would concentrate on operating aircrafts, and leave service industry tasks like catering to specialist companies. British Airways was an example, having handed over its short and medium haul catering at London's Heathrow airport to SSP.

Other related activities

SAS had also begun to offer a dedicated service to US magazine publishers wishing to distribute their products in Europe. The airline offered a fast freight and delivery service at a reasonable price through a single distribution system, and management believed this to be a growing market. This new activity allowed otherwise unused cargo capacity to be put to productive use.

The role of Vingresor, an SAS subsidiary since 1971 and Sweden's largest tour-operator, was also expanded considerably. All-inclusive tours on charter flights from Sweden and Norway remained the basic service offered. Additional service products such as Vingresor's resorts with hotels in Europe and Africa had been developed, as well as a travel programme including the Vingresor family concept.

New group structure

In March 1986 SAS was reorganized into five independent business units: the airline, SAS Service Partner, SAS International Hotels, SAS Leisure (Vingresor), and SAS Distribution (see Exhibit 9). The rationale was that each of these businesses faced very different strategic demands and, therefore, each was required to have its own management team to allow for more aggressive business development in an increasingly competitive climate. The same philosophy was pushed further down the line: for example, the new organization restructured the airline's route sectors into separate business units functioning as independent profit centres. The SAS group management, consisting of the chief executive officer, three executive officers and three executive vice-presidents representing Denmark, Norway, and Sweden, was expected to focus primarily on overall development of the SAS group's business areas.

It had been planned to introduce the new organization as early as 1984, but Carlzon had felt that the time was not ripe because the airline was involved in a public debate on air safety and there were problems with various trade union groups. 'Now, I fear we might have waited too long. It has become clear that the two jobs cannot be combined. The burdens of the day-to-day operation of the airline and work on the future development of it and other business units are simply too heavy,' he commented in 1986.

Exhibit 9   SAS group structure.

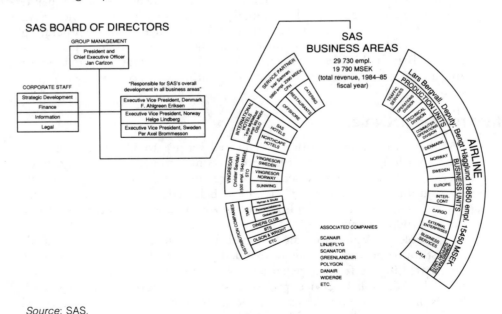

Source: SAS.

1988: FACING THE FUTURE

Looking ahead to the turn of the century, management of SAS was concerned about the future of the company. The globalization trend in the airline industry was gaining momentum, exemplified by the actions of giants like British Airways and American Airlines. BA had made it clear that it did not intend to stop growing after its acquisition of British Caledonian and the so-called 'marketing merger' with United Airlines, in which the two carriers agreed to co-ordinate flight schedules and marketing programmes, offer joint fares, and share terminals in four US cities. American Airlines was moving into Europe, having recently closed a leasing deal covering 40 new wide-body aircraft. 'Globalisation is inevitable,' commented Carlzon. 'Nobody will fly European unless we have a shake-out and become more efficient.' This underlined the threat of being relegated to a regional carrier, and SAS's need to unite with other airlines to create a 'Pan-European' system.

Aircraft replacement was another threat to SAS. The average age of its 60-strong DC-9 fleet (exclusive of the newer MD-80s) was 25 years, and an upcoming EEC directive on noise levels could, if put into effect in 1992, ground 30 aircraft. The required investment in new aircraft was estimated at Skr.40 billion over the next decade, which translated into one new plane per month from 1988 until the year 2000. This process of replacement had started, with the purchase of nine Boeing 767s for transatlantic traffic. To be able to finance these projects, the airline had to attain a gross profit level of 13% (before depreciation), compared to 11% in 1986. This increase was difficult to achieve in an increasingly competitive environment and one in which SAS had a cost disadvantage with respect to other airlines.

Partnerships or mergers with other airlines was clearly an attractive option, but the company had been frustrated in its attempts to develop such relationships. In the spring of 1987 SAS entered into negotiations with Sabena of Belgium with the goal of merging the operations of the two companies. Sabena was 52% state-owned and the Belgian government had expressed an interest in selling part of its holding to the private sector. With US$3.3 billion in sales, the merged carrier would have been Europe's fourth largest. Sabena chairman Carlos Van Rafelghem had stated that any accord with SAS would involve combining medium- and long-distance networks in a system based on hubs in Copenhagen and Brussels. The negotiations failed, however, mainly on the issue of the degree of integration. SAS wanted to include all of Sabena's operations, including hotels and catering, while the Belgian carrier was only interested in merging the airline systems.

In the fall of that same year, SAS launched a bid to acquire a major shareholding in British Caledonian Airways. SAS was eager to expand its traffic base and gain access to BCal's American, African, and Middle East destinations, and to the carrier's Gatwick Airport hub outside London. A battle for control with British Airways ensued, with BA emerging the winner, having paid £250 million, more than double the original bid. A major issue during the takeover battle was the implication of SAS gaining control of a British airline. The question of national control was important because of bilateral agreements. If Bcal were deemed to be non-British, the foreign partner in an agreement might revoke the airline's licences on routes to that country.

By the middle of 1988, it was clear to the corporate management of SAS that, while past actions had led to a sound base for the future, they were not sufficient by themselves to ensure long-term viability of the company. Within the rapidly changing environment, a new thrust was necessary, and had to be found without much delay.

SUGGESTED QUESTIONS

1. Between 1981 and 1986, SAS went through a dramatic and visible process of strategic change. How was this turnaround achieved? Why did it succeed? What can we learn from the process?
2. Why was the 'second wave' necessary? How do you feel about the direction SAS is following? Will the second round of change work? What might Carlzon do to make it work?
3. How do you evaluate the role played by Carlzon since 1981? What has he done well? With the benefit of hindsight, what might he have done differently? What lessons do you draw from the case about the roles and tasks of general managers in large worldwide companies?

21

Sportis: challenge and response in post-communist Poland

Case written by Max Boisot

SYSKY'S SOLILOQUY: PART I

Michael Sysky, Sales Manager of Sportis, chuckled to himself as his car reached the outskirts of Marki, 20 kilometers outside Warsaw, where his firm's headquarters were located. The journey to work had given him the time to savour the irony of the current situation at Sportis.

Here they were, a small private concern employing little over 300 people, barely one year after the Polish 'Big Bang' in which prices were freed up and the zloty devalued, facing the total collapse of their traditional domestic market. But what can Sportis do about it? Recognizing the need to develop its activities outside Poland in order to survive as a firm, in one bold leap Sportis enters the one major foreign market in which it knows it has a strong competitive advantage: not that of the US, Japan, or Western Europe, of course – what chance would a small Polish firm like Sportis stand there? – but that of Poland's former political master, the Soviet Union. By western standards Sportis may be lacking in funds and in know how, mused Sysky, but as this move shows, it certainly is not short on entrepreneurship.

Of course, Sysky acknowledged, westerners may have found it difficult to work with the Soviets – differences in culture as well as in economic philosophy were likely to cause problems. But, he believed, the Poles may have the necessary flexibility to succeed where westerners may not.

The 'people' problem, however, was by no means the end of it. The joint venture agreement which Sysky had signed on 2 March 1991 on behalf of Sportis had, as Soviet partners, the fishing company of **Murmanrybprom**, and a garment repair firm called **Silouhette**. Both were located in the city of Murmansk, some 200 miles north of the Arctic circle. The last time Sysky was in town, the temperatures were 45°C below zero.

There are so many barriers to entry against western competition, reflected the sales manager as he passed through the company gates. After all, which US, German, Japanese or British company in their right mind would brave this frozen desolation, the anachronistic caprices of 'old believers', and the now galloping entropy of the Soviet business system, in pursuit of a market which, if anything, was probably shrinking? Had not Gosplan just announced that domestic production had dropped by 11% last year and was it not common knowledge that in 'Sovietspeak' 11% really means 16% or more, making due allowance for the duplicity and ignorance of central planners?

However, as any Pole worth his vodka will tell you, a shrinking market is not bereft of profitable opportunities. It may not offer much sustenance to a Siemens or an IBM, but it is a square meal to a Polish firm of 300 people; a firm that is 'streetwise' in the Soviet Union and knows where to look. Like many Poles, Sysky felt he had got to know the Soviets – their way of thinking and their priorities – quite well. Geography had made the two countries neighbours and history had provided numerous opportunities to get acquainted – albeit not always happy ones.

Many Polish firms had come to realize that, in spite of the recent demise of Comecon and the Soviet's lack of hard currency, the Soviet market remained potentially a huge one for them (see Exhibit 1 for a brief example of another such firm) and, paradoxically, for the very reasons that made the market unattractive to western investors. Supplies there are scarce and consumers are therefore not too choosy about quality. Western standards of quality are a luxury well beyond their foreign exchange allowance and, more generally, their financial reach. Polish, Czeck, and Hungarian goods which would not be given shelf space in sophisticated western markets, are well received and often much sought after in the Soviet Union. For East European firms that have the patience and the flexibility, such a market could be theirs for the taking.

Sportis certainly had the patience and the flexibility needed, thought Sysky, but he wondered, under current circumstances, whether it had the stamina. As he drew up in front of his office, he could not help recalling that Sportis's remuneration for its minority participation in the Murmansk joint venture would be in fish – even dividend payments in the Soviet Union are made in the form of barter. 'How many clothing manufacturers in western countries, can list fish on the balance sheet as part of their current assets and still stay in business?' he asked himself.

SPORTIS: ORIGINS AND GROWTH

Life could be somewhat bleak for recently graduated young engineers in Poland in the late 1970s and early 1980s. Although they were required to

Exhibit 1   WZT.

Sportis forms part of the small firm sector in Poland which today accounts for approximately 18% of economic activity. Some light may be thrown on the prospects of this sector by a brief description of the situation faced by a larger firm in the state-owned sector.

WZT is a medium sized state-owned firm located about 15 kilometers from the centre of Warsaw and manufacturing televisions and professional recording equipment such as videocameras. The firm employs 5000 people and is currently being prepared for privatization in the second half of 1991.

The firm's sales and output figures for 1988—90 are as follows:

Year	Sales ($)	Output volume	Black and White TV Sets (%)
1988	52 million	379 000 TVs	70
1989	70 million	402 000 TVs	50
1990	96 million	370 000 TVs	20

WZT accounts for 50% of TV sets manufactured in Poland and currently has 30% of the domestic market. Its nearest competitor in Gdansk accounts for 30% of domestic production and 25% of the domestic market. Foreign competition, however, is increasing as western firms set up local production. One US/South Korean joint venture, Curtis International, is already producing 100 000 sets a year locally at prices that WZT cannot hope to match. Its productivity per employee is too low – about one-third that of Philips. The firm is clear that if it is to survive after privatization it has to find a foreign partner.

Joint venture discussions are currently under way with several prospective partners – Sharp, Sony, Hitachi, from Japan, and Siemens, Philips, and Thomson from Europe, as well as a Taiwanese firm – on the manufacture of video equipment and a new TV chassis. These prospective partners are all seeking to build up strong positions in a rapidly growing domestic market and to use Poland as a platform from which to launch into the Soviet Union. None of them are in Poland to exploit low labour costs. WZT has maintained its links with its former Russian trading partners and is in the process of setting up a distribution network with private distributors in the western part of the Soviet Union. The firm, however, faces the same problems as western firms in the Soviet Union: how to get paid.

WZT perceives its main attraction to prospective joint venture partners to be its technically qualified staff and the domestic distribution network it is in the process of building up. Eighteen months ago, the firm thought of itself primarily as a manufacturer and owned just two retail outlets in Warsaw. It now owns eight retail outlets directly and has signed up distribution agreements with another 70 throughout the country.

Given its current product range and its technical base, the firm does not feel able to target western markets yet. If anything, the share of its output that is exported has been declining – 12% of output in 1989, 7% in 1990. Discussions with prospective joint venture partners have also made it clear that the kind of technologies that would allow WZT to be more export-competitive are not on offer.

In preparation for its privatization, the firm's top management has been changed. The old Nomenklatura appointees have been replaced by younger managers – the new managing director, for example, is 33 years old and has no line management experience – although qualified people are not easy to find. This is hardly surprising when it is realized that an experienced research engineer is paid US$300 a month by WZT – less than half of what he can earn at Sharp's or in the blossoming private sector.

work for a state-owned enterprise for a minimum of three years as a condition for studying at all, they knew, upon entering their respective firms, that unless they were prepared to sign up with the party and then bind themselves tightly to the **nomenklatura**, they were headed for nowhere as fast as their talents would carry them there. To preserve their sanity and that minimum level of motivation that imparts meaning to life, many resorted to moonlighting in those many eddies of the command economy that the state plan majestically sails by. Others, less concerned with job security, simply took time off.

So it was with Thomas Holc, a recent graduate in electrical engineering, who at the age of 20 was spending most of his time sailing and generally messing about in boats instead of crouching over a drawing board, as he should have been doing, designing lighting equipment for an obscure state engineering company. During his stolen leisure hours – and of these, at least, there was no shortage – Holc developed a great many contacts in the world of sailing and gained some insight into its functioning. He resolved that, when he was released from his current servitude, he would put this clandestine experience to some profitable and, hopefully, enjoyable use.

Although Poland at the beginning of the decade did not offer a particularly hospitable environment for such heretical entrepreneurial thoughts – martial law was only a few months away and the economy, weighed down with external debts, was taking one of its periodic nosedives – there were signs of a new attitude towards private business by the authorities, albeit one forced upon them by the dire circumstances that they then confronted. As far back as 1976 legislation had been passed encouraging the creation of private business in Poland by 'foreigners' of Polish origin. Thomas Holc had a brother, Andrew Holc, living in London, who would be willing to 'front' for him should he decide to try something in this new climate. In 1980, therefore, Holc started collecting market data on a casual basis as well as investigating manufacturing processes. He did not have much money to invest at the time, but after seeing other budding entrepreneurs taking a chance and subsequently succeeding, he decided to have a try with an initial investment of 1 000 000 zlotys and £1000 sterling. Sportis was created in 1983.

Shortly after the firm's creation, Holc came across an old ruin in the small village of Serock some 30 kilometers outside Warsaw, not far from a lake on which he used to sail. The local authority was willing to let him have the ruin for a nominal rent of two US dollars a month on condition that he restored it to its earlier condition. Once renovated, it was to be Sportis's first production facility.

Holc had originally intended to manufacture sails and life jackets there, primarily for exports, but he was thwarted in this strategy by small Far Eastern producers, located mainly in Hong Kong, who were able to sell a finished product on the world markets for a lower price than he would pay for his inputs in Poland – courtesy of the state pricing system. Yet, since the renovation of his new building was now nearing completion, and local staff had already been recruited and were being trained, Holc felt under pressure to get going with something, even if that something was not quite along the lines he had initially envisaged. Was not the ability to adapt, after all, the essence of entrepreneurship? Thus it was that for the first nine months of its existence Sportis found itself in the business of making trousers.

Gradually, however, the firm was able to shift to the manufacture of life jackets as originally planned, but for the domestic rather than the export market. Its product range consisted of fairly basic designs, mostly copied from catalogues, whose colours and shapes were slightly modified to suit the requirements of the Polish market. The Polish navy turned out to be an important customer for these life jackets, but the firm soon branched out into new product areas such as windproof clothing, tracksuits, and windcheaters.

Although Sportis was directly in touch with some end users such as the country's sea rescue services – 70% of its sales at the time were in lifejackets – the bulk of its clients were state distributors such as Interster, Stoteczne Przedsiebiurstwo Handlv, Wewnetrzengo, and Handlomor, or state-owned or funded sports clubs acting as distributors. Having little or no direct contact with the market, the firm was unwilling to anticipate market demands and hence to invest in producing for stock. It would therefore only manufacture to order. Given the nature of the Polish economic environment, this turned out to be not such a bad strategy: the firm has been growing every year since outset.

This growth creates its own problems. In a political system committed to the public ownership of the means of production, whatever private sector exists – and in Poland at the time it did not exceed 5% of economic activity – does so because it is tolerated rather than encouraged. Consequently, not only did Sportis, during those years, receive no support whatever from state or local government – apart from the ruin it was offered in Serock – but its growth actually had to be covert if it was not to attract the disapproving gaze of the authorities. The Polish communist party continued to view the private sector – particularly that segment of it that could boast foreign connections – as a breeding ground for spies and a hotbed of capitalist corruption, and for that reason severely constrained its growth. The Warsaw city authorities were responsible for granting Sportis its production licence and would only do so if it was prepared to limit the size of its establishment to 60 employees and get its products approved. The firm, however, in line with current practice elsewhere, would be allowed to take on part-timers beyond its full-time staffing allocation, a concession which allowed it to share some staff with another firm, Christine, created almost at the same time as Sportis itself and owned by Thomas Holc's British wife. Christine was a manufacturer of women's clothes and it employed production processes not very different to those of Sportis and on a similar scale. There was clearly some scope for synergy between the two firms.

Continued growth and opportunities to diversify into survival suits and inflatable rescue boats led Sportis in 1989 to create a wholly owned subsidiary in the hamlet of Bojano, some 15 kilometers outside Gdansk and three hours by train from Warsaw. Production facilities are located in an extension of an old chicken hut and are reached by a dirt track. Ludwig Vogt, the director of the subsidiary and the inspiration behind it, had been a captain in the merchant navy and had spent time working in a testing station for sea rescue equipment. He had had dealings with Sportis for a number of years when acting as an adviser to the firm's clients and was recruited by Sportis largely on account of his detailed knowledge of customer requirements with respect to the products that the Bojano factory would be producing.

The choice of Gdansk as a location was strongly influenced by the fact that expansion could no longer be sensibly accommodated on the Serock site and that labour practices and attitudes in the Gdansk region seemed to be more flexible than around Warsaw. Another influencing factor was that Ludwig Vogt lived in Gdansk.

SPORTIS: CURRENT PERFORMANCE

Sportis today finds itself in a radically different economic environment to that which confronted it nearly a decade ago. The opportunities discernible on the horizon for many Polish firms following the collapse of the communist order, are now counterbalanced by a number of looming threats. The fog of confusion that currently shrouds the country's real economic performance is undermining the fragile consensus so necessary for the difficult policy decisions that lie ahead. Indeed, even western counsels are divided on the matter of how well the country is doing and where it is headed for. Inflation, at 5% a month, has improved greatly since 1990 but with the zloty now pegged to the dollar, it remains a major headache for firms which, having to turn outward towards exports, are caught in a vicious cost squeeze.

Official figures on the Polish economy may make grim reading – industrial production, it is claimed, fell by a third in 1990 – but how reliable are they? Official statistics are designed to measure the state economy. Private industry is for the most part ignored. In a communist system in which the private sector was largely made up of Marx's 'petty commodity traders' and never allowed to exceed more than 5% of national output, such neglect was understandable and probably not particularly harmful. Yet the Polish government's statistical office believes that the output of private industry (excluding farming) grew by over 50% in 1990 and now accounts for 18% of national income, up from 11% in 1989. And in the latter year, the government's statisticians estimate, the number of people employed in private enterprise grew by more than 500 000, bringing the total to 1.8–2 million people. These figures merely confirm what casual empiricism thrusts before the gaze of all foreign visitors to the country today: every Polish town now has its street markets where everything from imported toothpaste to once unavailable

Polish ham can be bought; the area around Warsaw's palace of culture, for example, has been transformed into a vast oriental souk. Queues in post-communist Poland have virtually disappeared.

Yet if many of these mushrooming small private firms are doing well it is because they have positioned themselves at the consumer end of what was an archaic state distribution system and have been able to respond as nimble traders do everywhere to pent up consumer needs. Sportis as a production organization, by contrast, is placed upstream of the state distributors on which it has relied for a regular flow of orders as well as detailed feedback on what end users of its products required in terms of quality and performance.

The state distribution system on which Sportis was so dependent has now collapsed and it is of no consolation to the firm that its main state-owned competitor has collapsed along with it. Sportis is in the paradoxical position of being the sole domestic producer – indeed, with only modest imports in these products the firm has virtually a monopoly – in a market to which it currently has almost no access.

Sportis confronts this situation with no marketing organization to speak of. Michael Sysky, the Sales Manager, joined Sportis in 1985 but, until very recently, he was the only person in the organization involved in the selling function. As Sysky explains, marketing as such was never needed under the old system. The firm produced to order and luckily there were always orders in the distributor's pipeline. Exactly where the pipeline led to had never much bothered anyone.

To build up its marketing capacity, Sportis has now recruited a sales-man who reports to Ludwig Vogt in Bojano and whose job it is to contact retailers directly. This is proving more difficult than expected: retailers are hard to identify and in the current economic climate as many are going out of business as are opening up. A further complication lies in trying to assess the current level of demand for Sportis products given the income levels that prevail in Poland at present (for one measure of Polish income see Exhibit 2). Per capita income continues to decline, but no one seems to be able to say at exactly what rate. The traditional users of the firm's main products are all facing hard times – deep sea fishing firms in Poland are now selling off a large part of their fleets and many face bankruptcy – but with the reforms new market segments are also making their appearance, especially in the field of leisure.

Given the overall gloomy outlook, sales and profit levels at Sportis may offer some surprises. On paper, at least, it does not seem to be doing as badly as its domestic circumstances would suggest (see Exhibit 3). There are two explanations for this.

The first is that in the last year Thomas Holc has reoriented Sportis towards external markets as originally intended (Exhibit 3 shows the firm's foreign currency earnings). In addition to a growing Soviet business, the firm has started manufacturing under contract for Compass, a Swedish firm producing vest and life jackets for sailors. In 1990 Compass, facing rising labour costs at home, relocated its production in the

Exhibit 2   Post-communist poverty.

Economists have been quarrelling for years about how poor the Soviet Union and Eastern Europe really are. The following chart shows new estimates by PlanEcon, a consultancy and authoritative communist-watcher based in Washington, DC.

To calculate incomes per head and GNP in dollar terms, an exchange rate has to be applied to local-currency figures (which are themselves pretty unreliable). Some estimates use the exchange rates available to businesses. This is unsatisfactory. The region's assorted economic policies mean that commercial exchange rates are volatile and distorted. Exchange rates based on purchasing-power parity are better; these compare incomes in terms of the goods that people buy with some allowance for quality. This is the measure used by PlanEcon.

The Soviet Union's GNP for 1990 comes out at roughly $1.5 trillion, giving a GNP per head of about $5000. Soviet incomes vary widely by republic: from $6740 in Latvia, $6240 in Estonia, $5960 in Belorussia, and $5880 in Lithuania to $2750 in Uzbekistan and $2340 in Tadzhikistan (all these figures are for 1989). Poland, Eastern Europe's boldest reformer, is one of its poorest, with an income per head of just $3910. In the region, only Romania and Albania are worse off.

The Economist, 12 January 1991

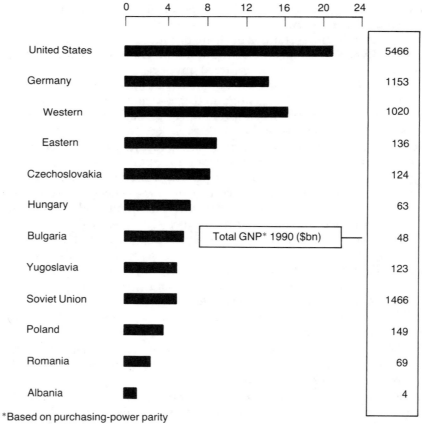

GNP* PER HEAD, 1990 ($ thousands)

	Total GNP* 1990 ($bn)
United States	5466
Germany	1153
Western	1020
Eastern	136
Czechoslovakia	124
Hungary	63
Bulgaria	48
Yugoslavia	123
Soviet Union	1466
Poland	149
Romania	69
Albania	4

*Based on purchasing-power parity
Source: Plan Econ.

Exhibit 3   Sportis: sales figures, 1986–90.*

1986	1987	1988	1989	1990	
278.300.030	162.579.541	348.879.482	1.053.822.169	10.650.296.550	Total sales (zloty)
278.118.067	144.552.311	326.502.545	1.004.546.738	3.897.554.145	Domestic sales
181.963	18.027.230	22.376.937	49.275.431	6.752.742.405	Exports
	USD 21.784,83	GBP 8.321,70	GBP 6.867	GBP 4.168,70	
	NLG 14,476	DEM 480		USD 46.993,60	
	DKK 6.119,62	SEG 75.258	Skr. 113.200	Skr. 20.000	
				DKK 121.536	
				RBL 2.783.955	
	295.081.970	275.739.020	309.431.480		

*This is a direct transcription from the document supplied by the Sportis bookkeeper and is a fair representation of Holc's information base.

Bojano plant and just held on to the design and marketing function. Bojano now produces between 120 000 and 150 000 pieces a year for its new Swedish client.

Sportis is also manufacturing under contract for Musto Ltd of Benfleet, in Essex (UK). Keith Musto, the owner, is an old friend of Thomas Holc from their sailing days. His firm, like Compass, specializes in protective clothing for sailors. He had originally intended to subcontract production operations to a Hong Kong firm but found the geographical distance too great for effective co-ordination. He then approached Sportis with a trial order, supplying it with both the designs and the raw materials. The firm now carries out six months worth of production for Musto each year and a joint venture between the two firms is currently under discussion. Both sides remain cautious on this matter, however, for they agree that Sportis is not yet sufficiently cost effective to be a viable joint venture partner.

A second possible reason why the sales and profit figures look so good is that the firm has no accounting system to accurately track and describe its present or past financial performance. Small private businesses in Poland were required to adopt the same socialist bookkeeping and accounting procedures as the larger state-owned enterprises. True to communist doctrine, the emphasis was on what was produced rather than on what was sold, and performance was judged on the value of outputs rather than the value of sales. In state-owned enterprises, of course, whether the firm made a profit or not was of no great account since any losses were usually made up by state subsidies. Furthermore, the financial data collected was placed at the service of the supervising authorities located externally rather than within the enterprises themselves, with the result that few firms knew how to convert a morass of bookkeeping data into usable accounting information that could help with managerial decision making.

Thomas Holc made a clear distinction between the figures that he used for external reporting – which usually showed either a loss or a small profit – and those that described the 'real' business which he kept in his head. In the past, the supervisory authorities had required two quite

Exhibit 4 Sportis: staffing levels.

	Numbers
Location: Serock	
Production (direct)	39
Production (indirect)	9
Administration	8
Total	56
Location: Bojano	
Production (direct)	85
Production (indirect)	4
Administration	15
Total	104

Note: Some Administrative staff work for both Sportis and Christine.

distinct sets of books: one for the tax office and one for the state statistical office. Holc had little faith in the relevance of either set of data. Yet the figures that Holc kept in his head and which he used for the day-to-day running of the business, as he himself acknowledges, were often themselves only tenuously related to its performance. Like most Polish managers brought up under the old system, he was unfamiliar with the managerial use of balance sheets, income statements, and flow of funds statements. These were documents that the firm produced – after a fashion – but it did so only for the tax office. They were never used internally. To keep track of his business Holc made use of productivity data in the raw form in which it was collected by Sportis's bookkeeper: measures of the productivity of different work teams; measures of time use by the staff; measures of direct and indirect costs; data on value added; summary data on monthly production; and so on.

Sportis's bookkeeper was trained in socialist bookkeeping methods. Holc would not describe her as an accountant in the western sense; he perceived her role primarily in terms of external reporting. She played a key role within the firm since only she was in a position to follow and interpret the myriad changes in financial regulations that affected it. She was happy to make bookkeeping data available to the Sportis managers but only on a request basis and usually only in the form in which it was collected. Indeed, who in the firm would know how to specify an alternative form? The result was that no one in Sportis was in a position to build up an overall picture of the firm's financial performance. Holc is well aware of the problems this could pose. A short while back, his wife's company, Christine, found itself in some difficulty when it turned out it had been running at a loss instead of making a profit as was believed.

He also knows that to get the firm's productivity up to competitive levels he must quickly establish a better control of costs. Until recently, this hardly seemed necessary. Inputs, including labour, were cheap, and were of an acceptable quality for the domestic market. Unrelenting inflation and the urgent need to find new markets abroad have changed all that. The point was driven home when Sportis was visited by the US firm Levi's, which was seeking out potential Polish subcontractors. In the course of discussions, it was discovered that, while it took Sportis 30 minutes to produce a pair of denims, the US firm could produce them in six-and-half minutes. 'They thought that they would make us feel better by telling us not to be too despondent since, after all, it had taken Levi's a hundred years to reach such a level of productivity,' commented Sysky ruefully.

The absence of an effective accounting system poses a more subtle challenge to Sportis than simply improving current productivity levels. With the company's growth and diversification – it is currently preparing to move into the production of oil booms based on the technology it is using for inflatable rescue boats – Holc increasingly feels the need to decentralize some management decisions. Some first steps have been taken. The sharing of staff with Christine – bookkeeper, sales manager, production manager, deliveries, purchasing, and administrative staff, and not least, Thomas Holc himself – was coming to an end. Sportis would maintain its head offices on Christine's production site at Marki but from now on the two firms would be run on an 'arm's length' basis. (Exhibit 4 gives Sportis's staffing levels). At the same time, Holc was preparing to delegate day-to-day responsibility for operations in Bojano to Ludwig Vogt. Major investments and decisions on product policy would remain with Holc but the rest would soon be handed over to Vogt.

Yet since Sportis had no planning or budgeting system to speak of, and since most of the knowledge required to manage the firm remained locked in Holc's head, he wondered how the decentralization would work out in practice.

SPORTIS: STRATEGIC AND ORGANIZATION ISSUES

Given the new opportunities and challenges that it faces, how does Sportis see the future? Perhaps it would be more relevant to ask how Thomas Holc sees the future since he is the classic owner-manager and for the time being takes all the strategic decisions himself (Sportis is legally a 'single-owner firm' and is not required by law to have a board of directors). Holc as Chief Executive nevertheless works closely with the Sales Manager (Sysky), the head of the Bojano operations (Vogt), and the bookkeeper, but he does so on a purely informal basis.

'Sportis is what westerners call a niche player,' comments Holc, 'producing differentiated products for a specialized market. I would like to see Sportis expand but not by switching to mass production techniques. This would bring about more changes than I could currently handle: a move towards automation and capital intensive production, greater investments in machinery and stocks, and, of course, bank loans. The current rate of interest on zloty loans is over 80%. Who needs it? I am not seeking the quiet life, but I don't want to die young either. Except for a small part of our production sold directly to retailers – about 10–15% of our total sales – we shall go on manufacturing to order'.

Holc recognizes that such an expansion strategy is not without its problems. The domestic market offers uncertain – although by no means negligible – prospects and while Sportis considers itself the most competitive (because it is the only) domestic producer, a number of the new distributors in its product markets are turning to imports rather than sourcing domestically.

The Soviet market which Sportis began to investigate a year ago is also full of pitfalls. 'Many Polish firms were spoilt in their dealing with the Soviet Union,' observes Sysky, 'In the days of the centrally planned economy, selling to the Russians was a picnic. Everything was routed through a few large state trading organizations and all that a Polish manager had to do was to drop in and pick up his cheque. It was all routine. Today there are no more cheques. The main challenge is to find a customer who can pay you – in Vodka, Russian bears, or black market submarines, anything at all, in fact, but roubles. Unsurprisingly there is a lot of corruption about. Over there at present, it's everyone for himself'.

'To do business with the Soviets,' Sysky continued, 'it is essential to build up mutual trust. Too many problems, both large and small, have to be overcome for people to trust a complete stranger. Take, for example, our new joint venture with Murmanrybprom: we drew up a legal agreement with them. Yet we know and they know many issues will arise that could not be anticipated by the agreement, and that once the joint venture has been officially registered – any day now – our dealings with each other will be guided entirely by the quality of our personal relationship'.

'In spite of such difficulties,' Sysky then added, 'the Soviet market remains a potentially attractive one for Sportis given the fragility of the domestic one. An added consideration is that western competitors are now showing their faces in the Polish market and this can only reduce the viability of small domestic producers working on their own'.

'Given the Soviet Union's current problems, westerners are unlikely to show up there quite yet, thank God, and since Soviet customers are generally still quite undemanding – we are to them what the West has always been for us: an Eldorado that we can only dream about – our price/quality offering remains quite acceptable to them.'

Did internationalization mean anything more for the firm than the Soviet Union or manufacturing subcontracts? Apparently not. Neither Holc nor Sysky felt that Sportis would be in any position to move into western markets for a long while yet. According to Holc:

> To enter western markets – many of them already saturated – with simple products like ours, would require greater marketing and organizational capacity than we currently dispose of. We would be dealing with new market segments sensitive to branding and fashion trends, and we currently lack the design capacity to respond.
>
> We might stand a better chance in the more industrial markets for protective wear and inflatables, where branding plays less of a role,

but there we often meet protectionism disguised as mandatory technical standards. Sportis manufactures these products to established international standards, but many countries such as the US, Great Britain, and Germany, still insist on local retesting, greatly adding to our product costs and hurting our competitiveness.

Given its current lack of competitiveness in western markets, the subcontracting work that Sportis was currently undertaking for Compass and Musto was considered something of a sideline activity and not central to the firm's future business. Holc explained:

Compass closed down its Swedish operations on account of labour problems such as recurring absenteeism and high social security costs. It transferred both its production and equipment to the Bojano site. But the firm really only sees us as a way of keeping down its labour costs. It does not appear willing to involve us in the higher value added parts of its operation. We remain a source of low cost inputs.

'In fact, not that low cost,' Holc continued, 'If our wage rates are low then so is our productivity. For this reason it is still unclear that the joint venture that we are currently discussing with Musto in the UK will prove profitable for either party'.

Improving productivity remains the firm's major headache. It is caught in a major cost squeeze which it is finding hard to analyse and to deal with. Direct costs went up by 250% in the first 11 months of 1990 but productivity failed to increase at all. Worse, the local authority that leased Sportis the Serock site for a 10 year period now wants to increase the rent from US$2 a month to US$2000 a month – and this 18 months before the rental agreement is due to expire. But with the zloty exchange rate now pegged to the dollar, none of these increases in operating costs can be passed on to the firm's foreign customers.

SYSKY'S SOLILOQUY: PART II

As he entered his car for the journey home at the end of the day, Michael Sysky sighed audibly. His thoughts returned once more to the Russian joint venture that he had negotiated.

Was this an advance or a retreat for Sportis?

From one perspective the firm was exploiting a competitive advantage by 'working with the devil it knew'. But for what benefit? Western and Japanese firms were not exactly queuing up to get into the Soviet Union and it was obvious why: earning an honest rouble, or preferably an honest dollar, there was proving to be more trouble than it was worth. Sysky had heard that these same firms also had their fingers burnt in China and for much the same reasons. Yet it seemed that South China was now overrun by small, nimble-footed entrepreneurs from Hong

Kong, all discreetly making money in out of the way places, mostly beyond the reach of the Chinese bureaucracy. Could not the Murmansk operation be of the latter kind?

From another perspective, however, the move east for Sportis could be viewed as an escape from the new challenge from the west. The firm did not feel that it could be competitive in western markets – indeed, it was not even sure how much of its domestic market it would be able to hold on to if foreign competition hotted up there.

To become truly competitive in western markets, mused Sysky, Sportis would need to undergo a cultural transformation. People would have to pull together and co-operate with each other to an extent until now unknown in Polish firms. At present everyone just attends to his own job in the organization – perhaps a consequence of paying people on piece rate – and teamwork is virtually non existent. 'We must be operating at least 40% below our existing productive potential because of poor work discipline and other work-related problems,' he muttered to himself as he drove off. Things would be hard to change without making the management more professional. But how were they going to do that? Polish managers are all like Christine's recently departed production manager; if they are good enough to run your organization, then they are also good enough to run from it and to start their own, and that is exactly what they will do. No amount of bribery or blandishments will keep them loyal once they get an entrepreneurial twinkle in their eye.

Sysky wondered about the changes that Sportis would have to make to its organization in order to attract and retain the right people. Would Thomas Holc, the final arbiter of the firm's fate, be prepared to swallow them? Would Sysky himself be prepared to?

SUGGESTED QUESTIONS

1. What is the most likely motivation of a state owned firm in seeking a foreign partner? How is it likely to differ from that of a small private firm?
2. Would a foreign investor seeking access to the Polish market do best tying up with a state owned firm or a private one or neither? What about investors looking for cheap inputs?
3. Is a small private firm in a planned economy 'entrepreneurial' in the same way as in a market economy? How would Sportis differ from a larger state owned firm supplying the same domestic market?
4. Has Sportis correctly perceived its prospects in the West and in the former Soviet Union? What does the firm's international strategy tell us about its internal culture?
5. What modifications to Sportis's system of governance would a formalization of its management style bring about? What changes to the firm's structure might it entail? How would Holc's personal position be affected?

22

Storehouse plc (A)

Case written by John Hendry

When the boards of British Home Stores and Habitat–Mothercare had announced the terms of an agreed merger in November 1985, City opinion had been divided. British Home Stores was a stable, cash–rich business with an excellent network of UK retail outlets, but was suffering from slow growth and image problems. Terence Conran's Habitat–Mothercare group were leaders in store and product design with a fast-expanding worldwide retail presence, hungry for further growth but short of cash to fund it. According to some commentators, and according to the companies themselves, the merger represented a fusion of complementary strengths, from which both companies could only benefit. Others, however, were inclined to see it more in terms of Conran's hunger for power and British Home Stores' fear of a hostile takeover bid following the recent acrimonious takeover of retailers Debenhams by the Burton Group. They questioned both the logic of the merger and its prospects for success, given the very different approaches and cultures of the two companies.

The big question for observers of Storehouse (the name given to the new holding company) was whether Conran's team could do anything about BHS's lacklustre performance. In the summer of 1986, presenting the first annual report of the new combine, Conran himself reassured them: 'Give us a couple of years,' he said, 'and you'll see the best family store in the High Street.' A year later, with no sign yet of any significant progress, takeover rumours began to mount. A property company, Mountleigh, declared its intention of bidding for Storehouse with a view to breaking it up into its constituent parts, and although this was never followed through it did prompt a highly leveraged break-up bid from Benlox, a small engineering company about one-fortieth the size of Storehouse itself. This bid was eventually rejected by Storehouse share-

This case was prepared by John Hendry as the basis for class discussion rather than to illustrate either effective or ineffective handling of an administrative situation.

holders, but the company was effectively on trial. By the summer of 1988, with Conran's 'couple of years' expired, the benefits were still not showing through. Moreover, the Habitat–Mothercare side itself seemed to have caught the stagnation bug. A year later, and profits throughout the group were declining dramatically. Conran and his new Chief Executive, Michael Julien, remained convinced that Storehouse could and would be a success. But time was running out if they were to prove it.

THE CONRAN STORY

Terence Conran was born in 1931. As a schoolboy at Bryanston he was attracted to both art and technology, and wanted for a while to be a gunsmith. Discovering that this required a 10-year apprenticeship, he went instead to a central London art college to study textile design. Even this took too long for the young Terence, however, and he left after just 18 months. Over the next couple of years he worked on a magazine for the Rayon Industry, in the interior design practice of Dennis Lennon, and on window displays for Simpsons of Piccadilly. Meanwhile he had also started to design modern furniture, sharing a studio with the sculptor Eduardo Paolozzi, and having made some furniture for Simpsons he was given a small display area in the store. In 1953 he set up business as Conran & Co and published a furniture catalogue, but not for the last time in his life he found his ambitions frustrated by a lack of capital needed for premises and machinery.

Talking about his problems with his landlord, Ian Storey, they decided that the quickest way to make money was to start up restaurants. Conran came up with a design concept, and they soon opened the first of a chain of Soup Kitchens. With pine-clad walls, cane furniture, and ceramic tiled table tops, these served good but very simple, and cheap, food: soup, bread, coffee, cheese, apple pie. They appealed to the new youth culture of the rock 'n' roll age and were a great success, and when Storey wanted to progress to more elaborate menus and restaurants, Conran sold out his share of the business for a small capital gain.

By 1960 Conran was employing 12 people, with two small factories, but he was not making much money, and was still short of capital. This time it was London Transport who came to his rescue, by compulsorily purchasing one of his properties and so starting a chain of developments which ended with the whole business moving to Thetford in Norfolk. Profits from London property sales enabled Conran to launch a proper range of domestic furniture. By 1963 this was selling in 200 shops, including the John Lewis chain, but Conran was far from satisfied. Looking at the shops he was depressed by the quality of the displays and the fact that there only ever appeared to be any customers on Saturday mornings. While working with Mary Quant on the design of her own new shop, he caught the retail bug himself, and in 1964 he opened the first Habitat (the name was chosen for the combination of its sound, its meaning, and its international applicability), next to the Michelin building in London's Fulham Road. In order to overcome the bleakness of most furniture departments, the furniture was displayed along with other merchandise such as lighting, textiles, and kitchen ware. The whole store was bright, cheerful, and young: like Mary Quant and Biba, a landmark of the swinging sixties.

HABITAT

Further Habitats followed, but not quickly enough for Conran, who once again found himself short of capital. In 1967 he discussed the possibility of going into a joint venture with the Reed Paper group, but this fell through, and on the rebound – or so it seemed later – he agreed to a full merger with the office equipment retailers Ryman. In terms of turnover and profits the two companies were comparable. Conran was by then turning over £3.4 million with profits of about £0.4 million, while Ryman's figures were £4 million and £0.6 million respectively. But Ryman had by far the stronger asset base, and Conran ended up with just 20% of the merged company.

The logic of the merger was simple. Ryman, a well established but rather dowdy public company, wanted Conran's design flair and the benefit of Habitat's trendy image. Conran for his part was interested in Ryman's cash resources and extensive network of retail outlets. When it came to implementing the merger, however, it quickly became clear that for Conran at least it had been thoroughly ill-conceived. Whereas Conran's organization was informal and people-oriented (Conran himself was known and addressed by everyone as Terence, as indeed he still is), the Ryman organization was a paternalistic bureaucracy. The senior Conran staff found that they simply could not work within this organization, and many soon left. The influence of the Conran company suffered, and while Ryman continued to expand its own retail operation, Habitat continued to be starved of investment funds. In 1969 Ryman acquired a mail order firm, Lupton Morton, and the following year it bought another retail chain, Straker Bedser, both of which were themselves short of capital. By 1970 the total turnover of the company had doubled since the merger, but Habitat had not expanded. In desperation Conran offered to buy it back, and his offer was accepted.

The new Habitat company comprised the seven existing Habitat stores, Conran's design company Conran Associates, and the foundation of a mail order operation based on Lupton Morton. The Thetford factory, comprising a large part of the original Conran operation, continued to manufacture for Habitat but was retained by Ryman, in which Conran himself remained a major shareholder. At the time of the sale Habitat had not been highly valued by Ryman, who apparently thought it was making a loss. But when the group accounts were fully untangled it became clear that it was in fact trading quite profitably, and that Conran had got a good bargain. Without the manufacturing side he now had a thriving design and retail business, with sufficient assets to secure funds for further growth. When shortly afterwards Ryman was aquired by the Burton Group, Conran was able to realize his shareholding for £1.5 million.

For the next 10 years Habitat expanded steadily until by 1981 it had a turnover of £66 million and profits of £4.8 million. Besides a growing chain of UK stores it also had outlets in France and in the US (where it traded as Conran's), which between them contributed over 40% of the company's turnover. Growth had not been without its problems, especially as regards the overseas operations. The US business, begun in 1977, was still not showing a profit. But the company was confident that the problems of adapting to the American marketplace could be overcome and that the basic Habitat philosophy of supplying well-designed, reasonably priced goods in a pleasant and well-designed shopping environment could be applied worldwide. In order to finance the further expansion this implied, Conran decided to go public and in October 1981 he launched the company on the Stock Exchange. Just two months later, in December 1981, Habitat announced an agreed merger – in fact a reverse takeover of Mothercare, a public company with twice its own market capitalization.

THE MOTHERCARE ACQUISITION

Mothercare had been created in 1961 by Selim Zilkha, a Syrian businessman with American nationality. The basic concept was that of a retail outlet dedicated specifically to the needs of mothers and babies, as well as mothers-to-be: 'everything for the mother to be and her baby and children under 5'. It was a runaway success. Concentration on the niche market gave Mothercare buying power and high margins – up to 17% in the mid-1970s. In 1972 the company went public, and by the middle of the decade there were about 200 Mothercare shops in the UK, all bright, clean, efficient, and profitable, and the company was beginning to move into Europe and the US. But neither overseas operation was particularly successful, and while the company could cut its losses on European shops, which were acquired gradually and could be disposed of if unsuccessful, the American operation posed greater problems.

Hoping to repeat its UK success on a larger scale, Mothercare had in 1976 taken over an existing, loss-making chain of 110 maternity stores in the US. By 1981 it had added a further 90 stores. But the whole operation was still trading at a loss, with little prospect of a turnaround, and in the six months to September 1981 losses exceeded £1 million. The original stores were very small, with an average floor area of just 600 square feet, and with a property boom in America forcing prices up, the larger sites acquired since 1976 were not in ideal locations. The 200 stores were spread right across the US, making the centralized control on which Mothercare's UK efficiency had been built virtually impossible. And the American maternity market was much more highly developed than that in the UK. Items like pushchairs, which accounted for a large slice of UK profits, offered minimal margins, while maternity and especially infant wear were a part of the fashion industry. Mothercare had built up its UK business on the basis of simple, functional wear, and was completely ill-equipped to compete in a fashion market where product lifecycles were of the order of months rather than years.

Meanwhile, the late 1970s had also seen an end to the company's growth in the UK. In 1981 Mothercare UK was still a successful and profitable business, but market share was declining as chains like Marks & Spencer, Boots, C&A, British Home Stores, and Littlewoods began to take the nursery market seriously. The birth rate was also declining, and so were the profits. Profits for the year to March 1981 were 8% down on the previous year, and the half-year to September saw a further decline. Within a year the share price halved. With changing tastes and fashions the orange and white shops were beginning to look tacky, and the infant and maternity wear cheap and common: a market survey conducted after the merger with Habitat revealed that Mothercare clothes were perceived as 'slimy nylon'.

Zilkha's response to these problems appears to have been the decision to retire from the fray and hand over to someone else: 'I have been doing it for twenty years,' he said, 'I felt that we needed a breath of fresh air.' He also wanted to spend more time on his other business concerns in America. And rather than promote his number two, Barney Goodman, or recruit an outsider, he decided to cash in the bulk of his shareholding and hand over the reins to Terence Conran. Conran accepted and, although the Habitat share price dropped like a stone on the news, falling 25% in a month, the merger duly went ahead.

From Zilkha's viewpoint there were some very good reasons for the merger, not the least of which were his own respect for Conran and the similarity of the Mothercare and Habitat concepts and operations. The styles of the two leaders were very different, Terence Conran's relaxed informality contrasting with Selim Zilkha's autocratic formality. But beneath that style, both were autocrats in their way, and both were entrepreneurs, with worldwide ambitions. Defending his choice of Conran, Zilkha emphasized their shared view of the future: 'We have the whole world still to conquer.' Both men kept a close eye on all aspects of their businesses, vetting and often influencing individual product designs, and specifying detailed operational and systems requirements.

The two companies also had much in common. Both were designer–retailers, selling only their own brand of goods but commissioning their manufacture from independent suppliers. Both based their success upon unique retailing concepts, each of which was backed up by a brilliant choice of name. Both had substantial mail order operations. Both were leaders in merchandising systems. Mothercare had pioneered a computerized stock–control system in the early 1960s while Habitat was in the midst of installing an advanced EPOS (electronic point of sale) system that would link its own computerized stock control system directly to the electronic tills in the stores.

If pursued further, however, the similarities began to take on a more ominous aspect. Both companies had sought to apply their concepts in Europe and the US, and both had run into difficulties. True, Habitat appeared to have overcome its problems in Europe, but it was still making losses in America: was Habitat the right company to solve Mothercare's much larger American problems? Moreover, while the potential benefits to Mothercare of the Conran design team were clear enough (and Conran Associates were already working for two of Mothercare's competitors, Boots and Marks & Spencer), what was there in the merger for Habitat? Conran would admit to being hungry for growth and for new challenges, but to many observers the appearance was one of greed rather than hunger, and the question everybody asked was whether he was biting off more than he could chew. Would Mothercare respond to the Habitat treatment, or would the end result be 'Habi-Tat', as one journalist suggested?

HABITAT–MOTHERCARE

Zilkha's decision to pull out from Mothercare had come as a severe shock to his senior managers, and it left a vacuum into which Conran could have stepped himself, if he had wished. As events showed, however, that was not his style – if only because he had, as always, too much else going on at the same time. He was at this time setting up the Boilerhouse industrial design project at the Victoria and Albert museum, and was also a very active non-executive Chairman of J Hepworth, the menswear retailers. Under his guidance Hepworth had bought, in 1981, a chain of 80 menswear outlets, which Conran Associates were in the process of converting into the 'Next' chain of design-led fashion shops focusing upon the needs of women in the 25–40 age range.

With all this going on at the same time, and with Mothercare still trading profitably, the approach of Conran and his staff to the Mothercare organization was that of designers who work with their clients, understanding their needs and seeking a common agreement on how to meet them, rather than imposing any hasty or preconceived solutions. Instead of interfering with Mothercare in the short term, Conran appointed Zilkha's deputy, Barney Goodman, who had recently been concentrating on the American operation, as Chief Executive, and left him to run the operational side of the business. With the problems in America, the UK side had been allowed to let slip in the last couple of years, and by improving efficiency and making some relatively straightforward changes to the merchandising mix so as to push the shops up-market, it proved possible to boost margins and arrest the profit decline.

Meanwhile a Habitat design team began work on a new image for the Mothercare shops, and on new ranges of more fashion-sensitive products. John Stephenson, who as Design and Marketing Director (a post he held previously in Habitat) masterminded the operation, was able to build up a good relationship with the Mothercare Marketing Director, Rosemary Good, and in the course of 1983 the fruits of the review began filtering through to the shops. The old bright orange and white decor was replaced by a soft blue fascia with pastel blue, pink, and green interiors. New clothing and other product designs began to appear, continuing the move up-market. Some of the smaller stores were closed and others expanded or resited. By the summer of 1984 the shop refits, which had cost £10 per square foot, were complete, as was the initial round of merchandise redesign.

Meanwhile, in the autumn of 1983, Mothercare opened the first of a new chain of shops trading under the name 'Now'. Influenced by the success of Next with its concept of narrowly defined customer markets, Now was aimed at school-children up to 16 years old, who wanted to choose their own fashion clothes and accessories, but whose parents still held the purse-strings. The idea was to appeal to the children themselves as a fashion store, while still being acceptable to the parents through providing quality and value for money in the Mothercare tradition.

In order to try and stem the losses in America, the Mothercare operation there was reorganized into four regional divisions each with its own vice-president. The attempt to reproduce the British Mothercare concept in America was abandoned. A new merchandise director was appointed and a start made on building up a team of buyers focusing on the fashion side. Meanwhile the Conran designers began work on a new look for Mothercare America.

It wasn't until 1986 that Mothercare's American operation finally edged into profitability, but Mothercare in Britain responded well to its new treatment and was soon showing a healthy profits growth. And at the same time Habitat itself was growing, with new stores in Britain, Europe, and America, and joint ventures or franchises in other parts of the world. The French business, having boomed in the early 1980s, suffered a setback in 1983–84 when government taxation measures hit both volume and margins and the liquidation of a newly nationalized furniture chain flooded the market with heavily discounted stock. This was only a temporary setback, however, and Habitat's ability to survive it and quickly start restoring profits seemed to confirm the underlying strength of a European operation that accounted for roughly a third of Habitat's overall turnover. The American operation moved into profit in 1983 and entered a period of rapid expansion.

The year 1983 also saw two more major acquisitions for the Habitat–Mothercare group. One was Heal & Son, owners of a large and famous up-market furniture store in central London, which had been trading at a loss for several years and was acquired for just £5 million. Heals was a natural base for extending the Habitat concept beyond the range of the typical Habitat customers, who were young couples setting up home for the first time. Whereas the median age of these customers was just 29, Conran saw Heals as appealing to a more affluent group of customers in their mid-thirties, furnishing their second home: 'Our customers at this stage want something different from Habitat, but they don't want to shop at Waring and Gillow or Times Furnishing, and they don't have the time to look for the alternative of antique second-hand furniture.' As Heals' massive product range was cut down to an efficiently manageable size, the shop floor space was also cut, enabling the prestigious building to act as a new headquarters for Habitat–Mothercare and accommodation for Conran Associates. For the future the plan was to gradually redesign the stock and then open new branches outside central London.

The second acquisition of 1983 was Richard Shops, a well-established chain of womenswear retailers which came onto the market when Hanson Trust took over United Drapery Stores, of which it had been part. The sale actually took the form of a management buy-out, but with Habitat–Mothercare putting in about £18 million for a 48% share of the equity. Following the success of Next, Conran's aim here was to do for his own company what he had already done for Hepworth, and resigning from the Hepworth board he set about redesigning and repositioning Richard Shops so as to compete directly with Next.

MERGER WITH BRITISH HOME STORES

By the beginning of 1985, the refitting of Richard Shops under the new name of Richards ('Richards working wardrobe') was well under way, the central London Heals had been transformed and a new branch was due to open in Croydon. In Britain, both Mothercare and Habitat appeared to be performing well, and while profits in Europe were still low and those in America, taken across the group, non-existent, the prospects in both areas seemed to be looking up. The Habitat–Mothercare share price was soaring, and on the lookout for further expansion opportunities, Conran talked to Bob Thornton, Chairman of the department store retailers Debenhams, about a possible merger. Debenhams were not interested, and Conran did not pursue the possibility, but when Ralph Halpern, Chairman of the Burton group of fashion retailers, launched a hostile bid for Debenhams later in the year, Conran emerged as a supporter of that bid. The agreement reached was that, if the bid were successful, Habitat–Mothercare would have options on 20% of the Debenhams shares and 20% of the floorspace, while Conran Associates would get a contract to redesign the Debenhams flagship store in London's Oxford Street. After a long and acrimonious battle, Burtons did eventually win control of Debenhams, but no sooner had this happened than Conran announced an agreed merger between Habitat–Mothercare and British Home Stores, a direct competitor of the Burton Group, with whom Conran Associates had been working for the past 18 months. After a lot of public argument, the Burtons options were rescinded.

Talking about the BHS merger at the time, Conran admitted that 'changing the face of the British High Street has always been my dream,' and after several years of takeover activity in the retail sector British Home Stores was one of the few groups with a strong high street presence still 'in play' in takeover and merger terms. He also noted that constant rumours about hostile bidders for BHS had 'helped focus the minds of the BHS board' when he had re-approached them in the autumn after initial talks in the spring had come to nothing. But he also claimed a strong logic for the merger.

British Home Stores was known to many of the British public as 'the poor man's Marks & Spencer'. Like Marks & Spencer, and like Mothercare, it offered a combination of quality and value for money, but at a somewhat lower price–quality level than Marks & Spencer. It had 127 stores across Britain, with floor space of 3.2 million square feet, and employed about 18 000 staff. The bulk of its turnover was in clothing, but it also sold lighting and other home furnishings as well as food, and had a small and highly profitable chain of in-store restaurants. Also profitable was Savacentre, a small chain of enormous out-of-town hypermarkets operated as a joint venture with Sainsbury's the grocery chain. In the last few years BHS had recorded a steadily rising turnover with good margins and profits increasing by the order of 10% a year, but the figures for 1985 were looking less promising, with fair profits growth but very little increase in turnover, and the possibility of a fall in real terms. There was a feeling both in the City and within parts of the company itself that it was failing to compete with Marks & Spencer and the fashion retailers such as Burtons, and that both its image and its performance were in need of livening up. Turnover in the year to March 1985 had been £550 million, with trading profits of £55 million.

Habitat–Mothercare, by comparison, had a turnover for the same period of £447 million and trading profits of £44 million. It had about 2.8 million square feet of selling space including nearly 500 Mothercare and Now shops, and over 90 Habitat or Conran's stores, together with the Mothercare and Habitat mail order operations. Besides Heals and the half share in Richards, it also had the design company, now called the Conran Design Group; the Conran Shop, a design showcase on the site of the first Habitat; a share in Conran's Octopus, a small publishing company; and 20% of FNAC, a French retailing chain supplying records, books, cameras, and consumer electronics.

As with the earlier Mothercare merger, the potential benefit to BHS was clear. In common with the Habitat–Mothercare companies, BHS sold only its own brand of goods, but it seemed to have lost its way in terms of brand image. It needed a new image, and it needed repositioning up-market. It was even reported that, when senior staff heard of the merger, they applauded, rejoicing in anticipation of the Conran touch. But in other respects BHS was no Mothercare. It had no name to trade on, no former image to resurrect. Organizationally it was a big company bureaucracy, very different from anything in the Habitat–Mothercare group. And the market to which it appealed was very different from anything the Conran team had designed for.

On the Habitat–Mothercare side, the merger offered further growth (though with a dilution of control: with each merger Conran's own personal shareholding declined significantly, and this one would bring it down to just 8% of the combined group), a possible source of cash for investment, and a network of prime High Street sites. But while there might be some gains to Mothercare in this last respect, BHS looked an unlikely vehicle for any other expansion of Habitat's activities, and an unlikely candidate for overseas expansion: even Marks & Spencer had experienced enormous difficulty in this respect. Finally there was the question mark over whether the American Mothercare operations were really out of the wood, or whether there was still more trouble to come. Was Conran's ambition getting the better of his judgement?

STOREHOUSE

Despite continuing rumours of a counter-bidder, none emerged, and the Habitat–Mothercare–BHS marriage was consummated at the beginning of 1986 under the new name of Storehouse. Many commentators assumed that this was a temporary name to be replaced by something more exciting in due course. In fact, though, it was a true reflection of the new company's operational philosophy, which was very much that underlying Habitat–Mothercare. The group was to be one of operationally auto-nomous businesses, linked by a general commitment to value for money, quality and design in their products, and to pleasant well-designed shop-ping environments, supported by common design resources and other group services such as credit card marketing, distribution, and data processing.

Presenting the first Storehouse annual report for the year to March 1986, Conran reinforced this message, and set out the group's priorities for the coming period. In the short term it had been decided to pull BHS out of food retailing, an area that had already been under review and was clearly not going to meet its profit targets. Thereafter the aim was 'to differentiate BHS from the rest of the High Street' and to make it 'the best family store in the High Street', a task for which Conran gave himself just two years. The designers were already at work on a new BHS image with a view to relaunching the chain in September. The earlier work by Conran Associates was beginning to filter through to the BHS product lines and was already having an effect on turnover, with sales of menswear and women's outerwear rising sharply. And the designers would now be working through the whole BHS product range over the next 18 months to two years. Savacentre, which was showing steeply rising profits, would be developed.

Meanwhile the development of the Habitat–Mothercare companies would continue, and Habitat would begin looking for out-of-town sites, where other retailers in furnishings and do-it-yourself were already meet-ing with tremendous success. But the Now business would cease to trade as a separate entity. The concept had not worked, with the shops being too closely associated in children's minds with Mothercare. The ten Now shops sited alongside or within Mothercare shops had performed very poorly, and while the 18 shops sited in fashion centres had performed better they had clearly been hampered by the restricted age range to which they appealed, the parental element being largely absent from these stores. Conran insisted, however, that he would try again, and pointed to the Italian Benetton chain as an example of a design-led store with international appeal to young people in their teens and twenties.

In terms of its direct impact on the Storehouse results, the failure of the Now shops was of minor importance. But it appears to have marked the beginning of a change in critics' perceptions of Storehouse and Conran. The question that began to be asked was: Was Conran losing his flair? In September, when BHS was relaunched with its new brand image, the question was asked again, for the change of image fell distinctly short of public expectations. The new shops were redesigned in a more contemporary style and with better use of the floorspace than in the old ones, but the new brand image that had been promised seemed to amount to little more than, as one journalist put it 'something "very exciting" happening to the "h".' BHS, as the stores had long been known, became BhS, with a lower-case, italic and multicoloured 'h'. But it still sounded the same.

Nine months later, with the publication of the results to March 1987, criticism mounted. Group profits were up by 16%, with BhS's trading profits up 18%. But this reflected increased margins rather than increased turnover, and as BhS's sales per square foot had been exceptionally low it was to turnover that the City had been looking for improvement. Moreover Mothercare's profits were actually down 9%, following transitional problems with the implementation of a new centralized distribution system, and here too turnover was static in real terms, despite the opening of over 30 new shops in the US. Pushchairs and nappies were doing very well, but when Conran waxed lyrical about Mothercare's design leadership in these areas the City was not impressed: it was just another case of designer enthusiasm seeming to them to part company with financial reality. Habitat managed a more respectable performance, and opened its first two out-of-town stores, but commentators were by now more interested in why Habitat had failed to go out of town five years earlier (which would have been a fairly obvious move) than in the fact that it had at last done so. Richards was very successful, but accounted for only a small part of the group's business.

Within weeks of the publication of the 1987 results, takeover rumours abounded, with Sears, Dixons, Woolworths, indeed most of the large retail companies being tipped as possible contenders. In July a property company, Mountleigh, declared its intention of making a bid, but in the end it was a small engineering company, Benlox, that put in a leveraged bid with a view to breaking Storehouse up into its component parts. The bid was eventually turned down by the Storehouse shareholders, and no other formal bid was made, but Storehouse was in a state of siege for several months and the message from the City was clear: whatever Conran's view of the logic of the merger, they placed a higher value on the group as a set of separate companies than as an ongoing business.

The public attention directed on Storehouse during this period also brought to light some of the organizational problems of the merger.

Doubts had been expressed at the time of the merger as to how the young BhS management team would take to what seemed in effect to be a Conran takeover. In the first year of the merger the consensus of public opinion had been that the Habitat–Mothercare and BhS management were in fact getting on well together, and in particular that Denis Cassidy, the Chief Executive of BhS and Deputy Chairman of the new group, was getting on well with his new Chairman and Group Chief Executive, Conran. Appearances were, however, illusory. British Home Stores had been run as an empire with its divisions controlled as fiefdoms, while Habitat was a more fluid and informal organization. The two groups found it very difficult to work together, and Conran's wish to preserve the operational autonomy of BhS had meant merely that these problems were not resolved early on.

At the time of the merger, Conran had stressed how professional and well-managed BhS was, and how it would bring to the merger a proven ability to manage a large cost base that Habitat–Mothercare lacked. In a 'staff annual review' distributed the following summer, however, a different tone emerged. In the 12-page review, 10 pages were devoted to extolling the glories of Habitat–Mothercare, and the message to BhS staff, though intended to be encouraging, was something of a put-down, especially to the management. 'Come on lets do it,' it urged: 'We have, I'm sure you'll agree, much to do: lets do it with pleasure and cheerfulness – quickly.' On the theme of corporate planning: 'Planning is not a chore but a creative discipline for chief executives which has been ignored by too many of Britain's retailers. This has resulted in the present High Street revolution, which has allowed those who know where they are going to acquire those who have lost their way!' This seemed to be the language of the takeover rather than the merger, and it is perhaps not surprising that it met with strong resistance from the BhS management.

The crunch came when, under pressure from the city, Conran decided to appoint a new chief executive, and decided that this would not be Cassidy. Cassidy and one of his assistant managing directors resigned. Geoff Davy, who had been in charge of Habitat UK, was appointed Chief Executive of BhS, and after a few months delay Michael Julien was appointed Group Chief Executive, a position shared in practice with Conran.

Julien's appointment was well received in the City. After a career at BICC he had been Finance Director at the Midland Bank from 1983–87 and had spent very short periods with Eurotunnel and Guinness before joining Storehouse. He had also been a non-executive director at Littlewoods during a crucial recovery period for the firm's retail business. He did not join Storehouse in time to have much effect on the figures for the year to March 1988, however, and those figures were not encouraging. Despite the introduction of new product ranges, BhS's turnover and trading profit remained unchanged in real terms over the previous year. Mothercare's profits slumped a further 40%, or £13 million, largely as a result of the distribution problems (though nappies and prams continued to do well). Even Habitat's profits failed to rise.

Conran and Julien remained convinced of the future for Storehouse. Following Julien's appointment, a new management structure was in place and, just as important, Conran now had someone to work with on the financial and systems side – something he had lacked since his former financial director and close colleague Ian Peacock had retired at the time of the BHS merger. As Conran admitted, 'financial and systems organizations are not my strong point'. As part of a new organization structure, a retail services division was being set up to provide distribution, information technology, and credit services across the whole group. This was expected to provide significant economies on the distribution side, to combine the best practices from the individual retail divisions, and to ensure that disasters such as that which had befallen the implementation of the new Mothercare system were not repeated. A space management project had also been launched, to improve space utilization across the group, and especially in the BhS shops. It was hoped to unlock a full million square feet of selling space through this project, increasing the group selling space to 8 million square feet out of a total premises of 13 million square feet.

Meanwhile, the Mothercare stock ordering and distribution system was up and working, as was a Habitat system that had been put in around the same time but without the same problems. A new Mothercare venture, 'Mothercare+', in which selected stores stocked a range of additional merchandise, was coming into operation. Conran's was expanding in America, and the European Habitat and Mothercare operations were being rationalized prior to a further drive to expand both businesses, and BhS, in Europe. The Habitat out-of-town programme was accelerating, and there were plans for more Savacentres. Richards was booming, and there were two new, as yet very small, fashion chains with scope for rapid growth: Anonymous, a joint venture with a firm called Melmart, who designed and supplied the clothes, aimed at women in their twenties; and Blazer, a menswear fashion chain bought for about £5 million from its founder David Krantz. The intention was to develop Anonymous primarily through concessions in BhS (as part of the space management project), and Blazer through a mixture of new sites and BhS concessions.

On the other hand, fashion retailing was becoming increasingly competitive, and with leading design consultants now retained by all the leading firms it was open to question whether Storehouse still had any specific competitive advantages in the market. Competition between the large retailers for the limited High Street market was also intense. Chains like BhS, Marks & Spencer, C&A, and Littlewoods could not all gain market share, and there was no sign of the brand image concept of BhS proving a significant weapon in this respect. Moreover, as competition at this level increased, stores such as Marks & Spencer were increasingly looking for niche markets to exploit and in the process eliminating the cost advantages of Mothercare. In a fragmented furniture market in which only five firms could claim more than 1% market share, Habitat and Heals should perhaps have been able to grow, but they had made relatively little headway in the past and many observers thought that their current market share of about 3% was as high as they were likely to get. Europe and America provided growth potential, but given the group's record there the risks were also considerable.

The view in the City at this time was that, whatever Storehouse was going to do, it had little time to do it: if it could not show much better results to March 1989 it was going to be very vulnerable to takeover. In fact the results for 1988–89 were, as even Conran had to admit, appalling. A few months before the year end Julien warned of an exceptional write-off of about £50 million which, it was claimed, should have been made at the time of the merger. But if this was bad, there was a lot worse to come. Operating profits crashed from £128 million to £76 million as, despite continued expansion, sales dipped and costs rose well ahead of inflation. None of the divisions was exempt. Habitat continued to increase turnover, but suffered a dramatic 60% fall in profits as its systems failed to deliver the goods customers wanted. Mothercare profits continued their rapid slide of the previous year and Richards, hit by trading problems affecting the whole of the fashion industry, turned in a loss. Despite all the efforts made to reposition and revitalize BhS, profits there fell by half on a declining real turnover.

Despite these results the balance sheet remained healthy, as the disposal of Storehouse's 50% share in Savacentre (£123 million) and its 20% of Fnac (£19.9 million) raised a surplus of over £50 million. But while Julien argued that these holdings were diverting attention from the core businesses, and that with a long-term contract to supply Savacentre the benefits of involvement in that venture would be retained, some analysts observed that the group was selling off its only profitable businesses. The acquisition in April 1989 of Jacadi SA, a French childrenswear distributor with an extensive retail franchise operation, for an initial outlay of £13 million, was better received, but seemed to do little to address the group's core problems.

Storehouse was in a sorry state, but with the outlook for retailing looking poor it was ironically in too bad a state to attract a takeover. In the winter of 1988–89 an American, Arthur Edelman, built up an 8% stake, and a threatened bid hung over the company for the first half of 1989. When Edelman did bid in June, however, it was conditional on Storehouse's and Conran's support, which was not forthcoming, and under pressure from the Stock Exchange he finally stated his intentions not to bid for the company. The stake remained in play, however, and available for sale to other potential bidders.

Immediately after the year end, in April 1989, Storehouse also entered into a joint venture with a property company, London and Edinburgh Trust, to acquire and develop a £100 million portfolio of Storehouse properties. Meanwhile, two new executive directors were appointed from outside the group, to take charge of marketing and design and home furnishings, and in presenting the 1988–89 accounts David Julien made clear his recognition that the group systems were in need of radical surgery. It had become a standing joke that Habitat could never supply the goods on display, and even within the group stories were told of people going into Mothercare stores and asking, before going any further, 'what **do** you have in stock at the moment?'

Julien also recognized that key aspects of the original Storehouse concept had not worked. The autonomy of the divisions had proved costly and inefficient, and had allowed cultural conflict to continue unresolved. The attempt to take BhS up market had failed, and even the latest and most successful refitting (the third in as many years) was producing increases of less than 10% in sales per square foot, where, with margins having declined steeply, a doubling was needed for profitability. If design had done little for BhS (except of course to increase its overheads), BhS had done nothing for Habitat–Mothercare, whose inability to operate advanced computer systems was as marked as ever.

Critics of Storehouse said that the group should be split up before any further damage was done. Conran and Julien persisted in taking the opposite view, and were now set on pulling the group more tightly together. But they faced an uphill struggle if they were to prove their point, and the odds against them retaining control long enough to succeed were lengthening rapidly.

SUGGESTED QUESTIONS

1. Why did Habitat–Mothercare merge with British Home Stores? How sound was the logic behind the merger, and to what extent was it clouded by other factors?
2. How successful has this merger been? What problems has it run into and why? In what ways could it have been better implemented?
3. What is Storehouse's strategy now, and what do you think it should be? How should it be implemented?

Exhibit 1   British Home Stores and Habitat–Mothercare: five-year record.

Year to end March	1981 (£ thousand)	1982 (£ thousand)	1983 (£ thousand)	1984 (£ thousand)	1985 (£ thousand)
British Home Stores					
Turnover: (inc. VAT)					
Merchandise	350 653	366 198	394 301	434 762	486 124
Food	74 292	73 134	78 884	81 099	88 277
Restaurants	26 643	27 308	29 544	30 989	34 180
Total turnover (excl. VAT)	410 099	427 563	455 684	494 394	550 444
Trading profit	40 549	39 669	42 783	48 086	54 026
Profit before tax	39 658	42 562	48 874	55 193	60 981
Sales area (thousand square feet)	2 859	2 929	2 992	3 033	3 148
Number of stores	116	120	123	124	128
Average no. of employees	26 617	25 239	25 260	24 085	24 354
Average no. employees (full-time equivalents)	15 438	14 655	14 891	14 291	14 296
Habitat–Mothercare					
Turnover (excl. VAT):					
Habitat UK	37 172	42 841	52 515	73 353	
Habitat France & Belgium	22 119	28 916	38 164	41 003	
Habitat USA	6 635	9 497	12 952	21 525	
Conran Associates	1 239	1 439	1 850	2 066	167 400
Mothercare UK			157 967	185 417	
Mothercare Europe		172 668	16 265	15 070	
Mothercare USA			29 982	36 977	279 400
Total turnover (excl. VAT)		255 361	309 695	375 410	446 733
Trading profit:					
Habitat UK	4 094	3 847	5 598	8 026	
Habitat France & Belgium	1 196	2 253	2 063	585	
Habitat USA	(493)	(278)	177	732	
Conran Associates	467	521	546	545	11 300
Mothercare UK			19 871	25 567	
Mothercare Europe		14 282	267	(112)	
Mothercare USA			(1 061)	(170)	
Total trading profit		20 625	27 461	35 173	43 887
Profit before tax		18 468	22 947	30 617	36 501
Sales area (thousand square feet)		1 864	2 120	2 318	2 454
Number of stores		481	506	521	546
Average no. of employees			9 148	10 418	10 959
Average no. employees (full-time equivalents)			6 306	7 068	7 436

Exhibit   409

Exhibit 2 British Home Stores and Habitat–Mothercare: profit and loss accounts.

Year to end March	1985 (£ thousand)	1984 (£ thousand)
British Home Stores		
Turnover (excl. VAT)	550 444	494 394
Cost of sales	(484 219)	(435 640)
Administration costs	(12 199)	(10 668)
Trading profit	54 026	48 086
Related companies share of profit	4 855	4 390
Net interest received	2 100	2 717
Taxation	(23 334)	(21 184)
Extraordinary items		(2 734)
Profit	37 647	31 275
Dividends	(14 045)	(12 436)
Retained profit	23 602	18 839
Habitat–Mothercare		
Turnover (excl. VAT)	446 733	375 410
Cost of sales	(372 543)	(312 246)
Distribution costs	(11 095)	(8 726)
Administration costs	(19 208)	(17 265)
Trading profit	43 887	35 173
Interest etcetera	(7 386)	(4 556)
Taxation	(12 896)	(11 393)
Deferred tax provision		(4 500)
Profit	23 605	14 724
Translation adjustment	1 145	(858)
Dividends	(8 463)	(6 877)
Retained profit	16 287	6 989

Exhibit 3   British Home Stores and Habitat–Mothercare: balance sheets.

Year to end March	1985	1984
British Homes Stores		
Fixed assets: tangible	215 622	170 848
investments	32 497	23 199
	248 119	194 047
Current assets: stocks	60 594	57 281
debtors	9 448	8 682
cash	46 583	73 886
Current liabilities	(87 067)	(79 695)
Total assets less current liabilities	277 677	253 201
Long term creditors: loan capital	(28 236)	(28 674)
taxation	(16 686)	(15 913)
Deferred taxation provision	(1 634)	(2 662)
	231 121	205 952
Called up share capital	52 346	52 137
Share premium account	4 024	2 666
Revaluation reserve	2 463	2 502
Other reserves	3 861	3 861
Profit and loss account	168 427	144 786
	231 121	205 952
Habitat–Mothercare		
Fixed assets: tangible	151 486	127 277
investments	15 583	16 682
	167 079	143 959
Current assets: stocks	82 352	68 690
debtors	17 919	13 941
cash	8 008	9 867
Current liabilities: bank loans	(16 266)	(12 414)
dividends	(5 924)	(4 760)
taxation	(15 857)	(12 410)
creditors	(61 246)	(55 644)
Total assets less current liabilities	176 063	151 229
Long-term creditors:		
loans	(32 123)	(22 394)
convertible loan stock	(39 088)	(39 088)
deferred taxation provision	(3 285)	(4 265)
	101 557	85 482
Share capital	10 579	10 579
Share premium account	8 603	8 603
Other reserves	38 422	38 634
Profit and loss account	43 953	27 666
	101 557	85 482

Exhibit 411

Exhibit 4 Storehouse: six-year record.

	1984 (£ million)	1985 (£ million)	1986 (£ million)	1987 (£ million)	1988 (£ million)	1989 (£ million)
Summary of turnover and profits:						
Turnover (excluding sales taxes)	869.8	997.2	1 057.8	1 120.6	1 170.6	1 221.2
Profit from retail operations	89.7	103.1	115.7	133.3	128.2	76.4
Interest and other items	(5.3)	(6.3)	(9.3)	(10.2)	(15.1)	(65.4)
Property profits	1.4	0.9	9.7	6.1	8.0	0.3
Profit before taxation	85.8	97.7	116.1	129.2	121.1	11.3
Taxation	(32.6)	(36.2)	(36.5)	(40.1)	(38.0)	(5.3)
Profit after taxation	53.2	61.5	79.6	89.1	83.1	6.0
Extraordinary items	(7.2)		(24.1)	(0.7)	(11.9)	52.8
Profit for the financial year	46.0	61.5	55.5	88.4	71.2	58.8
Summary of balance sheets:						
Fixed assets	338.0	416.4	459.5	542.1	596.0	576.5
Net current assets	66.4	42.5	23.8	39.8	23.5	67.5
Creditors falling due after one year	(106.1)	(116.5)	(62.1)	(114.9)	(115.4)	(110.8)
Provisions for liabilities and charges	(6.9)	(11.9)	(18.7)	(10.1)	(11.4)	(20.8)
Total net assets	291.4	330.5	402.5	456.9	492.7	512.4
Capital expenditure (£ million)	54.8	98.1	108.1	112.7	98.9	97.7
Number of stores	645	674	711	894	950	1 021
Net selling space (thousands, sq ft)	5 351	5 602	6 046	6 647	7 061	7 100
Average number of employees	34 503	35 313	35 269	33 604	32 404	32 208
Number of full-time equivalents	21 359	21 732	21 654	20 243	19 593	19 922

Exhibit 5 Storehouse: profit and loss account and balance sheet, 1986–89.

Year to end March	1989 (£ million)	1988 (£ million)	1987 (£ million)	1986 (£ million)
Profit and Loss acount				
Turnover (excl. VAT)	1221.2	1170.6	1120.6	1057.8
Cost of sales	(1097.7)	(1002.5)	(956.5)	(912.4)
Administrative costs	(60.5)	(50.8)	(40.1)	(34.0)
Share of results of related companies	13.4	10.9	9.3	4.2
Trading profit	76.4	128.2	133.3	115.7
Interest etc.	(16.0)	(15.1)	(10.2)	(9.3)
Exceptional items*	(49.4)			
Property profits	0.3	8.0	6.1	9.7
Taxation	5.3	(38.0)	(40.1)	(36.5)
Extraordinary items**	52.8	(11.9)	(0.7)	(24.0)
Profit	58.8	71.2	88.4	55.5
Dividends	(36.1)	(35.9)	(34.9)	(30.5)
Retained profit	22.7	35.3	53.5	25.0

At year end March	1989 (£ million)	1988 (£ million)	1987 (£ million)	1986 (£ million)
Balance sheet				
Fixed assets: tangible	566.3	532.8	503.1	401.8
investments	10.2	63.2	39.0	57.8
	576.5	596.0	542.1	459.6
Current assets: stocks	176.8	195.6	182.7	161.5
debtors	91.8	68.3	61.0	44.9
cash	113.4	46.3	53.0	45.2
Current liabilities	(314.5)	(286.7)	(256.9)	(227.7)
Total assets less current liabilities	644.0	619.5	581.9	483.4
Long-term creditors	(110.8)	(115.4)	(114.9)	(62.1)
Provisions for liabilities and charges	(20.8)	(11.4)	(10.1)	(18.7)
	512.4	492.7	456.9	402.5
Called up share capital	40.9	40.8	40.4	39.8
Share premium account	12.4	10.1	3.4	
Acquisition and merger reserves	110.2	110.9	122.6	122.7
Other reserves		12.6		
Profit and loss account	348.9	318.3	290.5	236.0
	512.4	492.7	456.9	402.5

*Stock provision £13.9m; reorganization costs £5.6m; fixtures and fittings £16.3m; systems and computers £9.2m.

**For 1989, includes surpluses on sale of shares in Savacentre (£59.9m) and Fnac (£9.8m) as well as losses on closure of European operations.

Exhibit   413

Exhibit 6   Storehouse: breakdown of results.

		1989 (£ million)	1988 (£ million)	1987 (£ million)
Turnover by division:	BhS	568.6	560.3	536.4
	Mothercare	399.8*	302.9	306.4
	Habitat	252.8	226.8	210.7
	Fashion		80.6	37.1
Trading profit:	BhS	40.2	83.9	79.5
	Mothercare	18.0*	22.1	35.9
	Habitat	5.1	14.9	14.8
	Fashion		7.3	3.9
Turnover by area:	UK	1047.7	997.8	953.0
	Europe	92.8	95.4	88.6
	USA	80.7	77.4	79.0
Trading profit:	UK	56.1	119.7	126.0
	Europe	5.0	5.1	4.2
	USA	2.2	3.4	3.1

* Includes fashion.

Exhibit 7   Storehouse: group profile, 1989.

Company	Stores	Franchises (overseas)	Sales area (million sq feet)
BhS	139	22	3.3
Mothercare UK	249	36	
Mothercare Europe	35		1.5
Mothercare USA	235		
Habitat UK	57	26	
Habitat Europe	29		
Conran's USA	16		1.8
Heal's	6		
Conran Shop	1		
Richards	215	12	
Blazer	18		0.5
Anonymous (81%)	23		
Jacardi	3	273	
Conran Design Group			

Exhibit 8   Extract from *Storehouse Annual Report*, 1988.

Your company has a portfolio of first-class retail businesses, each clearly distinguished and targeted, and supported by the best possible group-wide services of design, property and space management, distribution, information systems and technology and direct marketing, motivated by a unique business culture developed by the transfer of key executives between businesses.

Our priorities are:

- to complete the repositioning of BhS and improve sales densities;
- to recover Mothercare's profitability and increase market share;
- to push through Habitat's out of town programme;
- to build on the success of Richards and develop Blazer.

Exhibit 9   Storehouse organization, 1989.

Division	Companies	Division CEO	CEO's previous positions
Retail divisions			
BhS	BhS	Geoff Davy	CEO Habitat UK
Specialty Retail	Mothercare UK Mothercare Europe Mothercare USA Richards Blazer Anonymous (81%)	Kevyn Jones	CEO Mothercare UK
Home furnishing	Habitat UK Habitat Europe Habitat France Heals Conran's USA The Conran Shop	Michael Harvey	Recruited May 1989
Support divisions			
Marketing and design	Conran Design Group Conran Octupus (50%)	John Braddel	Recruited February 1989
Property	Storehouse Properties	Terry Goddard	Finance Director Habitat
Retail Services	Distribution Storecard Information Systems and Technology	Pat Diamond	Habitat

Exhibit 10   Furniture retailers: market shares, 1986.

Harris Queensway	12.7%
MFI	9.6%
Gillow	3.2%
Habitat	3.1%
Courts	1.2%
All others under 1%	

23

Taurus Hungarian Rubber Works: implementing a strategy for the 1990s

Case written by Joseph Wolfe, Gyula Bosnyak, and Janos Vecsenyi

Many major decisions had been made by Taurus in the two years since its top management planning session. Yet the basic implementation of its diversification strategy had not been accomplished. Gyula Bosnyak, Director of Corporate Development Strategic Planning, recognized both the timing and the enormity of the events and issues involved. In 1988 the Hungarian government had passed its Corporation Law which put all state-owned firms on notice to privatize and recapitalize themselves. Not only did the firm have to deal with the mechanics of going public, it had to obtain the ideal mix of debt and equity capital to ensure solid growth for a company which was operating in a stagnant economy and a low growth industry. Top management was also concerned about the route it should follow to invigorate the company. It was accepted that Taurus had to maintain or even improve its international competitiveness, and that it had to diversify away from its traditional dependence on the manufacturing of truck and farm tyres.

Rather than viewing this situation as a threat, Gyula had seen this as an opportunity for Taurus to deal with its working capital problem as well as to begin serious diversification efforts away from its basically non-competitive and highly threatened commercial tyre manufacturing operation. Now, in spring 1990, he was beginning to sort out his company's options before making his recommendations to Laszlo Geza, Vice President of Taurus's Technical Rubber Products Division, and Laszlo Palotas, the company's newly elected President.

Mechanical goods
Latex foam products
Shoe products
Athletic goods
Toys
Sponge rubber
Insulated wire and cable
Footwear
Waterproofed fabrics
Hard rubber products
Flooring
Cements
Drug sundries
Pulley belts
Waterproof insulation
Conveyor belts
Shock absorbers and vibration dampeners

Fig. 1   Major non-tyre rubber uses

Upon the nationalization of all rubber firms after the Second World War, the Hungarian government pursued a policy of extensive growth for a number of years. From 1950 to 1970 annual production increases of 12.5% a year were common while the rubber sector's employment and gross fixed asset value increased on average approximately 6.2% and 15.7% per year. Although growth was rapid, great inefficiencies were incurred. Utilization rates were low and productivity lagged by about 1.5–3.0 times that obtained by comparable socialist and advanced capitalist countries. Little attention was paid to rationalizing either production or the product line as sales to the Hungarian and CMEA countries appeared to support the sector's activities. At various times the nationalized firm produced condoms, bicycle and automobile tyres, rubber toys, boots, and raincoats (see Figure 1).

During this period the government also restructured its rubber industry. In 1963 Budapest's five rubber manufacturers, PALMA, Heureka, Tauril, Emerge, and Cordatic, were merged into one company called the National Rubber Company. Purchasing, cash management, and investment were centralized, and a central trade and research and development apparatus was created. Contrary to the normal way of conducting its affairs, however, the company pioneered the use of strategic planning when the classic type of centralized planning was still the country's ruling mechanism.

In 1973 the company changed its name to the Taurus Hungarian Rubber Works, operating rubber processing plants in Budapest, Nyiregyhaza, Szeged, Vac, and Mugi as well as a machine and mould factory in Budapest.

As shown in Exhibit 1 and Tables 7–9, Taurus operated four separate divisions while engaging in a number of joint ventures. Sales increased annually to the 20.7 billion forint mark with an increasing emphasis on international business.

Exhibit 1   Taurus Hungarian Rubber Works: organization structure.

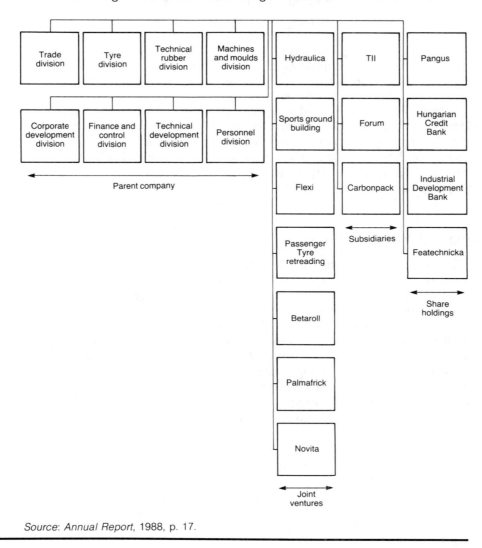

Source: *Annual Report*, 1988, p. 17.

Tyre division

The tyre division manufactured tyres for commercial vehicles after having phased out its production of automobile tyres in the mid-1970s. Truck tyres, as either cross-ply or all-steel radials, accounted for about 34.0% of the division's sales. Farm tyres were its other major product category as either textile radials or cross-ply tyres. Farm tyres were about 20% of the division's sales in 1988. A smaller product category included tyre retreading, inner tubes, and fork lift truck tyres. About 58.0% of the division's volume were export sales, of which the following countries constituted the greatest amount (in millions of forints):

United States	351.7
Algeria	298.2
Czechoslovakia	187.3
West Germany	183.5
Yugoslavia	172.0

The division had finished a capacity expansion financed by the World Bank in the all-steel radial truck tyre operation. Eleven new tyres within the 'Taurus Top Tyre' brand were scheduled for the market of which two were completed in 1988 and another three in early 1990. The division was also developing a new supersingle tyre under a licensing agreement with an American tyre manufacturer.

Technical rubber division

This division manufactured and marketed an assortment of rubber hoses, air-springs for trucks and buses, conveyor belts, waterproof sheeting, and the PALMA line of camping gear. The PALMA camping gear line had a 15.0% world market share while the company's rotary hose business was a world leader with 40.0% of all international sales. The demand for high-pressure and large-bore hoses was closely related to offshore drilling activity while the sale of air-springs for commercial vehicles was expected to increase as this technology gained increasing acceptance with vehicle manufacturers. The Soviet Union was this division's largest customer with 1988 sales of 380.0 million forints. In recent years, sales within the division had been distributed in the following fashion:

Large-bore high-pressure hoses	6.7%
Rotary hoses	27.1%
Hydraulic hoses	14.7%
Camping goods	18.0%
Waterproof sheeting	13.9%
Air springs	5.3%
Conveyor belts	14.3%

Machine and moulds division

This division manufactured products which were used in-house as part of Taurus' manufacturing process as well as products used by others. About 70.0% of its sales were for export and its overall sales were distributed as follows in 1988:

Technical rubber moulds	24.0%
Polyurethane moulds	17.0%
Machines and components	25.0%
Tyre curing moulds	34.0%

Bridgestone Corporation: Bridgestone's acquisition of the Firestone Tire and Rubber Company in 1988 for $2.6 billion vaulted it into a virtual tie with Goodyear as the world's second largest tyre company, behind Michelin. The acquisition proved troublesome for Bridgestone, with Firestone losing about $100.0 million in 1989 causing the parent company's 1989 profits to fall to about $250.0 million on sales of $10.7 billion. Bridgestone had already invested $1.5 billion in upgrading Firestone's deteriorated plants and an additional $2.5 billion would be needed to bring all operations up to Bridgestone's quality standards. North American sales were $3.5 billion and the firm planned to quadruple the output of its La Vergen, Tennessee plant. Bridgestone was attempting to increase its share of the American tyre market, while slowly increasing its share of the European market as Japanese cars increased their sales there. In mid-1989 nine top executives were forced to resign or accept reassignment over disputes about the wisdom of the company's aggressive growth goals. Bridgestone was a major player in Asia, the Pacific, and South America where Japanese cars and trucks were heavily marketed.

Continental Gummi – Werke AG: Continental was West Germany's largest tyre manufacturer and was number two in European sales. It purchased General Tyre from Gencord in June 1987 for $625.0 million and was known as a premium quality tyre manufacturer. Continental entered a $200 million joint radial tyre venture in 1987 with the Toyo Tyre and Rubber Company and Yokohama Rubber Company for the manufacture of tyres installed on Japanese cars being shipped to the American market. Another part of the venture entailed manufacturing radial truck and bus tyres in the United States.

Cooper Tire and Rubber Company: This relatively small American firm had been very successful by specializing in the replacement tyre market. This segment accounted for about 80.0% of its sales and nearly half its output was sold as private-labelled merchandise. Cooper had recently expanded its capacity by 12.0% with about 10.0% more capacity completed in 1990. About 60% of its sales were for passenger tyres while the remainder were for buses and heavy trucks. The company was attempting to acquire a medium truck tyre plant in Natchez, Mississippi to enable it to cover the tyre spectrum more completely.

Goodyear Tire and Rubber Co: Goodyear diversified into chemicals and plastics, and a California to Texas oil pipeline, as well as into the aerospace industry. Automotive products, which included tyres, accounted for 68.0% of sales and 76.0% of operating profits. Recent sales growth had come from African and Latin American tyre sales where the company had a dominant market share. Plant expansions were made in Canada and South Korea (12 000 tyres daily per plant) during 1991. Goodyear was attempting to sell off its All America pipeline for about $1.4 billion to reduce its $275.0 million per year interest charges on $3.5 billion worth of debt.

Michelin et Cie: Although it lost $1.5 billion between 1980 and 1984, Michelin had become profitable again. In late 1988 the company acquired Uniroyal/ Goodrich for $690.0 million which made it the world's largest tyre company. Uniroyal had merged in August 1986 with the B F Goodrich Company, creating a company where 29.0% of its output was in private brands. Passenger and light truck tyres were sold in both the United States and overseas, and sales grew 44.5% although profits fell 11.1%. Michelin entered a joint venture with Okamoto of Japan to double that company's capacity to 24 000 tyres a day. While a large company, Michelin was much stronger in the truck tyre segment than it was in the passenger tyre segment.

Pirelli: After having been frustrated in its attempts to acquire Firestone, Pirelli purchased the Armstrong Tyre Company for $190.0 million in 1988 to gain a foothold in the North American market. Armstrong had been attempting to

Fig. 2   Recent activities of various tyre and rubber companies

diversify out of the tyre and rubber industry by selling off its industrial tyre plant in March 1987. Pirelli, which was strong in the premium tyre market, obtained a company whose sales were equally divided between the original equipment and replacement markets and one which had over 500 retail dealers. In the acquisition process Pirelli obtained a headquarters building in Connecticut, three tyre plants, one tyre textile plant, and one truck tyre factory. Armstrong's 1988 sales were $500.0 million.

Fig. 2   continued

Trade division

The Trade Division conducted CMEA purchases and sales for Taurus as well as performing autonomous distribution functions for other firms. Its activities served other Taurus divisions as well as those outside the company. It was expected that this division would continue to function as the Taurus purchasing agent while increasing its outside trading activities; its status regarding CMEA trafficking was in a state of flux.

IMPLEMENTING THE TAURUS STRATEGY OF STRATEGIC ALLIANCES

Gyula Bosnyak could see that the general rubber industry had fallen from a better than average industry growth performance in the 1960–70 period to one that was far inferior to the industrial average during the 1980–87 period. He also saw that other industries, such as data processing, aircraft, medical equipment, and telecommunication equipment, had obtained sizeable growth rates from 1977–87. Moreover, he was extremely aware of the increasing concentration occurring in the tyre industry through the formation of joint ventures, mergers, co-operative arrangements, and acquisitions (see Figure 2). It was obvious that at least the rubber industry's tyre segment had passed into its mature stage. In response to this, most major rubber companies had diversified away from the heavy competition within the industry itself, as well as attempting to find growth markets for their rubber production capacity. For the year

Goodrich (USA) and Uniroyal (Great Britain) operate as a joint venture.

Pirelli (Italy) acquired Armstrong (USA).

Firestone (USA) acquired by Bridgestone (Japan) which has another type of alliance with Trells Nord (Sweden).

General Tire (USA) acquired by Continental Tyre (West Germany) which, in turn operates in co-operation with Yokohama Tyre (Japan). Continental also owns Uniroyal Englebert Tyre.

Toyo (Japan) operates in co-operation with Continental Tyre (West Germany) while also operating a joint venture in Nippon Tyre (Japan) with Goodyear (USA).

Michelin (France) operates in co-operation with Michelin Okamoto (Japan).

Sumitoma (Japan) operates in co-operation with Nokia (Finland), Trells Nord (Sweden), and BTR Dunlop (Great Britain).

Fig. 3   Strategic alliances in 1987

Rubber company	Non-tyre sales (%)	Major diversification efforts
Goodyear	27.0	Packing materials, Chemicals
Firestone	30.0	Vehicle service
Cooper	20.0	Laser technology
Armstrong	N.A.	Heat transmission equipment
General Tire	68.0	Electronics, Sporting Goods
Carlisle	88.0	Computer technology, Roofing materials
Bridgestone	30.0	Chemicals, Sporting goods
Yokohama	26.0	Sporting goods, Aluminium products
Trelleborg	97.0	Mining, Ore processing
Artimos	N.A.	Food processing
Nokia	98.0	Electronics, Inorganic chemicals

Source: Corporate annual report for citations of diversifications. Source for non-tyre sales volume in Davis, B (1989) No Clear-Cut Winner in Tire Crown Fight, *Rubber and Plastics News*, 21 August, p. 18.

Fig. 4 Major 1988 rubber company diversifications, 1988

1987 alone Gyula listed the various strategic alliances shown in Figure 3, while Figure 4 reviews the diversification activities of the company's major tyre competitors in 1989.

Within the domestic market, various other Hungarian rubber manufacturers had surpassed Taurus in their growth rates as they jettisoned low profit lines and adopted newer ones possessing greater growth rates. Taurus' market share of the Hungarian rubber goods industry had slowly eroded since 1970 and this erosion increased greatly in the decade of the 1980s due to the creation of a number of smaller start-up rubber companies encouraged by Hungary's new private laws. While the company's market share stood at about 68.0% in 1986, Gyula estimated that it would only fall another 4.0% by 1992. Table 12 displays the figures and estimates he created for his analysis.

With the aid of a major consulting firm, Taurus had recently conducted an in-depth analysis of its business portfolio (see Exhibit 2). It was concluded that the company operated in a number of highly attractive markets, but that its competitive position needed to be improved for most product lines. Accordingly, emphasis was to be placed on improving the competitiveness of the company's current product lines and businesses. With 1991 as the target year, Taurus was to implement two types of projects: software projects dealing with quality assurance programmes, management development and staff training efforts, and the implementation of a management information system; and hardware projects dealing with upgrading the agricultural tyre compounding process as well as upgrades in the infrastructures of various plants.

Fundamental to the desire for Taurus to be more growth oriented was its newly-enunciated strategy shown in Figure 5. The company was seeking strategic alliances for certain business lines rather than growth

Exhibit 2   Taurus product portfolio.

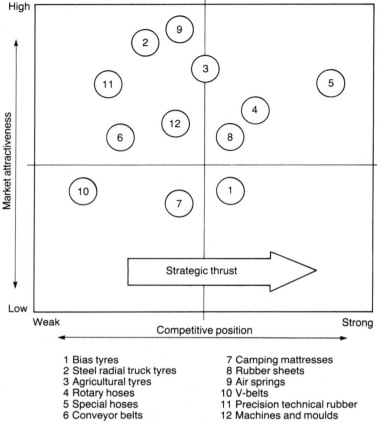

1 Bias tyres
2 Steel radial truck tyres
3 Agricultural tyres
4 Rotary hoses
5 Special hoses
6 Conveyor belts
7 Camping mattresses
8 Rubber sheets
9 Air springs
10 V-belts
11 Precision technical rubber
12 Machines and moulds

Source: Company documents and consulting group's final report.

through internal development which had been its previous growth strategy. While it was felt that internal development possessed lower risks, as it basically extended the company's current areas of expertise, benefited the various product lines already in existence, and better served its present customer base while simultaneously using the company's store of management knowledge and wisdom, internal development possessed a number of impediments to the current desires within Taurus for accelerated growth. Paramount was the belief that management was too preoccupied with current activities to pay attention to new areas outside the specific areas of expertise.

Now ranked at thirtieth in size in the rubber industry, Taurus found it was facing newly formed international combinations with enormous financial strength, strong market positions, and diverse managerial assets. Given the high degree of concentration in the rubber industry, and that

The decade of the 1990s is predicted to be a busy period for the rubber sector worldwide.

There are strong factors of concentration in traditional manufacturing businesses and particularly in tyre operations. The role of substitute products is growing in several areas. On the other hand, the fast end-of-century growth of industrial sectors is expected to stimulate the development of sophisticated special rubber products. In the face of these challenges, Taurus bases its competitive strategy on the following:

A continuous structural development programme has been started aimed at **increasing the company's competitive advantage** with scope to cover a range from manufacturing processes, through quality assurance, to the reinforcement of strengths and elimination of weaknesses.

Efficiency is a prerequisite of any business activity. The company portfolio must be kept in good balance.

Associated with profitability, the company keeps developing its sphere of operations, determining the direction of diversification according to the criteria of potential growth and returns.

Our pursuit of competitive advantages and diversification must be supported by a powerfully expanding **system of strategic alliance and co-operation**.

Source: Taurus Annual Report 1988, p. 3.

Fig. 5   Taurus's strategy for the 1990s

even the largest firms had to accomplish international co-operative relationships, Taurus determined that it too should seek co-operative, strategic alliances. In seeking these affiliations, the company would be open and responsive to any type of reasonable alternative or combination that might be offered, including participation with companies in the creation of new, jointly held companies, whether they were related or unrelated to the rubber industry. The only real criteria for accepting an alliance would be its profitability and growth potential.

In pursuing strategic alliances Gyula noted that the bargaining position differed greatly between the various business lines in the Taurus portfolio. As an aid to understanding its bargaining strategy with potential allies, the Taurus businesses were placed into one of three categories as shown in Figure 6. Category I types were those where the Taurus bargaining position was relatively weak as it felt it had little to offer a potential suitor. Category II types were those where Taurus could contribute a sizeable 'dowry' and had much to offer the potential ally, while Category III types were those businesses with mixed or balanced strengths and weaknesses.

The problem was how to restructure the company's current divisional activities to make them into rational and identifiable business units to outside investors, as well as serving Taurus's own needs for internal logic and market focus. Which product lines should be grouped together and what should be the basis for their grouping? Gyula saw several different ways to do this. Products could be grouped based on a common production process or technology. They could be based on their capital requirements, grouped by markets served, or trade relations which have already

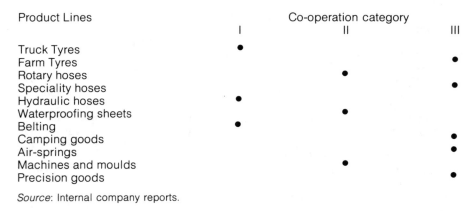

Product Lines	Co-operation category		
	I	II	III
Truck Tyres	●		
Farm Tyres			●
Rotary hoses		●	
Speciality hoses			●
Hydraulic hoses	●		
Waterproofing sheets		●	
Belting	●		
Camping goods			●
Air-springs			●
Machines and moulds		●	
Precision goods			●

Source: Internal company reports.

Fig. 6   Cooperation potentials by product line

been established by Taurus. Depending on how he defined the company's new SBUs, he knew he would be making some major decisions about the attractiveness of the company's assets as well as defining the number and the nature of Taurus's potential strategic alliances. As he explained:

> If I create an SBU which manufactures hoses, a good joint venture partner might be someone who manufacturers couplings for hoses – this would be a match that would be good for both of us and it would be a relatively safe investment. If on the other hand I create a business which can use the same hoses in the offshore mining and drilling business, and this is a business that is really risky but one that could really develop in the future, what do I look for in partners? I need to find an engineering company that is undertaking large mining exploration projects. For every type of combination like this where I can create, I have to ask myself each time 'What are the driving questions?'

In reviewing the company's portfolio he immediately saw three new SBUs that he could propose to Laszlo Geza. One SBU would serve the automobile industry through the manufacture of rubber profiles (rubber seals and grommets which provide watertight fits for car windows), V-belts for engines and engine components such as their air conditioning, power steering, and electrical units, and special engine seals. Another unit would serve the truck and bus industry by manufacturing the bellows for articulated buses and air springs for buses, heavy duty trucks, and long-haul trailers. The last new SBU would target the firm's adhesives and rubber sheeting at the construction and building industry where the products could be used to waterproof flatroofs as well as serving as chemical-proof and watertight liners in irrigation projects and hazardous waste landfill sites.

Although top management knew that 'the house wasn't on fire' and that a careful and deliberate pace could be taken regarding the company's restructuring, Gyula wanted to make sure the proposals he was about to make to the Technical Rubber Products Division were sound and reasonable. Moreover, the success or failure of this restructuring would set the tone for future diversification efforts.

REFERENCES

Benway, S J, (1989) Tire & Rubber Industry, *The Value Line Investment Survey*, 22 December, p. 127.

Greek, B F, (1988) Modest Growth Ahead for Rubber, *Chemical & Engineering News*, **66** (12), 21 March, pp. 25–29.

Thompson, A A, Jr, (1990) Competition in the World Tire Industry, in Thompson, A A Jr, and Strickland, A J *Strategic Management: Concepts and Cases*, Homewood, IL: R D Irwin, pp. 518–48.

SUGGESTED QUESTIONS

1. What are the key success factors in the rubber industry? Does Taurus possess them? Can it acquire them through the strategic alliances it is seeking?
2. What are the growth areas in the rubber industry?
3. How should the creation of new strategic business units be accomplished? Is the Director of Strategic Management going about the process in an appropriate way?
4. What are the advantages and disadvantages of Taurus's stated criteria for entering into strategic alliances?
5. What are the advantages and disadvantages of joint venturing? Is it an appropriate strategy for Taurus in its attempt to improve competitiveness?

Table 1 Predicted demand for synthetic rubbers in 1992 (non-socialist countries in thousands of metric tons)

Synthetic rubber	Forecast
Styrene-butadiene*	2819
Carboxylated styrene-butadiene	1015
Polybutadiene	1142
Ethylene-propylene diene	556
Polychloroprene	268
Nitrile	238
All others**	1025
Total	7063

*In both liquid and solid forms.
**Includes polyisoprene and butyl.
Source: International Institute of Synthetic Rubber Products as cited in Greek, BF (1988) Modest Growth Ahead for Rubber, *Chemical and Engineering News*, **66** (12), 21 March, p. 26.

Table 2 Predicted world consumption of rubber (in millions of metric tonnes, 2205 pounds/tonne)

Type	1986	1987	1988	1989	1990	1991	1992
Synthetic	9.5	9.8	9.8	9.9	9.9	10.0	10.0
Natural	4.5	4.6	4.9	5.1	5.4	5.7	5.9
Total	14.0	14.4	14.7	15.0	15.3	15.7	15.9

Source: Derived from data in Greek, BF (1988) Modest Growth Ahead for Rubber, *Chemical and Engineering News*, **66** (12), 21 March, pp. 25–26.

Table 3 Predicted changes in rubber demand by geographic area (in thousands of metric tons)

Geographic Area	1987	1992	Change (%)
North America	3 395	3 432	1.09
Latin America	788	944	19.80
Western Europe	2 460	2 953	20.04
Africa and Middle East	259	324	25.10
Asia and Oceania	3 060	3 541	15.72
Socialist Countries	4 057	4 706	16.00
Total	14 019	15 900	13.42

Source: Greek BF, (1988) Modest Growth Ahead for Rubber, *Chemical and Engineering News*, **66** (12), 21 March, p. 26.